300 Best
Blender
Recipes

Using Your Vitamix®

300 Best Blender Recipes

Using Your Vitamix®

Robin Asbell

Robert
ROSE

For complete cataloguing information, see page 320.

Disclaimers
300 Best Blender Recipes Using Your Vitamix® is an independent publication of Robert Rose Inc. and has
not been authorized, sponsored or otherwise approved by any other party, including Vita-Mix Corporation,
and Robert Rose Inc. is not a licensee of or otherwise associated with Vita-Mix Corporation.

The recipes in this book have been carefully tested by our kitchen and our tasters. To the best of our
knowledge, they are safe and nutritious for ordinary use and users. For those people with food or other
allergies, or who have special food requirements or health issues, please read the suggested contents of
each recipe carefully and determine whether or not they may create a problem for you. All recipes are
used at the risk of the consumer. Consumers should always consult their manufacturer's manual for
recommended procedures and cooking times. We cannot be responsible for any hazards, loss or damage
that may occur as a result of any recipe use. For those with special needs, allergies, requirements or
health problems, in the event of any doubt, please contact your medical adviser prior to the use of
any recipe.

Design and production: Daniella Zanchetta/PageWave Graphics Inc.
Editor: Sue Sumeraj
Recipe editor: Jennifer MacKenzie
Proofreader: Kelly Jones
Indexer: Gillian Watts
Photographer: Colin Erricson
Associate photographer: Matt Johannsson
Food stylist: Michael Elliott
Prop stylist: Charlene Erricson

Cover image: Mixed Berry Probiotic Blast (page 228)

The publisher gratefully acknowledges the financial support of our publishing program
by the Government of Canada through the Canada Book Fund.

Published by Robert Rose Inc.
120 Eglinton Avenue East, Suite 800, Toronto, Ontario, Canada M4P 1E2
Tel: (416) 322-6552 Fax: (416) 322-6936
www.robertrose.ca

Printed and bound in USA

1 2 3 4 5 6 7 8 9 CK 25 24 23 22 21 20 19 18 17

CONTENTS

INTRODUCTION

This morning, I went to the gym. In between sets, I scarfed an energy bar that I made in my Vitamix. When I got home, I used my Vitamix to whip up a facial and a body scrub made from fresh, organic foods. Then I slathered on a pure, additive-free lotion, also made in the Vitamix. By then I was hungry again, so I made a nutritious, whole-food smoothie in the Vitamix.

As the day progressed, I ground grains for fresh flour and made a loaf of bread, quickly and easily, in the Vitamix. For lunch, I had a deceptively decadent creamy soup and a big salad with a nutty, flavorful salad dressing emulsified in the Vitamix. I prepared marinades and a nut milk for tomorrow's meals. I had whole juice for a snack, then made a hearty pasta sauce and tasty veggie-packed burgers for my dinner guests, along with a moist, rich chocolate cake and frosting, with ice cream to serve on top. For the adults, I prepared blended cocktails, and the kids got a virgin version.

There was hardly time for the container to dry between jobs.

Chances are, you bought a Vitamix to make one thing. Maybe it was smoothies. Or perhaps you saw a chef demo at a cooking school and came away craving the ultra-creamy soup you sampled. But your Vitamix can do so much more. It can be a true workhorse in the kitchen, making quick work of everything from breakfast through dessert and drinks, with some skin-care products thrown in for good measure.

If you are looking for a way to eat fresh, wholesome foods but find yourself short on time, the Vitamix is the answer. This amazing high-power machine makes smoothies and juices from whole fruits and vegetables with the flip of a switch. No chopping, no chewing — just a convenient and nearly instant way to get those servings of fruits and vegetables that many of us have been skipping. It also chops, grinds and minces, so you don't have to spend time laboring over the cutting board.

Grinding your own flours is now within your reach, and it takes 60 seconds. Instead of buying flours that were ground months ago, you can grind your own for maximum flavor and nutrition, and mix up bread, pancakes, muffins and scones while the flour is at its peak. You are no longer bound by what your grocery store carries, because you can make flour from any grain or bean you choose. Want to try an ancient wheat, like farro or spelt flour? Or to make fresh buckwheat flour for pancakes? There's a wide world of grains, beans and nuts open to you for making flours. If you are avoiding gluten, or have allergies or intolerances to flours used in baked goods, you can grind your own flours, tailored to your needs.

Your powerful blender can help you at all stages of your life. Pregnant women may find that a sweet, digestible smoothie is a better way to answer cravings for ice cream, with more nutritious ingredients. And once the baby is ready for solid foods, the Vitamix is the tool of choice for making baby food, ensuring that your baby gets the best, freshest foods. Research shows that introducing vegetables in the formative months shapes the tastes of children as they grow, so early exposure to healthy vegetables will create vegetable eaters for life.

As your family grows, the speed and convenience of your super-powered blender will make feeding them easy. Kids love smoothies, ice pops and the smooth texture of blended foods. Even picky eaters can learn to consume healthful foods when they are blended. Many of the recipes in this book are designed to put more vegetables on the plate, whether in a veggie-packed meatloaf or a creamy soup with less cream.

Life is about celebrations and special meals, too, and the treats and splurge foods your family loves are a snap to make in the Vitamix. And when you make them yourself, you can be sure there are no weird ingredients.

At some point in life, you may decide to get into plant-based eating. Whether you have a vegan family member or just want to keep your cholesterol in check, whipping up your own cashew cheese, almond milk and vegan goodies is easy in your Vitamix.

After all this delicious, healthful food, you may want to celebrate with a cocktail. As long as you are having a drink, why not make it a good one? The best cocktail bars have blenders to make fresh juices and juice purées for high-end drinks. Your Vitamix allows you to use the best fresh fruits to make delicious cocktails, with none of the artificial flavors and colors found in many purchased cocktail mixes. Many of these blended drinks can also be made without alcohol, so everyone can enjoy them.

And if you're looking for the healthiest products to use on your skin, your Vitamix is equally adept at making natural body-care products, often from foods you already have in your kitchen. If you have ever read the label on a typical bottle of lotion or face cream, you have seen the long list of chemicals that are added to most products. Making your own gives you control over what goes on your body, as well as in it.

All this is within your reach, and recipes often take only a few minutes with your Vitamix and this book. You'll be amazed by how quickly and easily you can change the way you eat, feed your family and care for your skin.

VITAMIX BASICS

You, too, can make your Vitamix the main workhorse in your kitchen. Give the machine its own spot on the counter so you don't have to drag it out of a cupboard to use it. Then work your way through the chapters of this book and try some recipes you have never made in a blender. It will be a fun project. Once you are comfortable with the way the machine works, you can experiment with converting your old recipes into Vitamix recipes. You can even create brand-new ones.

You will likely find that the Vitamix can replace your other appliances, at least some of the time:

- The Vitamix does the work of a food processor, but not in the same way. In the Vitamix, the liquids should go in first, so that the blades can spin easily and gravity can pull the other ingredients into the vortex. The low-profile containers behave most like a food processor because of the wider base.
- The Vitamix does the work of a grain mill, but in small batches. Never grind more than 2 cups (500 mL) of a grain, or you will overheat both the machine and the grain.
- The Vitamix is a juicer, and it incorporates all the fiber into the juice.
- The Vitamix makes non-dairy milk.
- The Vitamix makes nut butters.
- The Vitamix crushes ice.
- The Vitamix makes ice creams and sorbets.

Models

The Vitamix comes in a variety of models, from mini to basic to professional. If you know what you plan to do with your Vitamix, you should be able to pick the right machine for you. Any model with variable speeds will have the versatility to allow you to explore all of the recipes in this book.

S Series

The S-series machines are the mini Vitamixes, designed for people with small kitchens. With a footprint only 5.6 inches (14 cm) wide, this appliance can slip in between the coffeemaker and the fridge. They have a less powerful motor than the larger models, too. The S series is the way to go if you want to make small batches of things like vinaigrette, or one or two servings of smoothies, juices, soups or sorbets. The S-series models have only 20- and 40-ounce (600 mL and 1.2 L) containers, which are not interchangeable with the other containers or larger machines.

C Series

The C stands for "classic," and most Vitamix owners have a C-series blender. It is built on a base with a 2-horsepower motor and comes in options from a minimalist two-speed version all the way up to a model with 10 variable speeds plus a High setting, five preprogrammed settings and a pulse function. These models come with the classic tall 64-ounce (2 L) container.

The Turbo Blend 2 Speed is the least expensive model in the full-sized line. It has a switch that flips between High and Low. If you are going to use your Vitamix to make smoothies, blended drinks and vinaigrettes, this is a fine option. If you want to move beyond these simple items, it's worth the extra cost to move up to a model with variable speeds.

The 5200 Standard Model has 10 speeds and a High setting, which will give you the control you want, allowing you to use the machine for many more types of recipes and finesse what is going on in that powerful blender.

The next step up is the Professional Series 500, which adds a pulse feature and some preprogrammed settings for smoothies, soups and frozen desserts. The pulse feature is handy, although you can also pulse at high speed in the C series by turning the machine on and off. It will not be moving as fast as the pulse on the Pro, but it still works.

G Series

The big difference with the G series is a more powerful 2.2-horsepower motor and a low-profile 64-ounce (2 L) container. All the G-series machines have the pulse feature, too. These machines are designed for making larger batches of food and have more power to keep going with a larger load in the container. The G series is also designed to be a little quieter, which many people appreciate.

The 7500 is the most basic of the G series, with variable speed, High and Pulse functions. It has no preprogrammed settings.

The Professional Series adds in some preprogrammed settings, which allow you to walk away while the machine does its work.

The high end of the series is the 780, which features an LED touch screen control panel that lights up, as well as five preprogrammed settings.

Accessories

Your Vitamix came with a container, a lid, a tamper and some instructional materials. This is all you need to get started, but as you learn about putting the machine to use, you may want a few accessories. If you want to make smaller batches, there are smaller containers that will work more efficiently. If you want your blender to fit under the cupboards more easily, a low-profile container may be on your wish list. If you want to grind flours and coffee, the dry grinding container is the most efficient way to do so.

Go ahead and get started with your blender, exploring the recipes in this book. Then you'll know whether you need some of the more specialized tools that make your Vitamix more versatile.

Spatulas

The first and most crucial accessory is the proper spatula. A white plastic spatula made from stiff plastic, with a rounded head about 1 inch (2.5 cm) wide, is the one that will make your blending life easiest. Some narrow rubber spatulas will fit in the space between the blade and the walls of the container, but a stiff plastic

---

Certified Reconditioned Blenders

The Vitamix corporation makes it easy and affordable to buy a reconditioned machine. They have a program to take back machines that break and exchange them for reconditioned ones. Once you have invested in a Vitamix, if your machine stops working, it costs about $200 to exchange it for a comparable model that has been rebuilt. That is cheaper than shipping your machine to the factory to be fixed, and it simplifies the process. You won't have to wait for your blender to be repaired; instead, the company will send you a reconditioned one right away.

Because Vitamixes are so durable, and because older Vitamixes are always being reconditioned, there are many makes and models still working away in homes all over the world. They all function a little bit differently, but you can learn to work with yours to make all of the recipes in this book.

one does the best job of scraping out thick mixtures, like bread dough. This style of spatula is sold on the Vitamix website and is available online.

Containers

The Vitamix designers recommend using only the container that came with your machine, but in practice you can use the tall, short and dry grinding containers on any of the C-series or G-series blenders. The S-series blenders are smaller and have their own containers that won't fit on the larger machines.

The classic tall 64-ounce (2 L) container works the best for most average-sized recipes. It is designed so that the blades create a vortex in the narrow base of the container, pulling the ingredients down and pulverizing them. The recipes in this book were tested in this container unless otherwise noted, and most Vitamix recipes you will find online are written for it as well.

The low-profile 64-ounce (2 L) container is designed to hold about one and a half times the volume of the standard, narrower 64-ounce container. The low-profile container is paired with the Pro models, which also have a little more horsepower to blend through big batches. It has the advantage of being short and squat, so you can fit the assembled blender under your cabinets.

For smaller batches, the 48-ounce (1.5 L) container is short, like the low-profile 64-ounce (2 L) container, and will fit under your cabinet. It is recommended for making medium-sized batches of food.

The smallest container for the C-series and G-series blenders is a 32-ounce (1 L), low-profile one. If you want to make small batches with less scraping down and starting again, this is the container for you.

Because of their wider base, the low-profile containers are better than the narrow containers for making doughs and batters, as there is more room to spin the mixture around in the bottom. These containers function more like a food processor bowl.

Dry Grinding Container

The dry grinding container is a valuable addition to your kitchen. If you find yourself grinding flour, coffee or herb mixes more than a few times a year, you should definitely invest in one of these. The blades are designed to make quick work of the hard kernels and beans. They also put less wear and tear on your machine, as they sail through the work more efficiently.

The shape of the blades is also designed for kneading bread doughs, and it actually throws the mass of dough away from the blades, rather than creating a vortex as the other containers do. This helps to knead bread dough properly.

The dry grinding container does not come with a tamper.

Tampers

Your machine comes with a container and a tamper that fits it. You can buy other containers, and they will also come with a tamper. Each tamper is designed to reach just far enough into the container to push food into the blades without making contact with the blades. Never try to use a long tamper made for the tall container in a low-profile container; it will engage with the blades and be ground into bits of plastic in your food. If your tamper gets damaged, you can order a new one for your specific container.

Rubber or Silicone Mat

A rubber or silicone mat to put under your Vitamix is a good idea, both to protect your counter and to slightly dampen the noise. Move the Vitamix away from the wall so that the engine noise isn't amplified. All that power does make for a bit of volume. If it bothers you, slip in some earplugs while blending.

Nut Milk Bag

Despite its unappealing name, a nut milk bag is a valuable tool for making soy milk, nut milk or anything you want to strain really well. Nut milk bags are available in various sizes online. You will find that, even when you're making small batches, a larger bag is easier to use: you have more fabric to twist and hold on to while wringing out the liquids. Organic fabrics are preferable to plastic mesh and should be easy to wash and dry after use.

For very large batches, some people recommend buying inexpensive paint-straining bags at the paint store. These are plastic and have larger openings in the mesh, but if you are straining gallons of liquid on a regular basis, they might come in handy.

Digital Scale

In the baking and desserts chapters, I have provided weights for some of the dry ingredients because weights are much more accurate than volume measurements. Ingredients such as grains and flour can be compressed, making for a denser volume measurement than intended. If you don't want to weigh flours, be careful to fluff and spoon them lightly into a dry (nesting-style) measuring cup, just barely to the rim, rather than scooping and packing, or rounding the ingredients above the rim.

Tips for Success

- The instructions in this book are written for the most popular C-series Vitamix. If you have a different model, you might need to adjust the times a bit. Follow the visual cues in the recipes ("until smooth," for example). If your blender speeds go from 1 to 10 and there is no High setting, consider 10 to be High.

- If you don't have a Pulse button, just turn the machine on and off at the speed specified.

- An important habit to start as soon as you get a Vitamix is automatically flipping the switch from High to Variable and turning the speed to 1 when you're done using the machine. If you leave it on High and think it is on Variable, you will experience a violent pulse when you turn it on.

- The Vitamix test kitchen recommends placing the container on the countertop to load the ingredients, then placing it on the base. This has the advantage of making the container lower and easier to see inside, and you will have an easier time securing the lid. In addition, any spills will be on the countertop, rather than on your machine base, for easier cleanup.

- You can mince foods by dropping them through the hole in the lid. This is an excellent way to mince carrots and onions, for example. You simply run the machine on a medium speed and drop each piece of food through the hole, adding the next piece only when the previous one is minced. This is a very fast process, and it is very easy to overprocess an onion into a paste, but if you move quickly, you can have the work of mincing vegetables done in seconds (see page 15 for further instructions).

- If your ingredients are flying up and sticking to the sides of the container, stop and scrape them down. You may have to do this a few times. All blenders function best when working with either completely dry or very wet mixtures, in which gravity pulls the ingredients down into the blades and the shape of the container creates a vortex at the center. With mixtures that are in between these two extremes, you may need to assist gravity by scraping bits of food down into the blades to be processed.

- Lower speeds are sometimes better for keeping food in contact with the blades. When making a recipe like an energy ball, with dried fruit and nuts, you'll get the best results by slowly increasing the speed only to the point that the food stays engaged with the blades and moves around the bottom of the container. It may be tempting to blast up to High speed, but that will just fling the food up out of the blades.

- As long as the food is in contact with the blades, the highest speed that works is recommended. When the directions say "gradually increase the speed," you should do so as quickly as you can, as long as the food is engaged and flowing around the blades. That may be a little slower for some recipes, a little faster for others.

- The tamper is your friend. There is a phenomenon called an "air bubble," which is when the ingredients hover above the blades and only air is moving underneath. When this happens, insert the tamper through the hole in the lid and press the food down into the blades, releasing the air bubble. If that doesn't work, turn off the machine and use your spatula to scrape the mixture into the center of the container, then start again at speed 1.

- The machine is at peak efficiency when running at high speed, because that is when the cooling fan is activated. Running the machine on a lower speed for more than 2 minutes can overheat the motor and add wear and tear to the machine. Try to avoid overheating the machine, but don't worry too much: your machine has an overload sensor and will simply shut down if it gets overheated. If that happens, take the container off the base, unplug it and let the motor cool down for 30 to 45 minutes or so. (If the room is very hot, it may take longer.) Once it's cooled down, your Vitamix should start right up again.

- With the preprogrammed settings, which allow you to select Smoothie, Hot Soup, Puree, Frozen Dessert or Cleaning, you can select a setting and walk away while the machine gradually increases the speed, as you would, then runs for the amount of time an average recipe of that type from the Vitamix test kitchens would take. If you don't need to walk away, you can probably do a more accurate job by staying beside your blender and manipulating the speed as needed.

- Cleaning your Vitamix container is easy. Just fill it halfway with warm water, add a drop of dish soap and secure the lid. Select variable speed 1, turn the blender on and gradually increase to 10, then High. Run for 30 to 60 seconds. Rinse the container and let it air-dry.

- In a few instances, such as when you have ground raw meat, you will want to sanitize the container after cleaning it. Fill the container halfway with warm water, add $1\frac{1}{2}$ teaspoons (7 mL) bleach, and repeat the cleaning process. Then rinse well and air-dry.

- If your container becomes stained or filmy, pour in 1 cup (250 mL) white vinegar, then fill the container halfway with warm water. Let it stand for several hours, then pour out the vinegar solution. Use a gentle scrubber to clean the inside of the container, being careful of the blades. Rinse the container and let it air-dry.

BASIC TECHNIQUES

Powdering Sugar

You've run out of powdered sugar (confectioners' or icing sugar)? No problem. Just grind some granulated sugar to powder in the Vitamix. The cornstarch or arrowroot keeps the sugar from forming lumps, but if you are using the sugar right away, you can skip it.

1. Place 1 cup (250 mL) sugar in the Vitamix container and secure the lid. With the switch on Variable, select speed 1 and turn the machine on. Gradually increase the speed to 10, then flip the switch to High and blend for 30 seconds.

2. Let the powder settle for a few seconds, then remove the lid and add 2 tsp (10 mL) cornstarch or arrowroot starch (if desired). Secure the lid. With the switch on Variable, select speed 1 and turn the machine on. Gradually increase the speed to 10 and blend for 10 seconds.

3. Remove the container from the base and tap the bottom lightly on the counter to knock the sugar to the bottom; let settle for a few seconds before transferring the powdered sugar to a measuring cup or storage container. Keeps for 1 month, tightly covered.

Tip

Whenever you have ground something to a powder, tap the bottom of the container lightly on the counter to help clear the powder from the sides, then give it a few seconds to settle.

Whipping Cream

Whipping cream takes seconds in your Vitamix.

1. Pour 2 cups (500 mL) heavy or whipping (35%) cream into the Vitamix container and secure the lid. With the switch on Variable, select speed 1 and turn the machine on. Gradually increase the speed to 10 and blend for 10 seconds.

2. Remove the lid and use a spatula to lift the whipped cream and gauge the texture. For firmer peaks, put the lid back on, remove the lid plug and whip, pulsing on speed 10 for 1 second at a time and pressing down with the tamper, just until the desired stiffness is reached. Serve immediately. Makes 2$1/4$ cups (550 mL).

Tips

Use cream right out of the refrigerator, as cold cream holds air better than warm cream.

For sweetened whipped cream, add 2 tbsp (30 mL) powdered sugar (or to taste) to the cream before whipping.

---

2. Flip the switch to High and blend for about 1 minute, using the tamper to press the cream into the blades. You will see water splashing on the sides of the container as the whey churns out of the butter.

3. Scrape the butter into a fine-mesh sieve set over a bowl and drain. Use a spatula to work the butter and press out the liquid. It's important to get all the whey out, to prevent spoilage, so you may even want to pat the butter dry with a folded paper towel.

4. Use immediately or transfer to a jar or wrap tightly in plastic wrap. Store in the refrigerator and use within a couple of weeks. Makes 6 oz (175 g).

Tips

Use cream right out of the refrigerator, as cold cream holds air better than warm cream, and the butter will churn more easily.

For salted butter, add $1/4$ tsp (1 mL) fine salt to the cream before churning.

Flavor your butter by adding minced herbs, dried fruit, extracts or spices after the butter is well drained.

Churning Butter

If you have never made your own butter, you will be pleasantly surprised by the sweet, fresh taste.

1. Pour 2 cups (500 mL) heavy or whipping (35%) cream into the Vitamix container, secure the lid and remove the lid plug. With the switch on Variable, select speed 1 and turn the machine on. Gradually increase the speed to 10 and blend for 10 seconds.

Chopping Cheese

If you want cheese to melt quickly, the fine, granular chop you can achieve in the Vitamix will expedite the process. There are two methods: one for firm, aged cheeses, like Parmesan, Gruyère and aged manchego, and another for medium-firm cheeses, like Cheddar and Swiss. Always chop the cheese cold, and don't try to chop more than 4 oz (125 g) at a time.

Firm Cheese

Cut 2 to 4 oz (60 to 125 g) cheese into 1-inch (2.5 cm) cubes. Place cheese cubes in the Vitamix container and secure the lid. With the switch on Variable, select speed 5 and pulse 10 times. Remove the lid and inspect the size of your cheese bits. If desired, continue pulsing just enough to get a finer mince. Use immediately or store in an airtight container in the refrigerator for up to 1 week.

Medium-Firm Cheese

Cut 2 to 4 oz (60 to 125 g) cheese into 1-inch (2.5 cm) cubes. Secure the lid of the Vitamix container and remove the lid plug. With the switch on Variable, select speed 5 and turn the machine on. Drop the cheese, one cube at a time, through the lid opening. Turn the machine off as soon as all the cheese is chopped. Use immediately or store in an airtight container in the refrigerator for up to 1 week.

Dry-Chopping Vegetables or Fresh Herbs

Your Vitamix is a powerful blender, and that's why it is often used to turn vegetables into smooth purées. Chopping vegetables instead means controlling all that power. All it takes is the right speed setting and a judicious application of the Pulse function.

Onions

Cut 2 onions into pieces that will fit through the lid opening. Secure the lid of the Vitamix container and remove the lid plug. With the switch on Variable, select speed 3 and turn the machine on. Drop the onion pieces, one at a time, through the lid opening, using the tamper if they are not falling into the blades. Turn the machine off as soon as all the onion is chopped.

Celery or Carrots

Place 2 celery stalks, cut into chunks, or 2 large carrots in the Vitamix container and secure the lid. With the switch on Variable, select speed 1 and turn the machine on. Gradually increase the speed to 5. Turn the machine off as soon as all the vegetables are chopped.

Fresh Herbs

Place 2 cups (500 mL) fresh herb leaves in the Vitamix container and secure the lid. Remove the lid plug and insert the tamper. With the switch on Variable, select speed 5 and pulse five times, using the tamper to press the leaves into the blades. Scrape the sides of the container and pulse three or more times, just until the desired mince size is achieved.

> **Tip**
>
> Firmer herbs, such as thyme, rosemary, oregano, chives or flat-leaf (Italian) parsley will mince; tender herbs, like basil or cilantro, will purée.

Wet-Chopping Vegetables

If you don't mind your chopped vegetables being wet, this is a fantastic way to chop them quickly. If you are planning on adding them to soup or sautéing them, a little dampness is not a problem. This technique is recommended for chopping cabbage for slaw or potatoes for hash browns; just drain well.

You can use 1 lb (500 g) cabbage, cut into $\frac{1}{2}$-inch (1 cm) slices (or fill the container up to the 4-cup/1 L mark), or 1 lb (500 g) potatoes, cut into 2-inch (5 cm) cubes. Or, for mirepoix, try this technique with 1 carrot, 2 stalks celery and 2 onions.

1. Place the vegetables in the Vitamix container and add cold water until the vegetables are lifted above the blades. Secure the lid. With the switch on Variable, select speed 5 and pulse until the desired chop size is achieved.

2. Transfer the vegetables to a fine-mesh sieve and drain well. If desired, spread on a kitchen towel to absorb any excess water.

Crushing Ice

If you've ever wished for the fine ice they use to make snow cones, or to quickly cool a drink on a hot summer day, you're in luck: you can crush ice almost instantly in your Vitamix.

1. Place a fine-mesh sieve in a bowl or in the sink.

2. Place the desired amount of ice cubes in the Vitamix container and add cold water until the ice cubes are floating above the blades. Secure the lid. With the switch on Variable, select speed 1 and turn the machine on. Gradually increase the speed to 10, then turn off the machine.

3. Drain the ice through the sieve and use immediately.

Grinding Coffee

Coffee is best when brewed from freshly ground beans, so grind just enough for a few days at a time. The dry grinding container is best for this, but you can make do with the standard blender container. Ten seconds should be just enough for a coarse grind; pulse for a few seconds longer for a fine grind.

1. Place up to 1 cup (250 mL) whole coffee beans in the Vitamix container and secure the lid. With the switch on Variable, select speed 1 and turn the machine on. Gradually increase the speed to 10 and grind for 10 seconds.

2. If desired, pulse a few more times to make a fine espresso grind.

Brewing Hot Cocoa

Warm up and ease a chocolate craving with comforting hot cocoa. Your Vitamix will warm the milk and melt the chocolate in under 3 minutes, with no powdered mixes.

1. Place 1 cup (250 mL) milk, 1/4 tsp (1 mL) vanilla extract and 2 oz (60 g) semisweet chocolate, cut into chunks, in the Vitamix container and secure the lid. With the switch on Variable, select speed 1 and turn the machine on. Gradually increase the speed to 10, then flip the switch to High and blend for 2 minutes.

2. Remove the lid and check whether the cocoa is as hot as you want. If you want it hotter, replace the lid, gradually increase the speed to High again and blend for 1 minute. **Makes 1 serving.**

Tips

Buy good dark chocolate bars and look at the weight on the package. It's easy to break a 4-oz (125 g) bar in half to get the amount you need for this recipe.

Replace some of the milk with cream for a richer drink.

Add 1 tsp (5 mL) granulated sugar to make your cocoa sweeter.

NUT BUTTERS and CHEESES

TIPS FOR SUCCESS

- The classic 64-ounce (2 L) container is best for making nut butters. The low-profile container is good for large double batches (4 cups/1 L of nuts is ideal), and not as good at making regular-sized batches. Do not use the dry grinding container to make nut butters.
- Making a batch of nut butter with less than 1 cup (250 mL) of nuts or seeds is a frustrating experience because the blades just can't engage fully with such a small amount. Use 1 to 3 cups (250 to 750 mL) of nuts or seeds.
- Nuts and seeds can be tough to grind, so you may want to add some oil or honey to make it easier. If you are grinding and pressing the nuts into the blades and not getting the results you want, turn off the machine, add 1 tbsp (15 mL) oil or honey and scrape the nuts to the center of the container, then start again at speed 1.
- If your nut butter is not grinding as quickly as you'd like, stop to scrape the container as many times as you need to.
- Don't grind a stiff butter for more than 2 minutes — it will be hard on the machine. Stop and let the machine and the mixture cool off for 10 minutes.
- If your Vitamix turns itself off while you are grinding, you have overheated it. Unplug it and leave it alone for 30 minutes, then plug it back in; it should start right up.
- Keep your fresh nut and seed butters in the refrigerator to keep their healthful oils from spoiling. They may be too stiff to spread when cold, so you may want to scoop out a serving and let it come to room temperature, or warm it gently in the microwave.

Almond Butter

You may well have bought your Vitamix just to make almond butter. It's truly a treat to enjoy it fresh, warm and smelling like almond heaven. Make it on a weekend morning and serve toast with freshly ground almond butter — your family will thank you!

MAKES ABOUT 2¹/₂ CUPS (625 ML)

4 cups	whole raw almonds	1 L
¹/₄ tsp	salt (optional)	1 mL
¹/₄ cup	canola oil	60 mL

Tips

Try toasting the almonds for your butter. Spread the nuts on a baking sheet and roast at 350°F (180°C) for 10 minutes or until fragrant and toasted. Immediately transfer to a bowl and let cool before grinding.

Because of a few cases of bacterial contamination of almonds, pasteurized almonds are now sold, and they make delicious almond butter.

1. Place the almonds in the Vitamix container and add salt (if using). Secure the lid, remove the lid plug and insert the tamper. With the switch on Variable, select speed 1 and turn the machine on. Gradually increase the speed to 10, then flip the switch to High and, using the tamper to push the nuts into the blades, grind for about 2 minutes or until the mixture is flowing around the blades.

2. Turn the machine off and scrape the mixture down. Add the oil and replace the lid and tamper. Gradually increase the speed to High again and blend for 30 seconds, pressing the butter into the blades.

3. Transfer the nut butter to a jar and use immediately or store in the refrigerator for up to 1 month.

Pistachio Butter

Yes, pistachios are pricey little nuts, but they are also one of the most uniquely flavorful nuts you can buy, and worth every penny. They make a deep green butter, rich and full of exotic flavor.

MAKES ABOUT 1¹/₂ CUPS (375 ML)

2 to 3 tbsp	canola oil or olive oil	30 to 45 mL
2 cups	shelled raw pistachios	500 mL
Pinch	salt	Pinch
1 tbsp	liquid honey (optional)	15 mL

Tips

Look for raw pistachios in the refrigerated bulk section at your natural foods store. They will be the freshest.

If you can find pistachio oil, use it for all or part of the oil in this recipe, for even more pistachio flavor.

1. Place 2 tbsp (30 mL) oil in the Vitamix container, then add the pistachios and salt. Secure the lid, remove the lid plug and insert the tamper. With the switch on Variable, select speed 1 and turn the machine on. Gradually increase the speed to 10, then flip the switch to High and, using the tamper to push the nuts into the blades, grind for about 1 minute or until the sound of the machine changes and it starts to labor and the mixture is moving around the blades.

2. Turn the machine off and taste the pistachio butter. If you want a creamier texture, add 1 tbsp (15 mL) more oil or honey and replace the lid and tamper. Gradually increase the speed to High again and blend for 30 seconds.

3. Transfer the nut butter to a jar and use immediately or store in the refrigerator for up to 1 month.

Peanut Butter

Fresh peanut butter is one of the joys of owning a Vitamix. The machine will crush the roasted peanuts to a warm butter, perfect for slathering on toast, right out of the machine. If you don't add oil, the butter will be quite thick and chunky.

MAKES ABOUT 1 CUP (250 ML)

2 cups	roasted unsalted peanuts	500 mL
1/4 tsp	salt (optional)	1 mL
1 tbsp	canola oil (optional)	15 mL

Tip

If you plan to make peanut butter regularly, buy skinned raw peanuts by the pound and keep them in the freezer. Toast them before using them in place of the roasted peanuts: Let them come to room temperature and spread on a baking sheet. Toast in a 350°F (180°C) oven for about 10 minutes or until fragrant and lightly toasted. Let cool before grinding.

1. Place the peanuts in the Vitamix container and add salt (if using). Secure the lid, remove the lid plug and insert the tamper. With the switch on Variable, select speed 1 and turn the machine on. Gradually increase the speed to 10, then flip the switch to High and, using the tamper to push the peanuts into the blades, grind for about 1 minute or until the sound of the machine changes and it starts to labor.

2. Turn the machine off and taste the peanut butter. If you want a creamier texture, add the oil and replace the lid and tamper. Gradually increase the speed to High again and blend for 30 seconds, pressing the butter into the blades.

3. Transfer the peanut butter to a jar and use immediately or store in the refrigerator for up to 1 month.

Variation

For a really chunky peanut butter, use 1 to 2 tbsp (15 to 30 mL) oil to make a thinner butter, then chop 1/2 cup (125 mL) additional roasted peanuts by hand and stir them into the finished peanut butter.

Peanut Sesame Butter

Give your peanut butter habit a little kick in the pants by adding the distinctive flavor of sesame. Sesame seeds are high in calcium, so this is a good way to make sure you are keeping your bones strong. Adding the optional oil will make your butter easier to spread, especially when cold.

MAKES ABOUT 1$^1/_2$ CUPS (375 ML)

2 cups	roasted unsalted peanuts	500 mL
1 cup	brown sesame seeds	250 mL
$^1/_4$ tsp	salt (optional)	1 mL
1 to 2 tbsp	canola oil (optional)	15 to 30 mL

Tip

For a deeper sesame flavor, toast the sesame seeds before grinding. Place them in a medium skillet and swirl over medium heat until fragrant and toasty. Immediately transfer to a bowl and let cool before grinding.

1. Place the peanuts and sesame seeds in the Vitamix container and add salt (if using). Secure the lid, remove the lid plug and insert the tamper. With the switch on Variable, select speed 1 and turn the machine on. Gradually increase the speed to 10, then flip the switch to High and, using the tamper to push the peanuts into the blades, grind for about 2 minutes or until the mixture is flowing around the blades.

2. Turn the machine off and scrape the mixture down. Add 1 tbsp (15 mL) oil (if using) and replace the lid and tamper. Gradually increase the speed to High again and blend for 30 seconds, pressing the butter into the blades.

3. Turn the machine off and check the texture of the butter. If desired, repeat step 2, blending in another 1 tbsp (15 mL) oil.

4. Transfer the peanut butter to a jar and use immediately or store in the refrigerator for up to 1 month.

Variation

Use sesame, peanut or olive oil in place of the canola oil to give the butter a different flavor.

Chocolate Hazelnut Butter

Unlike brand-name chocolate hazelnut spread, this one is free of dairy products and has real dark chocolate, for serious chocolate flavor. Adding dark chocolate to your morning toast is all about eating extra antioxidants, right?

MAKES ABOUT 1 CUP (250 ML)

- **Preheat oven to 325°F (160°C)**
- **Rimmed baking sheet**

1 cup	raw hazelnuts	250 mL
4 oz	semisweet chocolate, coarsely chopped	125 g
1/4 cup	powdered sugar (see page 13)	60 mL
1/2 tsp	salt	2 mL
1 tbsp	canola oil	15 mL
1/2 tsp	vanilla extract	2 mL

Tips

Semisweet chocolate is any chocolate with more than 60% cacao content. Depending on how much you like the strong, slightly bitter flavor of dark chocolate, you can go as high as 98% cacao for this butter. You can always add more sugar if it's too bitter for your taste.

If a dairy-free product is important to you, check the label of the chocolate to make sure it is, in fact, free of dairy ingredients.

This nut butter will be easier to spread at room temperature, so scoop out a portion and let it warm up before serving, or warm it gently in the microwave.

1. Spread the hazelnuts on the baking sheet and roast in preheated oven for 10 minutes or until fragrant and toasted. Immediately transfer to a folded kitchen towel, rub the skins from the nuts and let them cool. If some of the hazelnuts stubbornly refuse to give up their skins, return them to the baking sheet and roast for another 5 to 10 minutes, then try again.

2. Place the skinned hazelnuts in the Vitamix container. Add the chocolate, powdered sugar, salt, oil and vanilla. Secure the lid, remove the lid plug and insert the tamper. With the switch on Variable, select speed 1 and turn the machine on. Gradually increase the speed to 5 and, using the tamper to push the nuts into the blades, grind until the nuts begin to make a paste and the chocolate is melted, about 30 seconds.

3. Turn the machine off and scrape the nut butter from the corners of the container. Replace the lid, gradually increase the speed to High again and blend for 30 seconds.

4. Transfer the nut butter to a jar and use immediately or store in the refrigerator for up to 1 month.

Cinnamon Walnut Butter

This butter smells and tastes so fantastic warm, just out of the blender, that you may have a hard time saving any for another day. The combination of walnuts and cinnamon may remind you of your favorite cookies as you spread it on a virtuous slab of whole-grain toast.

MAKES ABOUT 1$^1/_2$ CUPS (375 ML)

3 cups	raw walnut pieces and/or halves	750 mL
2 tsp	ground cinnamon	10 mL
Pinch	salt (optional)	Pinch
3 tbsp	liquid honey	45 mL
1 tbsp	melted coconut oil or canola oil	15 mL

Tip

Walnut pieces are less expensive than unbroken halves, so save a few cents and use the cheaper ones for grinding.

1. Place walnuts, cinnamon, salt (if using), honey and oil in the Vitamix container. Secure the lid, remove the lid plug and insert the tamper. With the switch on Variable, select speed 1 and turn the machine on. Quickly increase the speed to 10, then flip the switch to High and, using the tamper to press the nuts into the blades, blend for 1 minute or until the machine makes a high-pitched chugging sound, the butter starts to flow freely and the machine's noise changes to a low, laboring sound.

2. Transfer the nut butter to a jar and use immediately or store in the refrigerator for up to 1 month.

Variation

Pecans are also fantastic in this recipe, with pure maple syrup instead of honey, for the taste of pecan pie in a spread.

Tahini

Versatile tahini is an essential ingredient in hummus and other Middle Eastern foods and has found its way into Asian recipes, too. Once you make it yourself, you will realize how much oil the manufacturers of the thin, pourable tahini have to be adding.

MAKES ABOUT 2/3 CUP (150 ML)

1 cup	sesame seeds	250 mL
2 to 4 tbsp	canola oil or extra virgin olive oil	30 to 60 mL
Pinch	salt (optional)	Pinch

Tips

Use brown (unhulled) sesame seeds for a deep sesame flavor or white (hulled) seeds for a milder flavor.

For the most neutral, pale tahini, skip step 1 and use the raw seeds.

1. In a medium skillet over medium heat, toast the sesame seeds, stirring often, for about 5 minutes or until fragrant and toasty. Immediately transfer to a bowl and let cool slightly.

2. Place the oil in the Vitamix container, then add the sesame seeds. Secure the lid, remove the lid plug and insert the tamper. With the switch on Variable, select speed 1 and turn the machine on. Using the tamper to push the seeds into the blades, gradually increase the speed only enough to keep the paste moving and engaged with the blades.

3. Turn the machine off and scrape the mixture down, then replace the lid and start over at speed 1, repeating as many times as it takes to make a smooth paste. If desired, add the salt and blend to mix.

4. Transfer the tahini to a jar and use immediately or store in the refrigerator for up to 2 weeks.

Variation

Untoasted almond oil, sold as a cooking and massage oil, would be a good substitution for the oil in this recipe.

Pepita Butter with Cumin and Chiles

Pepitas, or hulled pumpkin seeds, are a deep green, oval seed from a completely different kind of pumpkin than your jack-o'-lantern. They are big, plump and full of minerals and healthy fats. Their distinctive flavor pairs perfectly with cumin and chiles in this spreadable celebration.

MAKES ABOUT 1 CUP (250 ML)

2 cups	raw green pumpkin seeds (pepitas)	500 mL
4 tsp	canola oil (approx.)	20 mL
1/2 tsp	ground cumin	2 mL
1/2 tsp	hot pepper flakes	2 mL
1/2 tsp	salt	2 mL

Tip

Make sure you are buying raw pumpkin seeds, not roasted or salted seeds. Your butter will be much better if made with freshly toasted seeds.

1. In a large skillet over medium-high heat, swirl the pumpkin seeds until they start to pop and smell toasty, about 3 minutes. Immediately transfer to a bowl and let cool completely.

2. Place the oil in the Vitamix container, then add the pumpkin seeds, cumin, hot pepper flakes and salt. Secure the lid, remove the lid plug and insert the tamper. With the switch on Variable, select speed 1 and turn the machine on. Using the tamper to push the seeds into the blades, gradually increase the speed to 10. Grind for about 2 minutes, stopping the machine twice to scrape down the container and add more oil as needed for a creamy texture.

3. Transfer the seed butter to a jar and use immediately or store in the refrigerator for up to 1 month.

Variation

You can certainly leave out the spices, for a plain pumpkin seed butter.

Raw Cashew Cream

Cashew cream is the vegan answer to dairy cream, and can be made either savory or sweet. Make the savory version to use in Vegan Alfredo Sauce (page 32) or to stir into soups and pastas for added creamy richness. Make the sweet variation to use as a topping for fresh fruit or vegan desserts.

∾∾∾∾∾∾∾∾∾∾∾∾∾∾∾∾∾∾∾∾∾∾∾∾∾∾∾∾∾∾∾

MAKES ABOUT 1¼ CUPS (300 ML)

1 cup	raw cashews	250 mL
	Cool water	
½ cup	water	125 mL
1 tbsp	freshly squeezed lemon juice	15 mL
½ tsp	salt	2 mL

Tip

Rinsing the soaked nuts removes any bitterness and gives you the mildest, sweetest flavor.

1. Place the cashews in a 2-cup (500 mL) measure and add cool water up to the 2-cup mark. Let soak overnight at room temperature or in the refrigerator. Drain and rinse well.

2. Place the cashews, ½ cup (125 mL) water, lemon juice and salt in the Vitamix container. Secure the lid, remove the lid plug and insert the tamper. With the switch on Variable, select speed 1 and turn the machine on. Using the tamper to push the nuts into the blades, gradually increase the speed to 4 or 5. Grind for about 30 seconds or until a coarse purée forms and is moving freely.

3. Gradually increase the speed to 10 and blend for 1 minute or until the mixture is silky smooth and creamy.

4. Transfer the cashew cream to a jar and use immediately or store in the refrigerator for up to 1 week.

Variations

Sweet Cashew Cream: Use ¼ cup (60 mL) agave nectar or pure maple syrup in place of the lemon juice, and replace the salt with an equal amount of vanilla extract.

Cheesy Cashew Cream: Add ½ tsp (2 mL) garlic powder and 1 tbsp (15 mL) nutritional yeast to the savory version.

Vegan Almond Cheese

Dairy cheeses are made by fermenting milk and aging it to build complex flavors. Vegan "cheese" makers have been employing a similar strategy for years, using various sources for the lactobacilli needed to populate a nut purée like this one. In this recipe, convenient and easy-to-find probiotic bacteria capsules deliver active bacteria to give the cheese some tangy undertones. Serve as you would a spreadable cheese: on crackers, in a panini or crumbled on pizza or pasta.

MAKES ABOUT 1 CUP (250 ML)

- **Small wire-mesh sieve**
- **Cheesecloth**

1 cup	slivered almonds	250 mL
	Cool water	
1/2 cup	water (approx.)	125 mL
1	probiotic bacteria capsule (see tip, page 28)	1
1/2 tsp	salt	2 mL
2 tbsp	melted refined coconut oil	30 mL
	Fine salt or Meyer Lemon Salt (page 77)	

1. Place the almonds in a 2-cup (500 mL) measure and add cool water up to the 2-cup mark. Let soak overnight at room temperature or in the refrigerator. Drain and rinse well.

2. Place the almonds and 1/2 cup (125 mL) water in the Vitamix container. Secure the lid, remove the lid plug and insert the tamper. With the switch on Variable, select speed 1 and turn the machine on. As the mixture engages the blades, gradually increase the speed to 3, using the tamper to press the nuts into the blades, and grind until the nuts are very finely minced. If the mixture starts flying up the sides or sticking in the corners, turn off the machine, scrape the nuts to the center of the container and replace the lid before starting over at speed 1.

3. Decrease to speed 1 and blend until the mixture is smoothly puréed, adding 1 to 2 tbsp (15 to 30 mL) more water through the lid opening, if necessary.

4. Remove the lid, open the probiotic capsule and empty it into the nut mixture, discarding the capsule shell. Replace the lid and blend again, gradually increasing the speed as long as the mixture stays engaged with the blades, until well combined.

5. Scrape the purée into a medium bowl and cover with a lint-free kitchen towel so there is air circulation but the purée is protected from dust. Let stand at room temperature for 2 days (or 1 day if it is very warm in the room). The mixture will bubble a bit, develop a slightly tangy smell and may form a little crust. At this point, stir in the salt and coconut oil.

6. Line the sieve with two layers of cheesecloth, leaving enough overhang to fold back over the top. Place the sieve over a medium bowl. Scrape the purée into the sieve and smooth the top, then fold the cheesecloth over it. Place a large can or other weight on top of the cheesecloth and place the whole thing in the refrigerator.

7. Each day, unwrap the cheesecloth, then rewrap it (this keeps the cloth from sticking). After 3 to 7 days, the cheese should have a slight tangy smell and should have shrunk a bit. Remove the cheesecloth and sprinkle the cheese with fine salt or coat with seasoned salt. Transfer the cheese to a storage container and store in the refrigerator for up to 2 weeks.

Variation

Once you try your hand at this cheese, you can substitute other nuts, such as pistachios or raw pine nuts, for a different appearance and flavor.

Cashew Chèvre

For a less involved non-dairy cheese, with the option of a short fermentation or no fermentation, try this creamy spread. You'll supplement the tanginess of fermentation with a little lemon juice and nutritional yeast, for instant complexity. Keep this cheese in the refrigerator, ready to smear on a bagel or sprinkle on pasta.

∾ ∾

MAKES ABOUT ³/₄ CUP (175 ML)

1 cup	raw cashews	250 mL
	Cool water	
¹/₄ cup	water	60 mL
1	probiotic bacteria capsule (see tip)	1
2 tbsp	nutritional yeast (optional)	30 mL
1 tsp	salt	5 mL
2 tbsp	melted refined coconut oil	30 mL
1 tbsp	freshly squeezed lemon juice	15 mL

Tips

When purchasing probiotic capsules, look for brands with more than one kind of bacteria and a high CFU (colony forming units) count. Check the expiration date to make sure they are fresh.

Nutritional yeast is a cheesy-tasting, completely inactive form of yeast, bred and cultivated specifically to be an excellent source of vitamin B₁₂ for vegans. It's also a good source of umami and provides a bit of a cheesy mouthfeel.

Variation

Like chèvre, this cheese is delicious with add-ins such as diced sun-dried tomatoes, chopped fresh basil or thyme, or minced green onions.

1. Place the cashews in a 2-cup (500 mL) measure and add cool water up to the 2-cup mark. Let soak overnight at room temperature or in the refrigerator. Drain and rinse well.

2. Place the cashews and ¹/₄ cup (60 mL) water in the Vitamix container and secure the lid. With the switch on Variable, select speed 1 and turn the machine on. As the cashews are minced, gradually increase the speed to 7 and blend, stopping to scrape down the container if the nuts are sticking to the sides and not engaging the blades, for 2 to 3 minutes or until the mixture is smooth.

3. Remove the lid, open the probiotic capsule and empty it into the nut mixture, discarding the capsule shell. Replace the lid and blend again, gradually increasing the speed as long as the mixture stays engaged with the blades, until well combined.

4. If you wish to skip the fermentation step, add the nutritional yeast (if using), salt, coconut oil and lemon juice to the container and blend to mix, then proceed with step 6.

5. To ferment, scrape the purée into a jar or bowl and cover with a lint-free kitchen towel. Secure with a rubber band and let stand at room temperature for at least 24 hours or up to 2 days (it will ferment more quickly in the summer; in winter, it may need a couple of days). When the mixture smells tangy, stir in nutritional yeast (if using), salt, coconut oil and lemon juice.

6. Transfer the cheese to a jar or other storage container and use immediately or store in the refrigerator for up to 2 weeks.

SAUCES

Fast Fresh Italian Tomato Sauce

When you want real tomato flavor, make your own sauce from truly ripe tomatoes. This is a good sauce to make in the fall, when tomatoes are plentiful and inexpensive. It freezes well, and you will be glad that you saved a piece of summer. Serve with pasta, on pizza or in a casserole.

MAKES ABOUT 3¹/₂ CUPS (875 ML)

2 tbsp	extra virgin olive oil	30 mL
1	large onion, quartered	1
1	stalk celery, cut into 2-inch (5 cm) chunks	1
¹/₂	medium carrot, cut into 1-inch (2.5 cm) chunks	¹/₂
1	clove garlic, chopped	1
2 lbs	very ripe tomatoes, cored (and halved if very large)	1 kg
2	large bay leaves	2
¹/₂ tsp	salt	2 mL
¹/₂ tsp	freshly ground black pepper	2 mL
1 tsp	granulated sugar (optional)	5 mL
¹/₂ cup	lightly packed fresh basil, chopped	125 mL
2 tbsp	lightly packed fresh oregano, chopped	30 mL

Tip

To measure fresh herbs, pluck the leaves and place them in the measuring cup or spoon, pressing them down gently as you go, until the lightly compressed herbs reach the volume you need. If using the tender stems of herbs like basil or cilantro, add them as you measure. Don't use thyme or rosemary stems for anything but stock.

Variation

Add a generous pinch of hot pepper flakes when sautéing the vegetables for a diavolo sauce.

1. In a large sauté pan, heat oil over low heat.

2. Secure the lid of the Vitamix container and remove the lid plug. With the switch on Variable, select speed 3 and turn the machine on. Drop in the onion pieces, one at a time, using the tamper if they are not falling into the blades. Process for a few seconds, until the onions are chopped (but not puréed). Scrape the onions into the pan.

3. Place the celery, carrot and garlic in the Vitamix container and secure the lid. With the switch on Variable, select speed 1 and turn the machine on. Gradually increase the speed to 5. Turn the machine off as soon as all the vegetables are chopped and scrape them into the pan.

4. Increase the heat to medium-high and cook, stirring often, for about 10 minutes or until vegetables are softened.

5. Meanwhile, place the tomatoes in the Vitamix container and secure the lid. With the switch on Variable, select speed 1 and turn the machine on. Gradually increase the speed to 10, then flip the switch to High and purée for about 10 seconds or until smooth.

6. Pour tomato purée into the pan and stir in bay leaves, salt and pepper; bring to a boil. Reduce heat and simmer, stirring occasionally, for about 30 minutes or until thickened. Taste for seasoning and add sugar, if desired. Stir in basil and oregano; simmer for 2 minutes. Discard bay leaves.

7. Serve immediately or transfer to an airtight container and let cool, uncovered, then cover and store in the refrigerator for up to 1 week or freeze for up to 3 months.

Veggie Bolognese

Yes, Bolognese sauce is all about a very thick, meaty companion to sturdy pasta. This vegan version employs umami-rich, meaty minced mushrooms in place of beef for a surprisingly meaty-tasting result. Your Vitamix will make short work of the mincing, so you can enjoy your pasta in no time.

MAKES ABOUT 3 CUPS (750 ML)

8 oz	mushrooms, trimmed	250 g
1	onion, quartered	1
1	large carrot, cut into chunks	1
1	clove garlic, chopped	1
2 tbsp	extra virgin olive oil	30 mL
1	can (28 oz/796 mL) whole tomatoes, with juice	1
1 tsp	salt	5 mL

Tips

Have a light hand when chopping with the Vitamix; this is one time to keep its power in check. Just process the minimum amount of time needed to chop the vegetables.

For even more meaty flavor, try using cremini (baby bella) mushrooms in place of the white button mushrooms.

1. Secure the lid of the Vitamix container and remove the lid plug. With the switch on Variable, select speed 5 and turn the machine on. Drop in the mushrooms, one at a time, using the tamper if they are not falling into the blades. Process for a few seconds, until the mushrooms are chopped (but not puréed). Scrape the mushrooms into a bowl.

2. Repeat step 1 with the onion, then the carrot and garlic. Scrape the vegetables into the bowl.

3. In a large pot, heat oil over medium-high heat. Add mushroom mixture and cook, stirring, for about 3 minutes or until it starts to sizzle. Reduce heat to medium-low and cook, stirring often, for 10 to 15 minutes or until the pan is dry and the carrots are soft.

4. Meanwhile, place the tomatoes in the Vitamix container and secure the lid. With the switch on Variable, select speed 1 and turn the machine on. Gradually increase the speed to 10, then flip the switch to High and purée for about 10 seconds or until smooth.

5. Pour tomato purée into the pot and stir in salt; bring to a simmer over medium-high heat. Reduce heat to medium-low and simmer, stirring occasionally, for about 30 minutes or until thickened.

6. Serve immediately or transfer to an airtight container and let cool, uncovered, then cover and store in the refrigerator for up to 1 week or freeze for up to 3 months.

Vegan Alfredo Sauce

If you haven't tried cashew cream, you will be amazed by how incredibly creamy and rich it is. With some sprightly lemon and parsley, it takes on all the qualities of creamy Alfredo, with none of the dairy.

MAKES ABOUT 2 CUPS (500 ML)

1	batch Raw Cashew Cream (page 26)	1
1 tbsp	nutritional yeast	15 mL
1/2 tsp	salt	2 mL
2 tsp	grated lemon zest	10 mL
1 tbsp	extra virgin olive oil	15 mL
1	clove garlic, chopped	1

Tip

Keep raw cashews handy, stored in a jar in the freezer, for all your creamy vegan needs.

1. In a small bowl, combine cashew cream, yeast, salt and lemon zest.

2. In a large sauté pan, heat oil over medium heat. Add garlic and cook, stirring, for 30 to 60 seconds, just until fragrant. Add cashew cream mixture and stir well. Reduce heat to low and cook, stirring, for 2 to 3 minutes, just until warm.

3. Serve immediately or transfer to an airtight container and let cool, uncovered, then cover and store in the refrigerator for up to 1 week.

Variation

Rosemary Alfredo Sauce: Add 1 tbsp (15 mL) chopped fresh rosemary with the garlic.

Recipe Suggestion

Cook 8 oz (250 g) fettuccine in a large pot of boiling salted water until tender but firm, adding 1 julienned large carrot for the last 3 minutes. Drain well and add to sauce in pan, tossing to coat. Add 1 to 2 tbsp (15 to 30 mL) water to thin, as desired. Serve sprinkled with 1/4 cup (60 mL) chopped fresh parsley leaves (or other fresh herbs). Makes 4 servings.

Creamy Vegan Artichoke Sauce

You don't have to be vegan to love this sauce. Creamy avocado and a sparkle of lemon carry the artichoke hearts in a seriously flavorful and easy sauce. It's great for pasta, or you can smear it on crostini, toss boiled new potatoes in it or stir it into hot cooked grains.

MAKES ABOUT 2 CUPS (500 ML)

1/2 cup	unsweetened almond milk	125 mL
1 tbsp	freshly squeezed lemon juice	15 mL
1	can (14 1/2 oz/400 mL) artichoke hearts, drained and trimmed	1
1	large avocado, halved and pitted	1
1/4 cup	lightly packed fresh parsley, coarsely chopped	60 mL
1 tbsp	extra virgin olive oil	15 mL
1	large onion, chopped	1
1	clove garlic, chopped	1

Tip

Always drain artichoke hearts and trim the tips of the leaves. The leaves are often sharp and far too fibrous to eat.

1. Place the almond milk, lemon juice, artichoke hearts, avocado and parsley in the Vitamix container. Secure the lid, remove the lid plug and insert the tamper. With the switch on Variable, select speed 1 and turn the machine on. Using the tamper to push the ingredients into the blades, gradually increase the speed to 5. Process for 30 seconds. Scrape down the container and purée for a few more seconds, if necessary, until smooth. Leave the mixture in the container.

2. In a large sauté pan, heat oil over medium-high heat. Add onion, reduce heat to medium and cook, stirring, for about 5 minutes or until softened. Add garlic and cook, stirring, for 1 minute.

3. Scrape the artichoke mixture into the pan and cook, stirring, over medium heat just until warmed through.

4. Serve immediately or transfer to an airtight container and let cool, uncovered, then cover and store in the refrigerator for up to 2 days.

Variation

Use other fresh herbs or greens, such as basil, arugula or mint, in place of the parsley for a different flavor.

Recipe Suggestion

Cook 8 oz (250 g) cavatappi or spiral pasta in a large pot of boiling salted water until tender but firm. Drain well and return to the pot over medium heat. Add sauce and toss gently to coat. Cook, stirring, just until heated through. Fold in 1 cup (250 mL) chopped tomatoes. Makes 4 servings.

Creamy White Bean and Eggplant Sauce

Velvety puréed white beans make a surprisingly rich and creamy sauce for pasta. Studded with tender bits of eggplant and fragrant with rosemary and garlic, this sauce will become a favorite, even among meat lovers.

MAKES ABOUT 3 CUPS (750 ML)

1/3 cup	extra virgin olive oil	75 mL
1 lb	eggplant, peeled and cubed	500 g
2	cloves garlic, chopped	2
1	medium shallot, chopped	1
1 tbsp	fresh rosemary, chopped	15 mL
1/2 tsp	hot pepper flakes	2 mL
1 tsp	salt	5 mL
1 cup	dry white wine	250 mL
1	can (14 to 15 oz/398 to 425 mL) navy beans, drained and rinsed	1
1/2 cup	grape tomatoes	125 mL
	Water	
1/2 cup	lightly packed fresh parsley	125 mL

Tips

If you can only find larger cans of beans, use 1 1/2 cups (375 mL) rinsed drained beans, reserving the remainder for another use. You can also soak and cook the beans yourself, starting with about 1/2 cup (125 mL) dried navy beans.

Your Vitamix is powerful enough that you can use some of the tender parsley stems; it will buzz right through them.

1. In a large sauté pan, heat oil over medium-high heat. Add eggplant and stir, turning to coat. Cook, stirring constantly, for about 5 minutes or until eggplant starts to shrink and get some browned spots. Reduce heat to medium and add garlic, shallot, rosemary, hot pepper flakes and salt. Cook, stirring often, for 10 minutes or until eggplant is soft and golden. Reduce heat to low.

2. Place wine, beans and tomatoes in the Vitamix container and secure the lid. With the switch on Variable, select speed 1 and turn the machine on. Gradually increase the speed to 10 and purée for about 20 seconds or until smooth.

3. Pour purée into the pan and stir, scraping the bottom of the pan, to gently fold the bean purée into the eggplant mixture. If it seems too thick, add water 1 tbsp (15 mL) at a time. Stir in parsley and cook for 30 to 60 seconds or until heated through.

Variation

Replace the eggplant with cubed zucchini or yellow summer squash, or even green beans.

Recipe Suggestion

Cook 1 lb (500 g) farfalle pasta in a large pot of boiling salted water until tender but firm. Drain well and serve topped with hot sauce. Makes 6 servings.

Instant Creamy Spinach Sauce

If the thought of making a cream sauce on a weeknight seems crazy to you, you need this recipe. No stirring, no whisking; just a few spins in the Vitamix and you have a sauce. In this case, you have a vegetable, too, with brilliant green spinach puréed right in.

MAKES ABOUT 2¹/₄ CUPS (550 ML)

4 oz	aged Gruyère cheese, cubed	125 g
¹/₂ cup	half-and-half (10%) cream	125 mL
4 oz	cream cheese or Neufchâtel, softened	125 g
5 oz	packed fresh spinach (about 5 cups/1.25 L)	150 g
1 cup	lightly packed fresh basil	250 mL
¹/₂ tsp	salt	2 mL
¹/₂ tsp	freshly ground black pepper	2 mL

Tips

Buy bagged salad spinach for this, and you will have dinner on the table in minutes.

Because your machine is so powerful, you can use tender stems as well as leaves, and get the most out of your spinach and basil.

1. Secure the lid on the Vitamix container and remove the lid plug. With the switch on Variable, select speed 5 and turn the machine on. Drop in the Gruyère, one cube at a time. Insert the lid plug and process for a few seconds, until the cheese is finely ground. Transfer the cheese to a small bowl.

2. Place the cream, cream cheese, spinach, basil, salt and pepper in the Vitamix container. Add the ground Gruyère on top. Secure the lid and insert the tamper. With the switch on Variable, select speed 1 and turn the machine on. Using the tamper to push the ingredients into the blades, gradually increase the speed to 5. Purée for about 30 seconds or until smooth.

3. Gradually increase the speed to 10, then flip the switch to High and let the machine run for 4 minutes, until the sauce is steaming hot. Serve immediately.

Variation

In place of the Gruyère cheese, try Parmesan, Asiago or manchego.

Recipe Suggestion

Cook 1 lb (500 g) pasta in a large pot of boiling salted water until tender but firm. Drain well and return to the pot over medium heat. Add sauce and toss gently to coat. Cook, stirring gently, until slightly thickened. Makes 4 to 6 servings.

Arugula Goat Cheese Sauce

Now that arugula is a popular salad green, you can use it by the handful in sauces like this one. It's a fantastically healthy and delicious herb with a nutty flavor. Creamy goat cheese adds a bit of tanginess and great depth of flavor. This sauce can be used for pasta, pizza or vegetables, or drizzled over a roasted chicken breast.

MAKES ABOUT 1 1/2 CUPS (375 ML)

1 oz	Parmesan cheese, cubed	30 g
1/2 cup	half-and-half (10%) cream	125 mL
4 oz	creamy goat cheese (chèvre), softened	125 g
1	clove garlic, sliced	1
3 cups	packed arugula (about 3 oz/90 g)	750 mL
1/2 tsp	salt	2 mL
1/2 tsp	freshly ground black pepper	2 mL

1. Secure the lid on the Vitamix container and remove the lid plug. With the switch on Variable, select speed 1 and turn the machine on. Drop in the Parmesan, one cube at a time, then gradually increase the speed to 10 and flip the switch to High for 5 seconds or until the cheese is finely ground. Transfer the cheese to a small bowl.

2. Place the cream, goat cheese, garlic, arugula, salt and pepper in the Vitamix container. Add the ground Parmesan on top. Secure the lid and insert the tamper. With the switch on Variable, select speed 1 and turn the machine on. Using the tamper to push the ingredients into the blades, gradually increase the speed to 5. After about 10 seconds, the mixture will be flowing around the blades and you can gradually increase the speed to 10 and flip the switch to High for a few seconds, until smooth. Serve immediately.

Variation

The arugula can be supplemented with fresh basil, parsley or spinach; just make sure to use 3 cups (750 mL) total.

Recipe Suggestion

Cook 8 oz (250 g) penne pasta in a large pot of boiling salted water until tender but firm, adding 1 chopped large carrot and 1 cup (250 mL) thawed frozen peas for the last 2 minutes. Drain well and return to the pot over medium-low heat. Add sauce and toss gently to coat. Cook, stirring, just until heated through. Makes 4 servings.

Creamy Cheddar Sauce

This decadent cheese sauce hides a nutritious secret: puréed into the mix is a combination of cauliflower and carrot that blends to a creamy orange hue and stands harmoniously behind just enough tangy Cheddar to keep it cheesy. Serve hot over vegetables or pasta.

MAKES ABOUT 2½ CUPS (625 ML)

- Steamer basket

1½ cups	chopped cauliflower	375 mL
1	medium carrot, chopped	1
1 cup	whole milk	250 mL
8 oz	sharp or extra-sharp (old or extra-old) Cheddar cheese, cubed	250 g
½ oz	Parmesan cheese, chopped	15 g
¾ tsp	salt	3 mL

Tip

Use a well-aged Cheddar, so the cheese flavor will carry through and mask the vegetable flavors.

1. In a steamer basket set over a pot of boiling water, steam cauliflower and carrot until very tender, about 10 minutes.
2. Transfer the vegetables to the Vitamix container and add milk, Cheddar, Parmesan and salt. Secure the lid. With the switch on Variable, select speed 1 and turn the machine on. Gradually increase the speed to 10, then flip the switch to High and blend for 1 minute or until the sauce is creamy and warm. If desired, blend for another 2 minutes to heat the sauce further.

Variation

Try this with other aged cheeses, such as Mimolette or manchego.

Recipe Suggestion

Macaroni and Cheese: Cook 8 oz (250 g) macaroni in a pot of boiling salted water until tender but firm. Drain and combine with the sauce in an 8-cup (2 L) glass baking dish. Top with 1 cup (250 mL) buttered crumbs and bake in a 400°F (200°C) oven for 20 minutes or until bubbly. Makes 4 servings.

Classic Swiss Fondue

Making fondue on the stovetop involves quite a bit of stirring, and if you turn your back on it for a moment, you might have a disaster on your hands. The Vitamix takes all the worry out of the process: the friction of the blades melts the cheese and cooks the sauce to creamy perfection.

MAKES ABOUT 2 CUPS (500 ML)

1 tsp	extra virgin olive oil	5 mL
1 cup	chopped onion	250 mL
1/2 cup	dry white wine	125 mL
1/4 cup	milk	60 mL
8 oz	Emmental cheese, cubed	250 g
2 tsp	arrowroot starch	10 mL
1 tbsp	water	15 mL
	Bread and vegetables (see tip)	

Tips

For the vegetables, try boiled new potatoes, baby carrots or chopped broccoli or cauliflower.

Take a little longer with the onions, if you can. Half an hour of cooking will only improve the flavor of your fondue with some caramelization.

1. In a medium sauté pan, heat oil over medium-high heat. Add onion and cook, stirring, reducing the heat to low as the onion starts to soften, for at least 10 minutes (see tip) or until golden brown.

2. Scrape the onions into the Vitamix container and add wine, milk and cheese cubes. Secure the lid and remove the lid plug. With the switch on Variable, select speed 1 and turn the machine on. Gradually increase the speed to 10 and blend for 5 minutes. There will be steam rising from the cheese mixture.

3. In a cup, combine arrowroot starch and water. With the machine running, pour the starch mixture through the lid opening and process for 1 minute. Serve with bread and vegetables for dipping.

Variation

Other cheeses make wonderful fondue; just make sure they are good melting cheeses, such as Gruyère, Appenzeller, Tête de Moine, Comté and other variations on Swiss cheese.

Basic Salsa

A tasty fresh salsa can make the meal, whether you use it to top grilled chicken or rice and beans, or just as a dip for chips.

MAKES ABOUT 1 CUP (250 ML)

1	clove garlic, cut into pieces	1
1	large jalapeño pepper, seeded	1
8 oz	plum (Roma) tomatoes (2 large), halved and cored, divided	250 g
1 tbsp	freshly squeezed lime juice	15 mL
1/2	green bell pepper, cut into eighths	1/2
2 tbsp	chopped fresh cilantro	30 mL
1 tsp	salt	5 mL
1/2 tsp	freshly ground black pepper	2 mL

Tip

Have everything ready to go and, in step 3, be careful to just process enough to chop, not purée.

1. Place the garlic and jalapeño in the Vitamix container and secure the lid. With the switch on Variable, select speed 1 and turn the machine on. Roughly chop the garlic and jalapeño, increasing the speed to 3 for a few seconds. Scrape down the container.

2. Add 1 of the tomatoes and the lime juice. Secure the lid. With the switch on Variable, select speed 1 and turn the machine on. Gradually increase the speed to 10 and purée for about 30 seconds or until smooth.

3. Add the remaining tomato, green pepper, cilantro, salt and pepper. Cover tightly and, on speed 10, pulse to roughly chop the vegetables. Do not overprocess.

4. Transfer to a bowl and use immediately, or store in an airtight container in the refrigerator for up to 1 day.

Variation

This is a medium salsa. For a little more heat, you can add more jalapeño or substitute hotter chile peppers, such as serranos.

Spanish Salsa Verde

This fresh green sauce is perfect over fish or chicken, tossed with rice or pasta, or even as a topping for eggs. There are just a few anchovies in the mix, adding umami and a salty richness. It's entirely possible that even people who think they don't like anchovies will love this sauce.

MAKES ABOUT 1¼ CUPS (300 ML)

½ cup	extra virgin olive oil	125 mL
¼ cup	red or white wine vinegar	60 mL
4	large anchovies, drained	4
2	cloves garlic, peeled	2
2 cups	lightly packed fresh basil leaves	500 mL
2 cups	lightly packed fresh parsley leaves	500 mL
1 cup	lightly packed fresh mint leaves	250 mL
2 tbsp	drained capers	30 mL
½ tsp	salt	2 mL

Tips

Use a salad spinner to wash and dry the herbs. Simply pick the leaves from the stems and lightly pack them into the measuring cup, then dump them into the salad spinner. Cover with cold water and swish the leaves to remove any grit. Lift out the spinner basket and pour out the water, then spin-dry.

If you prefer, you can replace some of the parsley with additional mint.

1. Place the oil, vinegar, anchovies, garlic, basil, parsley, mint, capers and salt in the Vitamix container. Secure the lid, remove the lid plug and insert the tamper. With the switch on Variable, select speed 1 and turn the machine on. Gradually increase the speed to 10, then flip the switch to High. Using the tamper to press the ingredients into the blades, purée for 30 to 40 seconds or until smooth.

2. Transfer to a bowl and use immediately, or store in an airtight container in the refrigerator for up to 2 days.

Basil Pesto

Pesto is a classic sauce to toss with pasta, and could be the purest expression of the glory of basil. But pesto is more than just a pasta sauce; it is a versatile time-saver, whether you use it to top a piece of chicken or fish, make vegetables irresistible or elevate pizza, crostini or a bagel.

MAKES ABOUT 1$\frac{1}{4}$ CUPS (300 ML)

$\frac{1}{2}$ cup	extra virgin olive oil	125 mL
2	cloves garlic, peeled	2
2 oz	Parmesan cheese, sliced	60 g
2 cups	lightly packed fresh basil	500 mL
1 cup	lightly packed fresh spinach	250 mL
$\frac{1}{2}$ cup	pine nuts, toasted (see tip)	125 mL
$\frac{1}{2}$ tsp	salt	2 mL

Tips

Because your machine is so powerful, you can use tender stems as well as leaves, and get the most out of your basil and spinach.

To toast pine nuts, place a small skillet over medium-low heat. Add the pine nuts and cook, stirring constantly, until fragrant and toasted, about 3 minutes.

1. Place the oil, garlic, Parmesan, basil, spinach, pine nuts and salt in the Vitamix container. Secure the lid, remove the lid plug and insert the tamper. With the switch on Variable, select speed 1 and turn the machine on. Gradually increase the speed to 7, using the tamper to press the ingredients into the blades, and blend for about 30 seconds or until very smooth.

2. Transfer to a bowl and use immediately, or transfer to an airtight container and store in the refrigerator for up to 3 days or in the freezer for up to 3 months.

Variations

Substitute arugula for the basil.

Replace half the basil with parsley.

Try walnuts or almonds in place of the pine nuts.

Chimichurri

Chimichurri, the pesto of Argentina, has now become the property of the world. In this version, citrusy cilantro comes to the fore, so make sure your guests are cilantro lovers before you serve it, or prepare the variation. Serve over grilled steaks, chicken or fish.

MAKES ABOUT 1¹/₂ CUPS (375 ML)

6	cloves garlic, peeled	6
1 cup	chopped onion	250 mL
2 cups	lightly packed fresh cilantro (see tip)	500 mL
1 cup	lightly packed fresh parsley (see tip)	250 mL
2 tbsp	fresh oregano leaves	30 mL
1 tbsp	dried thyme	15 mL
1 tbsp	ground cumin	15 mL
¹/₂ tsp	salt	2 mL
¹/₂ tsp	hot pepper flakes	2 mL
¹/₂ cup	white vinegar	125 mL
¹/₂ cup	extra virgin olive oil	125 mL

Tip

Your Vitamix is powerful enough that you can use some of the tender parsley and cilantro stems; it will buzz right through them.

1. Place the garlic, onion, cilantro, parsley, oregano, thyme, cumin, salt and hot pepper flakes in the Vitamix container. Secure the lid, remove the lid plug and insert the tamper. With the switch on Variable, select speed 1 and turn the machine on. Using the tamper to press the ingredients into the blades, gradually increase the speed to 5.

2. Drizzle in the vinegar through the lid opening, then use the tamper to press down the ingredients. Drizzle in the oil and blend for about 30 seconds or until the mixture is smooth.

3. Transfer to a bowl and use immediately, or store in an airtight container in the refrigerator for up to 3 days.

Variation

If you don't like cilantro, just use additional parsley in its place.

Green Pipián Sauce

This sauce is often used to top boiled eggs, but you can also drizzle it over chicken or fish, or use it as a dip for chips. It has tons of flavor from roasted seeds and a lively combination of spices and herbs.

MAKES ABOUT 2 CUPS (500 ML)

2	whole cloves	2
2	whole allspice berries	2
1¼ cups	ready-to-use chicken or vegetable broth, divided	300 mL
2	jalapeño peppers, halved and seeded	2
2	cloves garlic, peeled	2
½	large onion, thickly sliced	½
½ cup	grape tomatoes	125 mL
½ cup	raw green pumpkin seeds (pepitas)	125 mL
¼ cup	sesame seeds	60 mL
½ cup	lightly packed fresh cilantro leaves and stems	125 mL
1 tsp	kosher salt	5 mL
1 tbsp	apple cider vinegar	15 mL
1 tbsp	canola oil	15 mL

1. Place the cloves and allspice in the Vitamix container and secure the lid. With the switch on Variable, select speed 1 and turn the machine on. Quickly increase the speed to 10, then flip the switch to High and grind the spices to powder, about 10 seconds. Leave them in the container and add 1 cup (250 mL) broth.

2. Heat a skillet over medium-high heat. Add jalapeños, garlic, onion and tomatoes. Cook, turning every 30 seconds or so, until the peppers are blistered, the onions are blackened and soft, and the tomatoes are wrinkled and collapsing. The mixture will stick to the pan and burn a little; reduce the heat to medium if it starts to smoke, and roll the tomatoes around on the dark spots on the pan. Transfer the mixture to the Vitamix container.

3. Wash the skillet and dry it well. Place over medium-high heat. Add pumpkin seeds and swirl until they start to pop, about 2 minutes. Add sesame seeds and swirl until fragrant, about 1 to 2 minutes. Transfer the seeds to the Vitamix container.

4. Add cilantro, salt and vinegar to the Vitamix container and secure the lid. With the switch on Variable, select speed 1 and turn the machine on. Gradually increase the speed to 10, then flip the switch to High and blend for about 30 seconds or until very smooth.

5. Return the skillet to medium heat and heat oil. Stir in sauce and cook, stirring and scraping the bottom of the pan with a spatula almost constantly to keep it from sticking, for about 5 minutes or until very thick and lumpy-looking. Stir in the remaining broth and cook, stirring, until heated through.

6. Use immediately or transfer to an airtight container and let cool, uncovered, then cover and store in the refrigerator for up to 4 days or freeze for up to 4 months.

Variation

For a hotter sauce, double the jalapeños or substitute a hotter pepper, such as serranos.

Tip

This sauce is also amazing over rice, tofu or vegetables.

Raspberry Chipotle Sauce

Sweet, hot, spicy and smoky, this sauce has it all. It's a disarming shade of raspberry red, with just a hint of heat. When raspberries are in season, make this your go-to sauce for Mexican meals.

MAKES ABOUT 2 CUPS (500 ML)

4 cups	fresh or frozen raspberries (about 1 lb/500 g)	1 L
2 tbsp	granulated sugar	30 mL
1/2 tsp	chipotle chile powder	2 mL
2 tbsp	freshly squeezed lime juice	30 mL
2	green onions, chopped	2

Tip

You can substitute canned chipotle peppers in adobo sauce for the chipotle chile powder. Start with 1 tsp (5 mL) chile and sauce, and add more to taste.

1. In a medium pot, combine raspberries, sugar, chile powder and lime juice. Bring to a boil over medium heat, stirring until raspberries break down and bubble. Reduce heat and simmer for about 5 minutes or until thickened.

2. Pour the raspberry mixture into the Vitamix container and secure the lid. With the switch on Variable, select speed 1 and turn the machine on. Quickly increase the speed to 10, then flip the switch to High and blend for 1 minute or until smooth. Add green onions and pulse on High twice, just to mix.

3. Use immediately or transfer to an airtight container and let cool, uncovered, then cover and store in the refrigerator for up to 1 week.

Variation

Other berries, such as blackberries or blueberries, would be tasty in this sauce and would create a very different and dramatic color.

Ancho Chile and Plantain Mole

When you hear mole, you probably think of the one made with chocolate, but there are actually many variations on mole sauce. This streamlined version is quite sweet and tangy, and not too hot. Serve it with roasted chicken or turkey.

MAKES ABOUT 2¹/₂ CUPS (625 ML)

4	whole allspice berries	4
4	whole cloves	4
1 tsp	whole coriander seeds	5 mL
1 tsp	whole cumin seeds	5 mL
3 oz	dried ancho chile peppers (about 6 whole)	90 g
2 tbsp	coconut oil, divided	30 mL
3	cloves garlic, peeled	3
¹/₂	medium onion, thickly sliced	¹/₂
1	small plantain, peeled and sliced	1
¹/₂	medium apple, peeled and cut into chunks	¹/₂
3 cups	ready-to-use chicken broth, divided	750 mL
1 tbsp	apple cider vinegar	15 mL
¹/₂ cup	prunes	125 mL
¹/₂ tsp	salt	2 mL

Tips

This sauce can be spread over meats at the end of grilling, like barbecue sauce, but it burns easily, so just baste it on for a quick turn over the heat.

Scrape the pan thoroughly in step 8; the sauce will stick if you aren't vigilant.

Variation

For a little more heat, use hotter chiles, like guajillos, or even throw in a few chipotles.

1. In a medium saucepan over medium heat, toast allspice, cloves, coriander seeds and cumin seeds, swirling for about 2 minutes or until fragrant. Transfer the spice mixture to the Vitamix container.

2. In the same pan, toast the ancho chiles, using tongs to turn and press them on the hot pan, for about 2 minutes or until puffed and softened. Transfer to a cutting board and let cool until you can handle them, then remove and discard the seeds and stems. Transfer to the Vitamix.

3. In the same pan, heat 1 tbsp (15 mL) coconut oil over medium-high heat. Add garlic and onion; cook, stirring, for 5 minutes or until browned. Using a slotted spoon, transfer the garlic and onion to the Vitamix, leaving the oil in the pan.

4. Add plantain and apple to the pan and cook, stirring, for 3 minutes or until browned and softened. Transfer to the Vitamix.

5. Add 1 cup (250 mL) broth, vinegar, prunes and salt to the Vitamix container and secure the lid. With the switch on Variable, select speed 1 and turn the machine on. Gradually increase the speed to 10, then flip the switch to High and blend for 1 minute or until very smooth.

6. In the same pan, heat the remaining oil over medium heat and pour in the ancho mixture.

7. Add the remaining broth to the Vitamix container and secure the lid. With the switch on Variable, select speed 5, turn the machine on and run for 10 seconds, then pour broth into the pan, whisking to combine.

8. Bring the sauce to a simmer, stirring and scraping the pan often, for about 10 minutes or until thickened.

Creamy Romesco with Hazelnuts

I learned to make this sauce from a woman named Isabel, a native Catalonian, on a trip to Barcelona. Most Romesco sauces I'd encountered before were based on roasted red bell peppers, but this one relies on a mild dried chile, which gives it much more depth of flavor. Serve with grilled veggies and Spanish dishes, such as grilled whole green onions, roasted potatoes, wedges of egg tortilla or grilled shrimp.

∽∽∽∽∽∽∽∽∽∽∽∽∽∽∽∽∽∽∽∽∽∽∽∽∽∽∽∽∽∽

MAKES ABOUT 1¼ CUPS (300 ML)

- **Preheat oven to 350°F (180°C)**
- **Rimmed baking sheet**

1	large dried ancho chile pepper	1
	Hot water	
8	cloves garlic, peeled	8
¼ cup	extra virgin olive oil, divided	60 mL
½ cup	hazelnuts	125 mL
¼ cup	slivered almonds	60 mL
1	large tomato, cored and halved	1
½ tsp	salt (approx.)	2 mL

Tip

To seed the ancho chile, remove it from the soaking water and place it on a cutting board. Use a paring knife to slice down one side and around the base of the stem. Open the chile and hold it flat as you scrape out the seeds. Discard the stem and seeds.

1. Place the ancho chile in a bowl and cover with hot water. Let stand for about 30 minutes or until soft.

2. Place garlic on a square of foil and drizzle with 1 tbsp (15 mL) oil. Fold into a packet. Roast in preheated oven for 30 minutes or until cloves are tender. Let cool.

3. Meanwhile, spread hazelnuts on the baking sheet. Toast in the oven for 10 minutes or until fragrant. Transfer to a folded kitchen towel and let cool, then rub the skins off the hazelnuts with the towel.

4. Spread the almonds on the baking sheet. Toast in the oven for 8 to 10 minutes or until golden and fragrant. Immediately transfer to a bowl and let cool.

5. Drain ancho chile and discard the stem and seeds (see tip).

6. Pour the remaining oil into the Vitamix container and add ancho chile, roasted garlic, hazelnuts, almonds, tomato and salt. Secure the lid. With the switch on Variable, select speed 1 and turn the machine on. Gradually increase the speed to 10, then flip the switch to High and blend for about 1 minute or until smooth and velvety. Taste and add a little more salt if desired.

7. Scrape the sauce into a bowl and serve immediately, or store in an airtight container in the refrigerator for up to 4 days or in the freezer for up to 4 months.

Variation

Omit the hazelnuts and use ¾ cup (175 mL) almonds for a simple almond Romesco sauce.

African Peanut Sauce

Thai chefs aren't the only ones making tasty peanut sauces. African cuisine is adept at turning the lowly groundnut into delicious soups and sauces with a hint of heat. This sauce can transform a bowl of millet and some roasted sweet potatoes and veggies into a meal. Or serve with sweet potato fries or over rice and beans.

MAKES ABOUT 1 1/2 CUPS (375 ML)

1 tbsp	canola oil	15 mL
1	large onion, chopped	1
2	jalapeño peppers, halved and seeded	2
1	clove garlic, chopped	1
1 tbsp	chopped gingerroot	15 mL
1 tsp	paprika	5 mL
1 tsp	ground coriander	5 mL
1 tsp	freshly ground black pepper	5 mL
1	large tomato, cored and halved	1
1/2 cup	unsalted roasted peanuts	125 mL
1/2 tsp	salt	2 mL

Tip

Make sure your peanuts are unseasoned and unsalted, or they will make the sauce too salty.

1. In a medium sauté pan, heat oil over medium-high heat. Add onion and cook, stirring, for about 5 minutes or until starting to soften. Add jalapeños, garlic and ginger; cook, stirring, for about 5 minutes or until jalapeños are softened. Add paprika, coriander and pepper; cook, stirring, just until the spices are fragrant, about 1 minute.

2. Transfer the onion mixture to the Vitamix container and add tomato, peanuts and salt. Secure the lid. With the switch on Variable, select speed 1 and turn the machine on. Gradually increase the speed to 7 and blend for 30 seconds. Scrape down the container, then blend on speed 7 for a few more seconds, just until puréed.

3. Scrape the sauce into a bowl and serve immediately, or transfer to an airtight container and let cool, uncovered, then cover and store in the refrigerator for up to 1 week or in the freezer for 4 months.

Variations

For a hotter sauce, add a few pinches of cayenne pepper with the paprika.

Substitute 1 cup (250 mL) chopped roasted eggplant for the tomato, for a very different flavor.

Curried Sweet Potato Coconut Sauce

When you go to an Indian restaurant, you often get to choose from different proteins, all of which will be cooked and bathed in a spicy sauce that is kept warm on the stove. You can use the same trick to serve all of your friends and family by making this tasty, creamy sauce that is equally good on chicken, fish, shrimp, pork, beans and tofu.

MAKES ABOUT 3½ CUPS (875 ML)

1 tbsp	coconut oil	15 mL
1 tbsp	brown mustard seeds	15 mL
2	large red chile peppers, seeded and chopped	2
1 tbsp	chopped gingerroot	15 mL
1 tbsp	whole cumin seeds	15 mL
1 tsp	ground turmeric	5 mL
1 lb	sweet potatoes, cubed (about 3 cups/750 mL)	500 g
1 tsp	packed brown sugar	5 mL
½ tsp	salt	2 mL
1	can (14 oz/400 mL) full-fat coconut milk	1
½ cup	lightly packed fresh mint leaves, chopped	125 mL
1 tbsp	freshly squeezed lemon juice	15 mL
¼ cup	toasted unsweetened shredded coconut (see tip)	60 m

Tips

To cube a sweet potato, slice a thin sliver off one long side and place that side down on the cutting board to form a stable base. Cut the sweet potato lengthwise into planks, stack them, and cut into strips. Turn the strips so that you can slice across them, making cubes.

To toast shredded coconut, place a small skillet over medium-low heat. Add the coconut and toast, shaking the pan constantly, for about 3 minutes or until the coconut is golden in spots and smells delicious.

1. In a large sauté pan, heat oil over medium-high heat. Add mustard seeds and cook, swirling the pan and stirring, for 30 to 60 seconds or until they start to pop and turn gray. Add chiles and ginger; cook, stirring, for 20 seconds, just to soften. Add cumin seeds and turmeric, stirring for a few seconds, until fragrant.

2. Add sweet potatoes, stirring to coat with spices. Add brown sugar, salt and coconut milk; bring to a boil, stirring. Reduce heat to low, cover and simmer for 10 to 15 minutes or until sweet potatoes are tender.

3. Using a slotted spoon, transfer 2 cups (500 mL) of the sweet potatoes to a measuring cup and set aside. Transfer the remaining sweet potato mixture to the Vitamix container. Secure the lid and hold it closed with a folded kitchen towel. With the switch on Variable, select speed 1 and turn the machine on. Gradually increase the speed to 10 and purée for about 30 seconds or until smooth.

4. Scrape the sauce back into the pan and stir in the reserved sweet potatoes, mint and lemon juice. Cook, stirring, over medium heat just until warmed through. Serve sprinkled with toasted coconut.

Variations

Cubed squash will also work in this in place of the sweet potatoes.

You can always add more chiles for heat.

Thai Blackened Chile Sauce

If burning the chiles sounds like a big mistake, you are in for an eye-opening experience. In this classic sauce, sweet shallots and garlic become golden and caramelized as the dried chiles take on deep mahogany tones. The transformation gives the oil deep flavor, and there is enough sugar to balance the heat. Serve as a side with any Thai meal, or even as a sandwich spread.

MAKES ABOUT ³/₄ CUP (175 ML)

1/2 cup	canola oil	125 mL
10	large dried red chile peppers (such as chile de árbol, cayenne or Chinese thin red chiles), stemmed	10
1	head garlic, cloves peeled and thickly sliced	1
1/2 cup	sliced shallots	125 mL
1/4 cup	granulated sugar	60 mL
1 tsp	salt	5 mL

Tip

Always wear gloves when handling chiles. Be very careful about inhaling the fumes from these chiles as they cook; do this under a vent hood or in a well-ventilated room, and stand back when stirring and when opening the Vitamix after puréeing.

1. In a small pot, heat oil over medium heat for about 1 minute, until warm but not hot. Add chiles, garlic and shallots; cook, stirring often, for 8 to 10 minutes or until chiles are slightly blackened and garlic and shallots are turning golden. Transfer to a heatproof bowl and let cool completely.

2. Transfer the chile mixture to the Vitamix container and add sugar and salt. Secure the lid. With the switch on Variable, select speed 1 and turn the machine on. Gradually increase the speed to 8 and blend for about 1 minute or until a coarse paste forms.

3. Transfer to a jar and let cool. Use immediately or store in the refrigerator for up to 2 months.

Variations

For a milder version, use milder chiles, such as guajillos.

For a deeper flavor, try brown sugar or palm sugar in place of the granulated sugar.

Cashew Sambal

Sambals are the required condiments for an Indonesian, Malaysian or Sri Lankan meal. This one is simple and easy — you can use preroasted cashews and not even turn on a burner. Serve with rice, flatbreads, beans or chicken.

ᘒ ᘒ

MAKES ABOUT ³/₄ CUP (175 ML)

3	large serrano peppers, halved and seeded	3
1	plum (Roma) tomato, cored and halved	1
¹/₂ cup	unsalted roasted cashews	125 mL
1 tbsp	packed brown sugar	15 mL
2 tbsp	freshly squeezed lime juice	30 mL
2 tbsp	unsalted tamarind paste (see tips)	30 mL
1 tbsp	soy sauce	15 mL

Tips

Wear gloves to handle serrano peppers; they are hotter than jalapeños.

Buy tamarind that has already been seeded and strained, sold in jars as tamarind paste, purée or concentrate. If it is very thick, use less, adjusting to taste.

Taste your tamarind paste before use, as some are quite salty. If you can only get salted tamarind, start with 1 tsp (5 mL) of soy sauce and add more to taste.

1. Place the serranos, tomato and cashews in the Vitamix container and secure the lid. With the switch on Variable, select speed 1 and turn the machine on. Mince the ingredients and gradually increase the speed to 7 as the mixture becomes smooth.

2. Scrape down the container, then add brown sugar, lime juice, tamarind and soy sauce. Secure the lid. With the switch on Variable, select speed 1 and turn the machine on. Gradually increase the speed to 10 and blend just until mixed to a coarse paste, about 20 seconds.

3. Scrape the sauce into a bowl and serve immediately, or transfer to an airtight container and let cool, uncovered, then cover and store in the refrigerator for up to 1 week.

Variation

Peanuts, raw green pumpkin seeds (pepitas) or hazelnuts would be a delicious replacement for the cashews.

Homemade Sriracha

Sriracha is the new standard hot sauce, available as a condiment in restaurants across North America. It won our hearts and palates with a garlicky, vinegary kick that adds zip to everything from salad dressings to steaks, and even desserts. Grow a few pepper plants this summer and you can make your own Sriracha to hold you over — for at least a month.

MAKES ABOUT 1¼ CUPS (300 ML)

- Gloves
- Nonreactive container, with lid
- Sterilized pint (500 mL) jar, with storage lid

1 lb	red Fresno peppers or red jalapeño peppers	500 g
3/4 cup	whole peeled garlic cloves	175 mL
1/4 cup	granulated sugar	60 mL
1 tbsp	salt	15 mL
2 cups	distilled white vinegar	500 mL
1/2 cup	apple cider vinegar	125 mL
	Water (optional)	

Tip

Always be very careful about handling hot chiles and inhaling their steam as they cook.

Make this sauce in a well-ventilated kitchen with the vent hood on to draw the capsaicin-laden fumes away.

1. Wearing gloves, cut peppers in half lengthwise, then cut out and discard stems and seeds. Place in the nonreactive container. Cut garlic cloves into thick slivers and add to the peppers.

2. In a cup, stir together sugar, salt, white vinegar and cider vinegar until sugar is dissolved. Pour over pepper mixture and stir to coat. Cover and refrigerate for 24 hours.

3. Transfer pepper mixture to a medium saucepan and place over medium-high heat. Bring to a boil, stirring. Reduce heat to low, cover and simmer for 30 to 40 minutes, stirring every 10 minutes, until peppers are very soft. Uncover and simmer gently for about 10 minutes or until the liquid is thick and syrupy.

4. Transfer to the Vitamix container, being careful not to inhale the vinegary steam. Secure the lid and place a folded kitchen towel on top. With the switch on Variable, select speed 1 and turn the machine on. Gradually increase the speed to 10, then flip the switch to High and blend for about 1 minute, until smooth. If the mixture is too thick, blend in water, 1 tbsp (15 mL) at a time, through the lid opening.

5. Transfer to the sterilized jar and let cool. Use immediately or store in the refrigerator for up to 1 month.

Variation

If you are feeling adventurous, try an assortment of fresh red chiles, ranging from sweeter, milder Italian banana peppers all the way to incendiary Scotch bonnets.

Ginger Mango Sriracha

For a taste of the tropics without leaving home, make this sauce. The creamy mango purée is spiked with ginger and just enough heat to make it interesting. This is a fantastic accompaniment to grilled foods, and also makes a great dipping sauce for egg rolls, sweet potato fries or fish cakes.

MAKES ABOUT 1 CUP (250 ML)

1	large mango, cut into chunks	1
1	slice fresh turmeric	1
1 tbsp	chopped gingerroot	15 mL
1/2 tsp	salt	2 mL
2 tbsp	agave nectar or liquid honey	30 mL
1 tbsp	freshly squeezed lemon juice	15 mL
2 tsp	Sriracha (store-bought or see recipe, page 51)	10 mL

Tip

Select a ripe mango that yields to a gentle squeeze. If all the mangos are hard and green, let yours ripen in a sunny window for a few days to develop its flavor.

1. Place mango, turmeric, ginger, salt, agave nectar, lemon juice and Sriracha in the Vitamix container. Secure the lid, remove the lid plug and insert the tamper. With the switch on Variable, select speed 1 and turn the machine on. Using the tamper to press the ingredients into the blades, gradually increase the speed to 5 and process for about 30 seconds or until very smooth.

2. Transfer to a bowl and use immediately, or store in an airtight container in the refrigerator for up to 4 days.

Variation

For a slightly different spin, use lime juice instead of lemon, or try a different hot sauce.

Chamoy Sauce

If you are looking for something new to do with fruit, this sauce is a spicy, sweet and sour way to make plain fruit more appealing. Use it as a dip for fresh fruit or drizzle it on fruit salads. Try it on sliced cucumber too!

MAKES ABOUT 2 CUPS (500 ML)

2	medium dried ancho chile peppers	2
	Hot water	
1 cup	apricot jam	250 mL
2	small limes, peeled	2
3 tbsp	packed dark brown sugar	45 mL
1 tsp	salt	5 mL

Tip

Wear gloves when handling chiles, especially if you have sensitive skin.

1. Heat a heavy skillet over medium-high heat. Add ancho chiles and, using tongs, press them flat on the pan. Cook, turning every few seconds, for about 2 minutes or until chiles have changed color slightly and become soft and puffed.

2. Transfer chiles to a medium bowl and add enough hot water to cover. Let soak for about 5 minutes or until softened. Drain and pat dry, then remove the stems and seeds.

3. Place the chiles in the Vitamix container and add apricot jam, limes, brown sugar and salt. Secure the lid, remove the lid plug and insert the tamper. With the switch on Variable, select speed 1 and turn the machine on. Using the tamper to press the ingredients into the blades, gradually increase the speed to 5 and blend for 20 seconds. Increase the speed to 10, then flip the switch to High and purée for about 30 seconds or until smooth.

4. Transfer to a bowl and serve immediately, or store in an airtight container in the refrigerator for up to 1 week.

Variation

Orange marmalade would be delicious in place of the apricot jam.

Blackberry Lime Coulis

Thanks to your Vitamix, it takes just minutes to make an intensely flavorful and colorful sauce from berries. The sauce needs no cream or butter, just pure fruit and a bit of sugar. Try it over crêpes, ice cream, cake or fresh fruit.

MAKES ABOUT 2 CUPS (500 ML)

- **Fine-mesh sieve**

12 oz	fresh or frozen blackberries (about 2$\frac{1}{2}$ cups/625 mL)	375 g
$\frac{1}{2}$ cup	granulated sugar (see tip)	125 mL
2 tsp	grated lime zest	10 mL
3 tbsp	freshly squeezed lime juice	45 mL

Tip

Frozen berries are perfectly fine for this, but if you want to use fresh, taste them for sweetness. Local berries are sometimes quite tart, and you may need an additional 1 to 2 tbsp (15 to 30 mL) sugar for a balanced flavor.

1. Place blackberries, sugar, lime zest and lime juice in the Vitamix container and secure the lid. With the switch on Variable, select speed 1 and turn the machine on. Gradually increase the speed to 10, then flip the switch to High and purée for about 45 seconds or until smooth.

2. Place the sieve over a large bowl and pour in the purée. Use a spatula to press the purée through the sieve, leaving the seeds behind.

3. Use immediately or store in an airtight container in the refrigerator for up to 3 days.

Variation

Raspberries would also be delicious here, and/or you could use lemon zest and juice instead of lime.

Mango Orange Coulis with Mint

When your menu is leaning toward Asian or Indian, try this quick dessert sauce to make simple coconut sorbet (page 180) or fresh fruit into an exciting closer. Mango and orange combine for a brilliant orange sauce that looks gorgeous on the plate.

MAKES ABOUT 3 CUPS (750 ML)

2 tbsp	freshly squeezed lemon juice	30 mL
1 tbsp	grated orange zest	15 mL
2	large mangos, peeled and pitted	2
1	large orange, peeled and seeded	1
$\frac{1}{4}$ cup	granulated sugar	60 mL
$\frac{1}{2}$ cup	lightly packed fresh mint leaves	125 mL

1. Place lemon juice, orange zest, mangos, orange and sugar in the Vitamix container. Secure the lid, remove the lid plug and insert the tamper. With the switch on Variable, select speed 1 and turn the machine on. Using the tamper to press the ingredients into the blades, gradually increase the speed to 10, then flip the switch to High and purée for about 30 seconds or until very smooth. Add mint and pulse four times to chop the mint and mix.

2. Transfer to a jar or airtight container and refrigerate for about 3 hours, until chilled, or for up to 4 days.

DRESSINGS, MARINADES and SPICE BLENDS

Balsamic Vinaigrette

Ditch the bottled dressings, with their gums and mystery ingredients. Your Vitamix makes it easy to make a vinaigrette with only fresh, high-quality foods. This tasty dressing is a perfect item to keep on hand in the refrigerator, and makes weeknight salads a snap.

MAKES ABOUT 1 CUP (250 ML)		
2	small shallots	2
1	clove garlic	1
1/4 cup	lightly packed fresh basil leaves	60 mL
1 tsp	salt	5 mL
1 tsp	granulated sugar	5 mL
Pinch	freshly ground black pepper	Pinch
1 tbsp	Dijon mustard	15 mL
2 tbsp	balsamic vinegar	30 mL
1/2 cup	extra virgin olive oil	125 mL

Tips

If your shallots and garlic are not as finely minced as you would like after step 2, don't worry: they will be fully incorporated into the dressing by the end of step 3.

This recipe can be used as a template to make dressings with other fresh herbs, vinegars and oils. For example, try fresh dill in place of basil, and white wine vinegar instead of balsamic.

1. Secure the lid on the Vitamix container and remove the lid plug. With the switch on Variable, select speed 1 and turn the machine on. Drop the shallots and garlic, one at a time, through the lid opening.

2. Turn the machine off and scrape down the container. Replace the lid and turn the machine on. Gradually increase the speed to 3 and blend for about 10 seconds or until the shallots and garlic are minced.

3. Turn the machine off and add the basil, salt, sugar, pepper, mustard and vinegar. Replace the lid and turn the machine on at speed 3. Gradually increase the speed to 5 and purée until smooth. Reduce the speed to 3 and very slowly pour in oil through the lid opening, blending until the oil is incorporated.

4. Transfer the vinaigrette to a jar and use immediately or store in the refrigerator for up to 3 days.

Provençal Herb Light Vinaigrette

When you buy a low-fat dressing at the grocery store, it has been thickened with gums and lots of sugary syrup to cover for the lack of oil. In this clean homemade dressing, a bit of vegetable stock, thickened with arrowroot, stretches the flavor of good olive oil across more salads. It's light, but not painfully so!

MAKES ABOUT 1 CUP (250 ML)

¹/₂ cup	ready-to-use vegetable broth	125 mL
2 tsp	arrowroot starch	10 mL
1 tbsp	fresh thyme leaves	15 mL
1 tbsp	fresh rosemary leaves	15 mL
1	small shallot	1
1	clove garlic	1
¹/₂ tsp	salt	2 mL
2 tbsp	red wine vinegar	30 mL
1 tbsp	liquid honey	15 mL
3 tbsp	extra virgin olive oil	45 mL

Tips

Keep small Tetra Paks of ready-to-use vegetable broth in the pantry or make Almost Instant Vegetable Stock (page 102) and freeze it in small portion sizes for easy access.

If you don't have arrowroot starch, you can substitute cornstarch.

Other vinegars, such as champagne or balsamic vinegar, can be swapped in.

1. Pour broth into a small saucepan and whisk in arrowroot. Bring to a boil over medium-high heat, whisking constantly. When it bubbles and thickens slightly, remove from heat and let cool.

2. Place the thyme and rosemary in the Vitamix container. Secure the lid and remove the lid plug. With the switch on Variable, select speed 1 and turn the machine on. Gradually increase the speed to 5. Drop the shallot and garlic, one at a time, through the lid opening and blend until minced.

3. Turn the machine off and scrape down the container. Add the salt, vinegar, honey and broth mixture. Secure the lid and turn the machine on at speed 5. Blend for about 40 seconds or until the herbs are minced into tiny bits. Reduce the speed to 3 and very slowly pour in oil through the lid opening, blending until the oil is incorporated.

4. Transfer the vinaigrette to a jar and refrigerate for at least 1 hour, until chilled, or for up to 3 days.

Hazelnut Vinaigrette

Hazelnuts give this dressing a rich, toasty flavor and a boost in nutritious fats and protein. They also serve to hold the dressing together after you purée it, and will create a more stable emulsion than just oil and vinegar alone.

MAKES ABOUT 1¼ CUPS (300 ML)

- **Preheat oven to 350°F (180°C)**
- **Rimmed baking sheet**

1/4 cup	raw hazelnuts	60 mL
1/2	large lemon, peeled and seeded	1/2
1/4 cup	lightly packed fresh parsley	60 mL
2 tsp	granulated sugar	10 mL
1/2 tsp	salt	2 mL
3/4 cup	extra virgin olive oil	175 mL

Tip

Roast some extra hazelnuts while you are at it, so you can chop them to sprinkle on the salad at serving time. They keep, tightly covered, in the refrigerator for a month.

1. Spread hazelnuts on baking sheet and roast in preheated oven for 10 minutes or until fragrant and toasted. Immediately transfer to a folded kitchen towel, rub the skins from the nuts and let cool. If some of the nuts stubbornly refuse to give up their skins, return them to the pan and roast for another 5 to 10 minutes, then try again.

2. Place the hazelnuts, lemon, parsley, sugar and salt in the Vitamix container. Secure the lid, remove the lid plug and insert the tamper. With the switch on Variable, select speed 1 and turn the machine on. Gradually increase the speed to 5, using the tamper to press the ingredients down into the blades, and blend for about 30 seconds or until the nuts are very finely minced. Remove the tamper, reduce the speed to 3 and very slowly pour in oil through the lid opening, blending until the oil is incorporated.

3. Transfer the vinaigrette to a jar and use immediately or store in the refrigerator for up to 1 week.

Variation

Roasted pecans or walnuts can stand in for the hazelnuts.

Strawberry Balsamic Dressing

If you love strawberries, make this beautiful pink dressing, then pile some fresh berries on your green salad and drizzle it with even more berry flavor. The berry purée keeps the dressing from separating as quickly, and gives it a natural sweet-tart flavor that will go with all sorts of springy vegetables, like asparagus and baby spinach.

MAKES ALMOST 1 CUP (250 ML)

4	large strawberries	4
1/4 cup	sliced shallot	60 mL
1/2 tsp	granulated sugar	2 mL
1/2 tsp	salt	2 mL
3 tbsp	balsamic vinegar	45 mL
1/2 cup	extra virgin olive oil	125 mL

Tip

Pick the least attractive berries to use in the dressing; save the pretty ones for the salad or another use.

1. Place strawberries, shallot, sugar, salt and vinegar in the Vitamix container. Secure the lid and remove the lid plug. With the switch on Variable, select speed 1 and turn the machine on. As the berries break down, gradually increase the speed to 4 and blend until smooth. Reduce the speed to 3 and very slowly pour in oil through the lid opening, blending until the oil is incorporated. Gradually increase the speed to 10 and blend for a few seconds.

2. Transfer the dressing to a jar and refrigerate for at least 1 hour, until chilled, or for up to 2 days.

Variation

A small peach could be a great end-of-summer sub for the strawberries.

Japanese Miso Ginger Dressing

When serving sushi or other Japanese fare, a salad with miso dressing is the perfect accompaniment. Even when you are just having a bowl of rice and beans, this tasty drizzle can season the whole dish.

MAKES ABOUT 1 CUP (250 ML)

1/4 cup	chopped gingerroot	60 mL
2	large garlic cloves, chopped	2
1/4 cup	red miso	60 mL
2 tbsp	liquid honey	30 mL
1/2 cup	canola oil	125 mL

Tips

Red miso, the most popular of the miso pastes, makes a great addition to soups, salad dressings, sauces and other foods. Just mix it with a little water to thin it and stir it in.

Darker misos have a stronger flavor and are wonderful in this dressing when you're intending to pair it with cooked vegetables or a seaweed salad.

1. Secure the lid on the Vitamix container and remove the lid plug. With the switch on Variable, select speed 1 and turn the machine on. Drop the ginger and garlic, a little bit at a time, through the lid opening. Gradually increase the speed to 3 and blend for about 30 seconds or until the ginger and garlic are minced.

2. Turn the machine off and scrape down the container. Replace the lid, select speed 1 and turn the machine on. Blend for about 30 seconds or until the ginger and garlic are finely minced.

3. Turn the machine off and add the miso and honey. Replace the lid and turn the machine on. Gradually increase the speed to 3. Very slowly pour in oil through the lid opening, blending until the oil is incorporated.

4. Transfer the dressing to a jar and use immediately or store in the refrigerator for up to 3 days.

Avocado Green Goddess Dressing with Basil

The creamy, lush texture of avocado is perfect for a salad dressing. Just remember that it will start to turn brown if exposed to air or kept for more than a day or two.

∽∾ ∽∾ ∽∾ ∽∾ ∽∾ ∽∾ ∽∾ ∽∾ ∽∾ ∽∾ ∽∾ ∽∾ ∽∾ ∽∾ ∽∾ ∽∾ ∽∾ ∽∾

MAKES ABOUT 1 CUP (250 ML)

1	large avocado	1
2 tbsp	white vinegar	30 mL
2	cloves garlic, chopped	2
1 cup	lightly packed fresh basil	250 mL
1/2 cup	lightly packed fresh parsley	125 mL
1/2 tsp	salt	2 mL
1/2 cup	extra virgin olive oil	125 mL

Tips

To pit the avocado, sink the blade of a chef's knife into the side of the pit, then twist it out.

Because your machine is so powerful, you can use tender stems as well as leaves, and get the most out of your basil and parsley.

1. Halve the avocado, remove the pit and scoop the flesh into the Vitamix container. Add vinegar, garlic, basil, parsley and salt. Secure the lid, remove the lid plug and insert the tamper. With the switch on Variable, select speed 1 and turn the machine on. Gradually increase the speed to 3, using the tamper to press the ingredients into the blades. Increase the speed to 5 and blend, using the tamper, for about 40 seconds or until smooth.

2. Remove the tamper, reduce the speed to 3, and very slowly pour in oil through the lid opening. Gradually increase the speed to 10 and purée for about 5 seconds or until smooth.

3. Transfer the dressing to a jar and use immediately or store in the refrigerator for up to 2 days.

Variation

Try making this dressing with lemon juice instead of vinegar, or with other fresh herbs, such as mint or cilantro.

Recipe Suggestion

Green Goddess Salad: Chop 1 head romaine lettuce and place in a large salad bowl with 2 oz (60 g) broccoli sprouts and 2 sliced large tomatoes. (If desired, add sliced avocado to the salad for even more green goddess magic!) Drizzle the dressing over the salad and toss to coat. Serve immediately. Makes 8 servings.

Greek Yogurt Dressing

Greek yogurt has taken over the world, with its concentrated nutrition and thick, creamy texture. Here, it lends great body and richness to a host of herbs and a splash of extra virgin olive oil. Drizzle it over swaths of spinach, tomatoes, olives and feta for a fantastic Greek salad.

MAKES ABOUT 1 CUP (250 ML)

1/2 cup	plain Greek yogurt	125 mL
1/4 cup	red wine vinegar	60 mL
2	cloves garlic, chopped	2
1/4 cup	lightly packed fresh parsley	60 mL
1/2 tsp	dried dillweed	2 mL
1/2 tsp	coarsely cracked black pepper	2 mL
1/2 tsp	salt	2 mL
1/4 cup	extra virgin olive oil	60 mL

Tips

Use finesse when blending in step 1 and take your time to make sure everything gets minced.

In place of Greek yogurt, you can use fat-free, low-fat or whole-milk yogurt here, for a different texture.

If you have fresh dill on hand, go ahead and use 1 tbsp (15 mL) — the fresh herb is so appealing!

1. Place the yogurt, vinegar, garlic, parsley, dill, pepper and salt in the Vitamix container. Secure the lid and remove the lid plug. With the switch on Variable, select speed 1 and turn the machine on. Gradually increase the speed to 3 as the mixture engages with the blades. After about 30 seconds, when the mixture is well minced, gradually increase to speed 5 and blend for 20 seconds or until very smooth. Reduce the speed to 3 and very slowly pour in oil through the lid opening, blending until the oil is incorporated.

2. Transfer the dressing to a jar and refrigerate for at least 1 hour, until chilled, or for up to 1 week.

Creamy Cucumber Dill Dressing

What could be more refreshing than a salad dressed with a creamy cucumber dill dressing? Puréeing some of the cucumber and using yogurt makes this version light, so you won't feel weighed down. This dressing is perfect on romaine or a bowl of veggies and chickpeas.

MAKES ABOUT 1¹/₂ CUPS (375 ML)

1 cup	plain Greek yogurt	250 mL
1 tbsp	champagne or white wine vinegar	15 mL
1 tbsp	liquid honey	15 mL
1	medium cucumber, peeled, halved lengthwise and seeded, divided	1
¹/₂ tsp	salt	2 mL
2 tbsp	lightly packed fresh dill, chopped	30 mL

Tips

You can vary the texture of this dressing by using regular yogurt (whole-milk, low-fat or fat-free).

Once you have a bunch of fresh dill, you may as well use some of the remaining fronds to garnish the salad, for a lovely presentation.

1. Place the yogurt, vinegar, honey, half the cucumber and salt in the Vitamix container and secure the lid. With the switch on Variable, select speed 1 and turn the machine on. Gradually increase the speed to 10 and blend for about 30 seconds or until smooth.

2. Cut the remaining cucumber into long strips, then into small pieces.

3. Add the chopped cucumber and dill to the Vitamix. Replace the lid, select speed 5 and pulse three times to combine.

4. Transfer the dressing to a jar and refrigerate for at least 1 hour, until chilled, or for up to 1 week.

Variation

Try making this dressing with fresh tarragon or basil in place of the dill, for a different herbal note.

Creamy Caesar Dressing

Caesar salad is everywhere, and the dressing is often disappointing. Ranging from overly acidic to bereft of the anchovy flavors that made it famous, the restaurant Caesar may make you want to go home and make it yourself. Enriched with a little cream, this dressing is satisfyingly thick, and carries the umami-rich anchovy purée to great effect. Serve over romaine, with plenty of croutons and shredded Parmesan.

MAKES ABOUT 1 CUP (250 ML)

2 tbsp	freshly squeezed lemon juice	30 mL
2 tbsp	heavy or whipping (35%) cream	30 mL
1 tsp	Worcestershire sauce	5 mL
3	cloves garlic, sliced	3
1 tbsp	anchovy paste or whole anchovies, packed into the spoon	15 mL
1/2 tsp	dry mustard	2 mL
1/2 tsp	freshly cracked black pepper	2 mL
1 oz	Parmesan cheese	30 g
1/2 cup	extra virgin olive oil	125 mL

Tip

Anchovy pastes, oil-cured anchovies and salt-cured anchovies vary in saltiness, but are usually all the salt you need for this dressing. If you taste it and think it needs a little salt, go ahead and add a pinch.

1. Place the lemon juice, cream, Worcestershire sauce, garlic, anchovy paste, mustard, pepper and Parmesan in the Vitamix container. Secure the lid, remove the lid plug and insert the tamper. With the switch on Variable, select speed 1 and turn the machine on. Gradually increase the speed to 5, using the tamper to press the ingredients into the blades, and blend for about 30 seconds or until smooth.

2. Remove the tamper and reduce the speed to 3. Very slowly pour in oil through the lid opening, blending until the oil is incorporated. Increase the speed to 5 and blend for 5 seconds.

3. Transfer the dressing to a jar and serve immediately or store in the refrigerator for up to 1 week.

Variation

It's your dressing, so if you want to use another aged cheese in place of the Parmesan, it would be delicious. Try aged Gruyère, manchego or Asiago.

Jamaican Jerk Marinade

This intensely flavorful, spicy marinade has been perfected by Jamaican cooks, who use it to flavor pork, chicken and seafood. In Jamaica, jerk is slowly grilled over pimento wood, from the tree that gives us allspice berries. But the marinade is so tasty, you can cook your jerk in the oven and still have something amazing.

MAKES ABOUT ¾ CUP (175 ML)

1 tbsp	allspice berries	15 mL
1 tbsp	whole black peppercorns	15 mL
¼ cup	white wine vinegar	60 mL
2 tbsp	soy sauce	30 mL
2	large green onions, chopped	2
1	small Scotch bonnet or habanero chile pepper, stem and seeds removed	1
½ cup	chopped onion	125 mL
1 tbsp	chopped gingerroot	15 mL
1 tbsp	fresh thyme leaves	15 mL
2 tsp	salt	10 mL
½ tsp	grated nutmeg (see tip)	2 mL

Tips

Always wear gloves when handling chile peppers, or your hands will absorb hot oils from the fruit, causing quite a bit of pain.

If you haven't tried fresh nutmeg, it is worth the effort for the fresh, vibrant flavor it adds to this marinade. Purchase fresh nutmeg at a spice shop and use a rasp grater, such as a Microplane, to grate it finely. The leftover chunk of nutmeg keeps well, tightly covered, in a small jar at room temperature.

This recipe makes enough to marinate 6 chicken breasts or 2 lbs (1 kg) shrimp. Marinate overnight, then grill or roast.

This is a great marinade for tofu or tempeh, too.

1. Place the allspice and peppercorns in the Vitamix container and secure the lid. With the switch on Variable, select speed 1 and turn the machine on. Gradually increase the speed to 10, then flip the switch to High and blend for about 1 minute or until the spices are finely powdered.

2. Turn the machine off and add the vinegar, soy sauce, green onions, chile, onion, ginger, thyme, salt and nutmeg. Replace the lid, select speed 1 and turn the machine on. Gradually increase the speed to 10, then flip the switch to High and blend until smooth.

3. Use the marinade immediately or transfer to an airtight container and store in the refrigerator for up to 1 day.

Thai Lime Ginger Marinade

Buzz up this simple, intense marinade in seconds and infuse Thai flavors into your chicken while you are at work. It works even more quickly on shrimp and fish: just marinate for 20 minutes before they meet the fire.

MAKES ABOUT 1 CUP (250 ML)		
2	large limes	2
1/4 cup	fish sauce	60 mL
2	large red chile peppers, seeded	2
2	cloves garlic, coarsely chopped	2
2 tbsp	coarsely chopped gingerroot	30 mL
2 tbsp	packed light brown sugar	30 mL

Tip

Red Fresno chiles or red jalapeños are the mildest red chiles and work well in this recipe. Other red chiles, such as red piquillo, cayenne or Thai, can also be used.

1. Grate the zest from one of the limes and place the zest in a small bowl. Cut off and discard the peels from both limes. Place the limes in the Vitamix container.

2. Add the fish sauce, chiles, garlic, ginger and brown sugar. Secure the lid, remove the lid plug and insert the tamper. With the switch on Variable, select speed 1 and turn the machine on. Gradually increase the speed to 3, using the tamper to press the ingredients into the blades and increasing the speed only as the mixture engages with the blades. As the mixture becomes fluid and well minced, increase the speed to 5.

3. Turn the machine off and add the lime zest. Replace the lid and pulse a few times on speed 5 to mix.

4. Use the marinade immediately or transfer to an airtight container and store in the refrigerator for up to 2 days.

Recipe Suggestion

To marinate 3 lbs (1.5 kg) bone-in skinless chicken thighs or 4 bone-in skinless chicken breasts, slash the flesh of each piece in a few places to allow the marinade to penetrate deeper. Halve the breasts if they are very large. Place the chicken in a large sealable plastic bag and pour in marinade. Seal the bag and massage the marinade over the chicken by squeezing and turning the bag. Refrigerate for at least 8 hours or overnight. Remove the chicken from the marinade, discarding excess marinade, and bake or grill as desired. Makes 4 to 6 servings. (Alternatively, marinate 2 lbs/1 kg skin-on salmon or deveined peeled large shrimp for about 20 minutes before grilling.)

Korean Bulgogi Marinade and Sauce

With the growing interest in Korean flavors, Korean barbecue has become a familiar sight on menus. It's an easy marinade, packed with exciting flavors of soy, sesame, ginger and pepper. It's also versatile and can be applied to all sorts of foods, not just beef.

MAKES ABOUT 1 CUP (250 ML)

1/4 cup	soy sauce	60 mL
2 tbsp	sesame oil	30 mL
1 tbsp	dark (cooking) molasses	15 mL
4	large cloves garlic, chopped	4
1	3-inch (7.5 cm) piece gingerroot (about 1 oz/30 g), sliced across the grain	1
1/2	large lemon, peeled and seeded	1/2
3 tbsp	granulated sugar	45 mL
1 tsp	whole black peppercorns	5 mL
1 tsp	hot pepper flakes	5 mL
4	green onions, minced	4
2 tbsp	sesame seeds	30 mL

Tip

This marinade isn't just for grilling; you can also pour it over your chosen food and roast in the oven, or use it to season vegetables in a stir-fry.

1. Place the soy sauce, oil, molasses, garlic, ginger, lemon, sugar, peppercorns and hot pepper flakes in the Vitamix container and secure the lid. With the switch on Variable, select speed 1 and turn the machine on. Gradually increase the speed to 10 and blend for about 1 minute or until finely minced.

2. Turn the machine off and add the green onions and sesame seeds. Replace the lid. Select speed 5 and pulse twice to mix.

3. Use the marinade immediately or transfer to an airtight container and store in the refrigerator for up to 1 week.

Recipe Suggestion

Soak 12 wooden skewers for at least 1 hour, then drain. Thread 1 1/2 lbs (750 g) cubed boneless beef sirloin steak, boneless skinless chicken, tofu or skinless salmon, or deveined peeled shrimp, onto skewers. Place in a shallow dish, pour in marinade and toss to coat. Cover and refrigerate for at least 1 hour (no longer for shrimp or fish) or up to 24 hours (for steak, chicken or tofu). Remove skewers from marinade, discarding marinade. Grill or broil as desired. Serve each skewer in a leaf of romaine lettuce, with a slice of lemon to squeeze over top. Makes 6 servings.

Barbecue Sauce

This easy sauce is perfect for brushing on a chicken breast on the grill, for the last couple of turns over the heat. It's also fun as a pizza topper, with pineapple and chicken or mock duck, or tossed with shredded meat for a barbecue sandwich. The secret to making it rival the bottled kind is in the smoky chipotle and paprika, which give it the whiff of the fire.

MAKES ABOUT 2 CUPS (500 ML)

1 tsp	canola oil	5 mL
1	large onion, chopped	1
2	cloves garlic, chopped	2
2 tsp	cumin seeds	10 mL
1/2 tsp	whole black peppercorns	2 mL
1	can (5 1/2 oz/156 mL) tomato paste	1
3/4 cup	unsweetened apple juice	175 mL
1/4 cup	apple cider vinegar	60 mL
1 tbsp	Worcestershire sauce	15 mL
2 tsp	Dijon mustard	10 mL
2 tbsp	packed light brown sugar	30 mL
1 tsp	chipotle chile powder	5 mL
1 tsp	salt	5 mL
1/2 tsp	dried oregano	2 mL
1/2 tsp	smoked paprika	2 mL

Tips

Cook the onions for as long as you can — up to 1 hour over low heat before adding the garlic — to caramelize them and build depth and sweetness for the sauce.

Sugars burn easily on the grill, so baste the food with this sauce after it is cooked through, just to glaze.

1. In a medium skillet, heat oil over medium-high heat. Add onion and cook, stirring, until it is starting to stick to the pan, then reduce the heat to medium-low and cook, stirring, for about 5 minutes or until softened. Add garlic, and cook, stirring often, for about 5 minutes or until fragrant and golden but not browned.

2. Meanwhile, place the cumin seeds and peppercorns in the Vitamix container and secure the lid. With the switch on Variable, select speed 1 and turn the machine on. Quickly increase the speed to 10 and blend for about 20 seconds or until the spices are powdered.

3. Turn the machine off and add the tomato paste, apple juice, vinegar, Worcestershire sauce, mustard, onion mixture, brown sugar, chipotle powder, salt, oregano and paprika. Replace the lid, select speed 1 and turn the machine on. Gradually increase the speed to 10, then flip the switch to High and blend for about 45 seconds or until smooth and well mixed.

4. Transfer the sauce to a jar and use immediately or store in the refrigerator for up to 2 weeks.

Variation

You can use honey or another sweetener in place of the brown sugar.

Vindaloo Simmer Sauce

Vindaloo is famous for being incredibly hot, and tangy with vinegar. When you make it at home, you can tame the heat or amp it up, whichever you prefer. This version is probably restaurant "medium"; a couple more or hotter chiles would take it up to "hot."

	MAKES ABOUT ³/₄ CUP (175 ML)	
6	cloves garlic, sliced	6
1	large onion, quartered	1
2 tbsp	canola oil, divided	30 mL
1 tbsp	cumin seeds	15 mL
1 tsp	coriander seeds	5 mL
1 tsp	whole black peppercorns	5 mL
1 tsp	ground turmeric	5 mL
1 tsp	ground cinnamon	5 mL
1 tsp	salt	5 mL
¹/₄ cup	apple cider vinegar	60 mL
3	large jalapeño peppers (or to taste)	3
2 tbsp	chopped gingerroot	30 mL
2 tsp	packed brown sugar	10 mL

1. Secure the lid of the Vitamix container and remove the lid plug. With the switch on Variable, select speed 3 and turn the machine on. Drop the garlic and onion quarters, one piece at a time, through the lid opening, using the tamper if they are not falling into the blades. Turn the machine off as soon as everything is chopped.

2. In a small skillet, heat half the oil over medium heat. Scrape in the onion mixture and cook, stirring, for about 5 minutes or until soft and golden. Remove from heat.

3. Rinse and dry the Vitamix container. Place the cumin seeds, coriander seeds, peppercorns, turmeric, cinnamon and salt in the container. Secure the lid and insert the lid plug. With the switch on Variable, select speed 1 and turn the machine on. Quickly increase the speed to 10, then flip the switch to High and blend for 15 seconds or until the spices are powdered.

4. Turn the machine off and add the vinegar, onion mixture, jalapeños, ginger and brown sugar. Replace the lid, select speed 1 and turn the machine on. Gradually increase the speed to 6 and blend for about 20 seconds, to a coarse purée. Increase the speed to 10 and purée for about 30 seconds or until very smooth.

5. Transfer the sauce to a jar and use immediately or store in the refrigerator for up to 1 week.

Variation

Add 1 tsp (5 mL) whole fenugreek with the whole spices before you grind them, for a unique perfume.

Recipe Suggestion

Rub the vindaloo over 4 to 6 bone-in skinless chicken breasts or 1¹/₂ lbs (750 g) lamb or beef stew meat. Cover and refrigerate for at least 12 hours or up to 24 hours. Transfer the meat and marinade to a large Dutch oven and add ¹/₂ cup (125 mL) ready-to-use broth or water. Bring to a boil over medium heat. Cover, reduce heat to low and simmer, stirring occasionally, for 40 to 60 minutes for chicken or up to 2 hours for stew meats to get tender, adding broth or water as needed to keep moist. When the meat is cooked, take it out and boil the liquids for a few minutes to thicken. Serve it all over rice. Makes 6 servings.

This is a great dish to make in the slow cooker, too. Just combine all ingredients in the stoneware, cover and cook on Low for about 6 hours for chicken or longer for stew meats to get tender.

Ssamjang Sauce

Ssamjang is an all-purpose basting and brushing sauce in the Korean kitchen. With miso and spicy gochujang sauce, it creates a flavor explosion however you use it. Think of it as a flavor-packed hot sauce and glaze, and use it to baste all types of meat, seafood and tofu or tempeh, or on roasted vegetables.

MAKES ABOUT 1 CUP (250 ML)

1/4 cup	red miso	60 mL
1/4 cup	gochujang sauce	60 mL
2 tbsp	unsweetened apple juice	30 mL
2 tbsp	tamari	30 mL
1 tbsp	sesame oil	15 mL
1 1/2 tbsp	granulated sugar	22 mL
2	large cloves garlic, sliced	2
2	medium green onions, thinly sliced	2
1	medium shallot, quartered	1

Tips

If you haven't tried gochujang, the favorite hot sauce of Korea, you absolutely should. If you don't have access to Asian markets with a Korean section, you can order it online. A tub lasts for months.

Try using ssamjang sauce to coat slices of winter squash before roasting.

1. Place the miso, gochujang, apple juice, tamari, oil, sugar, garlic, green onions and shallot in the Vitamix container and secure the lid. With the switch on Variable, select speed 1 and turn the machine on. Gradually increase the speed to 5 and purée for about 1 minute or until smooth. Gradually increase the speed to 10 and blend for a few more seconds.

2. Transfer the sauce to a bowl and use immediately or store in an airtight container in the refrigerator for up to 3 days.

Mild Thai Rendang Spice Paste

Thai curry pastes are concentrated sources of herbal flavor and chile heat, and the red and green versions are pretty easy to find. This variation is a little less common, and can easily be made a little less hot, with no loss of amazing Thai flavor.

MAKES ABOUT ³/₄ CUP (175 ML)

3	medium dried guajillo chile peppers	3
1 tsp	coriander seeds	5 mL
1 tsp	cumin seeds	5 mL
1 tsp	whole black peppercorns	5 mL
6	cloves garlic	6
2	stalks lemongrass, dry, hard leaves removed, root ends thinly sliced	2
1	large shallot	1
2 oz	piece gingerroot, sliced	60 g
	Grated zest of 1 large lime	
1 tsp	salt	5 mL
1 tsp	ground turmeric	5 mL

Tips

When you purchase fresh lemongrass, put it in a jar of water like a bouquet of flowers. This will keep the stalk from becoming too hard. If the lemongrass is really fresh, it may even start to sprout roots and grow.

Guajillos are relatively mild chiles. For a hotter sauce, you can replace a portion of the guajillos with a couple of dried chiles de Arbol or Thai bird peppers.

1. Place chiles in a bowl and pour in warm water to cover; let soak for 1 hour or until softened. Drain and remove stems and seeds.

2. Place the coriander seeds, cumin seeds and peppercorns in the Vitamix container and secure the lid. With the switch on Variable, select speed 1 and turn the machine on. Quickly increase the speed to 10 and grind the spices finely. Turn the machine off, tap the container on the counter gently and let the spices settle for a few seconds before removing the lid.

3. Add the drained chiles, garlic, lemongrass, shallot, ginger, lime zest, salt and turmeric. Replace the lid, select speed 1 and turn the machine on. Gradually increase the speed to 4 and blend to a coarse paste, stopping and scraping down the container repeatedly.

4. Transfer the paste to a jar and use immediately or store in the refrigerator for up to 1 week.

Curry Powder

Curry powder in a jar seems so standardized, almost as if it were really a single spice. Like most foods, you can make it fresher and customize it to your tastes when you do it yourself. Once you try this blend, add and subtract to your palate's content.

∽∽∽∽∽∽∽∽∽∽∽∽∽∽∽∽∽∽∽∽∽∽∽∽∽∽∽∽∽∽∽∽

MAKES ABOUT ⅓ CUP (75 ML)

1	small dried red chile pepper	1
2 tbsp	coriander seeds	30 mL
2 tbsp	cumin seeds	30 mL
1 tbsp	black mustard seeds	15 mL
1 tsp	fennel seeds	5 mL
1 tsp	fenugreek seeds	5 mL
1 tsp	whole black peppercorns	5 mL
½ tsp	cardamom seeds	2 mL
1 tsp	ground turmeric	5 mL
1 tsp	ground ginger	5 mL

Tips

Toasting the spices gives you the best flavor for use right away. If you want to use the blend over a period of months, skip the toasting. Just add all the spices to the Vitamix container and proceed with step 2. Untoasted powder will hold its flavor better, and you can store it for up to 3 months.

Buy spices in small amounts from stores that sell in bulk, so you don't have to buy a whole jar. That way, they will be as fresh as possible.

If you want a hotter curry, add another chile.

You can omit any spices you don't care for.

1. In a large skillet, combine chile pepper, coriander seeds, cumin seeds, mustard seeds, fennel seeds, fenugreek seeds and peppercorns. Place over medium-low heat and toast, stirring and swirling the pan constantly, for 4 minutes. As the seeds become fragrant, keep a close eye on them and press the dried chile down with your spoon to make sure it toasts evenly. Add cardamom seeds and toast, stirring, for a few seconds.

2. Transfer the spice mixture to the Vitamix container and add the turmeric and ginger. Secure the lid. With the switch on Variable, select speed 1 and turn the machine on. Gradually increase the speed to 10 and blend for about 1 minute or until the seeds are finely powdered. Turn the machine off, tap the sides of the container and let the spices settle for a few seconds before removing the lid.

3. Transfer the curry powder to a jar and use immediately or store, tightly closed, at room temperature for up to 1 month (see tip).

Recipe Suggestion

For a dry rub, mix 1 tbsp (15 mL) curry powder with 1 tsp (5 mL) brown sugar and 1 tsp (5 mL) salt. For a wet rub, stir 1 tbsp (15 mL) oil into the dry rub mixture. Use to coat 1½ lbs (750 g) potatoes, chicken, fish or pork.

Shichimi Togarashi

If your idea of a Japanese condiment is the wasabi that comes with sushi, prepare your taste buds for a wake-up call. This sprinkle is a flavor-packed combination of chile heat, citrus tang and the umami and salt of nori seaweed. Use it liberally to season everything from a simple bowl of rice to vegetables, chicken and seafood.

MAKES ABOUT 6 TBSP (90 ML)

1/2	large orange	1/2
1	8 1/3- by 7 1/2-inch (21 by 19 cm) sheet nori	1
1/2 tsp	ground ginger	2 mL
2 tbsp	hot pepper flakes	30 mL
2 tbsp	white sesame seeds	30 mL
1 tbsp	black sesame seeds	15 mL

Tip

Store nori in an airtight sealable storage bag in between uses, so it will stay crisp. That will make it easier to crumble.

1. Using a sharp paring knife, peel the zest from the orange half, removing only the orange part and leaving the white pith behind. Reserve the orange for another use. Chop the orange zest into 1/2-inch (1 cm) wide pieces.

2. Place the orange zest pieces in the Vitamix container and secure the lid. With the switch on Variable, select speed 1 and turn the machine on. Gradually increase the speed to 10, then flip the switch to High and blend for about 30 seconds or until finely minced.

3. Turn the machine off and scrape down the container. Crumble the nori into the container. Add the ginger and replace the lid. With the switch on Variable, select speed 1 and turn the machine on. Quickly increase the speed to 10, then flip the switch to High and blend for about 30 seconds or until finely minced.

4. Turn the machine off and add the hot pepper flakes, white sesame seeds and black sesame seeds. Replace the lid and pulse for 1 to 2 seconds on High, just to mix.

5. Transfer the spice mixture to a medium skillet. Place over medium heat and swirl the pan. Toast, stirring, for about 4 minutes or until dry-looking. Remove from heat, stir a few times and let cool in the pan, drying the mixture in the open air.

6. Transfer the spice mixture to a jar and use immediately or store, tightly closed, at room temperature for about 2 weeks.

Variation

For a slightly less fiery blend, replace the hot pepper flakes with 1 tbsp (15 mL) whole black peppercorns, adding them with the orange zest.

Gomasio

Gomasio is a simple seasoning that can turn a plain bowl of rice or greens into a savory meal. Sesame seeds are toasted, then ground with salt to make a crumbly sprinkle. Use it when you were going to reach for salt; you'll be adding nutty flavor, protein and calcium, and eating less sodium.

∽ ∽

MAKES ABOUT 1¼ CUPS (300 ML)

1 cup	sesame seeds	250 mL
1 tsp	coarse salt	5 mL

Tips

Pulse the seeds just to a coarse chop, or you will end up with tahini.

White, brown and black sesame seeds will all provide a different look and flavor.

1. Spread sesame seeds in a large skillet. Place over medium heat and swirl, taking care not to spill the seeds. Toast, swirling and stirring constantly, for about 4 minutes or until the seeds start to smell toasty and are hot to the touch.

2. Transfer the seeds to the Vitamix container and let cool for 5 minutes, then add salt and secure the lid. With the switch on Variable, select speed 10 and pulse three times.

3. Remove the lid and scrape the seeds from the corners of the container. Replace the lid and pulse twice more or until the seeds are coarsely chopped.

4. Transfer the seasoning mixture to a jar and let cool completely before using or covering tightly and storing in the refrigerator for up to 2 weeks.

Mushroom Umami Rub

Umami is a pleasing sense of meaty, satisfying richness that comes from certain chemicals in food. It is highest in protein foods, but there are certain plant foods that are also rich in umami, and this mixture is based on some concentrated sources.

∽∾ ∽∾

MAKES ABOUT $^1/_2$ CUP (125 ML)

2	dry-packed sun-dried tomato halves	2
1	$8^1/_3$- by $7^1/_2$-inch (21 by 19 cm) sheet nori, torn into pieces	1
1 cup	dried shiitake mushrooms	250 mL
1 tbsp	smoked salt	15 mL

Tips

Use this blend as a rub for tofu or tempeh before roasting, or sprinkle it over salads and pastas for an instant flavor boost.

The mushrooms and tomatoes must be very dry to grind easily. If your tomatoes are moist, let them sit out at room temperature for a few days to dry to a crunchy texture.

Try other mushroom varieties for a different flavor.

Sea vegetables such as dulse and thin kombu are also delicious in place of nori in this mixture. Use 2 tbsp (30 mL) dulse or kombu leaves, or 1 tbsp (15 mL) chopped dulse.

1. Place the sun-dried tomatoes, nori, shiitakes and salt in the Vitamix container and secure the lid. With the switch on Variable, select speed 1 and turn the machine on. Quickly increase the speed to 10, then flip the switch to High and blend for 30 seconds. Turn the machine off, tap the container to knock down the ingredients and let the powder settle for 10 seconds before opening the container. If there are any chunks left, process again.

2. Scrape the seasoning mixture into a jar and use immediately or store at room temperature for up to 2 months.

Thyme and Orange Salt and Pepper

This is sure to become your go-to seasoning for a simple piece of fish or chicken, or for root vegetables before roasting. It also livens up a salad or sautéed vegetables.

MAKES ABOUT ¹/₄ CUP (60 ML)

¹/₂	large orange	¹/₂
2 tbsp	fresh thyme leaves	30 mL
1 tbsp	whole black peppercorns	15 mL
1 tbsp	coarse salt	15 mL

1. Using a sharp paring knife, peel the zest from the orange half, removing only the orange part and leaving the white pith behind. Reserve the orange for another use. Chop the orange zest into ¹/₄-inch (0.5 cm) wide pieces.

2. Place the orange zest pieces in the Vitamix container and add the thyme, peppercorns and salt. Secure the lid. With the switch on Variable, select speed 1 and turn the machine on. Gradually increase the speed to 10, then flip the switch to High and blend for 40 seconds or until the zest and thyme are minced.

3. Transfer the seasoning mixture to a jar and use immediately or store in the refrigerator for up to 1 month.

Variation

Replace half of the thyme with fresh rosemary or sage.

> **Tip**
>
> Buy organic citrus fruits when you are going to use the zest, to minimize your exposure to chemicals.

Mrs. Smash Salt-Free Blend

There is a popular salt-free blend, which has been around for years, that has a winning combination of spices and dried vegetables. Its secret ingredient is nutritional yeast, an umami-rich form of yeast often used by vegans to add B vitamins to their food. In your version of this blend, a little nutritional yeast adds a slightly cheesy taste and a pleasant sense of meatiness.

MAKES ABOUT 3 TBSP (45 ML)

¹/₄ cup	dehydrated mixed vegetables	60 mL
2 tbsp	nutritional yeast	30 mL
¹/₂ tsp	whole black peppercorns	2 mL
¹/₂ tsp	dried thyme	2 mL
¹/₂ tsp	dried sage	2 mL
¹/₂ tsp	dried oregano	2 mL
¹/₂ tsp	dried basil	2 mL
¹/₂ tsp	dried minced garlic	2 mL

1. Place dried vegetables, yeast, peppercorns, thyme, sage, oregano, basil and garlic in the Vitamix container and secure the lid. With the switch on Variable, select speed 1 and turn the machine on. Gradually increase the speed to 10, then flip the switch to High and grind for about 20 seconds, until finely powdered. Turn the machine off, tap the sides of the container and let settle for a few seconds.

2. Transfer the seasoning mixture to a small jar and use immediately or store at room temperature for up to 1 month.

Meyer Lemon Salt

Meyer lemons are plentiful in wintertime, and this is a fun way to save that unique flavor in a seasoning salt. The yellow lemon zest and pink salt make a pretty sprinkle over a salad or a slice of avocado toast.

MAKES ABOUT $1/2$ CUP (125 ML)

1	large Meyer lemon	1
2 tbsp	fresh rosemary leaves	30 mL
$1/4$ cup	large chunk Himalayan pink salt	60 mL

Tip
Be patient; just keep scraping and pulsing until the zest and salt are very finely minced.

1. Using a sharp paring knife, peel the zest from the lemon, removing only the yellow part and leaving the white pith behind. Reserve the lemon for another use. Chop the lemon zest into $1/2$-inch (1 cm) wide pieces.

2. Place the lemon zest pieces in the Vitamix container and add the rosemary. Secure the lid. With the switch on Variable, select speed 1 and turn the machine on. Gradually increase the speed to 3 and blend, stopping every 30 seconds to scrape down the container, until the zest is very finely minced.

3. Turn the machine off and add the salt. Replace the lid, select speed 1 and turn the machine on. Gradually increase the speed to 10, then pulse in 10-second bursts until finely minced.

4. Turn the machine off and use a spatula to scrape out the corners of the container. If there are any large chunks of zest or salt, replace the lid and repeat step 3 until the mixture is evenly minced.

5. Transfer the seasoning mixture to a plate, spread out and let dry at room temperature for 24 hours. Use immediately or store in a jar at room temperature for up to 2 months.

Variation
Try another kind of citrus fruit, such as a tangerine.

Cheddar Cheese Powder

Cheese-flavored popcorn is an addictive snack, but it's laced with bright orange cheese powder of questionable origin. Using this recipe, you can make your own cheese powder and sprinkle it over hot popped corn for a fresher, less-processed version of your favorite salty treat.

MAKES ABOUT ¾ CUP (175 ML)

- **Preheat oven to 170°F (80°C)**
- **Baking sheet, lined with parchment paper**

2 oz	sharp (old) Cheddar cheese, finely shredded	60 g
1 tsp	water	5 mL
¼ cup	arrowroot starch	60 mL
2 tbsp	buttermilk powder	30 mL
¾ tsp	salt	3 mL
¼ tsp	granulated sugar	1 mL

Tip

Buttermilk powder is sold in well-stocked grocery stores, next to the powdered and canned milk (or sometimes in the baking section).

1. In a small saucepan, combine cheese and water. Place over medium-low heat and cook, stirring gently every couple of minutes, until the cheese is melted.

2. Transfer the cheese mixture to the Vitamix container and add the arrowroot, buttermilk powder, salt and sugar. Secure the lid. With the switch on Variable, select speed 1 and turn the machine on. Gradually increase the speed to 4 and blend for about 10 seconds, just until a paste forms.

3. Transfer the paste to the prepared baking sheet and break it into irregular pieces (the more pieces the better), using your fingertips to flatten the pieces to ¼ inch (0.5 cm) thick. Bake in preheated oven for 45 minutes or until very dry. Remove from the oven, leaving the oven on.

4. Meanwhile, wash and dry the Vitamix container.

5. Transfer the cheese pieces to the container and secure the lid. With the switch on Variable, select speed 1 and turn the machine on. Gradually increase the speed to 10 and grind for about 20 seconds, to make a powder.

6. Transfer the powder to the lined baking sheet, spreading it in an even layer. Bake for 15 minutes or until nearly dry. If desired, grind again for a finer texture. Let cool completely.

7. Transfer the cheese powder to a small jar and use immediately or store, tightly covered, in the refrigerator for up to 1 month.

Variation

Nacho Cheese Powder: Add ½ tsp (2 mL) chili powder and ½ tsp (2 mL) ground cumin with the cheese pieces in step 5.

DIPS and SPREADS

Mayonnaise with Herbs

Freshly made mayonnaise is so much better than store-bought, you will want to have it all the time. If you follow the tip on pasteurizing eggs, you can keep it for up to 3 days (if it lasts that long).

MAKES ABOUT 1 CUP (250 ML)

2	large egg yolks	2
2 tbsp	freshly squeezed lemon juice	30 mL
1/2 tsp	salt	2 mL
Pinch	cayenne pepper	Pinch
1/2 cup	canola oil	125 mL
1/4 cup	extra virgin olive oil	60 mL
2 tbsp	minced fresh basil, parsley or mint	30 mL

Tip

To pasteurize eggs, place them in a saucepan with enough cold water to cover. Bring the temperature of the water up to 140°F (60°C) over medium heat. Adjust the heat as necessary to hold the temperature at 140°F for 3 minutes. Drain the eggs and rinse with cold water. Store in the refrigerator for up to 3 days.

1. Place the egg yolks, lemon juice, salt and cayenne in the Vitamix container. Secure the lid and remove the lid plug. With the switch on Variable, select speed 1 and turn the machine on. Blend for 10 seconds, then increase the speed to 3. Very slowly pour the canola oil and olive oil through the lid opening, blending until the oils are incorporated and the mixture is thick.

2. Turn the machine off and add the basil. Replace the lid and turn the machine on. Blend on speed 5 for a couple of seconds.

3. Transfer the mayonnaise to a jar and use immediately or store in the refrigerator for up to 3 days.

Variation

Use the fresh herbs that complement your meal or mood. Tarragon, sorrel or other tender herbs would be delicious in this mayo.

Aquafaba Mayo

Giving up eggs needn't mean giving up mayo. "Aquafaba" (pseudo-Latin for "bean water") is the new way to replace eggs. A base of creamy chickpeas and water, seasoned with lemon and plenty of olive oil, is a pretty fair approximation of the mayo you grew up eating on your sandwiches. It's also good for potato salads and other salads that call for mayonnaise.

MAKES ABOUT 3/4 CUP (175 ML)

2 tbsp	dried chickpeas	30 mL
1 1/2 cups	water, divided	375 mL
2 tsp	Dijon mustard	10 mL
2 tsp	freshly squeezed lemon juice	10 mL
1/2 tsp	granulated sugar	2 mL
1/2 tsp	salt	2 mL
1/4 tsp	paprika	1 mL
1/8 tsp	ground turmeric	0.5 mL
1/4 cup	extra virgin olive oil	60 mL

Tip

Try using the chickpea mixture after step 3 as an egg replacer in baking; it makes 1/2 cup (125 mL) egg replacer, which replaces 2 large eggs.

1. Place the chickpeas in a small bowl and pour in 1/2 cup (125 mL) water. Let soak overnight. Drain and rinse.

2. Place the chickpeas and the remaining water in the Vitamix container and secure the lid. With the switch on Variable, select speed 1 and turn the machine on. Gradually increase the speed to 10, then flip the switch to High and blend for 1 minute.

3. Scrape the chickpea purée into a small saucepan and bring to a boil over medium heat, stirring often. Reduce heat and simmer, stirring often, for 20 minutes to cook the beans (the mixture will thicken slightly). Scrape the chickpea mixture into a measuring cup and, if necessary, add enough cold water to make 1/2 cup (125 mL). Let cool to room temperature.

4. Transfer the chickpea mixture to the Vitamix and add the mustard, lemon juice, sugar, salt, paprika and turmeric. Secure the lid. With the switch on Variable, select speed 1 and turn the machine on. Gradually increase the speed to 5 and blend until mixed, stopping to scrape down the container as necessary.

5. Remove the lid plug, reduce the speed to 3 and very slowly pour in oil through the lid opening, blending until the oil is incorporated.

6. Transfer the mayo to a jar and refrigerate for at least 2 hours, until set to a firmer texture, or for up to 1 week.

Variations

Aïoli: Add a clove of crushed garlic with the mustard in step 4.

Red Pepper Aïoli: Add half a drained roasted red pepper with the mustard in step 4.

Hot Artichoke Dip

Caramelized onions and canned artichokes conspire to be so flavorful that you won't even notice the tofu in this dip. It's baked with a layer of crunchy bread crumbs on top, for extra texture. Serve it at holiday parties, with crackers, crudités or toast.

MAKES ABOUT 3 CUPS (750 ML)

● **4-cup (1 L) shallow baking dish or glass loaf pan, lightly oiled**

2 tbsp	extra virgin olive oil	30 mL
2	large onions, thinly sliced	2
2	cloves garlic, sliced	2
1 tbsp	fresh thyme leaves	15 mL
2 tbsp	freshly squeezed lemon juice	30 mL
1	can (14 oz/398 mL) artichoke bottoms, drained	1
8 oz	extra-firm tofu (see tip)	250 g
1 tsp	salt	5 mL
1/2 tsp	freshly ground black pepper	2 mL

TOPPING

1/4 cup	toasted slivered almonds, minced	60 mL
1/4 cup	panko (Japanese bread crumbs)	60 mL
1/2 tsp	salt	2 mL
1 tbsp	extra virgin olive oil	15 mL
1 tsp	grated lemon zest	5 mL

Tip

To get the right texture for this dish, look for water-packed extra-firm tofu that is made with nigari (magnesium chloride). Do not use silken tofu.

1. In a large skillet, heat oil over medium-high heat. Add onions and cook, stirring, until starting to sizzle. Reduce heat to medium-low and cook, stirring every 5 minutes, for at least 45 minutes or up to 2 hours, until shrunken, golden brown and sweet. Add garlic and thyme; cook, stirring, for 5 minutes or until garlic is softened.

2. Meanwhile, preheat oven to 400°F (200°C).

3. Transfer the onion mixture to the Vitamix container and add the lemon juice, artichokes, tofu, salt and pepper. Secure the lid, remove the lid plug and insert the tamper. With the switch on Variable, select speed 1 and turn the machine on. Gradually increase the speed to 5, using the tamper to push the ingredients into the blades. As the mixture starts to flow, gradually increase the speed to 7, tamping and blending until the mixture is almost smooth (it's fine if there are some chunks left). Transfer to the prepared baking dish and smooth the top.

4. *Topping:* In a medium bowl, combine almonds, panko, salt, oil and lemon zest. Sprinkle over the artichoke mixture and pat down.

5. Bake in preheated oven for 25 minutes or until the crumb topping is browned and the dip is nice and hot. Serve immediately.

Variation

For a deep, sweet garlic flavor, use a head of roasted garlic in place of 1 of the onions and the sliced garlic. At the end of step 1, just sauté the thyme with the onions briefly. Add the roasted garlic with the artichokes in step 3.

Super-Creamy Guacamole

Mashing avocados by hand gives you a rustic version of guacamole, but using the Vitamix will give you the silkiest, smoothest guacamole you have ever tried. Give it a try; you may find that you like it better.

∽∾ ∽∾

MAKES ABOUT 1¹/₂ CUPS (375 ML)

2	ripe large avocados	2
1	clove garlic, chopped	1
2 tbsp	freshly squeezed lime juice	30 mL
¹/₂ tsp	salt	2 mL
1	large green onion, chopped	1
1	plum (Roma) tomato, seeded and chopped	1
2 tbsp	lightly packed fresh cilantro, chopped	30 mL

Tip

To store the dip, transfer it to a bowl or storage container, sprinkle the surface with lime juice, then place plastic wrap on the dip and use your fingers to make sure the wrap is in contact with the entire surface. Store in the refrigerator for no longer than 24 hours.

1. Halve the avocados, remove the pits and scoop the flesh into the Vitamix container. Add the garlic, lime juice and salt. Secure the lid, remove the lid plug and insert the tamper. With the switch on Variable, select speed 1 and turn the machine on. Using the tamper to push the ingredients into the blades, gradually increase the speed to 3 and blend for about 20 seconds or until smooth.

2. Turn the machine off and the add the green onion, tomato and cilantro, stirring them in with a spatula. Pulse once just to mix. Transfer to a bowl.

Variation

Spicy Guacamole: Add 1 minced seeded jalapeño pepper with the cilantro. (For an even spicier dip, leave in the seeds.)

Spicy Beet Dip

Shake up your dip routine with this creamy crimson spread. It's a perfect dip for your vegan friends and anyone who likes beets. Put a bowl alongside some Black Bean Hummus (page 88) and Super-Creamy Guacamole (page 83), for a beautiful color assortment.

MAKES ABOUT 1¼ CUPS (300 ML)

● **Steamer basket**

¹/₂ cup	raw cashews	125 mL
	Cool water	
1 lb	beets, peeled and cut into thick slices	500 g
¹/₂ cup	unsweetened almond milk	125 mL
2 tbsp	balsamic vinegar	30 mL
1 tsp	salt	5 mL
1 tsp	hot pepper flakes	5 mL

Tips

Keep an easy-to-wash plastic cutting board for working with beets, so you can keep from staining a wooden one.

Golden beets make a vibrant yellow version of this dip, which may complement your table even more than red.

1. Place the cashews in a 2-cup (500 mL) measure and add cool water up to the 1½-cup (375 mL) mark. Let soak overnight at room temperature or in the refrigerator. Drain and rinse well.

2. In a steamer basket set over a pot of boiling water, steam beets for 10 minutes or until tender. Let cool slightly.

3. Place the almond milk, vinegar, cashews, beets, salt and hot pepper flakes in the Vitamix container. Secure the lid, remove the lid plug and insert the tamper. With the switch on Variable, select speed 1 and turn the machine on. Using the tamper to push the ingredients into the blades, gradually increase the speed to 10 and blend for about 20 seconds or until very smooth.

4. Turn the machine off and scrape down the sides of the container to make sure everything is puréed. If there are any chunks remaining, replace the lid and blend on speed 10 again.

5. Scrape the dip into a bowl and serve immediately, or store in an airtight container in the refrigerator for up to 4 days.

Baba Ghanouj

Your meze spread is not complete without baba ghanouj, the eggplant dip that can convert even people who don't like eggplant. Enriched with nutty tahini and lightened with a generous spritz of lemon, this classic dip delivers great Middle Eastern flavor.

MAKES ABOUT 2 CUPS (500 ML)

- **Preheat oven to 400°F (200°C)**
- **Large rimmed baking sheet, lightly oiled**

1	medium eggplant (about 1 lb/500 g)	1
1/4 cup	freshly squeezed lemon juice	60 mL
1/2 cup	tahini	125 mL
2	cloves garlic	2
1/2 tsp	salt	2 mL
1/4 tsp	cayenne pepper	1 mL

Tip

The longer the eggplant cools in the skin, the more the color of the skin soaks into the flesh — something traditionalists want to avoid. To keep your eggplant dip light in color, scoop out the flesh as soon as it is cool enough to handle.

1. Cut eggplant in half lengthwise and place, cut side down, on the prepared baking sheet. Roast in preheated oven for about 30 minutes or until tender when pierced. Flip the eggplant halves over and let cool on pan on a wire rack.

2. Place the lemon juice in the Vitamix container. When the eggplant is cool enough to handle, scoop the flesh into the container and discard the skins. Add the tahini, garlic, salt and cayenne. Secure the lid, remove the lid plug and insert the tamper. With the switch on Variable, select speed 1 and turn the machine on. Using the tamper to push the ingredients into the blades, gradually increase the speed to 5. As the mixture becomes smoother, gradually increase the speed to 10, then flip the switch to High and blend for about 30 seconds or until creamy.

3. Transfer the dip to a bowl and serve immediately, or store in an airtight container in the refrigerator for up to 1 week.

Variation

Tahini is the classic flavor for this dip, but you can substitute your own fresh pistachio or almond butter (page 19 or 18) for a tasty improvisation on the theme.

Tapenade with Capers

Olives are such a concentrated source of savory flavor and richness that making them into a spread is an almost instant way to make a simple piece of toast into a sophisticated appetizer. You can also toss tapenade into hot pasta or drop a spoonful on top of a vegetable soup for a delicious garnish.

MAKES ABOUT 1 CUP (250 ML)

2	cloves garlic, coarsely chopped	2
8 oz	pitted kalamata olives, drained	250 g
2 tbsp	drained capers	30 mL
2 tbsp	lightly packed fresh parsley	30 mL
2 tbsp	fresh thyme leaves	30 mL
2 tbsp	extra virgin olive oil	30 mL

Tips

Buy pitted olives, to save time.

You can use this as a template to make delicious spreads from other kinds of olives, whatever variety appeals to you. Green olives are a little firmer in texture and may take a few seconds longer to purée.

1. Place the garlic, olives, capers, parsley and thyme in the Vitamix container. Secure the lid, remove the lid plug and insert the tamper. With the switch on Variable, select speed 1 and turn the machine on. Blend for a few seconds to chop, using the tamper to push the ingredients into the blades, then gradually increase the speed to 4 and blend for about 30 seconds to a coarse purée.

2. Turn the machine off and scrape down the container. If you would like a smoother paste, replace the lid and blend on speed 4 for 30 seconds. Scrape down the container again. Replace the lid, select speed 3 and turn the machine on. Very slowly pour in oil through the lid opening, blending until the oil is incorporated.

3. Transfer the dip to a bowl and use immediately, or store in an airtight container in the refrigerator for up to 1 week.

Cauliflower Hummus

Hummus has expanded from a simple paste made of chickpeas to a seemingly infinite number of variations. This one skips the beans, which may not agree with you, in favor of cauliflower. It adds a vegetable to your plate, with all the nutty flavor of tahini.

〜〜〜〜〜〜〜〜〜〜〜〜〜〜〜〜〜〜〜〜〜〜〜〜〜〜

MAKES ABOUT 1¹/₂ CUPS (375 ML)

● **Steamer basket**

3 cups	chopped cauliflower, including peeled and chopped stem	750 mL
1	clove garlic	1
¹/₄ cup	tahini	60 mL
2 tbsp	freshly squeezed lemon juice	30 mL
	Paprika	
¹/₂ tsp	salt	2 mL
	Extra virgin olive oil	

Tip

This is a great way to use the stem of the cauliflower. If you are planning to have a cauliflower dish later in the week, you can save most of the florets for that and make this spread mostly from stem.

1. In a steamer basket set over a pot of boiling water, steam cauliflower for about 10 minutes or until very tender.

2. Transfer the cauliflower to the Vitamix container and add the garlic, tahini, lemon juice, ¹/₂ tsp (2 mL) paprika and salt. Secure the lid, remove the lid plug and insert the tamper. With the switch on Variable, select speed 1 and turn the machine on. Using the tamper to push the ingredients into the blades, gradually increase the speed to 10, then flip the switch to High and blend for 40 to 60 seconds or until smooth.

3. Transfer the hummus to a bowl, drizzle with oil and sprinkle with paprika, if desired. Use immediately or store, tightly covered, in the refrigerator for up to 4 days.

Variation

For a greenish hummus, try broccoli in place of cauliflower, and decrease the steaming time to about 7 minutes.

Black Bean Hummus

Black beans have a slightly stronger flavor than chickpeas, and the addition of lime juice gives this hummus a Southwestern vibe. It is delicious with chips or pita triangles, or smeared on sandwiches.

∿∿∿∿∿∿∿∿∿∿∿∿∿∿∿∿∿∿∿∿∿∿∿∿∿

MAKES ABOUT 1³/₄ CUPS (425 ML)

1	can (14 to 15 oz/398 to 425 mL) black beans (see tip)	1
1	large clove garlic, chopped	1
2 tbsp	freshly squeezed lime juice	30 mL
¹/₄ cup	tahini	60 mL
2 tbsp	extra virgin olive oil	30 mL
¹/₂ tsp	ground cumin	2 mL
¹/₂ tsp	salt (approx.)	2 mL
	Extra virgin olive oil	
	Paprika	

Tips

If you can find only larger cans of beans, measure 1³/₄ cups (425 mL) beans with liquid for this recipe and reserve the remainder for another use.

Black beans are rich in antioxidants, especially the anthocyanins that protect us from free radicals, so enjoy them often. Red beans are also high in antioxidants and make a tasty variation on this hummus.

1. Drain the liquid from the can of beans, but don't rinse the beans. Reserve the liquid in case you need to thin the dip.

2. Place the beans, garlic, lime juice, tahini, oil, cumin and salt in the Vitamix container. Secure the lid, remove the lid plug and insert the tamper. With the machine on Variable, select speed 1 and start the machine. Using the tamper to push the ingredients into the blades, gradually increase the speed to 5 and blend for about 30 seconds or until smooth.

3. Turn the machine off and taste the hummus. If desired, thin the dip with some of the reserved bean liquid and/or add more salt, then replace the lid and blend again.

4. Transfer the hummus to a bowl, drizzle with oil and sprinkle with paprika, if desired. Use immediately or store, tightly covered, in the refrigerator for up to 4 days.

Guajillo and Red Bean "Refried" Beans

If you keep some dried chiles and canned beans in the pantry, you'll be minutes away from a tasty bean dip like this one. Dried chiles add a sweet and spicy flavor to beans, and enough complexity that you will not need to do much more than open a bag of chips. But you can also serve this spread on tostadas or in burritos.

MAKES ABOUT 2¹/₂ CUPS (625 ML)

1 oz	dried guajillo chile peppers (about 5 chiles)	30 g
2 cups	boiling water	500 mL
2	cans (each 14 to 15 oz/398 to 425 mL) red kidney beans	2
4 tsp	ground cumin	20 mL
1 tsp	salt	5 mL
2 tbsp	coconut oil	30 mL

Tips

To use dried beans in this recipe, soak 1 cup (250 mL) dried red kidney beans in water to cover overnight, then drain. Place in a medium pot with 4 cups (1 L) water and bring to a boil over high heat. Reduce heat and simmer for about 1 hour or until very soft. Drain, reserving the liquid, and measure 3 cups (750 mL) of cooked beans for this recipe.

Beans are incredibly healthful, with protein, fiber and minerals. If your family isn't that excited about whole beans, try a creamy bean dip or spread, and they may fall in love with beans.

1. Place chiles in a heatproof bowl, cover with boiling water and let soak for about 5 minutes or until pliable. Drain, reserving the soaking liquid, and place chiles on a cutting board. Using a paring knife, remove the stems, seeds and membranes.

2. Drain the liquid from the cans of beans, but don't rinse the beans. Reserve 1 cup (250 mL) liquid.

3. Place the chiles in the Vitamix container and add the beans, reserved bean liquid, cumin and salt. Secure the lid, remove the lid plug and insert the tamper. With the switch on Variable, select speed 1 and turn the machine on. Using the tamper to push the ingredients into the blades, gradually increase the speed to 10, then flip the switch to High and blend for about 30 seconds or until smooth.

4. In a large skillet, heat coconut oil over medium-high heat. Scrape in the bean mixture and cook, using a spatula to stir and turn the mixture in the pan and scrape the bottom thoroughly. Reduce the heat to medium and cook, scraping, for about 5 minutes or until the desired thickness is reached.

Variation

Ancho chiles can be substituted for a similar heat level. For more smoky heat, use ¾ oz (22 g) dried chipotles.

Feta Spinach Dip with Oregano

The classic Greek flavor pairing of feta and spinach is just as delicious in a dip as in a pie, and it takes much less time to make. This tangy dip is equally at home smeared on pitas or chips and as a sandwich filling or a pizza topping.

MAKES ABOUT 1½ CUPS (375 ML)

1 cup	plain Greek yogurt or sour cream	250 mL
1	clove garlic, sliced	1
2 cups	lightly packed fresh spinach	500 mL
1 cup	crumbled feta cheese (see tip)	250 mL
½ tsp	freshly ground black pepper	2 mL
2 tbsp	toasted pine nuts	30 mL

Tip

Look for feta made with sheep or goat milk, which are often creamier. Always rinse the cheese before crumbling, to remove the brine.

1. Place the yogurt, garlic, spinach, feta and pepper in the Vitamix container. Secure the lid, remove the lid plug and insert the tamper. With the switch on Variable, select speed 1 and turn the machine on. Using the tamper to push the ingredients into the blades, gradually increase the speed to 10 and blend for 30 to 40 seconds or until smooth.

2. Transfer the dip to a bowl and sprinkle with pine nuts. Serve immediately or cover tightly and refrigerate for about 1 hour, until chilled, or for up to 4 days.

Variation

Replace half the spinach with parsley and sprinkle with toasted pistachios.

Cheesy Jalapeño Queso

A Mexican-style cheese dip with a bag of chips and a can of refried beans is perfect for an easy meal. You can also drizzle queso over a plateful of nachos, to great effect.

MAKES ABOUT 2¼ CUPS (550 ML)

1 tsp	extra virgin olive oil	5 mL
1 cup	chopped onion	250 mL
½ cup	Mexican lager beer, boiling	125 mL
¼ cup	milk	60 mL
8 oz	sharp (old) Cheddar cheese, cubed	250 g
2 tsp	arrowroot starch	10 mL
1 tbsp	water	15 mL
1	medium jalapeño pepper, chopped	1

1. In a medium skillet, heat oil over medium-high heat. Add onion and cook, stirring and reducing the heat to medium-low as the onion starts to soften, for about 5 minutes or until onion is soft and light golden.

2. Transfer onion to the Vitamix container and add beer, milk and cheese. Secure the lid and remove the lid plug. With the switch on Variable, select speed 1 and turn the machine on. Gradually increase the speed to 10, then flip the switch to High and blend for 5 minutes.

3. In a small bowl, whisk arrowroot into water. Pour this slurry through the lid opening and blend on speed 10 for 1 minute.

4. Turn the machine off and add the jalapeño. Replace the lid and pulse to incorporate.

5. Transfer the queso to a bowl and serve warm.

Vegan Nacho Queso

Vegans need not be left out of the fun when it's time for nachos. This makes a party-size batch of dip that keeps well, so you can reheat it later in the week for another dipping session. Make sure to buy unsweetened almond milk (or make your own). Serve over chips, or as a dip.

MAKES ABOUT 2¹/₂ CUPS (625 ML)

1 cup	raw cashews	250 mL
	Cold water	
1¹/₂ cups	unsweetened almond milk	375 mL
¹/₄ cup	canola oil	60 mL
2 tbsp	red miso	30 mL
2 tsp	freshly squeezed lime juice	10 mL
2	cloves garlic, sliced	2
¹/₄ cup	nutritional yeast	60 mL
6 tbsp	arrowroot starch	90 mL
1 tsp	salt	5 mL
¹/₄ tsp	ground turmeric	1 mL
2	large jalapeño peppers, chopped	2

Tip

You can keep soaking the cashews in the refrigerator for up to 4 days; if you don't get around to making this dip, they won't go bad.

1. Place the cashews in a bowl and add cold water to cover; let soak for 6 hours (see tip). Drain well.

2. Place the almond milk, oil, miso, lime juice, cashews, garlic, yeast, arrowroot, salt and turmeric in the Vitamix container. Secure the lid, remove the lid plug and insert the tamper. With the switch on Variable, select speed 1 and turn the machine on. Using the tamper to push the ingredients into the blades, gradually increase the speed to 5 and blend for 20 seconds.

3. Flip the switch to High and blend for 4 minutes. When the mixture thickens, the machine will start to make a different sound. Turn the machine off and use a spatula to scrape all the way to the bottom of the container. The mixture should have thickened as it heated, and it will thicken at the bottom first. If it has not thickened, replace the lid, turn the machine on and blend on High for 1 minute or until thickened.

4. Turn the machine off and add the jalapeños. Replace the lid and pulse to incorporate.

5. Transfer the queso to a bowl and serve immediately.

Variation

If you like spice, add ¹/₂ tsp (2 mL) chipotle chile powder (or to taste) with the salt in step 2.

Fromage Fort Spread

The name of the thrifty French cook who came up with this idea has been lost to history, but it remains a perfect answer for using up all those bits and pieces of cheese that can end up in your fridge — too small to serve and too big to throw away. It's also delicious, with a kick of wine and plenty of garlic.

MAKES ABOUT 1¹/₂ CUPS (375 ML)

¹/₄ cup	dry white wine	60 mL
8 oz	leftover firm cheeses (Swiss, Cheddar, blue, etc.), cubed	250 g
4 oz	soft goat cheese (chèvre)	125 g
2	cloves garlic, chopped	2
¹/₄ cup	lightly packed fresh parsley leaves	60 mL

Tips

It's fine to trim some mold from hard cheeses, but softer cheeses that have become moldy will be contaminated all the way through and must be discarded.

A sweet wine can also be delicious in place of the dry wine, especially with blue or Cheddar cheese.

1. Place the wine, firm cheese, soft cheese, garlic and parsley in the Vitamix container. Secure the lid, remove the lid plug and insert the tamper. With the switch on Variable, select speed 1 and turn the machine on. Using the tamper to push the ingredients into the blades, gradually increase the speed to 5, then to 8 as the purée becomes smoother. Blend on speed 8 for about 60 seconds or until creamy.

2. Transfer the spread to a bowl and use immediately, or store in an airtight container in the refrigerator for up to 1 week.

Baked Shrimp and Brie Dip

This rich, creamy dip is studded with shrimp and spiked with fresh dill fronds, and it smells incredible coming out of the oven. It won't last long at your party once people start plunging in crackers or crusts of bread.

MAKES ABOUT 1¹/₂ CUPS (375 ML)

- **Preheat oven to 400°F (200°C), with a rack positioned in the upper third**
- **8- by 4-inch (20 by 10 cm) glass loaf dish or 2-cup (500 mL) casserole dish, buttered**

1 tbsp	unsalted butter	15 mL
1	large onion, chopped	1
1	clove garlic, sliced	1
2 tbsp	unbleached all-purpose flour	30 mL
2 tbsp	white wine	30 mL
8 oz	Brie cheese, rinds removed	250 g
4 oz	cooked shrimp, peeled and deveined	125 g
1 tbsp	fresh dill	15 mL

Tips

You don't have to splurge on the most expensive Brie for this, but do give the cheese a little sniff and a squeeze; it should be fragrant and soft when ripe.

After using your Vitamix to process seafood or meat, clean it as usual, then fill it halfway with water, add 1¹/₂ tsp (7 mL) liquid bleach and secure the lid. With the switch on Variable, select speed 1 and turn the machine on. Gradually increase the speed to 10 and run for 1 minute, then drain and air-dry. This will sanitize it for the next use.

1. In a large skillet, melt butter over medium heat. Add onion and garlic; cook, stirring often, for 10 minutes or until onion is golden and soft. Sprinkle in flour and stir to combine. Stir in wine and cook, stirring, for 1 minute.

2. Transfer the onion mixture to the Vitamix container and add the cheese, shrimp and dill. Secure the lid, remove the lid plug and insert the tamper. With the switch on Variable, select speed 1 and turn the machine on. Gradually increase the speed to 5, using the tamper to push the ingredients into the blades as the mixture starts to move and mix in the container, and blend for about 30 seconds or until well mixed but not perfectly smooth. Scrape into prepared dish.

3. Bake on upper rack in preheated oven for 20 minutes or until the dip is bubbly and the cheese is golden brown. Serve hot.

Variation

Cooked scallops or crab also make a delicious combo with Brie and dill in place of the shrimp.

Lemony Crab Dip

Unexpected guests? This dip is made from pantry staples and takes only minutes to assemble. It's also a nice spread for bagels in the morning.

ᘒᘓ ᘒᘓ

MAKES ABOUT 1¹/₂ CUPS (375 ML)

2 tsp	grated lemon zest	10 mL
2 tsp	freshly squeezed lemon juice	10 mL
1/4 tsp	Worcestershire sauce	1 mL
4 oz	brick-style cream cheese, softened	125 g
1	can (8 oz/227 g) crabmeat, drained	1
1/4 tsp	salt	1 mL
1	large green onion, chopped	1
	Paprika (optional)	

Tip

The best canned crab is sold in the refrigerated section by the fresh fish counter, labeled "pasteurized crabmeat."

1. Place the lemon zest, lemon juice, Worcestershire sauce, cream cheese, crab and salt in the Vitamix container. Secure the lid, remove the lid plug and insert the tamper. With the switch on Variable, select speed 1 and turn the machine on. Using the tamper to push the ingredients into the blades, gradually increase the speed to 5 and blend for 5 to 10 seconds or until smooth.

2. Turn the machine off and scrape down the container. If the mixture is not smooth, replace the lid and blend until smooth.

3. Transfer the dip to a bowl and stir in green onion. Sprinkle with paprika, if desired. Use immediately or store, tightly covered, in the refrigerator for up to 4 days.

Variation

Replace the crab with cooked cocktail shrimp or even smoked salmon.

Salmon Mousse

This delicious mousse is decidedly old-school, and due for a renaissance. In your Vitamix, the gorgeous pink salmon is puréed to a creamy texture, then held in a sliceable form by just enough gelatin to set it. Unmold it onto a bed of baby spinach and thinly sliced radishes for a dramatic presentation, or just slice it and eat it on toast.

MAKES ABOUT 4 CUPS (1 L)

- 4-cup (1 L) mold or 9- by 5-inch (23 by 12.5 cm) loaf pan, lightly oiled

1/2 cup	ready-to-use chicken broth or fish stock	125 mL
2 tbsp	unflavored gelatin powder	30 mL
1 tbsp	freshly squeezed lemon juice	15 mL
3/4 cup	sour cream	175 mL
1 lb	cooked boneless skinless salmon fillet, flaked	500 g
1/2 tsp	salt	2 mL
2	small green onions, minced	2

Tips

Run hot water over the outside of the mold to help release the mousse neatly.

Gelatin is often recommended as a remedy for joint pain and fragile fingernails. This mousse is a tasty way to get a little gelatin in your diet.

1. Pour broth into a small saucepan and sprinkle gelatin over top; let stand for 10 minutes or until softened. Place the pan over low heat and stir constantly until gelatin is dissolved. Stir in lemon juice.

2. Transfer the gelatin mixture to the Vitamix container and add sour cream, salmon and salt. Secure the lid, remove the lid plug and insert the tamper. With the switch on Variable, select speed 1 and turn the machine on. Using the tamper to push the ingredients into the blades, gradually increase the speed to 10, then flip the switch to High and blend for about 45 seconds or until relatively smooth.

3. Turn the machine off and check the texture. If you want a smoother purée, replace the lid and blend on High for another 30 seconds. Turn the machine off and stir in green onions with a spatula.

4. Scrape the mousse into the prepared mold and smooth the top. Cover and refrigerate for at least 3 hours, until cold and set, or for up to 3 days.

Variation

For a smoky flavor, use 12 oz (375 g) cooked salmon and 4 oz (125 g) smoked salmon.

Chicken Liver Mousse

This classic pâté is perfect for tea sandwiches or slicing to build a super-sandwich. It's made from half thighs and half liver, so the liver flavor is more subtle than some liver pâtés.

MAKES ABOUT 4 CUPS (1 L)

• **4-cup (1L) mold or bowl, lightly buttered**

2 cups	ready-to-use chicken broth	500 mL
1/4 cup	unflavored gelatin powder	60 mL
2 tbsp	fresh thyme leaves	30 mL
1 tsp	whole black peppercorns	5 mL
2	cloves garlic	2
2	medium shallots, quartered	2
1/4 cup	unsalted butter	60 mL
6 oz	boneless skinless chicken thighs, chopped	175 g
6 oz	chicken livers, trimmed	175 g
1 tsp	salt	5 mL
2 tbsp	cognac	30 mL

Tips

Run hot water over the outside of the mold to help release the mousse neatly.

Ask your butcher for the freshest chicken livers. If they are cutting up chickens on-site, you will get livers that have not been languishing in the freezer.

If you prefer, you can use 12 oz (375 g) chicken livers instead of half livers and half thighs.

1. Pour broth into a small saucepan and sprinkle gelatin over top; let stand for 10 minutes or until softened. Place the pan over low heat and stir constantly until gelatin is dissolved. Remove from heat and set aside.

2. Place the thyme and peppercorns in the Vitamix container and secure the lid. With the switch on Variable, select speed 1 and turn the machine on. Quickly increase the speed to 10, then flip the switch to High and grind for about 20 seconds or until powdered.

3. Turn the machine off and add the garlic. Replace the lid and remove the lid plug. With the switch on Variable, select speed 1 and turn the machine on. Gradually increase the speed to 5. Drop the shallot quarters, one at a time, through the lid opening, using the tamper as needed to push the last pieces into the blades.

4. In a large skillet, melt butter over medium heat. Scrape the shallot mixture into the pan and cook, stirring, for about 5 minutes or until shallots are softened and almost dry. Add chicken thighs and cook, stirring often, for about 3 minutes or until almost cooked through. Add chicken livers, salt and cognac; cook, stirring and turning the livers, until the livers are browned but still pink inside. Remove from heat.

5. Transfer the broth mixture and the liver mixture to the Vitamix container. Secure the lid and insert the tamper. With the switch on Variable, select speed 1 and turn the machine on. Gradually increase the speed to 10, then flip the switch to High and blend for 1 minute or until very smooth and light.

6. Scrape the mousse into the prepared mold and smooth the top. Cover and refrigerate for at least 3 hours, until cold and set, or for up to 4 days.

Cinnamon Walnut Butter (page 23) and
Chocolate Hazelnut Butter (page 22)

Macaroni and Cheese with
Creamy Cheddar Sauce (page 37, recipe suggestion)

Spanish Salsa Verde (page 40)

Strawberry Balsamic Dressing (page 59)

Spicy Beet Dip (page 84), Black Bean Hummus (page 88)
and Super-Creamy Guacamole (page 83)

Baked Shrimp and Brie Dip (page 93)

Chilled Cucumber Watercress Soup (page 103)

Thai Red Curry Pumpkin Soup (page 112)

Smoky Deviled Chicken Spread

If you have a leftover piece of chicken breast, make it into this creamy spread with a whiff of smoke and heat. Suddenly you're excited about lunch again! Serve it in sandwiches or as a dip for crudités.

MAKES ABOUT 1½ CUPS (375 ML)

¼ cup	mayonnaise	60 mL
1 tbsp	freshly squeezed lemon juice	15 mL
2 tsp	Dijon mustard	10 mL
8 oz	cooked boneless skinless chicken breast, cut into 1-inch (2.5 cm) pieces	250 g
½ tsp	chipotle chile powder	2 mL
½ tsp	salt	2 mL
1	large green onion, chopped	1
2 tbsp	chopped fresh parsley	30 mL

Tips

If your chicken is a bit dry, this is a perfect way to use it, adding moisture and seasonings to make it appealing again.

Leftover turkey is also good this way, and this is a perfect way to use up that after-Thanksgiving turkey.

1. Place the mayonnaise, lemon juice, mustard, chicken, chile powder and salt in the Vitamix container. Secure the lid, remove the lid plug and insert the tamper. With the switch on Variable, select speed 1 and turn the machine on. Using the tamper to push the ingredients into the blades, gradually increase the speed to 3 and blend until the chicken is minced. Increase the speed to 5 and blend for a few seconds to a coarse purée.

2. Scrape the spread into a bowl and stir in green onion and parsley. Use immediately or store, tightly covered, in the refrigerator for up to 4 days.

Pumpkin Pie Dip with Gingersnaps

If you crave pumpkin pie but don't have time to bake one, just blend up this easy dip.
It's creamy and spicy and makes a perfect after-school snack in the fall.

∽ ∽

MAKES ABOUT 1³/₄ CUPS (425 ML)

8 oz	brick-style cream cheese, softened	250 g
1/2 cup	pumpkin purée (not pie filling)	125 mL
1/2 cup	powdered sugar (see page 13)	125 mL
2 tbsp	pumpkin pie spice	30 mL
2 tbsp	pure maple syrup	30 mL
	Gingersnap cookies	

Tips

The dip can be stored, tightly covered, in the refrigerator for up to 1 week.

You'll have some pumpkin purée left over from this recipe. Measure two 1/2-cup (125 mL) portions onto a baking sheet lined with parchment paper and freeze, then transfer to a sealable freezer bag to thaw whenever you need 1/2 cup (125 mL) pumpkin.

1. Place the cream cheese, pumpkin, sugar, pie spice and maple syrup in the Vitamix container. Secure the lid, remove the lid plug and insert the tamper. With the switch on Variable, select speed 1 and turn the machine on. Using the tamper to push the ingredients into the blades, gradually increase the speed to 3 and blend until the mixture starts to flow and become well mixed. Gradually increase the speed to 7 and blend for a few seconds.

2. Transfer the dip to a bowl and serve with gingersnaps.

Variation

For a more grown-up version, replace the cream cheese with soft goat cheese (chèvre).

Blueberry Mint Refrigerator Jam

If you've never made jam before, try this entry-level recipe. It relies on Pomona's Universal Pectin, a pectin created specifically for making low-sugar preserves, so you need to buy that brand. Other pectins require a higher percentage of sugar for the jam to set.

MAKES ABOUT 1 CUP (250 ML)

2 cups	fresh or thawed frozen blueberries	500 mL
1 tbsp	freshly squeezed lemon juice	15 mL
1 tsp	calcium water (see tips)	5 mL
1/4 cup	liquid honey or agave nectar	60 mL
3/4 tsp	low-methoxyl citrus pectin (Pomona's Universal Pectin)	3 mL
1 tbsp	packed fresh mint leaves, chopped	15 mL

Tips

You can make this jam any time of year. If you have a craving, just use frozen berries.

Every box of Pomona's Universal Pectin comes with a packet of white calcium powder that you can use to make calcium water. Mix 1/2 tsp (2 mL) calcium powder with 1/2 cup (water) in a small jar, seal and shake vigorously. Store the calcium water in the refrigerator so you can make jam any time. It keeps for several months.

Pomona's Universal Pectin is activated by calcium. Since you are unlikely to know exactly how much calcium is present in the fruit you are using, it is best to always add calcium water when making jam with this pectin.

1. Place the blueberries and lemon juice in the Vitamix container. Secure the lid, remove the lid plug and insert the tamper. With the switch on Variable, select speed 1 and turn the machine on. Using the tamper to push the ingredients into the blades, gradually increase the speed to 10 and blend for 30 seconds to a coarse purée.

2. Transfer the blueberry mixture to a small saucepan and bring to a simmer over medium heat, stirring occasionally. Stir in calcium water and heat, stirring, for 1 minute.

3. In a small bowl, stir together honey and pectin. Stir into the simmering berries and bring to a boil. Reduce heat and simmer, stirring, for 2 minutes. Remove from heat and stir in mint.

4. Transfer the jam to a jar and let cool completely. Use immediately or store in the refrigerator for up to 2 weeks.

Variation

Try this recipe with blackberries and basil, for a sophisticated spread.

Raspberry Agave Preserves

Small batches of preserves, like this one, are a convenient way to eat more fruit, without all the sugars in commercial spreads. Agave is an alternative to refined sugars and corn syrup, and because it is $1^1/_2$ times as sweet as sugar, you can use less.

MAKES ABOUT 1¹/₂ CUPS (375 ML)

1/2 cup	agave nectar	125 mL
2 cups	fresh or thawed frozen raspberries	500 mL
3 tbsp	chia seeds (see tip)	45 mL

1. Place the agave, raspberries and chia seeds in the Vitamix container and secure the lid. With the switch on Variable, select speed 1 and turn the machine on. Gradually increase the speed to 10, then flip the switch to High and blend for 1 minute to a smooth purée.
2. Transfer the raspberry mixture to a small saucepan and bring to a boil over medium heat, stirring constantly. Reduce heat to maintain a gentle simmer and cook, stirring, for 2 minutes. The mixture will thicken slightly.
3. Transfer the preserves to a jar and let cool completely. Cover and refrigerate for at least 3 hours, until chilled and set, or for up to 1 month.

Variation

Strawberries taste wonderful with the agave in these preserves.

Tip

Buy white chia seeds for a paler, less noticeable thickener.

Classic Cranberry Sauce

On a plate filled with meat, potatoes and cooked vegetables, a spoonful of this vibrant, fresh sauce provides a palate cleanser and a jolt of fruity tartness. It's a Thanksgiving tradition, made even easier by your Vitamix, but there is no reason to keep it as holiday-only fare.

MAKES ABOUT 2 CUPS (500 ML)

1	large orange	1
2 cups	fresh or thawed frozen cranberries (about 8 oz/250 g)	500 mL
1/2 cup	granulated sugar	125 mL

1. Pare the zest from half the orange and set aside. Peel the rest of the orange, paring away and discarding as much of the white pith and seeds as you can.
2. Place the orange in the Vitamix container and add the orange zest, cranberries and sugar. Secure the lid. With the switch on Variable, select speed 1 and turn the machine on. Gradually increase the speed to 10, then blend for 30 to 60 seconds, depending on how smooth you want your purée (it's okay to leave it a little chunky).
3. Transfer the sauce to a bowl and serve immediately, or transfer to an airtight container and refrigerate for 2 hours, until chilled, or for up to 4 days. Serve cold or at room temperature.

Variation

For a deeper, darker flavor, replace the granulated sugar with packed brown sugar.

SOUPS

Almost-Instant Vegetable Stock

Your Vitamix makes quick work of chopping the vegetables for stock so that you just need a 30-minute simmer to extract their flavors. This homemade stock is so easy, you may just get into the habit of making your own.

MAKES ABOUT 2 CUPS (500 ML)

- **Sieve or colander**

4 cups	water	1 L
3	stalks celery, cut into 2-inch (5 cm) chunks	2
2	large carrots, cut into 2-inch (5 cm) chunks	2
1	large onion, quartered	1
1	clove garlic	1
1/2 cup	fresh parsley stems	125 mL
3	stems fresh thyme	3
1	large bay leaf	1
1 tsp	whole black peppercorns	5 mL
1/2 tsp	salt	2 mL

Tip

Save parsley stems and the bases of celery bunches for use in stock. Just make sure to trim away any brown or wilted parts before using.

1. Pour the water into the Vitamix container and add the celery, carrots, onion, garlic and parsley stems. Secure the lid. With the switch on Variable, select speed 10 and pulse 4 or 5 times, just until the vegetables are chopped.

2. Transfer the vegetables to a medium pot and add thyme, bay leaf, peppercorns and salt. Bring to a boil over high heat, stirring often. Reduce heat and simmer for 30 minutes. (Do not boil, or the stock will be bitter.)

3. Strain the stock through the sieve into a heat-safe container, pressing lightly on the vegetables with the back of a spoon to press out the liquid; discard solids.

4. Taste the stock. If you want a more concentrated flavor, return it to the pot and bring to a boil over high heat. Reduce heat and boil gently until reduced as desired. Taste again and add more salt, if desired.

5. Use immediately or transfer the stock to airtight containers and store in the refrigerator for up to 1 week or in the freezer for up to 3 months.

Chilled Cucumber Watercress Soup

On a hot summer day, a refreshing cucumber soup hits the spot. This one is spiked with peppery watercress, which is both delicious and packed with nutrients. You can choose to go a little lighter by using yogurt or make the soup more filling by using sour cream.

MAKES 4 SERVINGS

4	large cucumbers, peeled and seeded	4
3 cups	plain full-fat yogurt or sour cream	750 mL
2 tbsp	freshly squeezed lemon juice	30 mL
4	large green onions, chopped	4
2 cups	watercress	500 mL
$1/2$ tsp	salt	2 mL
$1/2$ tsp	ground white pepper	2 mL

Tips

To seed a cucumber, halve it lengthwise and use a small spoon or melon baller to scoop out the seeds.

If watercress is unavailable, try this soup with arugula or 1 cup (250 mL) fresh basil.

1. Cut 1 cucumber lengthwise into thin strips, then cut the strips crosswise into small pieces. Set aside. Cut the remaining cucumbers into 3-inch (7.5 cm) chunks and place in the Vitamix container.

2. Add the yogurt and lemon juice to the container and secure the lid. With the switch on Variable, select speed 1 and turn the machine on. Gradually increase the speed to 10 and blend for about 10 seconds or until smooth.

3. Turn the machine off and add the green onions, watercress, salt and pepper. Replace the lid, select speed 1 and turn the machine on. Gradually increase the speed to 5 and blend for about 10 seconds or until the soup is flecked with chopped watercress but not puréed.

4. Transfer the soup to a bowl or airtight container and stir in the chopped cucumber. Cover and refrigerate for at least 3 hours, until chilled, or for up to 1 day. Serve cold.

Catalan Gazpacho

In North America, we have freely adapted the concept of gazpacho to encompass everything from watermelon to hot chiles. A visit to Barcelona, where refreshingly simple chilled gazpacho is sold by the cup in the market, set me straight.

$\infty \infty$

MAKES 4 SERVINGS

1 lb	tomatoes, cored and halved	500 g
2	cloves garlic, chopped	2
1	medium cucumber, peeled and quartered	1
1	medium red bell pepper, quartered and seeded	1
1	large Anaheim chile pepper, halved and seeded	1
1	medium onion, coarsely chopped	1
1 tsp	salt	5 mL
1/2 tsp	freshly ground black pepper	2 mL
1/2 cup	extra virgin olive oil	125 mL

Tips

Use the ripest, best-tasting tomatoes you can find, regardless of variety.

If Anaheim chile peppers are unavailable, look for Italian banana peppers or poblanos. If you don't want any heat, use 1/2 green bell pepper instead.

1. Place the tomatoes, garlic, cucumber, red pepper, chile, onion, salt and pepper in the Vitamix container. Secure the lid, remove the lid plug and insert the tamper. With the switch on Variable, select speed 1 and turn the machine on. Using the tamper to push the ingredients into the blades, gradually increase the speed to 10 and blend for about 45 seconds or until smooth. Reduce the speed to 5 and very slowly pour oil through the lid opening, blending until the oil is incorporated.

2. Transfer the soup to a bowl or airtight container, cover and refrigerate for at least 3 hours, until cold, or for up to 3 days. Serve cold.

Cheddar and Beer Soup

One of the best ways to pair beer with food is to cook with the same beer you are serving. In a soup like this, don't go with a hoppy, bitter beer unless you really like that flavor. A simple blond lager is a good complement to the cheese.

MAKES 4 SERVINGS

2 tbsp	unsalted butter	30 mL
1	large onion, chopped	1
1/4 cup	unbleached all-purpose flour	60 mL
1 cup	lager beer	250 mL
1 cup	vegetable stock (page 102) or ready-to-use vegetable or chicken broth	250 mL
4 oz	sharp (old) Cheddar cheese, cubed	125 g
1/2 tsp	salt	2 mL
1	large green onion, chopped	1

Tips

When using the speed of the machine to cook a cheese soup, as in this recipe, don't overprocess. If the blending goes on too long, the cheese can separate.

If you are a beer and cheese aficionado, try different combinations of beer and cheese.

1. In a medium skillet, melt butter over medium heat. Add onion and cook, stirring, for about 5 minutes or until light golden and tender. Sprinkle with flour and cook, stirring, for about 2 minutes or until the flour is dry-looking and lightly browned. Stir in beer, scraping up any browned bits from the bottom of the pan and incorporating all the flour. Remove from heat.

2. Place the onion mixture, stock, cheese and salt in the Vitamix container. Secure the lid, remove the lid plug and insert the tamper. With the switch on Variable, select speed 1 and turn the machine on. Using the tamper to push the ingredients into the blades, gradually increase the speed to 10.

3. Turn the machine off, remove the tamper and replace the lid plug. Flip the switch to High and turn the machine on. Blend for 4 minutes, then remove the lid to see if the soup is steaming. If it isn't, replace the lid and blend for 1 minute or until steaming.

4. Ladle the hot soup into warmed bowls and sprinkle with green onion.

Cream of Asparagus Soup

This creamy green soup is full of asparagus flavor and puts the stems to good use for the body of the soup. The secret ingredient is cauliflower, which thickens the soup without adding flour or carbs.

MAKES 4 SERVINGS

● **Steamer basket**

2 lbs	asparagus	1 kg
1 tbsp	extra virgin olive oil	15 mL
1	large onion, chopped	1
1 cup	chopped cauliflower	250 mL
4 cups	vegetable stock (page 102) or ready-to-use vegetable broth	1 L
2 cups	baby spinach	500 mL
1/2 tsp	salt (or to taste)	2 mL
1/2 tsp	freshly ground black pepper	2 mL
1 cup	milk	250 mL
1/4 cup	sliced almonds, toasted	60 mL

Tips

Don't worry about peeling the asparagus stems; the Vitamix makes quick work of them.

To toast almonds, spread them on a baking sheet and roast at 350°F (180°C) for 10 minutes or until fragrant and toasted. Immediately transfer to a bowl and let cool.

1. Trim the hard bottoms from the asparagus and discard. Cut off the tips in bite-size pieces and set aside. Chop the remaining stalks and set aside separately.

2. In a pot, heat oil over medium-high heat. Add onion and cook, stirring, for about 5 minutes or until starting to soften. Reduce heat to medium and cook, stirring, for at least 5 minutes or up to 10 minutes, until onion is tender and translucent.

3. Stir in asparagus stalks, cauliflower and stock. Cover and bring to a boil over high heat. Reduce heat to medium, cover and boil for 15 minutes or until asparagus is very soft.

4. Meanwhile, in a steamer basket set over a pot of boiling water, steam asparagus tips for 1 to 2 minutes or until tender-crisp. Transfer to a bowl and cover to keep warm.

5. Transfer the stock mixture to the Vitamix container and secure the lid. With the switch on Variable, select speed 1 and turn the machine on. Gradually increase the speed to 10 and blend for 20 seconds.

6. Turn the machine off and add the spinach, salt and pepper. Replace the lid, select speed 1 and turn the machine on. Gradually increase the speed to 10 and blend for 20 seconds. Remove the lid plug, pour in the milk through the lid opening and blend for 3 minutes, then remove the lid to see if the soup is steaming. If it isn't, replace the lid and blend for 1 minute or until steaming.

7. Ladle the hot soup into warmed bowls and garnish with asparagus tips and almonds.

Variation

For a tasty herbal flavor, add 1 tbsp (15 mL) dried tarragon at the end of step 6, pulsing just to combine.

Creamy Cabbage and Thyme Soup

This simple, peasant-style soup is a wonderful way to warm up on a cold day. It's easy to make, and any leftovers are sturdy enough to take to work and warm up for lunch.

MAKES 4 SERVINGS		
2 tbsp	unsalted butter	30 mL
1	large onion, chopped	1
2 tbsp	fresh thyme leaves, coarsely chopped	30 mL
8 oz	green cabbage, chopped (about 4 cups/1 L)	250 g
2	medium potatoes, cubed	2
1 tsp	salt	5 mL
1 1/2 cups	water	375 mL
1 cup	half-and-half (10%) cream	250 mL
1/2 cup	lightly packed fresh parsley, chopped	125 mL

Tips

Make a double batch of this soup when you have a big cabbage on hand; it freezes well.

You can always try out different herbs, such as rosemary or sage, in place of the thyme.

1. In a large skillet, melt butter over medium heat. Add onion and thyme; cook, stirring, for 5 minutes. Reduce heat to medium-low and cook, stirring often, for 10 minutes or until onions are soft and golden.

2. Stir in cabbage, potatoes and salt; increase heat to medium-high and cook, stirring, for about 5 minutes or until cabbage is softened. Stir in water, cover and bring to a boil, then reduce heat to medium and boil gently for 10 minutes or until potatoes are tender. Using a slotted spoon, scoop out 2 cups (500 mL) vegetables and set aside.

3. Transfer the remaining soup to the Vitamix container and add the cream. Secure the lid. With the switch on Variable, select speed 1 and turn the machine on. Gradually increase the speed to 10 and blend for about 10 seconds or until smooth.

4. Turn the machine off and add the reserved vegetables and parsley. Replace the lid and pulse once or twice just to mix. Serve hot.

Corn and Red Pepper Soup with Oregano

Sweet corn and sweet red peppers are a perfect pair, both on the tongue and to the eye. Keep frozen corn on hand so you can make this quick soup in a snap.

MAKES 4 SERVINGS

1 tbsp	butter or extra virgin olive oil	15 mL
1	large onion, chopped	1
1	medium yellow-fleshed potato, peeled and chopped	1
1¼ lbs	thawed frozen corn (about 2½ cups/625 mL), divided	625 g
1 cup	milk	250 mL
½ cup	vegetable stock (page 102) or ready-to-use vegetable or chicken broth	125 mL
	Salt	
½	large red bell pepper, chopped	½
1 tbsp	fresh oregano leaves, coarsely chopped	15 mL
	Freshly ground black pepper (optional)	

Tip

If you're in a hurry, thaw frozen corn by placing it in a colander and running hot water over it for a couple of minutes. Drain well before adding to the soup.

1. In a large skillet, melt butter over medium heat. Add onion and potato; cook, stirring, for about 10 minutes or until potato is tender. Remove from heat.

2. Set 1 cup (250 mL) corn aside. Place the milk, stock, onion mixture, the remaining corn and ¾ tsp (3 mL) salt in the Vitamix container. Secure the lid, remove the lid plug and insert the tamper. With the switch on Variable, select speed 1 and turn the machine on. Using the tamper to push the ingredients into the blades, gradually increase the speed to 10, then flip the switch to High and blend for 5 minutes or until steam comes out of the lid opening when you lift the tamper.

3. Turn the machine off and quickly add the reserved corn, red pepper and oregano, using the tamper to stir them down into the hot soup. Cover and let stand for about 4 minutes to soften the pepper. Taste and adjust the seasoning with salt and pepper as desired. Serve hot.

Variation

For a bit more weight and flavor, stir in some crumbled cooked bacon or smoked ham with the red pepper.

Creamy Parsnip and Apple Soup

The flavors of a brisk fall day are on full display in this soup, with sweet parsnips and tart apples melding in a creamy purée.

MAKES 4 SERVINGS		
1 tbsp	unsalted butter	15 mL
1	large onion, chopped	1
2	large apples, divided	2
2 lbs	parsnips, chopped	1 kg
3 cups	ready-to-use reduced-sodium chicken broth	750 mL
1 tbsp	fresh thyme leaves, chopped	15 mL
1 tsp	salt	5 mL
Pinch	cayenne pepper	Pinch
1 cup	plain full-fat yogurt or sour cream	250 mL
2	green onions, chopped	2

Tip

You can freeze this soup, as long as you don't add the yogurt or sour cream (or green onions). Let it cool completely, then transfer to an airtight container and freeze for up to 1 month. To finish, let it thaw in the refrigerator overnight, then heat the thawed purée and stir in the yogurt or sour cream. Serve sprinkled with green onions.

1. In a large pot, melt butter over medium-high heat. Add onion and cook, stirring, for about 3 minutes or until starting to sizzle. Reduce heat to medium and cook, stirring often, for at least 5 minutes, or up to 45 minutes, until onion is soft and golden.

2. Meanwhile, peel and slice 1 apple. Stir sliced apple and parsnips into the pot. Add broth, increase heat to high and bring to a boil. Reduce heat to medium, cover and boil for 10 minutes or until parsnips are very tender. Remove from heat and stir in thyme, salt and cayenne.

3. Transfer the soup to the Vitamix container and secure the lid. With the switch on Variable, select speed 1 and turn the machine on. Gradually increase the speed to 10 and blend for about 2 minutes or until very smooth. Remove the lid to see if the soup is steaming. If it isn't, replace the lid and blend for 1 minute or until steaming.

4. Turn the machine off and add the yogurt. Replace the lid, select speed 1 and turn the machine on. Gradually increase the speed to 5 and blend until yogurt is incorporated. Turn the machine off.

5. Chop the remaining apple, leaving the peel on. Add the chopped apple to the soup, stirring it in with a spatula. Cover and let stand for about 3 minutes to heat the apple.

6. Ladle the hot soup into warmed bowls and sprinkle with green onions.

Variation

For a pale orange soup, use carrots in place of some of the parsnips.

Creamy Potato and Spinach Soup

If you want a bowl of comfort, this velvety purée of potatoes and spinach will make you happy. Potatoes cook quickly, and the Vitamix cooks the spinach as it purées the soup to a lively green tint.

MAKES 4 SERVINGS

1 tbsp	extra virgin olive oil	15 mL
1	large onion, chopped	1
1 lb	potatoes, cubed	500 g
1	clove garlic, chopped	1
1 tbsp	fresh thyme leaves, chopped	15 mL
1 tsp	salt	5 mL
2 cups	water	500 mL
3 cups	packed fresh spinach	750 mL
1 cup	milk	250 mL

Tip

Use prewashed salad spinach, to save time. Just rinse it and spin dry before adding to the Vitamix.

1. In a large skillet, heat oil over medium-high heat. Add onion and cook, stirring, for about 5 minutes or until soft and golden.

2. Stir in potatoes, garlic, thyme, salt and water; bring to a boil over high heat. Reduce heat to medium-low, cover and simmer for 10 to 15 minutes or until potatoes are tender. Using a slotted spoon, scoop out 1 cup (250 mL) potatoes and set aside.

3. Transfer the remaining soup to the Vitamix container and add the spinach and milk. Secure the lid. With the switch on Variable, select speed 1 and turn the machine on. Gradually increase the speed to 10, then flip the switch to High and blend for 2 minutes. Turn the machine off and taste a spoonful to check the temperature; if you would like it hotter, blend for another 1 to 2 minutes.

4. Turn the machine off and, using a spatula, stir in the reserved potatoes. Cover and let stand for 2 minutes to heat the potatoes. Serve hot.

Variation

Other tender greens, such as sorrel, baby kale or arugula, are also good in place of the spinach.

Purple Potato Purée with Chiles

Purple potatoes are not just pretty, they are also loaded with antioxidant purple pigments that help protect your vision. This beautiful soup, known as *locro* in Peru, has a hint of chile heat.

MAKES 4 SERVINGS

1 tbsp	extra virgin olive oil	15 mL
1	large onion, chopped	1
2 lbs	purple potatoes, cubed (about 6 cups/1.5 L)	1 kg
3/4 tsp	salt	3 mL
2 cups	vegetable stock (page 102) or ready-to-use vegetable broth	500 mL
2	medium red Fresno chile peppers, seeded and chopped	2
1 cup	milk	250 mL
1/2 cup	hot cooked white quinoa	125 mL
1/2 cup	lightly packed fresh parsley, minced	125 mL

Tips

Purple potatoes have soft skins, so don't worry about peeling them. Your Vitamix will make quick work of the skins, saving time and making use of the nutrient-rich skin.

This soup can, of course, be made with other potatoes; it just won't be as pretty.

If you cannot find red Fresno chile peppers, you can use other hot red chile peppers, such as cayenne or Thai chiles, in their place.

1. In a large pot, heat oil over medium-high heat. Add onion and cook, stirring, for about 3 minutes or until starting to sizzle. Reduce heat to medium-low and cook, stirring occasionally, for 5 to 10 minutes or until soft and golden.

2. Stir in potatoes, salt and stock; increase heat to high and bring to a boil. Reduce heat to medium, cover and simmer, adjusting heat as necessary to prevent boiling, for about 10 minutes or until potatoes are tender. Using a slotted spoon, scoop out 2 cups (500 mL) potatoes and set aside.

3. Transfer the remaining soup to the Vitamix container and add the chiles and milk. Secure the lid, remove the lid plug and insert the tamper. With the switch on Variable, select speed 1 and turn the machine on. Using the tamper to push the ingredients into the blades, gradually increase the speed to 10 and blend for about 3 minutes or until smooth. Remove the lid to see if the soup is steaming. If it isn't, replace the lid and blend for 1 minute or until steaming.

4. Turn the machine off and, using a spatula, stir in the reserved potatoes. Cover and let stand for 2 minutes to heat the potatoes.

5. Ladle the hot soup into warmed bowls and top with quinoa and parsley.

Thai Red Curry Pumpkin Soup

Thai curry pastes have become easy to find, and they are a wonderful way to give your curries authentic, concentrated flavor. Sweet, meltingly tender pumpkin bathes in a creamy coconut curry soup, balanced with just enough hot, sweet, salty and sour.

	MAKES 4 SERVINGS	
1	large shallot, chopped	1
1	2-inch (5 cm) piece lemongrass, split and bruised	1
1/4	large lime, peeled	1/4
1	can (14 oz/400 mL) full-fat coconut milk	1
1/2 cup	vegetable stock (page 102) or ready-to-use vegetable or chicken broth	125 mL
1 tbsp	fish sauce (or to taste)	15 mL
2 tsp	Thai red curry paste (or to taste)	10 mL
1 1/2 lbs	fresh pumpkin, seeded, peeled and cubed (about 4 cups/1 L)	750 g
1/2 tsp	salt	2 mL
1/2 cup	lightly packed fresh cilantro leaves, torn	125 mL

Tips

To peel and seed a pumpkin, use a sharp chef's knife to cut it in half, then scoop out the seeds with a spoon. Place the halves, cut side down, on the cutting board. Slice the halves into 1-inch (2.5 cm) wide wedges. Place each wedge, cut side down, on the board and slice away the peel in sections.

Taste the soup after step 1; if you want more heat, add another 1 tsp (5 mL) red curry paste when it goes into the blender.

1. In a large pot or Dutch oven, combine shallot, lemongrass, lime, coconut milk, stock, fish sauce and curry paste, mashing the curry paste with a spatula. Bring to a boil over medium-high heat. Add pumpkin and salt; bring to a simmer, then reduce heat to medium. Cover and cook for about 10 minutes or until pumpkin is tender when pierced. Using a slotted spoon, scoop out 2 cups (500 mL) pumpkin and set aside.

2. Transfer the remaining soup to the Vitamix container. Secure the lid, remove the lid plug and insert the tamper. With the switch on Variable, select speed 1 and turn the machine on. Using the tamper to push the ingredients into the blades, gradually increase the speed to 10 and blend for about 30 seconds or until silky smooth.

3. Return the soup and the reserved pumpkin to the pan and reheat, if necessary. Adjust the salt and seasonings to taste. Serve topped with cilantro.

Variation

Other winter squash, such as kabocha, red kuri or even butternut, can be used in place of the pumpkin.

Pumpkin Sage Soup with Pears

Looking for a fabulous side dish at Thanksgiving? This soup has the pumpkin and sage flavors we associate with the holiday. It's incredibly easy to make in your Vitamix with canned pumpkin, saving you valuable kitchen time.

MAKES 4 SERVINGS		
1 tbsp	canola oil or butter	15 mL
1	large onion, chopped	1
2 tbsp	unbleached all-purpose flour	30 mL
1 cup	vegetable stock (page 102) or ready-to-use vegetable or chicken broth	250 mL
1 cup	milk	250 mL
1	can (15 oz/425 mL) pumpkin purée (not pie filling)	1
2 tsp	light brown sugar	10 mL
1 tsp	salt	5 mL
1	large pear, chopped	1
2 tbsp	lightly packed fresh sage leaves, chopped	30 mL

Tip

Keep canned pumpkin in the pantry, for this soup and all sorts of baking recipes.

1. In a medium skillet, heat oil over medium-high heat. Add onion and cook, stirring for 3 minutes or until starting to sizzle. Reduce heat to medium-low and cook, stirring often, for 5 to 10 minutes or until softened and golden. Sprinkle with flour and cook, stirring, for 1 minute. Stir in stock, scraping up any browned bits from the bottom of the pan.

2. Transfer the onion mixture to the Vitamix container and add the milk, pumpkin, brown sugar and salt. Secure the lid. With the switch on Variable, select speed 1 and turn the machine on. Gradually increase the speed to 10, then flip the switch to High and blend for 4 minutes. Remove the lid to see if the soup is steaming. If it isn't, replace the lid and blend for 1 minute or until steaming.

3. Turn the machine off and add the pear and sage, stirring them in with a spatula. Cover and let stand until pear is heated through. Serve hot.

Variation

Instead of sage, try fresh thyme or a handful of fresh parsley. A pinch or two of ground cinnamon would be lovely too.

Indian Spinach Kale Soup with Yogurt Raita

This is a soup you don't see in many Indian restaurants, so it may be a new experience for you. It's a celebration of savory spices and fresh greens, with a cooling dollop of yogurt raita at the end.

MAKES 4 SERVINGS

4 oz	kale	125 g
1 tbsp	butter or canola oil	15 mL
1	medium yellow-fleshed potato, chopped (about 1 cup/250 mL)	1
2	medium jalapeño peppers, seeded and chopped	2
2	cloves garlic, chopped	2
2 tbsp	sliced gingerroot	30 mL
1 tsp	ground cumin	5 mL
1 tsp	ground coriander	5 mL
1/2 tsp	ground turmeric	2 mL
3 cups	vegetable stock (page 102) or ready-to-use vegetable broth	750 mL
4 cups	packed fresh spinach (about 4 oz/125 g)	1 L
1 cup	cherry tomatoes	250 mL
1 tsp	salt	5 mL
1/2 cup	lightly packed fresh cilantro leaves, chopped	125 mL

YOGURT RAITA

1 cup	plain Greek yogurt	250 mL
1/2 cup	diced cucumber	125 mL
1 tsp	paprika	5 mL
Pinch	salt	Pinch

Tip

Use your fingers to strip the leaves from the kale stems; just pinch the stem at the base of the leaf and pull toward the tip.

1. Separate kale stems from leaves and set leaves aside. Chop stems into small pieces.

2. In a large pot, melt butter over medium heat. Add kale stems and potato; cook, stirring, for about 8 minutes or until potato is tender. Add jalapeños, garlic, ginger, cumin, coriander and turmeric; cook, stirring, for 10 seconds or until spices are fragrant.

3. Pour the stock into the Vitamix container and add the potato mixture, kale leaves, spinach, cherry tomatoes and salt. Secure the lid. With the switch on Variable, select speed 1 and turn the machine on. Gradually increase the speed to 10, then flip the switch to High and blend for 5 minutes. Remove the lid to see if the soup is steaming. If it isn't, replace the lid and blend for 1 minute or until steaming.

4. *Raita:* Meanwhile, in a bowl, stir together yogurt, cucumber, paprika and salt.

5. Stir cilantro into the hot soup and ladle into warm bowls. Serve each bowl with a dollop of yogurt raita.

Variation

Other greens are also good in this soup. If you have a bumper crop of Swiss chard or collard greens, use them in place of the kale and spinach here.

Cream of Tomato Soup with Basil

Canned soups will be in your rear-view mirror now that you have a machine that makes smooth and creamy soups in a snap.

MAKES 4 SERVINGS		
1 tbsp	extra virgin olive oil	15 mL
1	large onion, chopped	1
2 tbsp	unbleached all-purpose flour	30 mL
1	can (28 oz/796 mL) whole tomatoes, with juice	1
1 cup	half-and-half (10%) cream	250 mL
1/2 tsp	salt (or to taste)	2 mL
1 cup	lightly packed fresh basil leaves, chopped	250 mL
1/2 tsp	ground white pepper	2 mL
1/8 tsp	cayenne pepper	0.5 mL

Tip

Keep high-quality canned whole tomatoes in the pantry so you are always ready to make this soup.

1. In a medium skillet, heat oil over medium-high heat. Add onion and cook, stirring, for about 5 minutes or until soft and golden. Sprinkle with flour and stir to incorporate. Reduce heat to medium-low and cook, stirring, for 2 minutes.

2. Transfer the onion mixture to the Vitamix container and add tomatoes, cream and salt. Secure the lid. With the switch on Variable, select speed 1 and turn the machine on. Gradually increase the speed to 10, then flip the switch to High and blend for 4 minutes. Remove the lid to see if the soup is steaming. If it isn't, replace the lid and blend for 1 minute or until steaming.

3. Turn the machine off and add the basil, white pepper and cayenne. Replace the lid. With the switch on Variable, select speed 1 and turn the machine on. Gradually increase to speed 5 and blend for a few seconds, just to mix. Serve hot.

Variation

In a pinch, substitute 1/2 cup (125 mL) lightly packed fresh parsley, chopped, and 2 tsp (10 mL) dried basil for the fresh basil.

Garden Tomato, Zucchini and Basil Soup

When zucchini is snappingly fresh and abundant, make this soup. Tomatoes and basil should be plentiful at the same time, making this the perfect soup for summer.

MAKES 6 SERVINGS

2 lbs	plum (Roma) tomatoes (about 10), divided	1 kg
2	large cloves garlic, sliced	2
1	medium onion, quartered	1
1/4 cup	extra virgin olive oil	60 mL
1 lb	zucchini (about 4 medium), cut into 1/2-inch (1 cm) cubes	500 g
1 tsp	salt	5 mL
1/2 tsp	freshly ground black pepper	2 mL
2 cups	vegetable stock (page 102) or ready-to-use vegetable broth	500 mL
1 cup	lightly packed fresh basil leaves, chopped	250 mL

Tip

Cut the zucchini lengthwise into slices, then stack the slices and cut them into long strips. Cut across the pile to make little cubes.

1. Seed and chop 4 of the tomatoes and set aside.

2. Secure the lid on the Vitamix container and remove the lid plug. With the switch on Variable, select speed 3 and turn the machine on. Drop the garlic and onion quarters, one piece at a time, through the lid opening, using the tamper if they are not falling into the blades. Turn the machine off as soon as everything is chopped.

3. In a large pot, heat oil over medium-high heat. Scrape in the onion mixture and cook, stirring, for about 5 minutes or until starting to soften. Add zucchini and cook, stirring, for 5 minutes or until zucchini is browned slightly and tender throughout. Stir in chopped tomatoes, salt and pepper. Reduce heat to low.

4. Place the remaining tomatoes and stock in the Vitamix container, secure the lid and replace the lid plug. With the switch on Variable, select speed 1 and turn the machine on. Gradually increase the speed to 10 and blend for about 3 minutes or until smooth. Remove the lid to see if the soup is steaming. If it isn't, replace the lid and blend for 1 minute or until steaming.

5. Pour the purée over the zucchini mixture in the pot and stir it in. Increase heat to medium and simmer gently for 5 minutes, then stir in basil. Taste and adjust seasoning as desired. Serve hot.

Variation

Yellow summer squash is wonderful in place of the zucchini in this soup.

Persian Pistachio Soup

If you like rich, sweet pistachios, this soup is for you. It is a very simplified rendition of a traditional soup that would be served in small cups alongside a spread of Persian food. The pistachios purée into a silky soup that is as amazingly decadent as any cream soup, with all the health benefits of nuts.

MAKES 4 SERVINGS		
1 tbsp	extra virgin olive oil	15 mL
1	large onion, chopped	1
1	clove garlic, chopped	1
2 tsp	chopped gingerroot	10 mL
2 tsp	ground cumin	10 mL
1/2 tsp	ground coriander	2 mL
1/2 tsp	freshly ground black pepper	2 mL
1/8 tsp	ground turmeric	0.5 mL
1/8 tsp	cayenne pepper	0.5 mL
1/2 tsp	salt	2 mL
3 cups	vegetable stock (page 102) or ready-to-use vegetable or chicken broth, divided	750 mL
4	large red grapes, seedless or seeds removed	4
1 cup	raw shelled pistachios (see tip), divided	250 mL
1/4 cup	freshly squeezed orange juice	60 mL
1 tbsp	grated lime zest	15 mL
1 tbsp	freshly squeezed lime juice	15 mL

Tip

Look for raw pistachios at natural foods stores and Middle Eastern groceries, and always give them a sniff — they should smell sweet and nutty.

1. In a large skillet, heat oil over medium-high heat. Add onion and cook, stirring, for about 3 minutes or until starting to soften. Reduce heat to medium-low and cook, stirring, for about 5 minutes or until softened and golden. Add garlic and ginger; cook, stirring, for 3 minutes. Add cumin, coriander, black pepper, turmeric and cayenne; cook, stirring, for 2 minutes or until fragrant. Stir in salt and 1 cup (250 mL) stock, scraping up any browned bits from the bottom of the pan.

2. Transfer the onion mixture to the Vitamix container and add the remaining stock, grapes, 3/4 cup (175 mL) pistachios, orange juice and lime juice. Secure the lid. With the switch on Variable, select speed 1 and turn the machine on. Gradually increase the speed to 10, then flip the switch to High and blend for 2 to 3 minutes. Remove the lid to see if the soup is steaming. If it isn't, replace the lid and blend for 1 minute or until steaming.

3. Meanwhile, chop the remaining pistachios. In a small skillet over medium-low heat, toast pistachios and lime zest, stirring constantly, for about 3 minutes or until toasted and fragrant.

4. Ladle the hot soup into warmed small bowls and sprinkle with the toasted pistachio mixture.

African Peanut Soup

If you like peanut butter, you will love this soup. Using freshly ground peanuts gives it a wonderful nutty flavor that is complemented by the spices and tomatoes. Pass a bottle of hot sauce at the table so your diners can decide how hot to make it. Serve over brown rice or with flatbreads.

MAKES 4 SERVINGS

1 tbsp	extra virgin olive oil	15 mL
1	large onion, chopped	1
1	clove garlic, chopped	1
1 tsp	paprika	5 mL
1 tsp	ground coriander	5 mL
1/4 tsp	cayenne pepper	1 mL
2 cups	vegetable stock (page 102) or ready-to-use vegetable broth	500 mL
1 1/2 cups	unsalted roasted peanuts	375 mL
1/2 tsp	salt	2 mL
3 cups	lightly packed fresh spinach leaves, chopped	750 mL
1 cup	canned diced tomatoes, with juice	250 mL

Tip

Unsalted peanuts can be harder to find than salted ones, so keep an eye out for a good source. You'll want them for making peanut butter, too.

1. In a large pot, heat oil over medium heat. Add onion and cook, stirring, for about 5 minutes or until soft and golden. Add garlic and cook, stirring, for 2 to 3 minutes or until softened and golden. Add paprika, coriander and cayenne; cook, stirring, for about 1 minute or until fragrant.

2. Transfer the onion mixture to the Vitamix container and add the stock, peanuts and salt. Secure the lid. With the switch on Variable, select speed 1 and turn the machine on. Gradually increase the speed to 10, then flip the switch to High and blend for 3 minutes or until the soup is smooth. Remove the lid to see if the soup is steaming. If it isn't, replace the lid and blend for 1 minute or until steaming.

3. Turn the machine off and add the spinach and tomatoes, stirring them in with a spatula. Replace the lid and let the spinach wilt in the hot soup for 2 minutes. Pulse once or twice to mix. Serve hot.

Variation

Roasted cashews would be a delicious substitution for the peanuts.

Creamy White Bean Soup with Pan-Roasted Garlic and Basil

If you keep meaning to eat more healthful, money-saving beans but just can't get into it, try this soup. The purée of silky white beans is luxurious and savory, and might just convince you that this soup is spiked with cream.

MAKES 4 SERVINGS

3¹/₂ tbsp	extra virgin olive oil, divided	52 mL
5	large cloves garlic	5
1	large onion, chopped	1
1 cup	vegetable stock (page 102) or ready-to-use vegetable broth	250 mL
2	cans (each 14 to 15 oz/398 to 425 mL) cannellini (white kidney) beans, with liquid	2
¹/₂ cup	lightly packed fresh basil leaves	125 mL
1	large carrot, chopped	1
2 cups	broccoli florets	500 mL
1 tsp	dried thyme	5 mL
1 tsp	salt	5 mL
¹/₂ tsp	freshly ground black pepper	2 mL

Tips

If you can only find larger cans of beans, use two 19-oz (540 mL) cans and measure 3¹/₃ cups (825 mL) beans with liquid for this recipe, reserving the remainder for another use, or use one 28-oz (796 mL) can.

Canned beans are convenient, but you can also cook the beans yourself. For this recipe, soak and cook 1 cup (250 mL) cannellini beans and save about 1¹/₂ cups (375 mL) of the cooking liquid.

Other beans, such as navy (white pea) beans or even small red beans, will also work well in this soup.

1. In a large pot, heat 3 tbsp (45 mL) oil over medium-high heat. Add garlic and onion; cook, stirring, for 1 minute or until starting to sizzle, then reduce heat to medium-low and cook, stirring often, for 10 to 15 minutes or until garlic is soft when pierced.

2. Transfer the garlic mixture to the Vitamix container and add the stock, beans and basil. Secure the lid. With the switch on Variable, select speed 1 and turn the machine on. Gradually increase the speed to 10 and blend for about 30 seconds or until smooth and creamy.

3. In the same pot, heat the remaining oil over medium-high heat. Add carrot and broccoli; cook, stirring, for about 5 minutes or until softened. Add thyme and cook, stirring, for 1 minute. Pour in the purée and add salt and pepper. Reduce heat to medium and simmer, stirring often, just until heated through. Serve hot.

Creamy Red Pepper and Chicken Soup with Almonds

Sweet roasted peppers create a scarlet backdrop for a bit of cooked chicken. This is a great way to celebrate summer, when fresh red bell peppers can be had for a song at your local farmers' market.

MAKES 4 SERVINGS

- Preheat broiler, with the rack set 6 inches (15 cm) from the heat source
- Rimmed baking sheet, lined with foil

4	large red bell peppers	4
1 tbsp	extra virgin olive oil	15 mL
1	large onion, chopped	1
1	clove garlic, chopped	1
1 tbsp	fresh rosemary, chopped	15 mL
1^1/$_2$ cups	ready-to-use no-salt-added chicken broth	375 mL
^{1}/$_2$ cup	heavy or whipping (35%) cream	125 mL
1 tsp	salt	5 mL
1 lb	boneless skinless chicken breasts, cooked and shredded	500 g
^{1}/$_2$ cup	lightly packed fresh parsley, chopped	125 mL

Tips

Roasting peppers may seem like a chore, but they are essential to the flavor of this soup. It will save time next time if you roast twice what you need and freeze them.

If you have leftover cooked chicken on hand, you'll need about 3 cups (750 mL) shredded chicken for this recipe.

1. Place red peppers on the prepared baking sheet. Broil, turning once, for about 4 minutes per side or until blackened. Transfer peppers to a casserole dish or bowl, cover and steam for 10 minutes. Uncover and let cool, then peel peppers and discard stems, seeds and skins. Place the peeled peppers in the Vitamix container. Set aside.

2. In a medium skillet, heat oil over medium-high heat. Add onion and cook, stirring, until starting to sizzle, then reduce heat to medium-low and cook, stirring, for 5 to 10 minutes or until soft and golden. Add garlic and rosemary; cook, stirring, for 2 minutes or until softened. Transfer to the Vitamix.

3. Add the broth, cream and salt to the Vitamix and secure the lid. With the switch on Variable, select speed 1 and turn the machine on. Gradually increase the speed to 10 and blend for about 30 seconds or until smooth.

4. Pour the purée into a medium pot and place over medium heat. Add chicken and heat, stirring, until the soup is steaming and the chicken is hot.

5. Ladle the hot soup into warm bowls and sprinkle with parsley.

Variation

Other chopped leftover cooked meats, such as pork roast or turkey, would also be good in place of the chicken, or go veg with cooked cannellini (white kidney) beans instead. Whichever protein you choose, you'll need about 3 cups (750 mL).

BURGERS and LOAVES

Pecan and Beet Burgers

When you want satisfying burgers without beef, these are the perfect choice. The pecans give them an almost meaty texture and richness, and the beets add chewy sweetness and tint them a familiar beefy red. You'll hardly even notice the creamy tofu holding it all together once you slap them in a bun with some lettuce and tomato, and serve a crisp salad on the side.

MAKES 5 SERVINGS

- **Preheat oven to 400°F (200°C)**
- **Large baking sheet, lined with parchment paper and lightly oiled**

1 cup	raw pecans	250 mL
1	large onion, quartered	1
1 tbsp	canola oil	15 mL
9 oz	beets, peeled and cubed ($1^3/_4$ cups/425 mL)	270 g
5 oz	extra-firm tofu	150 g
2 tbsp	ground flax seeds (flaxseed meal)	30 mL
$1/_2$ tsp	salt	2 mL
2 tbsp	red miso	30 mL
1 tbsp	Dijon mustard	15 mL

1. Place the pecans in the Vitamix container and secure the lid. With the switch on Variable, select speed 5 and pulse 5 times, just until finely chopped. Transfer the nuts to a large bowl.

2. Secure the lid of the container and remove the lid plug. With the switch on Variable, select speed 3 and turn the machine on. Drop the onion quarters, one at a time, through the lid opening, using the tamper if they are not falling into the blades. Turn the machine off as soon as all the onion is minced.

3. In a large skillet, heat oil over medium-high heat. Add onion and cook, stirring occasionally, for about 5 minutes or until softened.

4. Meanwhile, secure the lid on the Vitamix container. Select speed 5 and turn the machine on. Drop the beet cubes, one at a time, through the lid opening, using the tamper if they are not falling into the blades. Turn the machine off as soon as all the beets are chopped into small pieces.

5. Add beets to the skillet and cook, stirring, for about 5 minutes or until beets are tender. Scrape into the bowl with the pecans.

6. Crumble tofu into the bowl (see tip) and add flax seeds, salt, miso and mustard. Knead gently with your hands, mixing well, until the mixture holds together when squeezed.

7. Using a $1/_2$-cup (125 mL) measure, scoop out 5 portions and place on the prepared baking sheet, spacing them evenly. With wet hands, gently flatten the portions to about $3/_4$ inch (2 cm) thick. Using your fingers, make the edges neat and round.

8. Bake in preheated oven for 40 minutes, carefully flipping the patties over halfway through, until firm and browned. Let cool on pan on a wire rack for 5 minutes before serving.

Variation

Walnuts can be used instead of pecans, for a slightly more assertive flavor.

Tips

If you're not vegan, you can use 1 large egg, beaten, in place of the flax seeds.

Crumbling the tofu by hand is essential to the texture of the patties. Don't worry about it being in big chunks; the process of kneading and mixing will finish the job.

Burgers are great make-ahead fare and can easily be reheated in the oven or microwave.

To freeze, see tip, page 123.

Tofu Veggie Burgers

Frozen veggie burgers try to be just like beef burgers, and can't help but fall short. Why pretend? These tasty patties are full of flavor, with fresh vegetables and herbs, and they don't try to be something they are not. They are much more interesting than a machine-made faux-burger, I promise. Serve on hamburger buns, with lettuce, sliced tomato and your condiments of choice.

MAKES 5 SERVINGS

- **Preheat oven to 400°F (200°C)**
- **Large baking sheet, lined with parchment paper and lightly oiled**

14 oz	extra-firm tofu	400 g
$\frac{1}{2}$ cup	large-flake (old-fashioned) rolled oats	125 mL
$\frac{1}{2}$ cup	raw green pumpkin seeds (pepitas)	125 mL
2	slices onion	2
1	large carrot, cut into chunks	1
1	leaf kale, torn into 1-inch (2.5 cm) pieces	1
1 tsp	dried thyme	5 mL
$\frac{1}{2}$ tsp	salt	2 mL
1 tbsp	Dijon mustard	15 mL
2 tsp	soy sauce	10 mL

1. Drain the tofu and wrap it in a kitchen towel. Place a cutting board or heavy pot on top of the tofu and place some heavy cans on top. Let stand for about 15 minutes to press out the water from the tofu.

2. Meanwhile, place the oats and pumpkin seeds in the Vitamix container and secure the lid. With the switch on Variable, select speed 1 and turn the machine on. Gradually increase the speed to 5 and blend for about 30 seconds or until the oats and seeds are finely ground. Transfer the mixture to a large bowl.

3. Place the onion, carrot and kale in the Vitamix. Secure the lid, remove the lid plug and insert the tamper. Select speed 1 and pulse, using the tamper to push the vegetables into the blades, about 20 times, until the vegetables are minced. Add to the bowl with the oat mixture.

4. Unwrap the tofu and crumble it into the bowl. Add thyme, salt, mustard and soy sauce. Knead gently with your hands, mixing well, until the mixture holds together when squeezed.

5. Using a $\frac{1}{2}$-cup (125 mL) measure, scoop out 5 portions and place on the prepared baking sheet, spacing them evenly. With wet hands, gently flatten the portions to about $\frac{3}{4}$ inch (2 cm) thick. Using your fingers, make the edges neat and round.

6. Bake in preheated oven for 20 minutes, then carefully flip the patties over. Bake for 10 minutes or until firm and browned. Let cool on pan on a wire rack for 5 minutes before serving.

Variation

Instead of kale, try another green leafy vegetable, like Swiss chard or collard greens.

Tips

Today's extra-firm tofu is much firmer than it used to be. Some manufacturers are making it so firm that you really don't need to press it. If you buy a brand that hardly gives off any water when you press it, feel free to skip step 1 next time and just wrap the tofu to dry the surface.

To freeze, place the cooled patties on a pan lined with parchment paper and place in the freezer for 2 hours, then transfer to an airtight container and freeze for up to 4 months. Thaw in the refrigerator overnight before reheating in the microwave or in a lightly oiled skillet over medium heat.

Tempeh Walnut Burgers

Tempeh is an underappreciated food made with fermented high-protein soy, often with whole grains added to the mix. The fermentation process makes the soy much more digestible and adds a meaty, mushroomy flavor that works well in burgers. Serve on hamburger buns, with sliced tomato, arugula and your condiments of choice.

MAKES 6 SERVINGS		

- Preheat oven to 400°F (200°C)
- Steamer basket
- Large baking sheet, lined with parchment paper and lightly oiled

1 lb	tempeh, cubed	500 g
1/2 cup	lightly packed fresh basil leaves	125 mL
1	clove garlic, chopped	1
1 cup	raw walnuts	250 mL
2 tbsp	nutritional yeast	30 mL
1 tbsp	arrowroot starch	15 mL
2 tbsp	tamari	30 mL
1 tbsp	Dijon mustard	15 mL
1 tbsp	tahini	15 mL
	Vegetable oil	

Tips

The more evenly you flatten the burgers, the better they will hold their shape when you flip them.

Meatless burgers are a great way to get your family and friends to eat more vegetables, in the familiar shape of meatier fare.

To freeze, place the cooled patties on a pan lined with parchment paper and place in the freezer for 2 hours, then transfer to an airtight container and freeze for up to 4 months. Thaw in the refrigerator overnight before reheating in the microwave or in a lightly oiled skillet over medium heat.

1. In a steamer basket set over a pot of simmering water, steam tempeh for 5 minutes. Transfer to a bowl and let cool.

2. Place basil and garlic in the Vitamix container and secure the lid. With the switch on Variable, select speed 1 and turn the machine on. Blend for 1 minute.

3. Turn the machine off and scrape down the container. Replace the lid and remove the lid plug. Quickly drop half the tempeh, one cube at a time, through the lid opening. Quickly drop in the walnuts, blending just until minced.

4. In a large bowl, combine nutritional yeast and arrowroot. Scrape the contents of the Vitamix into the bowl and add tamari, mustard and tahini.

5. Mince the remaining tempeh and add it to the bowl. Knead gently with your hands, mixing well, until the mixture still has a chunky texture but forms a ball easily.

6. Using a lightly oiled 1/2-cup (125 mL) measure, scoop out 6 portions and place on the prepared baking sheet, spacing them evenly. Using an oiled metal spatula, flatten the patties to 3/4 inch (2 cm) thick. (The spatula will make them nice and even.) Spritz or brush the tops of the patties with oil.

7. Bake in preheated oven for 20 minutes, then carefully flip the patties over. Bake for 10 minutes or until firm and browned. Let cool on pan on a wire rack for 5 minutes before serving.

Variation

Replace the basil with arugula or cilantro, to go with your meal.

Sweet Potato and Quinoa Fritters with Sriracha Salsa

Sweet potatoes go with quinoa the way peanut butter goes with chocolate — it was just meant to be. These simple fritters come together quickly, with a few pulses in the Vitamix and a few minutes in the pan.

⁓⁓⁓⁓⁓⁓⁓⁓⁓⁓⁓⁓⁓⁓⁓⁓⁓⁓⁓⁓⁓⁓⁓⁓⁓⁓⁓⁓

MAKES 9 SERVINGS

- **Preheat oven to 200°F (100°C) (optional)**
- **Oven-safe platter, lined with paper towels**

....

1	large egg	1
12 oz	sweet potato, baked and mashed (1¼ cups/300 mL mashed)	375 g
1 tsp	salt	5 mL
6 tbsp	all-purpose flour	90 mL
2 tsp	ground cumin	10 mL
½ tsp	baking powder	2 mL
2 cups	cooled cooked quinoa	500 mL
1	green onion, chopped	1
1 to 2 tbsp	canola oil	15 to 30 mL

SRIRACHA SALSA

1	clove garlic, chopped	1
½	medium lime, peeled	½
1½ cups	cherry tomatoes, divided	375 mL
½ tsp	salt	2 mL
1 tbsp	Sriracha (store-bought or see recipe, page 51)	15 mL

1. Place the egg, sweet potato and salt in the Vitamix container and secure the lid. With the switch on Variable, select speed 1 and turn the machine on. Gradually increase the speed to 5 and blend for about 1 minute or just until smooth. Turn the machine off.

2. In a small cup or bowl, combine flour, cumin and baking powder. Add the flour mixture to the Vitamix and replace the lid. Turn the machine on and blend for about 20 seconds or until incorporated.

3. Turn the machine off and add the quinoa and green onion. Replace the lid and select speed 5. Turn the machine on and blend for about 10 seconds or until incorporated. Transfer the quinoa mixture to a bowl. Wash and dry the Vitamix container.

4. *Salsa:* Place garlic, lime, 1 cup (250 mL) tomatoes, salt and Sriracha in the Vitamix container. Secure the lid, remove the lid plug and insert the tamper. With the switch on Variable, select speed 5 and pulse 4 times or until tomatoes are slightly puréed. Turn the machine off and add the remaining tomatoes. Replace the lid and pulse 3 or 4 times, just until tomatoes are chopped. Transfer the mixture to a medium bowl.

5. Heat a large skillet over medium-high heat. Add 1 tbsp (15 mL) oil and swirl to coat. Working in batches, use a ¼-cup (60 mL) measure to scoop fritters into the pan, spacing them evenly. Use the back of the cup to flatten to ½ inch (1 cm) thick. Cook for about 2 minutes or until golden on the bottom. Flip fritters over, reduce heat to medium-low and cook for about 2 minutes or until golden and hot in the center. Transfer fritters to the prepared platter and hold in the preheated oven for up to 1 hour, if desired, or serve immediately. Repeat with the remaining fritter mixture, adding more oil to the pan as necessary. Serve with salsa.

Variation

The salsa is delicious, but you might enjoy these fritters with any number of the sauces in this book, such as Chimichurri (page 42) or African Peanut Sauce (page 47).

Amazing Mushroom Loaf

Mushrooms are often used in place of meat in vegetarian recipes because they are high in the chemicals that trigger umami in the mouth. In this loaf, the Vitamix minces the mushrooms quickly and efficiently, so that you can sauté them to concentrated, meaty tenderness.

∽◌

MAKES 6 TO 8 SERVINGS

- Preheat oven to 400°F (200°C)
- 9- by 5- inch (23 by 12.5 cm) loaf pan, lightly oiled

1 cup	water	250 mL
1/2 cup	millet	125 mL
1/2 cup	slivered almonds, toasted (see tip)	125 mL
2	small onions, quartered	2
1 tbsp	canola oil	15 mL
1 lb	mushrooms, trimmed	500 g
2	cloves garlic, chopped	2
1 tsp	salt	5 mL
1/2 tsp	freshly ground black pepper	2 mL
2	large eggs	2
1	can (14 to 15 oz/398 to 425 mL) cannellini (white kidney) beans, drained, liquid reserved	1
2 tbsp	arrowroot starch	30 mL
1 tbsp	dried sage	15 mL
1/3 cup	ketchup	75 mL

1. In a small saucepan, bring the water to a boil over high heat. Add millet and return to a boil. Reduce heat to low, cover and simmer for 20 minutes or until all of the water is absorbed. Remove from heat, fluff with a fork and let cool, uncovered.

2. Place the almonds in the Vitamix container and secure the lid. With the switch on Variable, select speed 5 and pulse 5 times or until finely chopped. Transfer the nuts to a large bowl.

3. Secure the lid of the container and remove the lid plug. Select speed 3 and turn the machine on. Drop the onion quarters, one at a time, through the lid opening, using the tamper if they are not falling into the blades. Turn the machine off as soon as all the onion is chopped.

4. In a large skillet, heat oil over medium-high heat. Scrape in onions and cook, stirring, for about 3 minutes or until starting to sizzle. Reduce heat to medium-low and stir occasionally as you chop the mushrooms in step 5.

5. Secure the lid on the Vitamix, select speed 5 and turn the machine on. Drop one-quarter of the mushrooms, one at a time, through the lid opening, blending until just chopped. Transfer to the pan with the onions and stir. Repeat with three more batches of mushrooms.

6. Once all the mushrooms are in the pan, add garlic, salt and pepper. Increase heat to medium-high and cook, stirring, until the mushrooms release their liquids and the pan is soupy. Increase heat to high and boil off the liquids, stirring constantly until the pan is dry. Remove from heat and scrape the mixture into the bowl with the almonds.

Tips

To toast almonds, spread them on a baking sheet and roast at 350°F (180°C) for 10 minutes or until fragrant and toasted. Immediately transfer to a bowl and let cool.

The loaf will be easiest to cut into neat slices if made a day ahead and refrigerated. Reheat individual slices in the microwave, or reheat the whole loaf in a 350°F (180°C) oven for about 30 minutes.

Meatless loaves are a great way to get your family and friends to eat more vegetables, in the familiar shape of meatier fare.

7. Place the eggs, beans and arrowroot in the Vitamix and secure the lid. Select speed 1 and turn the machine on. Using the tamper to push the ingredients into the blades, gradually increase the speed to 6 and blend for 10 to 20 seconds or until the beans are coarsely chopped (not smoothly puréed). Scrape into the bowl with the mushrooms.

8. Add the sage to the bowl. Using your hands, knead the mixture until well mixed. Pack into the prepared loaf pan.

9. Bake in preheated oven for 50 to 60 minutes or until the top of the loaf is firm when pressed. Spread ketchup over the loaf and bake for 10 minutes. Let cool in pan on a wire rack for 10 minutes before slicing. Serve hot.

Variation

Try making this with black beans instead of white, for a darker loaf.

Herbed Veggie Meatloaf

Meatloaf is a perfect vehicle for some healthy, high-fiber veggies and oats. Your Vitamix will make quick work of mincing the add-ins, saving you time in the kitchen.

∽∾ ∽∾

MAKES 4 TO 6 SERVINGS

- **Preheat oven to 350°F (180°C)**
- **9- by 5-inch (23 by 12.5 cm) loaf pan, lightly oiled**

1/2 cup	large-flake (old-fashioned) rolled oats	125 mL
1	leaf kale, torn into 1-inch (2.5 cm) pieces	1
1	large carrot, cut into 1-inch (2.5 cm) chunks	1
1/2	large onion, quartered	1/2
1/2 cup	lightly packed fresh parsley, coarsely chopped	125 mL
1 lb	regular ground beef	500 g
1	large egg, beaten	1
2 tbsp	fresh thyme leaves, chopped	30 mL
1 tsp	salt	5 mL
1/2 tsp	freshly ground black pepper	2 mL
1/2 cup	tomato paste	125 mL
2 tbsp	liquid honey	30 mL

Tips

Don't worry if the vegetables are chopped in uneven pieces; they will cook to tenderness inside the loaf and slice easily with the meat.

Loaves are great make-ahead fare and can easily be reheated in the oven or microwave. They freeze well, too.

1. Place the oats in the Vitamix container and secure the lid. With the switch on Variable, select speed 1 and turn the machine on. Gradually increase the speed to 10 and blend for 20 seconds or until finely ground. Transfer the oats to a large bowl.

2. Place the kale in the Vitamix. Secure the lid, remove the lid plug and insert the tamper. Select speed 1 and turn the machine on. Blend, using the tamper to push the kale into the blades. Increase to speed 5, then drop the carrot, one chunk at a time, through the lid opening, mincing each chunk. Drop the onion quarters, one at a time, and parsley through the lid opening and blend for about 10 seconds or until finely chopped. Scrape the vegetables into the bowl with the oats.

3. Add beef, egg, thyme, salt and pepper to the bowl. Using your hands, mix thoroughly but gently to avoid crushing the beef. Pack the mixture into the prepared loaf pan.

4. Bake in preheated oven for 30 minutes.

5. In a small bowl, combine tomato paste and honey. Spread over the loaf and bake for 20 minutes or until an instant-read thermometer inserted in the center of the loaf registers 165°F (74°C). Let cool in pan on a wire rack for 5 minutes before slicing. Serve hot.

Variations

Replace the beef with ground turkey or chicken.

Use a different fresh herb in place of the thyme.

Walnut and Sweet Potato Loaf

Thanks to your Vitamix, you can quickly mince the walnuts and sweet potatoes for this flavorful loaf, saving you chopping time. The combination of tender sweet potatoes, walnuts and sage will remind you of Thanksgiving meals, but you can enjoy this loaf any time of year.

MAKES 6 TO 8 SERVINGS

- **Preheat oven to 400°F (200°C)**
- **9- by 5- inch (23 by 12.5 cm) loaf pan, lightly oiled**

2	slices whole wheat bread, toasted	2
1¹/₂ cups	raw walnuts	375 mL
1 lb	sweet potato, cut into 1-inch (2.5 cm) chunks	500 g
¹/₂	large onion, quartered	¹/₂
1 tbsp	extra virgin olive oil	15 mL
2 tbsp	fresh sage leaves, chopped	30 mL
2 tbsp	ground flax seeds (flaxseed meal)	30 mL
2 tbsp	water	30 mL
¹/₂ cup	lightly packed fresh parsley, chopped	125 mL
¹/₂ tsp	salt	2 mL
¹/₂ tsp	freshly ground black pepper	2 mL
¹/₃ cup	ketchup (optional)	75 mL

1. Place toast in the Vitamix container and secure the lid. With the switch on High, pulse 3 or 4 times to coarse crumbs. Measure 1 cup (250 mL) crumbs and transfer to a large bowl. Save any extra crumbs for another use.

2. Place walnuts in the container and secure the lid. With the switch on Variable, select speed 1 and pulse about 5 times, until finely chopped, with a few coarse chunks. Transfer nuts to the bowl with the crumbs.

3. Secure the lid on the container and remove the lid plug. Select speed 1 and turn the machine on. Drop half the sweet potato, one cube at a time, through the lid opening, blending until chopped.

Turn the machine off and scrape down the container. Replace the lid, turn the machine on and blend until the sweet potato is evenly chopped. Transfer to a separate bowl. Repeat with the remaining sweet potato.

4. Secure the lid of the container and remove the lid plug. Select speed 3 and turn the machine on. Drop the onion pieces, one at a time, through the lid opening, using the tamper if they are not falling into the blades. Turn the machine off as soon as all the onion is chopped. Transfer to the bowl with the sweet potatoes.

5. In a large skillet, heat oil over medium-high heat. Add the sweet potato mixture and sage; cook, stirring, for about 4 minutes or until hot and sizzling. Reduce heat to medium-low, cover and cook for 4 minutes or until sweet potato is tender but not falling apart.

6. Meanwhile, in a small bowl, combine flax seeds and water. Let stand for a few minutes to thicken.

7. Transfer the sweet potato mixture to the bowl with the nuts and crumbs. Add the flax mixture, parsley, salt and pepper, stirring to mix well. Pack into the prepared loaf pan and smooth the top.

8. Bake in preheated oven for 1 hour. If desired, spread ketchup over loaf after 30 minutes. Bake until an instant-read thermometer inserted in the center of the loaf registers 165°F (74°C). Let cool in pan on a wire rack for 5 minutes before slicing. Serve hot.

Variation

Try toasted and skinned hazelnuts in place of the walnuts, for a different nutty flavor.

Gyros with Yogurt Sauce

That giant column of sizzling gyro meat at the restaurant is pretty impressive, to be sure. It's also pretty easy to make your own, albeit smaller, gyro filling in a loaf pan. The key is to purée the meat so it has a smooth texture. That way, it slices into thin sheets, just like at the restaurant.

MAKES 4 TO 6 SERVINGS

- **Preheat oven to 350°F (180°C)**
- **9- by 5-inch (23 by 12.5 cm) loaf pan, lightly oiled**

2 tsp	dried rosemary	10 mL
2 tsp	dried marjoram	10 mL
1/2 tsp	whole black peppercorns	2 mL
4	cloves garlic, chopped	4
1	small onion, quartered	1
1 tsp	salt	5 mL
1 lb	regular ground lamb, divided	500 g
6	6 1/2-inch (16 cm) pitas	6

YOGURT SAUCE

1 cup	plain Greek yogurt	250 mL
1/4 cup	tahini	60 mL
2 tbsp	red wine vinegar	30 mL
1/2 tsp	salt	2 mL
1/2	large cucumber, cut into chunks	1/2
1/4 cup	lightly packed fresh mint leaves, chopped	60 mL

1. Place the rosemary, marjoram and peppercorns in the Vitamix container and secure the lid. With the switch on Variable, select speed 1 and turn the machine on. Gradually increase the speed to 10 and blend for up to 1 minute, until the herbs and spices are powdered.

2. Turn the machine off and scrape down the container. Replace the lid and remove the lid plug. Select speed 1 and turn the machine on. Drop the garlic and onion, one piece at a time, through the lid opening, then add the salt.

Insert the tamper and, using it to push the ingredients into the blades, gradually increase the speed to 5 and blend until the onion is puréed and wet. Scrape half the purée into a small bowl and set aside.

3. Add half the lamb to the purée remaining in the Vitamix. Secure the lid and insert the tamper. Select speed 1 and turn the machine on. Using the tamper to push the ingredients into the blades, gradually increase the speed to 5 and blend until the meat is smooth. Scrape the lamb mixture into a large bowl.

4. Return the reserved onion purée to the Vitamix and add the remaining lamb. Blend as in step 3, then add the mixture to the large bowl and mix well. Press the lamb mixture into the prepared pan.

5. Bake in preheated oven for 45 minutes or until an instant-read thermometer inserted in the center of the loaf registers 165°F (74°C). Let cool for at least 20 minutes in pan on a wire rack. For the densest gyro meat, place another loaf pan on top and put a couple of cans of food in the pan to press the loaf as it cools.

6. Meanwhile, wash and sanitize the Vitamix container (see tip) and let air-dry.

7. *Sauce:* Place the yogurt, tahini, vinegar and salt in the Vitamix container and secure the lid. With the switch on Variable, select speed 1 and turn the machine on. Quickly increase the speed to 10 and blend for 10 seconds. Turn the machine off and add the cucumber and mint. Replace the lid and pulse twice to mix. Scrape into a medium bowl.

8. Thinly slice the meat and serve in pitas with sauce.

FRESH FLOURS and BAKED GOODS

TIPS FOR SUCCESS

- If you are just getting started with your Vitamix, you may want to try grinding grains in the container that came with the machine before investing in a dry grinding container. But if you enjoy freshly ground flours and baked goods, it is worth buying the dry grinding container. It is designed just for grinding and kneading, and will do a better job, with less wear and tear on your machine.
- Don't try to grind more than $2^1/_2$ cups (625 mL) of any grain or bean at a time, or it may overheat the machine.
- Your Vitamix will usually finely grind flour in 1 minute. For very fine flour, place a fine-mesh sieve over a bowl and sift the fresh flour through the sieve, shaking it back and forth. Regrind any bits left in the sieve.
- For optimal freshness and nutrition, grind flours the day you will use them. You may notice that freshly ground flours are quite warm just after grinding. This is absolutely fine, but they will spoil more quickly than flours you purchase because the naturally occurring oils in grains and beans are sensitive to heat.
- If you need to make flours ahead of time, they can be stored in an airtight container in the refrigerator for up to 1 week.
- The flour in these recipes is meant to be measured with the spoon-and-sweep technique. Place a dry, nesting-style measuring cup on a level surface (place waxed paper underneath to catch any overflow, to keep things neat) and spoon the flour very lightly into the cup. Tap the cup once to fill in any empty spaces and use the flat side of a butter knife to sweep the flour level with the top of the cup. If you scoop the flour instead of spooning it, you can end up packing in quite a bit more flour.
- To measure dry grains, pour them just to the top rim of the dry measuring cup, not above it.
- Avoid using raw honey in yeast breads, as some varieties have antibiotic properties and might kill yeast.
- When you're making bread, if you don't have the dry grinding container, you may find it easier to mix and knead the dough with the low-profile Vitamix container, which has a wider base.
- There are two methods for mixing bread dough in the Vitamix: 1) You can grind the grain, let it cool in the container, then add the quick-rising (instant) yeast mixture with the machine running; or 2) You can dump the flour mixture into a bowl to cool while you stir together the liquids and quick-rising (instant) yeast in the container, then blend the flour and liquids. Both work, although it is a little easier to mix the dough using the second method. Try both and see which you prefer.
- The breads can be stored, tightly wrapped, at room temperature for up to 4 days.
- The scones and muffins can be stored, tightly covered, at room temperature for up to 4 days.

Flour Grinding Guide

When selecting grains and beans to grind, it pays to know how they perform as flours. Hard red winter wheat is the standard for making whole wheat flour for yeast breads, as it is the highest in gluten. Hard white wheat is a variety of winter wheat that has a pale outer bran layer and a slightly lower gluten level than red wheat, and it is very good for bread. Soft wheats, sometimes called spring wheats, also come in both red and white. They are "soft" because they have lower gluten levels, and are best used in pastries, which you want to be tender.

If you are looking for gluten-free grain and bean flours, your selection is often limited in stores. With your Vitamix, you can grind just about any grain or bean into a fine fresh flour. Have fun with trying new flours, from split pea to black bean, sorghum to quinoa.

To grind grains or beans, place them in the Vitamix dry grinding or regular container and secure the lid. With the switch on Variable, select speed 1 and turn the machine on. Gradually increase the speed to 10, then flip the switch to High and blend for 1 minute or until the flour is finely ground. Don't grind for more than 2 minutes or you will overheat the machine. If desired, you may sift the flour with a fine-mesh sieve, to remove any coarser pieces. Spread the flour on a plate to cool completely before storing.

Use this guide to make the volume of flour you need in your recipes.

Volume of Whole Grain or Bean	Weight	Volume of Flour
Wheat		
3/4 cup (175 mL) hard wheat berries	144 g	1 cup (250 mL)
1 cup (250 mL) hard wheat berries	192 g	1 1/2 cups (375 mL)
1 1/4 cups (300 mL) hard wheat berries	240 g	1 3/4 + 2 tbsp (455 mL)
1 1/2 cups (375 mL) hard wheat berries	280 g	2 1/3 + 1 tsp (580 mL)
1 3/4 cups (425 mL) hard wheat berries	336 g	2 1/2 cups + 3 tbsp (670 mL)
2 cups (500 mL) hard wheat berries	384 g	3 1/4 cups (800 mL)
1 cup (250 mL) soft wheat berries	186 g	1 1/2 cups (375 mL)
Other Grains		
1 cup (250 mL) Kamut	185 g	1 1/4 cups (300 mL)
1 cup (250 mL) spelt	180 g	1 3/4 cups (425 mL)
Beans		
1 cup (250 mL) dried chickpeas	175 g	1 1/4 cups (300 mL)
1 cup (250 mL) dried black turtle beans	180 g	1 1/4 cups (300 mL)
1 cup (250 mL) dried navy (white pea) beans	190 g	1 1/4 cups (300 mL)

Whole Wheat Bread

This is a great all-purpose loaf. Once you become familiar with the process, it will become a go-to recipe that allows you to have fresh bread anytime you want it.

MAKES 1 LOAF

- **Dry grinding container (see tip)**
- **9- by 5-inch (23 by 12.5 cm) metal loaf pan, greased**

2¹/₂ cups	hard wheat berries	625 mL
¹/₂ tsp	salt	2 mL
1¹/₂ cups	warm water	375 mL
2 tbsp	honey (see tip, page 132)	30 mL
2 tsp	quick-rising (instant) yeast	10 mL
2 tbsp	extra virgin olive oil	30 mL
1 tsp	apple cider vinegar	5 mL

1. Place the wheat berries in the dry grinding container and secure the lid. With the switch on Variable, select speed 1 and turn the machine on. Gradually increase the speed to 10, then flip the switch to High and blend for 1 minute or until the wheat is finely ground.

2. Transfer the flour to a medium bowl, using a spatula to scrape out the bits stuck in the corners of the container. Let cool for 10 minutes, then stir in salt.

3. Meanwhile, place the warm water, honey and yeast in the dry grinding container and stir with a spatula to dissolve the yeast. Let stand for 3 to 5 minutes or until foamy.

4. Add the oil and vinegar to the yeast mixture. Secure the lid and, with the switch on High, pulse once, just to mix.

5. Remove the lid and add the flour mixture. Replace the lid and pulse once. Turn the machine off and scrape the dough away from the walls of the container, stirring the dough up from the bottom of the blender, then replace the lid. Pulse, scrape and stir four more times. The dough will look wet. Let the dough rest, covered, for 5 minutes.

6. To knead the dough, use the spatula to pull it away from the sides of the container, then secure the lid. With the switch on High, quickly pulse five times. Turn the machine off and scrape the container, then pulse five more times. Scrape and pulse three more times. The dough will be smooth and slightly sticky.

7. Scrape the dough into the prepared pan, smooth the top and use the spatula or wet hands to shape it into a rounded shape. Cover with a damp towel and let rise in a warm, draft-free place for 30 minutes.

8. Meanwhile, preheat oven to 350°F (180°C).

9. Uncover and bake for 35 minutes or until the top of the loaf is golden brown, an instant-read thermometer inserted in the center registers 170°F (80°C), and the loaf sounds hollow when tapped with a finger. Let cool in pan on a wire rack for 10 minutes, then tap the loaf out onto the rack to cool completely.

Tips

For the most accurate measurements when making baked goods, weigh your dry ingredients. For this recipe, you'll need 458 g wheat berries.

The dry grinding container makes quick work of grinding the wheat berries, but if you don't have one, the regular container will work just fine.

There may be a few flecks of less-ground wheat bran and germ in the flour, which may be pleasing to you. If not, you can sift the flour through a fine-mesh sieve, then regrind any bits left in the sieve.

Double the amount of honey, for a honey wheat version.

Store the cooled bread, tightly wrapped, at room temperature for up to 4 days.

Gluten-Free Sandwich Loaf

This lovely loaf has the familiar grainy taste that many gluten-free loaves lack, because it relies on gluten-free whole grains as the basis of a flour blend.

MAKES 1 LOAF

- **Dry grinding container (see tip)**
- **9- by 5-inch (23 by 12.5 cm) metal loaf pan, greased**

1 cup	whole sorghum	250 mL
1/2 cup	long-grain brown rice	125 mL
2 tbsp	flax seeds	30 mL
3/4 cup	tapioca starch	175 mL
1/3 cup	potato starch	75 mL
1 tsp	salt	5 mL
1/4 tsp	guar gum	1 mL
3/4 cup	warm water	175 mL
2 tbsp	honey (see tip, page 132)	30 mL
1 tbsp	quick-rising (instant) yeast	15 mL
2	large eggs	2
1/4 cup	canola oil	60 mL
1 tsp	apple cider vinegar	5 mL

1. Place the sorghum, rice and flax seeds in the dry grinding container and secure the lid. With the switch on Variable, select speed 1 and turn the machine on. Gradually increase the speed to 10, then flip the switch to High and grind for 1 minute.

2. Transfer the flour to a large bowl, using a spatula to scrape out the bits stuck in the corners of the container. Let cool for 10 minutes, then stir in tapioca, potato starch, salt and guar gum.

3. Meanwhile, place the warm water, honey and yeast in the container and stir with a spatula to dissolve the yeast. Let stand for 3 to 5 minutes or until foamy.

4. Add the eggs, oil and vinegar to the yeast mixture and secure the lid. With the switch on Variable, select speed 1 and blend for 3 seconds, just to combine.

5. Turn the machine off and add the flour mixture. Replace the lid, select speed 1 and turn the machine on. Gradually increase the speed to 10 and blend for 15 seconds.

6. Turn the machine off and scrape the flour away from the corners of the container, stirring it in with the spatula. Replace the lid. Flip the switch to High, turn the machine on and blend for 10 seconds. Scrape and repeat two more times. The batter should be well mixed and thick.

7. Scrape the batter into the prepared pan and smooth the top. Cover with a damp towel and let rise in a warm, draft-free place for 45 minutes. Don't let the towel touch the top of the rising dough; check the rising progress every 10 minutes and when the dough is almost up to the top of the pan, remove the towel and continue to let rise uncovered.

8. Meanwhile, preheat oven to 350°F (180°C).

9. Bake for 35 minutes or until the top of the loaf is golden brown and an instant-read thermometer inserted in the center registers 170°F (80°C). Let cool in pan on a wire rack for at least 10 minutes before slicing.

Tips

For the most accurate measurements when making baked goods, weigh your dry ingredients. For this recipe, you'll need 200 g sorghum, 90 g brown rice, 20 g flax seeds, 90 g tapioca starch and 50 g potato starch.

The dry grinding container makes quick work of grinding the sorghum and rice, but if you don't have one, the regular container will work just fine.

Millet Demi-Loaf or Round

This petite loaf is a perfect addition to a family meal, or is enough for two people to dine on for a couple of days. The option to make a free-form round loaf gives you a little variety in your bread selection.

MAKES 1 SMALL LOAF

- **Dry grinding container (see tip)**
- **9- by 5-inch (23 by 12.5 cm) metal loaf pan, greased, or 4-cup (1 L) bowl, lined with a kitchen towel and dusted heavily with flour**
- **Baking stone (for round loaf)**

³/₄ cup	hard white wheat berries	175 mL
¹/₄ cup	millet	60 mL
1 cup	warm water	250 mL
1 tsp	granulated sugar	5 mL
1 tbsp	quick-rising (instant) yeast	15 mL
³/₄ cup	bread flour	175 mL
1 tsp	salt	5 mL
1 tbsp	coarse cornmeal (for the round loaf)	15 mL

Tips

For the most accurate measurements when making baked goods, weigh your dry ingredients. For this recipe, you'll need 150 g wheat berries, 50 g millet and 103 g bread flour.

The dry grinding container makes quick work of grinding grains, but if you don't have one, the regular container will work just fine.

Using a baking stone is a good way to ensure an even temperature and a good rise, whether or not you use a pan.

Store the cooled bread, tightly wrapped, at room temperature for up to 4 days.

1. Place the wheat berries and millet in the dry grinding container and secure the lid. With the switch on Variable, select speed 1 and turn the machine on. Gradually increase the speed to 10, then flip the switch to High and blend for 1 minute or until the wheat is finely ground.

2. Turn the machine off and fluff the flour with a spatula. Let cool for 10 minutes.

3. Meanwhile, in a 2-cup (500 mL) measuring cup, combine warm water, sugar and yeast. Stir well and let stand for 3 to 5 minutes or until foamy.

4. When the flour has cooled, add the bread flour and salt to the container. Replace the lid and remove the lid plug. With the switch on High, pulse once. Turn the machine on and slowly pour the yeast mixture through the lid opening, then blend for 10 seconds.

5. Turn the machine off and use a spatula to scrape the sides of the container. Replace the lid and pulse on High four times, stirring the dough up from the bottom of the blender each time. Let the dough rest, covered, for 5 minutes.

6. To knead the dough, use the spatula to pull it away from the sides of the container, then secure the lid. With the switch on High, quickly pulse five times. Turn the machine off and scrape the container, then pulse five more times. Scrape and pulse three more times. The dough will be soft and slightly sticky.

To make a loaf

7. Scrape the dough into the prepared pan, smooth the top and use the spatula or wet hands to shape it into a cylindrical shape. Cover with a damp towel and let rise in a warm, draft-free place for 30 minutes.

8. Meanwhile, preheat oven to 375°F (190°C).

9. Uncover and bake for 30 to 35 minutes or until the top is golden brown, an instant-read thermometer inserted in the center registers 190°F (88°C), and the loaf sounds hollow when tapped with a finger. Let cool in pan on a wire rack for 10 minutes, then tap the loaf out onto the rack to cool completely before slicing.

To make a round

7. Scrape the dough into the prepared bowl. Cover with a damp towel and let rise in a warm, draft-free place for 30 minutes.

8. Meanwhile, place the baking stone in the oven and preheat oven to 425°F (220°C).

9. Pull the rack with the hot stone halfway out of the oven and sprinkle with cornmeal. Remove the towel and quickly invert the bowl of dough onto the stone to drop the loaf onto it. Remove the bowl. Bake for 20 minutes or until the top is golden brown, an instant-read thermometer inserted in the center registers 190°F (88°C), and the loaf sounds hollow when tapped with a finger. Let cool on a wire rack for 10 minutes before slicing.

Variation

Use buckwheat groats instead of millet, for a hint of buckwheat flavor.

Veggie Kamut Bread

Kamut, or Khorasan wheat, is an ancient variety with long golden kernels. It has a buttery flavor that is worth seeking out.

∿∿∿∿∿∿∿∿∿∿∿∿∿∿∿∿∿∿∿∿∿∿∿∿∿∿∿∿∿

MAKES 1 LOAF

- Dry grinding container (see tip, page 136)
- 9- by 5-inch (23 by 12.5 cm) metal loaf pan, greased

1³/₄ cups	whole Kamut berries	425 mL
1 tsp	salt	5 mL
1¹/₄ cups	warm water	300 mL
2 tbsp	honey (see tip, page 132)	30 mL
2 tsp	quick-rising (instant) yeast	10 mL
2 tbsp	extra virgin olive oil	30 mL
1 tsp	apple cider vinegar	5 mL
1	green onion, minced	1
1 cup	shredded carrot	250 mL
3 tbsp	fresh parsley, chopped	45 mL

1. Place the Kamut berries and salt in the dry grinding container and secure the lid. With the switch on Variable, select speed 1 and turn the machine on. Gradually increase the speed to 10, then flip the switch to High and grind for about 1 minute or until the Kamut is finely ground.

2. Turn the machine off and fluff the flour with a spatula. Let cool for 10 minutes.

3. Meanwhile, in a 2-cup (500 mL) measuring cup, combine warm water, honey and yeast. Stir well and let stand for 3 to 5 minutes or until foamy, then stir in oil and vinegar.

4. When the flour has cooled, replace the lid on the container and remove the lid plug. With the switch on Variable, select speed 1 and turn the machine on. Gradually increase the speed to 5 and blend until a well forms in the center of the flour. Slowly pour the liquid through the lid opening into the center of the flour. When all of the liquid has been added, blend for 20 seconds.

5. Turn the machine off and use a spatula to scrape the sides of the container. Replace the lid. Flip the switch to High and pulse once. Remove the lid and scrape the dough away from the sides of the container, stirring it into the center. Pulse and scrape one more time. The flour should be incorporated; if it isn't, stir it with your spatula and pulse one more time. Let the dough rest, covered, for 5 minutes.

6. To knead the dough, use the spatula to pull it away from the sides of the container, then secure the lid. With the switch on High, quickly pulse once. Scrape and pulse three more times. The dough should be soft and elastic; if it isn't, scrape and pulse one more time.

7. Remove the lid and add the green onion, carrot and parsley to the container. Use the spatula to mix them in, scraping down to the bottom of the container and folding the dough over.

8. Scrape the dough into the prepared pan and smooth the top. Cover lightly with plastic wrap and let rise in a warm, draft-free place for 45 minutes or until the dough has risen to just above the top of the pan.

9. Meanwhile, preheat oven to 350°F (180°C).

10. Uncover and bake for 30 to 35 minutes or until the top of the loaf is golden brown, an instant-read thermometer inserted in the center registers 170°F (80°C), and the loaf sounds hollow when tapped with a finger. Let cool in pan on a wire rack for 10 minutes, then tap the loaf out onto the rack to cool completely.

Tip

For the most accurate measurements when making baked goods, weigh your dry and fresh ingredients. For this recipe, you'll need 323 g Kamut berries and 110 g carrot.

Kamut Rolls

These hearty whole-grain rolls are the perfect accompaniment to a soup or dip. Letting them rise and bake in muffin cups ensures an even shape.

MAKES 12 ROLLS

- **Dry grinding container (see tip, page 136)**
- **12-cup muffin pan, greased**

2 cups	whole Kamut berries	500 mL
1¼ cups	warm water	300 mL
2 tbsp	honey (see tip, page 132)	30 mL
1 tbsp	quick-rising (instant) yeast	15 mL
1 tsp	salt	5 mL
2 tbsp	extra virgin olive oil	30 mL
1 tsp	apple cider vinegar	5 mL

1. Place the Kamut berries in the dry grinding container and secure the lid. With the switch on Variable, select speed 1 and turn the machine on. Gradually increase the speed to 10, then flip the switch to High and grind for 1 minute or until the Kamut is finely ground.

2. Turn the machine off and fluff the flour with a spatula. Let cool for 10 minutes.

3. Meanwhile, in a 2-cup (500 mL) measuring cup, combine warm water, honey and yeast. Stir well and let stand for 3 to 5 minutes or until foamy.

4. When the flour has cooled, add the salt to the container and secure the lid. With the switch on Variable, select speed 5 and blend until a well forms in the center. Remove the lid plug and slowly pour the yeast mixture through the lid opening, then pour in the oil and vinegar, blending until the flour is incorporated.

5. Turn the machine off, flip the switch to High and pulse three times. Remove the lid and use a spatula to scrape the dough away from the sides of the container, stirring it into the center, then replace the lid. Pulse and scrape four more times, stirring the dough up from the bottom of the container each time. Let the dough rest, covered, for 5 minutes.

6. To knead the dough, use the spatula to pull it away from the sides of the container, then secure the lid. With the switch on High, quickly pulse five times. Turn the machine off and scrape the container, then pulse five more times. Scrape and pulse three more times. The dough will be soft and slightly sticky.

7. Scrape the dough onto a floured work surface. Using a bench scraper or chef's knife, divide the dough into 4 equal portions, then cut each of those into 3 equal portions, to make 12 portions. Using lightly floured hands, shape each portion into a ball and drop into a prepared muffin cup. Cover loosely with a damp towel and let rise in a warm, draft-free place for 30 minutes.

8. Meanwhile, preheat oven to 375°F (190°C).

9. Uncover and bake for 15 minutes or until the rolls are dark golden on top and sound hollow when tapped. Let cool in pan on a wire rack for 5 minutes, then gently run a butter knife around each roll and transfer rolls to the rack. Serve warm.

Tips

For the most accurate measurements when making baked goods, weigh your dry ingredients. For this recipe, you'll need 371 g Kamut berries.

If you prefer a more rustic look, you can place the rolls 2 inches (5 cm) apart on a parchment-lined baking sheet instead of in a muffin pan.

Store the cooled rolls, tightly wrapped, at room temperature for up to 5 days. To reheat, bake for 10 minutes in a 350°F (180°C) oven, or microwave 1 or 2 rolls on High for 45 seconds.

Basic Socca

Socca is a Provençal tradition, a simple, rustic flatbread made with chickpea flour. It's a fantastic option for gluten-free diners, and can even stand in for a pizza crust or crostini. Grind your own chickpea flour or branch out and grind any bean you like.

MAKES 6 TO 8 SERVINGS

- **Dry grinding container (see tip)**
- **Fine-mesh strainer**
- **10-inch (25 cm) cast-iron skillet**

1 cup	dried chickpeas	250 mL
1^1/$_4$ cups	water	300 mL
^{1}/$_4$ cup	extra virgin olive oil, divided	60 mL
1 tsp	salt	5 mL
^{1}/$_2$ tsp	freshly cracked black pepper	2 mL
2 tbsp	fresh rosemary leaves, chopped	30 mL

Tips

For the most accurate measurements when making baked goods, weigh your dry ingredients. For this recipe, you'll need 175 g chickpeas.

The dry grinding container makes quick work of grinding the chickpeas, but if you don't have one, the regular container will work just fine.

If you don't have a cast-iron skillet, you can use a 9-inch (23 cm) round or square metal baking pan, preheated for 3 minutes, but the crust will not be as crisp.

1. Place the skillet in the oven and preheat oven to 450°F (230°C).

2. Place the chickpeas in the dry grinding container and secure the lid. With the switch on Variable, select speed 1 and turn the machine on. Gradually increase the speed to 10, then flip the switch to High and blend for 1 minute.

3. Set the sieve over a medium bowl and sift the flour into the bowl. Return any bits left in the sieve to the container and secure the lid. Turn the machine on and grind on High for 30 seconds or until powdery. Add to the bowl.

4. Place the water, 2 tbsp (30 mL) oil, salt, pepper, rosemary and chickpea flour in the dry grinding container and secure the lid. With the switch on Variable, select speed 1 and turn the machine on. Gradually increase the speed to 10 and blend for about 30 seconds or until smooth.

5. Remove the hot skillet from the oven and place it on a wire rack, then quickly drizzle in the remaining oil, swirling to coat the pan. Pour in the batter and quickly spread to the edges.

6. Bake for 15 minutes or until the top is crackled and lightly browned and the bottom is golden brown and crisp. Carefully slide the socca onto a cutting board or platter, cut into wedges or squares and serve hot.

Variations

Grind other dried legumes, such as navy (white pea) beans, black beans or red lentils, to suit your taste.

For a simple pizza, top the finished socca with a smear of pesto and a sprinkling of shredded cheese, and bake for 5 minutes longer.

Gluten-Free Quinoa Flatbreads

When you need a quick gluten-free bread, these flatbreads are about as fast as it gets. Served fresh and hot from the pan, they will appeal to everyone, not just the gluten-avoiders.

∽∽∽∽∽∽∽∽∽∽∽∽∽∽∽∽∽∽∽∽∽∽∽∽∽∽∽∽∽∽∽

MAKES 4 FLATBREADS

- **Dry grinding container (see tip)**
- **Griddle or large cast-iron skillet**

3/4 cup	quinoa	175 mL
1/2 cup	tapioca starch	125 mL
1 tsp	baking powder	5 mL
1/2 tsp	salt	2 mL
1/4 tsp	xanthan gum	1 mL
1	large egg	1
6 tbsp	water (approx.)	90 mL
2 tbsp	extra virgin olive oil	30 mL
	Additional extra virgin olive oil	

Tips

For the most accurate measurements when making baked goods, weigh your dry ingredients. For this recipe, you'll need 126 g quinoa and 60 g tapioca starch.

The dry grinding container makes quick work of grinding the quinoa, but if you don't have one, the regular container will work just fine.

Keep xanthan gum in a tightly sealed container in the freezer, and it will last indefinitely.

These flatbreads are best served the same day they are made. If they cool down before you're ready to serve them, wrap them in foil and reheat them in a 350°F (180°C) oven for about 10 minutes.

Variation

Add a pinch of chili powder with the salt for a slightly spicy flatbread.

1. Place the quinoa in the dry grinding container and secure the lid. With the switch on Variable, select speed 1 and turn the machine on. Gradually increase the speed to 10, then flip the switch to High and grind for 1 minute.

2. Turn the machine off and fluff the flour with a spatula. Let cool for 10 minutes.

3. When the flour has cooled, add the tapioca, baking powder, salt and xanthan gum to the container and secure the lid. Turn the machine on and blend on High for 10 seconds to mix and form a well in the center of the flour.

4. In a 2-cup (500 mL) measuring cup, whisk together egg, water and oil until blended. Pour into the well in the flour mixture and secure the lid. With the switch on High, pulse three times. Remove the lid and use a spatula to scrape down the sides of the container, then replace the lid and pulse three times. Scrape and pulse three or four more times, until the mixture forms a smooth dough. If it is dry or has unblended flour, drizzle in 1 tbsp (15 mL) more water and pulse until mixed.

5. Scrape the dough onto a work surface dusted with tapioca starch and cut into 4 equal pieces. Roll each piece into a ball, then pat out to a 5½-inch (14 cm) round.

6. Heat the griddle over high heat until hot, about 3 minutes. Drizzle with a thin layer of oil. Using a large metal spatula, transfer a round to the griddle. Cook for about 2 minutes per side, until dry and lightly browned, then for about 1 minute per side, until speckled with brown spots. Transfer to a wire rack. Repeat with the remaining rounds, oiling the pan and adjusting the heat as necessary between batches to prevent burning. Serve warm.

Ancient Grain Tortillas

Ancient grains are grains that existed in their current forms before plant breeders started hybridizing wheat. Each has a unique story and plenty of great whole-grain nutrition to bring to your tortillas.

MAKES 6 TORTILLAS

- **Dry grinding container (see tip)**
- **Griddle or large cast-iron skillet**

. . . .

1/2 cup	whole Kamut berries	125 mL
1/3 cup	whole spelt berries	75 mL
1/3 cup	quinoa	75 mL
3/4 tsp	salt	3 mL
1/4 tsp	guar gum	1 mL
1/2 cup	warm water	125 mL
2 tbsp	melted coconut oil	30 mL

Tips

For the most accurate measurements when making baked goods, weigh your dry ingredients. For this recipe, you'll need 90 g Kamut berries, 60 g spelt berries and 57 g quinoa.

The dry grinding container makes quick work of grinding the Kamut, spelt and quinoa, but if you don't have one, the regular container will work just fine.

When you're rolling out the tortillas, the dough may start to resist being stretched. Let it rest for a few minutes, and it will relax and become easy to roll again.

Store the cooled tortillas, tightly wrapped, in the refrigerator for up to 4 days. They will harden as they cool, but warming them in the microwave for 20 to 30 seconds or, wrapped in foil, in a 350°F (180°C) oven for about 10 minutes will make them tender again.

1. Place the Kamut, spelt and quinoa in the dry grinding container and secure the lid. With the switch on Variable, select speed 1 and turn the machine on. Gradually increase the speed to 10, then flip the switch to High and grind for 1 minute.

2. Turn the machine off and add the salt and guar gum. Replace the lid and blend on High to mix and form a well in the center of the flour.

3. Remove the lid and pour the warm water and coconut oil into the well. Replace the lid and pulse three times. Remove the lid and use a spatula to scrape down the sides of the container, then replace the lid. Pulse and scrape until the dough is well mixed.

4. Scrape the dough onto a floured work surface. Divide into 6 equal pieces, then form each piece into a ball. Cover with plastic wrap and let rest for 10 minutes.

5. Using a floured rolling pin, roll each ball out into an 8-inch (20 cm) circle. Brush off any extra flour, as it will burn in the pan. Have a plate and a towel ready to keep the tortillas warm.

6. Heat the griddle over medium-high heat until hot, about 3 minutes. Place one tortilla in the pan and cook for about 45 seconds per side or until both sides have brown blisters and some puffy spots. Transfer to the plate and cover with the towel. Repeat with remaining tortillas, adjusting the heat as necessary between batches to prevent burning. Serve warm.

Variation

Instead of quinoa, try millet, buckwheat or sorghum, for some tasty variations on the theme.

Whole-Grain Pizza Crust

Pizza is one of the most popular foods on earth, but has a reputation for being junk food. If you grind your own whole wheat flour and turn it into a thick and tasty crust, you are starting out with a decidedly not-junk base. Pick a variety of veggies for the topping, and you start moving a decadent food into the healthy-food column.

MAKES ONE 14-INCH (35 CM) CRUST, ABOUT 4 SERVINGS

- Dry grinding container (see tip)
- 16- by 14-inch (40 by 35 cm) rimless baking sheet

1 cup	hard wheat berries	250 mL
1 cup	warm water	250 mL
1 tbsp	granulated sugar	15 mL
2 tsp	quick-rising (instant) yeast	10 mL
1/2 cup	unbleached all-purpose flour	125 mL
1 tsp	salt	5 mL
1 tbsp	extra virgin olive oil	15 mL
	Cornmeal	
	Additional extra virgin olive oil	
	Pizza sauce and toppings	

1. Place the wheat berries in the dry grinding container and secure the lid. With the switch on Variable, select speed 1 and turn the machine on. Gradually increase the speed to 10, then flip the switch to High and grind for 1 minute.

2. Turn the machine off and fluff the flour with a spatula. Let cool for 10 minutes.

3. Meanwhile, in a 2-cup (500 mL) measuring cup, combine warm water, sugar and yeast. Stir well and let stand for 3 to 5 minutes or until foamy.

4. When the flour has cooled, add the unbleached flour and salt to the container. Secure the lid and remove the lid plug. With the switch on Variable, select speed 6 and pulse two or three times to mix the flours, then run continuously until a well forms in the center of the flour. Slowly pour the yeast mixture through the lid opening and blend for 4 seconds.

5. Turn the machine off and use a spatula to scrape the dough away from the sides of the container, mixing any flour in the corners into the dough. Replace the lid and blend on speed 6 for 5 to 10 seconds to mix in any stray flour. Turn the machine off. Let the dough rest, covered, for 5 minutes.

6. Secure the lid and, with the switch on High, quickly pulse five times. Let the dough rest for a few seconds. Repeat four more times.

7. Brush oil in a 14-inch (35 cm) circle on baking sheet, then sprinkle lightly with cornmeal. Dump dough on top of cornmeal and use a wet spatula or wet fingers to spread the dough to a 14-inch (35 cm) circle. Let rise, uncovered, for 30 minutes.

8. Meanwhile, preheat oven to 425°F (220°C).

9. Spread crust with pizza sauce and top with desired toppings. Bake for about 20 minutes or until toppings are browned and the crust is crisp on the bottom. Slide pizza onto a cutting board and cut into slices.

Tips

For the most accurate measurements when making baked goods, weigh your dry ingredients. For this recipe, you'll need 192 g wheat berries and 57 g unbleached flour.

The dry grinding container makes quick work of grinding the wheat berries, but if you don't have one, the regular container will work just fine.

Don't load your crust down with too many toppings. About 1/2 cup (125 mL) sauce and up to 2 cups (500 mL) chopped veggies and meats, plus a light dusting of up to 1 1/2 cups (375 mL) shredded cheese will give you a great pizza without making the crust soggy.

Cauliflower Pizza Crust with Veggies and Goat Cheese

As a low-carb vegetable, cauliflower has emerged as the darling of the carbohydrate-averse set. In this pizza, you use your Vitamix to finely grind cauliflower, and, with the addition of some egg and Parmesan, it becomes a savory, chewy crust. You'll eat it with a fork and savor every bite.

MAKES 2 SERVINGS

- **Preheat oven to 375°F (190°C)**
- **Smooth-textured, lint-free kitchen towel or nut-milk straining bag**
- **Large baking sheet, lined with parchment paper**

6 cups	chopped cauliflower (1 small; 1½ lbs/750 g)	1.5 L
2 oz	Parmesan cheese, cut into cubes	60 g
1 tbsp	extra virgin olive oil	15 mL
½ tsp	salt	2 mL
1	large egg, beaten	1
	Additional extra virgin olive oil	

TOPPINGS

½ cup	pizza sauce	125 mL
½ cup	chopped broccoli	125 mL
½ cup	chopped red bell pepper	125 mL
3 oz	goat cheese (chèvre), crumbled	90 g

Tip

This is a great way to use the cauliflower stems and leaves — just grind them along with the florets. If you like, you can even cut up 2 cauliflowers, save the florets for other uses and make up the bulk of the cauliflower needed for this recipe with stems.

1. Place half the cauliflower in the Vitamix container and secure the lid. With the switch on High, pulse five or six times. Remove the lid and stir with a spatula to pull the bits out of the corners. Replace the lid and pulse once or twice, until finely ground. Transfer the cauliflower to a large bowl. Repeat with the remaining cauliflower. Set aside.

2. Secure the lid on the container and remove the lid plug. With the switch on Variable, select speed 4 and turn the machine on. Drop the Parmesan through the lid opening, one cube at a time, then flip the switch to High and blend for about 1 minute or until the cheese is finely ground. Set aside.

3. In a large skillet, heat oil over medium-high heat. Add cauliflower and salt; cook, stirring, for 2 to 3 minutes or until cauliflower is hot. Reduce heat to medium and cook, stirring occasionally, for about 10 minutes or until cauliflower is very soft. Remove from heat.

4. Spread the kitchen towel on the counter, or set the nut-milk straining bag in a sieve over a bowl, and transfer the cauliflower to the towel or bag. Let cool for 5 minutes. Gather up the towel or bag and hold it over a bowl, then use it to wring the liquid out of the cauliflower. Discard liquid. Return cauliflower to the large bowl and stir in Parmesan and egg, mixing well.

5. Spread a thin layer of oil in a 10-inch (25 cm) circle on prepared baking sheet. Mound the cauliflower mixture in the center and, using damp hands, pat it out to a 10-inch (25 cm) circle.

6. Bake in preheated oven for 25 minutes or until firm. Spread sauce over the crust and top with broccoli and red pepper, then sprinkle with goat cheese. Bake for 15 to 20 minutes or until cheese is melted and veggies are lightly browned. Cut into wedges and serve immediately.

Variation

Use another cheese in the crust, for a nice twist. Gruyère would complement a topping of olives and smoked salmon.

Gingerbread Scones

These hearty whole-grain scones are almost a meal in themselves, served with a steaming mug of coffee or tea. Fresh ginger gives them a peppery spark, and plenty of butter keeps them from veering too far into the healthy zone.

MAKES 12 SCONES

- Preheat oven to 400°F (200°C)
- Dry grinding container (see tip)
- Baking sheet, lined with parchment paper

1¹/₂ cups	soft wheat berries	375 mL
¹/₂ cup	unbleached all-purpose flour	125 mL
¹/₂ cup	large-flake (old-fashioned) rolled oats	125 mL
¹/₂ cup	packed light brown sugar	125 mL
2 tsp	ground cinnamon	10 mL
1 tsp	baking powder	5 mL
1 tsp	baking soda	5 mL
¹/₂ tsp	salt	2 mL
¹/₄ tsp	ground cloves	1 mL
¹/₂ cup	butter, chilled	125 mL
2 tbsp	grated gingerroot	30 mL
³/₄ cup	plain yogurt	175 mL
1 tbsp	dark (cooking) molasses	15 mL
¹/₄ cup	turbinado sugar	60 mL

Tips

For the most accurate measurements when making baked goods, weigh your dry ingredients. For this recipe, you'll need 279 g wheat berries, 57 g unbleached flour, 78 g oats and 110 g brown sugar.

The dry grinding container makes quick work of grinding the wheat berries, but if you don't have one, the regular container will work just fine.

Using a grater to shred the cold butter gives you a nice even distribution of butter pieces throughout the dough, which will make the scones flaky and tender.

1. Place the wheat berries in the dry grinding container and secure the lid. With the switch on Variable, select speed 1 and turn the machine on. Gradually increase the speed to 10, then flip the switch to High and grind for 1 minute or until the wheat is finely ground.

2. Transfer the flour to a large bowl and let cool to room temperature.

3. Add unbleached flour, oats, brown sugar, cinnamon, baking powder, baking soda, salt and cloves to the bowl, whisking to combine. Using the coarse side of a box grater, grate in the cold butter; toss to mix.

4. In a small bowl, whisk together ginger, yogurt and molasses. Pour over flour mixture and stir with a fork just until moistened.

5. Transfer dough to a lightly floured surface and cut into 2 equal pieces. Form each piece into a round and flatten to about 1 inch (2.5 cm) thick. Cut each round into 6 wedges. Sprinkle the tops with turbinado sugar, pressing to adhere. Place scones at least 2 inches (5 cm) apart on prepared baking sheet.

6. Bake in preheated oven for 12 to 15 minutes, just until golden around the edges. Transfer scones to wire racks to cool. Serve warm or let cool completely.

Variation

Gingerbread Date Scones: Stir in ¹/₂ cup (125 mL) chopped soft dates at the end of step 4.

Whole-Grain Muffins

These whole-grain muffins emerge from the oven golden brown and fragrant, sparkling with a topping of turbinado crystals. Pick your favorite add-in fruits and/or nuts, and customize the muffins for your family, the season or the meal.

MAKES 12 MUFFINS

- **Preheat oven to 400°F (200°C)**
- **Dry grinding container (see tip)**
- **12-cup muffin pan, lined with paper or silicone liners**

2 cups	whole Kamut berries	500 mL
1/2 cup	packed light brown sugar	125 mL
1 tsp	baking powder	5 mL
1/2 tsp	baking soda	2 mL
1/2 tsp	salt	2 mL
1	large egg	1
1 1/4 cups	buttermilk	300 mL
1/2 cup	canola oil	125 mL
1 cup	dried fruit (chopped as necessary) and/or chopped nuts	250 mL
1/4 cup	turbinado sugar	60 mL

Tips

For the most accurate measurements when making baked goods, weigh your dry ingredients. For this recipe, you'll need 371 g Kamut berries and 110 g brown sugar.

The dry grinding container makes quick work of grinding the Kamut, but if you don't have one, the regular container will work just fine.

Using dried fruit instead of fresh helps you control the moisture content of the muffins.

Store the cooled muffins, tightly covered, in the refrigerator for up to 4 days.

1. Place the Kamut in the dry grinding container and secure the lid. With the switch on Variable, select speed 1 and turn the machine on. Gradually increase the speed to 10, then flip the switch to High and grind for 1 minute or until the Kamut is finely ground.

2. Transfer the flour to a large bowl and let cool for 10 minutes.

3. Add brown sugar, baking powder, baking soda and salt to the bowl, whisking to combine. Set aside.

4. Place the egg, buttermilk and oil in the dry grinding container and secure the lid. With the switch on Variable, select speed 1 and turn the machine on. Gradually increase the speed to 5 and blend for 10 seconds.

5. Pour the egg mixture into the flour mixture and stir gently, just until almost moistened. Stir in fruit and/or nuts just until incorporated.

6. Scoop the batter into the prepared muffin cups, dividing equally, and sprinkle with turbinado sugar.

7. Bake in preheated oven for about 20 minutes or until a tester inserted in the center of a muffin comes out clean. Let cool in pan on a wire rack for 5 minutes, then transfer muffins to the rack to cool completely.

Variation

Add 2 tsp (10 mL) ground cinnamon or pumpkin pie spice for a spicy version, paired with dried cranberries and/or pecans.

Lemon Blueberry Muffins

These lively, lemony muffins are lightened with a balance of almost half unbleached flour. You can make them with purchased flour instead of grinding your own, if you prefer (see variation).

∽◯∽

MAKES 12 MUFFINS

- **Preheat oven to 375°F (190°C)**
- **Dry grinding container (see tip)**
- **12-cup muffin pan, lined with paper or silicone liners**

3/4 cup	soft wheat berries	175 mL
3/4 cup	unbleached all-purpose flour	175 mL
1/2 cup	granulated sugar	125 mL
1 1/2 tsp	baking powder	7 mL
1/2 tsp	baking soda	2 mL
1/2 tsp	salt	2 mL
1 1/2 tbsp	grated lemon zest	22 mL
1 cup	milk	250 mL
3 tbsp	freshly squeezed lemon juice	45 mL
1	large egg	1
1/4 cup	canola oil	60 mL
1 tsp	vanilla extract	5 mL
1 cup	fresh or frozen blueberries (not thawed)	250 mL
2 tbsp	turbinado sugar	30 mL

Tips

For the most accurate measurements when making baked goods, weigh your dry and fresh ingredients. For this recipe, you'll need 150 g wheat berries, 78 g unbleached flour, 100 g granulated sugar and 148 g blueberries.

The dry grinding container makes quick work of grinding the wheat berries, but if you don't have one, the regular container will work just fine.

To keep your blueberries from spilling juice into the batter and making purple muffins, fold them in gently. If using frozen berries, fold them in straight from the freezer, and expect to bake the muffins for about 30 minutes.

1. Place the wheat berries in the dry grinding container and secure the lid. With the switch on Variable, select speed 1 and turn the machine on. Gradually increase the speed to 10, then flip the switch to High and grind for 1 minute or until the wheat is finely ground.

2. Transfer the flour to a large bowl and let cool for 10 minutes.

3. Add unbleached flour, granulated sugar, baking powder, baking soda, salt and lemon zest to the bowl, whisking to combine. Set aside.

4. Place the milk and lemon juice in the dry grinding container and let stand for 3 minutes. Add the egg, oil and vanilla. Secure the lid. With the switch on Variable, select speed 1 and turn the machine on. Gradually increase to speed 5 and blend for 5 to 10 seconds or until well mixed.

5. Pour the milk mixture into the flour mixture and stir gently, just until almost moistened. Gently fold in blueberries.

6. Scoop the batter into the prepared muffin cups, dividing equally, and sprinkle with turbinado sugar.

7. Bake in preheated oven for 20 to 30 minutes or until the tops are golden brown and a tester inserted in the center of a muffin comes out clean. Let cool in pan on a wire rack for 5 minutes, then transfer muffins to the rack to cool completely.

Variations

To substitute whole wheat pastry flour instead of grinding wheat berries, use 1 cup + 2 tbsp (280 mL) flour and skip step 1.

Raspberries make a tangy and gorgeous replacement for the blueberries.

Apple Kale Muffins

These moist, fruity muffins hide a few surprises. One is the addition of a green leafy vegetable, chopped finely so it can nestle there unobtrusively. They are also vegan, and taste terrific, even with no dairy or eggs.

〜〜〜〜〜〜〜〜〜〜〜〜〜〜〜〜〜〜〜〜〜〜〜〜〜〜〜〜〜〜

MAKES 12 MUFFINS

- **Preheat oven to 375°F (190°C)**
- **Dry grinding container**
- **12-cup muffin pan, lined with paper or silicone liners**

2 cups	soft white or red wheat berries	500 mL
1 tbsp	ground cinnamon	15 mL
1 tsp	baking powder	5 mL
1 tsp	baking soda	5 mL
1/2 tsp	salt	2 mL
2	apples	2
3/4 cup	unsweetened almond milk	175 mL
1/2 cup	canola oil	125 mL
1 tbsp	freshly squeezed lemon juice	15 mL
3/4 cup	packed light brown sugar	175 mL
3 tbsp	ground flax seeds (flaxseed meal)	45 mL
4	leaves kale, stemmed and finely chopped	4

Tips

For the most accurate measurements when making baked goods, weigh your dry ingredients. For this recipe, you'll need 356 g wheat berries, 165 g brown sugar and 30 g ground flax seeds.

The dry grinding container makes quick work of grinding the wheat berries, but if you don't have one, the regular container will work just fine.

Adding a puréed apple to the liquid mixture makes the muffins more moist.

Once out of the pan, these muffins need to cool for at least 10 minutes before serving, or they will be too soft.

1. Place the wheat berries in the dry grinding container and secure the lid. With the switch on Variable, select speed 1 and turn the machine on. Gradually increase the speed to 10, then flip the switch to High and grind for 1 minute or until the wheat is very finely ground.

2. Transfer the flour to a large bowl and let cool for 10 minutes.

3. Add cinnamon, baking powder, baking soda and salt to the bowl, whisking to combine. Set aside.

4. Cut 1 apple into quarters and trim out core. Place in the dry grinding container. Peel and finely chop the remaining apple and set aside.

5. Add the almond milk, oil, lemon juice, brown sugar and flax seeds to the Vitamix container and secure the lid. With the switch on Variable, select speed 1 and turn the machine on. Blend for about 20 seconds or until smooth.

6. Pour the almond milk mixture into the flour mixture and stir gently, just until almost moistened. Gently fold in chopped apple and kale.

7. Scoop the batter into the prepared muffin cups, dividing equally.

8. Bake in preheated oven for about 25 minutes or until the tops are puffed and golden brown and a tester inserted in the center of a muffin comes out clean. Let cool in pan on a wire rack for 5 minutes, then transfer muffins to the rack to cool for at least 10 minutes before serving.

Variation

If you are baking for picky people, leave the kale out or substitute 2 cups (500 mL) lightly packed spinach, finely chopped.

Double Cornbread

This lightly sweet, tender cornbread is speckled with whole corn kernels, adding even more corn flavor. If you can find blue cornmeal, buy it for this bread. You'll love the lavender color and the way the yellow corn pops against the blue background.

MAKES 9 SERVINGS

- Preheat oven to 400°F (200°C)
- 9-inch (23 cm) square metal baking pan, greased

1 cup	blue or yellow cornmeal	250 mL
3/4 cup	unbleached all-purpose flour	175 mL
1/4 cup	granulated sugar	60 mL
1 tsp	baking powder	5 mL
1/2 tsp	salt	2 mL
2	large eggs	2
1 cup	plain yogurt	250 mL
1/4 cup	canola oil	60 mL
1 cup	cooked corn kernels (see tip)	250 mL

Tips

For the most accurate measurements when making baked goods, weigh your dry and fresh ingredients. For this recipe, you'll need 125 g cornmeal, 98 g unbleached flour, 50 g sugar and 165 g corn.

Use thawed frozen corn, canned corn (well drained) or cooled freshly cooked corn cut off the cob. If your corn is wet, pat it dry so it won't make the batter soggy.

Store the cooled cornbread, tightly covered, in the refrigerator for up to 4 days.

1. In a medium bowl, whisk together cornmeal, flour, sugar, baking powder and salt.

2. Place the eggs, yogurt and oil in the Vitamix container and secure the lid. With the switch on Variable, select speed 1 and turn the machine on. Gradually increase to speed 5 and blend for 5 seconds to mix.

3. Remove the lid and add the cornmeal mixture. Replace the lid and quickly pulse three times, just until evenly moistened. Remove the lid and add corn, stirring with a spatula just until incorporated. Spread batter in prepared pan.

4. Bake in preheated oven for 15 to 20 minutes or until the top is golden and a tester inserted in the center of the bread comes out clean. Let cool in pan on a wire rack for 5 minutes before cutting. Serve warm.

Variation

For an even more colorful bread, add 1/2 cup (125 mL) shredded Cheddar cheese and 1/2 red bell pepper, minced, with the corn kernels.

Whole Wheat Pancakes

Everybody loves these pancakes, which are light and fluffy and much more substantial than a white flour pancake. They are not sweetened at all, so they're a perfect vehicle to top with steamed vegetables and melted cheese, but they're also delicious with the usual fruit or syrup.

MAKES 12 PANCAKES

- Preheat oven to 250°F (120°C)
- Dry grinding container
- Griddle or large cast-iron skillet
- Oven-safe platter or plate

3/4 cup	soft wheat berries	175 mL
2 tsp	baking powder	10 mL
1/2 tsp	baking soda	2 mL
1/2 tsp	salt	2 mL
1	large egg	1
1 1/2 cups	buttermilk	375 mL
1 cup	large-flake (old-fashioned) rolled oats	250 mL
	Vegetable oil	

1. Place the wheat berries in the dry grinding container and secure the lid. With the switch on Variable, select speed 1 and turn the machine on. Gradually increase the speed to 10, then flip the switch to High and grind for 1 minute or until the wheat is finely ground.

2. Turn the machine off and fluff the flour with a spatula. Let cool for 10 minutes.

3. Add the baking powder, baking soda and salt to the dry grinding container and secure the lid. Pulse once to mix, then run for 3 seconds to form a well in the center.

4. Remove the lid and add the egg and buttermilk to the well in the flour, then secure the lid. With the switch on Variable, select speed 1 and turn the machine on. Gradually increase the speed to 8 and blend for about 5 seconds or until evenly moistened.

5. Turn the machine off and scrape down the sides of the container. Add the oats and replace the lid. Pulse about three times, until mixed. Let the batter stand, covered, for 5 minutes, to hydrate the flour.

6. Meanwhile, heat the griddle over medium heat for 3 to 5 minutes or until hot. Brush with a thin layer of oil.

7. Pulse the batter again to remix. Using a 1/4-cup (60 mL) measure, scoop batter onto the hot griddle, leaving at least 1 inch (2.5 cm) between pancakes. Cook for about 2 minutes or until the edges are browned and the top is evenly bubbled. Flip pancakes over and cook for about 1 minute or until browned. Transfer to platter and keep warm in preheated oven.

8. Repeat with the remaining batter, stirring the batter before each batch of pancakes so that the oats are evenly distributed, and oiling the pan and adjusting the heat as necessary to prevent burning. Serve hot.

Variations

Substitute 1 cup + 2 tbsp (280 mL) whole wheat pastry flour for the wheat berries and skip step 1.

For sweetened pancakes, add 2 tbsp (30 mL) granulated sugar and 1 tsp (5 mL) ground cinnamon with the baking powder.

Tips

For the most accurate measurements when making baked goods, weigh your dry ingredients. For this recipe, you'll need 150 g soft wheat berries.

The dry grinding container makes quick work of grinding the wheat berries, but if you don't have one, the regular container will work just fine.

Let the griddle or skillet fully preheat before oiling it and adding the first portion of batter to the pan. Your first pancake will be as good as your last.

Savory Spinach Waffles with Cheddar

Savory takes on traditionally sweet foods are always a good break from all the sweetness, especially at breakfast. These Cheddar-laced, spinach-dappled waffles are equally at home under an over-easy, runny-yolked egg or with sautéed apples and a drizzle of maple syrup.

MAKES ABOUT 12 WAFFLES

- **Preheat oven to 250°F (120°C)**
- **Dry grinding container (see tip)**
- **Waffle iron**
- **Wire rack set over a large baking sheet**

1¼ cups	hard wheat berries	300 mL
¼ cup	unbleached all-purpose flour	60 mL
2 tsp	baking powder	10 mL
1 tsp	salt	5 mL
2	large eggs	2
2 cups	milk	500 mL
½ cup	butter, melted	125 mL
1 cup	lightly packed fresh spinach, chopped	250 mL
4 oz	Cheddar cheese, shredded	125 g
	Vegetable oil	

Tips

For the most accurate measurements when making baked goods, weigh your dry ingredients. For this recipe, you'll need 240 g wheat berries and 28 g unbleached flour.

The dry grinding container makes quick work of grinding the wheat berries, but if you don't have one, the regular container will work just fine.

Save leftovers for waffle sandwiches and fill them with sliced cheese, meats and vegetables before baking or microwaving to melt the cheese.

1. Place the wheat berries in the dry grinding container and secure the lid. With the switch on Variable, select speed 1 and turn the machine on. Gradually increase the speed to 10, then flip the switch to High and grind for 1 minute or until finely ground.

2. Turn the machine off and fluff the flour with a spatula. Let cool for 10 minutes.

3. Add the unbleached flour, baking powder and salt to the dry grinding container and secure the lid. With the switch on Variable, select speed 10 and turn the machine on. Blend for 3 seconds to mix and form a well in the center of the flour.

4. Turn the machine off and add the eggs, milk and butter. Replace the lid, select speed 5 and quickly pulse three times to mix. Remove the lid and use a spatula to scrape down the sides of the container. Replace the lid and pulse once.

5. Scrape the batter into a large bowl and stir in spinach and cheese.

6. Preheat the waffle iron. Place the baking sheet with rack in the oven.

7. Brush or spray waffle iron with oil. Scoop about ½ cup (125 mL) batter (or according to the waffle manufacturer's directions) into the center of the waffle iron, then quickly spread the batter and close the lid. Cook according to manufacturer's directions until crisp and browned. Transfer to the rack in the oven to keep warm. Repeat with the remaining batter, oiling the waffle iron as necessary between batches.

Variation

For an herbed version, replace the spinach with 2 tbsp (30 mL) chopped fresh parsley and 1 tbsp (15 mL) chopped fresh thyme or rosemary. Serve with a cream sauce.

DESSERTS

Chocolate Bundt Cake

If you think all cakes involve lots of whipping and folding and other complex techniques, try this recipe. Your Vitamix makes quick work of blending the batter; just be careful not to overmix.

~~~~~~

MAKES 8 SERVINGS

- **Preheat oven to 350°F (180°C)**
- **10-inch (25 cm) Bundt pan, greased**

2 cups	unbleached all-purpose flour	500 mL
3/4 cup	unsweetened cocoa powder	175 mL
2 tsp	baking powder	10 mL
1 tsp	baking soda	5 mL
1/2 tsp	salt	2 mL
2	large eggs, at room temperature	2
1 cup	plain Greek yogurt	250 mL
1/2 cup	canola oil	125 mL
1 tsp	vanilla extract	5 mL
1 cup	granulated sugar	250 mL
1/2 cup	packed light brown sugar	125 mL
3/4 cup	hot water	175 mL
	Blender Chocolate Glaze (page 172)	

1. In a large bowl, whisk together flour, cocoa, baking powder, baking soda and salt. Set aside.

2. Place the eggs, yogurt, oil, vanilla, granulated sugar and brown sugar in the Vitamix container and secure the lid. With the switch on Variable, select speed 1 and turn the machine on. Gradually increase the speed to 10 and blend for about 20 seconds or until well blended.

3. Turn the machine off and pour in the hot water. Replace the lid and blend on speed 10 for 10 seconds.

4. Turn the machine off and add the flour mixture. Replace the lid and pulse three times. Turn the machine off and use a spatula to scrape the sides of the container. If any flour mixture is not mixed in, replace the lid and pulse two or three more times.

5. Scrape the batter into the prepared pan and smooth the top. Tap the pan on the counter to release any air bubbles.

6. Bake in preheated oven for 40 to 60 minutes or until the top is springy when pressed and has some cracks running across it and a tester inserted in the center comes out clean. Let cool in pan on a wire rack set over parchment paper for 10 minutes, then invert onto the rack to cool completely.

7. Pour the glaze over the cake, letting excess drip onto the parchment paper below. (Or transfer it to a cake plate and drizzle with glaze, letting it flow into deep puddles around and in the center of the cake.)

Variations

Chocolate Chip Bundt Cake: Stir in 3/4 cup (175 mL) mini chocolate chips after mixing in the flour mixture.

Mocha Bundt Cake: Use hot coffee in place of the hot water.

Instead of glazing the cake, you can let it cool, then dust it with powdered (icing) sugar just before serving.

Tips

For the most accurate measurements when making baked goods, weigh your dry ingredients. For this recipe, you'll need 230 g unbleached flour, 60 g cocoa, 200 g granulated sugar and 106 g brown sugar.

For the hot water, pour 3/4 cup (175 mL) boiling water into a heat-safe measuring cup and let it cool for a few seconds.

Apple Pecan Sheet Cake

This moist, lightly spicy apple cake is studded with pecans, for nutty goodness in every bite. Serve it for dessert, after-school snacks or brunch, with warm cider on the side, and enjoy all the flavors of fall in an easy-to-make cake.

MAKES 12 SERVINGS

- **Preheat oven to 350°F (180°C)**
- **13- by 9- inch (33 cm by 23 cm) metal baking pan, greased**

1¹/₂ cups	unbleached all-purpose flour	375 mL
³/₄ cup	whole wheat pastry flour	175 mL
1¹/₂ tsp	ground cinnamon	7 mL
³/₄ tsp	baking powder	3 mL
³/₄ tsp	baking soda	3 mL
¹/₂ tsp	salt	2 mL
¹/₄ tsp	ground nutmeg	1 mL
3	large eggs, at room temperature	3
³/₄ cup	canola oil	175 mL
2 tsp	vanilla extract	10 mL
1¹/₂ cups	packed light brown sugar	375 mL
2	large apples, diced	2
1¹/₂ cups	pecans, chopped	375 mL

Tips

For the most accurate measurements when making baked goods, weigh your dry ingredients. For this recipe, you'll need 175 g unbleached flour, 97 g whole wheat pastry flour, 330 g brown sugar and 200 g pecans.

Use firm baking apples for this. Granny Smith, Braeburn, Gala, Fuji and Golden Delicious are a few great options.

If you don't need a big cake, you can freeze half of this one, tightly wrapped, for up to 2 months. You'll be glad you did.

1. In a large bowl, whisk together unbleached flour, pastry flour, cinnamon, baking powder, baking soda, salt and nutmeg. Set aside.

2. Place the eggs, oil, vanilla and brown sugar in the Vitamix container and secure the lid. With the switch on Variable, select speed 1 and turn the machine on. Gradually increase the speed to 5 and blend for 3 to 4 seconds, just until the ingredients are blended.

3. Pour the egg mixture over the flour mixture and stir until almost moistened. Fold in apples and pecans just until incorporated.

4. Scrape the batter into the prepared pan and smooth the top.

5. Bake in preheated oven for about 40 minutes or until the top is golden brown and a tester inserted in the center of the cake comes out clean. Let cool completely in pan on a wire rack.

Variation

If you are not a nut lover, substitute 1 cup (250 mL) dried currants or cranberries for the pecans.

Blood Orange and Olive Oil Cake

Olive oil cake is a moist, lush dessert that lets you appreciate the flavor of olive oil in a sweet treat, which may surprise you. Pick a fruitier olive oil, to pair with the tart and sweet blood oranges, and celebrate the flavors of Spain.

MAKES 8 TO 10 SERVINGS

- **Preheat oven to 350°F (180°C)**
- **9-inch (23 cm) round metal cake pan, greased and floured**

2 cups	unbleached all-purpose flour	500 mL
1 1/2 cups	granulated sugar	375 mL
1 tsp	salt	5 mL
1/2 tsp	baking soda	2 mL
1/2 tsp	baking powder	2 mL
4	large eggs, at room temperature	4
1 cup	milk	250 mL
1 cup	extra virgin olive oil	250 mL
1 1/2 tbsp	grated blood orange zest	22 mL
1/2 cup	freshly squeezed blood orange juice	125 mL
	Powdered sugar (see page 13) and/or berries	

Tips

For the most accurate measurements when making baked goods, weigh your dry ingredients. For this recipe, you'll need 230 g unbleached flour and 300 g granulated sugar.

Always be alert for olive oil fraud. Look for bottles with a single place of origin, preferably a specific farm, not bulk mixes of oils from all over. Organic oils are better regulated and give you better odds that they are really extra virgin oil and not adulterated.

1. In a large bowl, whisk together flour, granulated sugar, salt, baking soda and baking powder. Set aside.

2. Place the eggs, milk, oil and orange juice in the Vitamix container and secure the lid. With the switch on Variable, select speed 1 and turn the machine on. Gradually increase the speed to 5 and blend for 15 to 20 seconds, just until the ingredients are blended.

3. Turn the machine off and add the orange zest. Replace the lid and pulse twice to mix.

4. Pour the egg mixture over the flour mixture and whisk gently to combine. Do not overmix.

5. Scrape the batter into the prepared pan and smooth the top.

6. Bake in preheated oven for about 70 minutes or until the cake is deep golden brown and puffed in the center and a tester inserted in the center comes out clean. Let cool in pan on a wire rack and serve warm or at room temperature.

7. Just before serving, sift powdered sugar over the cake, if desired, and/or serve with berries.

Variation

Other oranges, from standard navels to Cara Cara or even mandarins, make good substitutions for blood oranges; just add a squeeze of lemon juice to make up for the lack of acidity in sweeter oranges.

Zucchini Spice Cake

This cake is small enough to make for a family of two, and quick enough to blend and bake for an after-school snack. The Vitamix does a lightning-speed dice of the zucchini, so you can skip the time you would have spent grating it for other zucchini cake recipes.

MAKES 6 SERVINGS

- **Preheat oven to 350°F (180°C)**
- **9-inch (23 cm) round metal cake pan, greased**

1/2 cup	whole wheat pastry flour	125 mL
1/2 cup	unbleached all-purpose flour	125 mL
1/2 tsp	baking powder	2 mL
1/2 tsp	baking soda	2 mL
1/2 tsp	salt	2 mL
1/2 tsp	ground cinnamon	2 mL
1/2 tsp	ground cloves	2 mL
1/4 tsp	ground nutmeg	1 mL
1/4 cup	raw walnut halves	60 mL
6 tbsp	packed light brown sugar, divided	90 mL
1	small zucchini, trimmed and quartered	1
1	large egg, at room temperature	1
1/2 cup	buttermilk	125 mL
1/4 cup	canola oil	60 mL
1/2 tsp	vanilla extract	2 mL

Tips

For the most accurate measurements when making baked goods, weigh your dry and fresh ingredients. For this recipe, you'll need 65 g whole wheat pastry flour, 57 g unbleached flour, 28 g walnuts, 78 g brown sugar and 196 g zucchini.

To improvise some buttermilk, place 1 1/2 tsp (7 mL) apple cider vinegar in a liquid measuring cup and add milk to make 1/2 cup (125 mL). Let stand for 5 minutes, then use as directed.

The cooled cake can be stored, tightly covered, at room temperature for up to 4 days.

1. In a large bowl, whisk together pastry flour, unbleached flour, baking powder, baking soda, salt, cinnamon, cloves and nutmeg. Set aside.

2. Secure the lid of the Vitamix container and remove the lid plug. With the switch on Variable, select speed 3. Drop the walnuts and 2 tbsp (30 mL) brown sugar through the lid opening and pulse three times, just until the walnuts are coarsely chopped. Transfer the nut mixture to a small bowl.

3. Replace the lid on the container. Drop the zucchini quarters, one at a time, through the lid opening and pulse several times to chop the zucchini into small pieces. Scrape the zucchini into a medium bowl.

4. Place the egg, buttermilk, oil, vanilla and the remaining brown sugar in the container and secure the lid. Select speed 1 and turn the machine on. Gradually increase the speed to 10 and process for about 15 seconds or until well blended.

5. Pour the egg mixture over the flour mixture and stir until almost moistened. Fold in zucchini just until incorporated.

6. Scrape the batter into the prepared pan and sprinkle with the walnut mixture.

7. Bake in preheated oven for 20 minutes or until the top is golden brown and a tester inserted into the center of the cake comes out clean. Let cool in pan on a wire rack for at least 10 minutes before cutting.

Variation

Use yellow summer squash in place of zucchini for a sunny yellow-speckled cake.

Vegan White Cupcakes

Nobody needs to know that these light and tasty little cakes are vegan, except the vegans at the party.

∽ ∽

MAKES 12 CUPCAKES

- Preheat oven to 350°F (180°C)
- 12-cup muffin pan, greased or lined with silicone or paper liners

1³/₄ cups	unbleached all-purpose flour	425 mL
1 cup	granulated sugar	250 mL
1 tsp	baking soda	5 mL
¹/₂ tsp	salt	2 mL
1 cup	unsweetened almond milk	250 mL
1 tbsp	apple cider vinegar	15 mL
6 tbsp	canola oil	90 mL
1 tsp	vanilla extract	5 mL
	Powdered sugar (see page 13) or Blender Chocolate Glaze (page 172)	

Tips

For the most accurate measurements when making baked goods, weigh your dry ingredients. For this recipe, you'll need 203 g unbleached flour and 200 g granulated sugar.

Use organic sugar, which is required to be processed without the use of animal products.

It's better to mix that last bit of flour into the batter by hand than to overblend the batter. The speed of the Vitamix can encourage gluten to form and make the cupcakes tough.

1. In a medium bowl, whisk together flour, granulated sugar, baking soda and salt. Set aside.

2. Place the almond milk and vinegar in the Vitamix container and let stand for 2 minutes to curdle. Add the oil and vanilla. Secure the lid. With the switch on Variable, select speed 1 and turn the machine on. Gradually increase the speed to 5 and blend for 3 to 4 seconds, just until the ingredients are blended.

3. Turn the machine off and add the flour mixture. Replace the lid and pulse twice. Remove the lid and stir with a spatula to incorporate any unmixed flour mixture.

4. Pour the batter into the prepared muffin cups, dividing equally.

5. Bake in preheated oven for about 25 minutes or until the tops are lightly golden and a tester inserted in the center of a cupcake comes out clean. Let cool in pan on a wire rack for 5 minutes, then carefully transfer cupcakes to the rack to cool completely.

6. Just before serving, dust with powdered sugar or drizzle with glaze.

Variation

Vegan Chocolate Cupcakes: Replace ¹/₂ cup (125 mL) of the flour with unsweetened cocoa powder.

Pear and Lemon Cupcakes

These little cakes are studded with chunks of sweet pear and balanced with a touch of tangy lemon. They are so tender and delicious that you may not even need a topping, but go ahead and try the lemon glaze for an extra burst of lemony goodness.

MAKES 12 CUPCAKES

- **Preheat oven to 325°F (160°C)**
- **12-cup muffin pan, greased or lined with silicone or paper liners**

1 cup	cake flour	250 mL
1/2 cup	unbleached all-purpose flour	125 mL
2 tsp	grated lemon zest	10 mL
2 tsp	baking powder	10 mL
1/2 tsp	salt	2 mL
2	large eggs, at room temperature	2
1/2 cup	plain yogurt	125 mL
1/2 cup	unsalted butter, softened	125 mL
1/2 tsp	vanilla extract	2 mL
1 cup	granulated sugar	250 mL
1	large pear, peeled and chopped	1

GLAZE

1 cup	powdered sugar (see page 13)	250 mL
2 tbsp	freshly squeezed lemon juice (approx.)	30 mL
1/2 tsp	vanilla extract	2 mL

Tips

For the most accurate measurements when making baked goods, weigh your dry ingredients. For this recipe, you'll need 137 g cake flour, 57 g unbleached flour, 200 g granulated sugar and 120 g powdered sugar.

Cake flour gives cakes and pastries a delicate, tender texture because it is very low in gluten.

1. In a large bowl, whisk together cake flour, unbleached flour, lemon zest, baking powder and salt. Set aside.

2. Place the eggs, yogurt, butter, vanilla and sugar in the Vitamix container and secure the lid. With the switch on Variable, select speed 1 and turn the machine on. Gradually increase the speed to 7 and blend for about 30 seconds or until smooth.

3. Pour the egg mixture over the flour mixture and stir until almost moistened. Gently fold in pear just until incorporated.

4. Scoop the batter into the prepared muffin cups, dividing equally.

5. Bake in preheated oven for 27 to 30 minutes or until a tester inserted in the center of a cupcake comes out clean. Let cool in pan on a wire rack for 10 minutes, then carefully transfer cupcakes to the rack to cool completely.

6. *Glaze:* Place powdered sugar in a medium bowl and whisk in lemon juice and vanilla. If the mixture is too stiff to pour, stir in more lemon juice, 1 tsp (5 mL) at a time, to make a thick glaze.

7. When the cupcakes are completely cooled, drizzle glaze on top and let dry.

Variation

Other fruit that isn't too juicy (such as an apple) or whole berries (such as blueberries) are wonderful in these cupcakes in place of the pear.

Gluten-Free Brownies

These brownies are every bit as rich and fudgy as the wheat-based ones you love. They make use of the pulp leftover from making homemade almond milk, so you won't waste all that fiber and nutrition. Almond flour is a sweet, mild alternative flour, and is more digestible than some of the bean and grain flours you may have tried.

∽∾ ∽∾

MAKES 9 BROWNIES

- **Preheat oven to 350°F (180°C)**
- **8-inch (20 cm) square metal baking pan**

³/₄ cup	homemade almond flour (see tip)	175 mL
¹/₄ cup	arrowroot starch	60 mL
¹/₂ tsp	salt	2 mL
¹/₄ tsp	baking soda	1 mL
5 oz	semisweet chocolate, broken into chunks	150 g
¹/₂ cup	unsalted butter or coconut oil	125 mL
1 cup	packed light brown sugar	250 mL
1 tbsp	gluten-free vanilla extract	15 mL
2	large eggs	2
¹/₂ cup	chopped nuts or chocolate chips (optional)	125 mL
	Powdered sugar (see page 13) or frosting	

Tips

For the most accurate measurements when making baked goods, weigh your dry ingredients. For this recipe, you'll need 42 g almond flour, 26 g arrowroot starch, 220 g brown sugar and 85 g chocolate chips.

To make your own almond flour, save the pulp from making fresh almond milk and dry it in the oven. If you don't have time to dry it right away, you can freeze it and dehydrate it later. See page 212 for more details.

For neat slices, refrigerate the brownies in the pan before cutting.

1. Line the baking pan with foil or parchment paper, with overhanging handles at each end, then oil the bottom.

2. Place the almond flour, arrowroot, salt and baking soda in the Vitamix container. Secure the lid, remove the lid plug and insert the tamper. With the switch on Variable, select speed 1 and turn the machine on. Gradually increase the speed to 10, using the tamper to push down the flour as it flies up and sticks to the sides, and blend for 3 to 4 seconds.

3. In a small saucepan over low heat, or in the microwave on Medium-High (70%) power, melt chocolate and butter, stirring until smooth. Remove from heat and stir in brown sugar and vanilla.

4. Scrape the chocolate mixture into the Vitamix and add the eggs. Secure the lid, select speed 1 and turn the machine on. Gradually increase the speed to 10, then flip the switch to High. Turn the machine off and use a spatula to scrape down the sides of the container. Replace the lid and pulse three or four times, until the mixture is smooth and well mixed. Scrape into the prepared pan and sprinkle with nuts or chocolate chips (if using).

5. Bake in preheated oven for 32 to 35 minutes or until dry-looking and cracking on top and a tester inserted in the center comes out clean. Let cool completely in pan on a wire rack. Use the overhanging handles to lift brownies from pan, then peel foil or paper off.

6. Just before serving, sift powdered sugar on top or spread frosting over the brownies. Cut into 9 large squares.

Pecan and Beet Burgers (page 122)

Millet Demi-Loaf and Millet Round (page 136)

Pear and Lemon Cupcakes (page 159)

Mixed Berry Tart in a Hazelnut Crust (page 164)

Pistachio Gelato (page 177),
Chocolate Ice Cream (page 174) and
Cherry Vanilla Ice Cream (page 175)

Matcha Almond Butter Energy Bars (page 193)
and Mango Coconut Energy Balls (page 198)

Apple Oat Porridge (page 202), Leafy Greens (Spinach; page 200)
and Root Veggies (Carrots; page 201)

Horchata (page 222)

Vegan Chocolate Cashew Pie

Don't think this pie is just for vegans. It is creamy and rich with chocolate flavor, and you will be amazed by how well dates disappear into the fudgy crust. It is also very filling — it only takes a small slice to satisfy your dessert craving. Serve topped with chocolate sauce or berries.

MAKES 12 SERVINGS

- 9-inch (23 cm) round metal cake pan, lightly oiled

CRUST

2 tbsp	pure maple syrup	30 mL
1 to 2 tbsp	unsweetened apple juice	15 to 30 mL
8	Medjool dates, pitted	8
1/2 cup	raw pecan halves	125 mL
1/4 cup	raw walnut halves	60 mL
3 tbsp	unsweetened cocoa powder	45 mL
	Vegetable oil	

FILLING

1 1/2 cups	raw cashews, soaked (see tip)	375 mL
1/2 cup	agave nectar	125 mL
1/4 cup	melted coconut oil	60 mL
1/4 cup	unsweetened apple juice	60 mL
1 tsp	vanilla extract	5 mL
1/2 cup	unsweetened cocoa powder	125 mL
Pinch	salt	Pinch

Tips

For the most accurate measurements, weigh your dry ingredients. For this recipe, you'll need 50 g dates, 68 g pecans, 28 g walnuts, 15 g cocoa for the crust, 165 g cashews and 40 g cocoa for the filling.

Buy dates at a natural foods store, where they will be fresh and moist, not old and dried out.

To soak cashews, place them in a bowl and add enough water to cover by at least 1 inch (2.5 cm). Cover and let soak at room temperature for at least 6 hours or preferably overnight.

1. *Crust:* Place the maple syrup, apple juice, dates, pecans, walnuts and cocoa in the Vitamix container. Secure the lid, remove the lid plug and insert the tamper. With the switch on Variable, select speed 1 and turn the machine on. Using the tamper to push the ingredients into the blades, gradually increase the speed to 5 and blend for about 15 seconds or until smooth.

2. Scrape the crust mixture into the prepared pan. With lightly oiled hands, pat it evenly into the bottom of the pan. Freeze while you prepare the filling. Wash and dry the Vitamix container.

3. *Filling:* Drain the cashews and place in the container. Add the agave nectar, coconut oil, apple juice, vanilla, cocoa and salt. Secure the lid, remove the lid plug and insert the tamper. With the switch on Variable, select speed 1 and turn the machine on. Using the tamper to push the ingredients into the blades, gradually increase the speed to 5 and blend for about 15 seconds or until almost smooth. Flip the switch to High and blend for 15 seconds.

4. Pour the cashew mixture over the crust and smooth the top. Freeze for about 2 hours, until completely solid, or tightly wrapped for up to 1 week.

5. To serve, slice while frozen, then let stand in the refrigerator for 1 hour or on the countertop for 30 minutes.

Variation

You can play around with using other nuts in the crust, such as skinned roasted hazelnuts, if you are not concerned about the pie being fully raw.

Peanut Butter Pie

Peanut butter is one of the most beloved foods, in desserts as well as in sandwiches. Using your Vitamix to grind fresh peanut butter and then making it into a pie gives you even more peanutty flavor.

MAKES 8 SERVINGS

2 cups	unsalted roasted peanuts	500 mL
3/4 cup	pure maple syrup	175 mL
2 tsp	vanilla extract	10 mL
1 tsp	freshly squeezed lemon juice	5 mL
14 oz	firm tofu, drained and crumbled	400 g
6 tbsp	unsweetened soy milk	90 mL
1/4 cup	arrowroot starch or cornstarch	60 mL
1/8 tsp	salt	0.5 mL
1	9-inch (23 cm) graham cracker crumb pie crust	1
1/2 cup	chocolate chips	125 mL

1. Place the peanuts in the Vitamix container. Secure the lid, remove the lid plug and insert the tamper. With the switch on Variable, select speed 1 and turn the machine on. Gradually increase the speed to 10, then flip the switch to High and, using the tamper to push the peanuts into the blades, grind for about 1 minute or until the sound of the machine changes and it starts to labor.

2. Turn the machine off and taste the peanut butter. If it is not smooth, replace the lid and tamper. With the switch on Variable, select speed 1 and turn the machine on. Gradually increase the speed to 10 and blend until smooth. Scrape the peanut butter into a bowl (don't worry if you leave a little behind in the container) and set aside.

3. Place the maple syrup, vanilla, lemon juice and tofu in the container. Replace the lid and tamper. Select speed 1 and turn the machine on. Using the tamper to push the ingredients into the blades, gradually increase the speed to 5. Once the mixture

starts to flow, increase the speed to 10 and blend for about 20 seconds or until well puréed.

4. Turn the machine off and use a spatula to scrape down the sides of the container. If the mixture is not creamy, continue blending on speed 10 until creamy.

5. In a small saucepan, whisk together soy milk and arrowroot. Bring to a boil over medium heat, whisking constantly. Boil for about 1 minute or until very thick. Remove from heat.

6. Remove the lid of the Vitamix container and quickly scrape the hot soy milk mixture into the tofu mixture. Replace the lid, select speed 1 and turn the machine on. Quickly increase the speed to 10 and blend until incorporated.

7. Remove the lid and add the reserved peanut butter and salt. Replace the lid and blend on speed 10 until smooth.

8. Scrape the tofu mixture into the pie crust and smooth the top. Sprinkle with chocolate chips. Refrigerate for at least 3 hours, until chilled and firm, or tightly wrapped for up to 1 week. Slice and serve while cold.

Tips

For the most accurate measurements, weigh your dry ingredients. For this recipe, you'll need 260 g peanuts, 22 g arrowroot and 85 g chocolate chips.

Use a firm, water-packed tofu coagulated with nigari for a good texture. Silken tofu has a higher water content and would make a runny filling.

No-Bake Pumpkin Cream Cheese Pie

Baked pumpkin pies, with their labor-intensive crusts and dense, spicy filling, take time to make. This quick and easy pie may well become your favorite, with its light, fluffy filling cradled in a sweet and crunchy graham crust. The flavor of pumpkin shines through, with cream cheese and whipped cream holding it aloft. In this recipe, you can use a purchased pie crust as I did, or make your favorite recipe for a graham crust and prebake it.

MAKES 8 SERVINGS

1	can (14 oz/398 mL) pumpkin purée (not pie filling)	1
8 oz	brick-style cream cheese, softened	250 g
1 cup	packed light brown sugar	250 mL
2 tsp	pumpkin pie spice	10 mL
Pinch	salt	Pinch
1/4 cup	unsweetened apple juice	60 mL
1 tbsp	unflavored gelatin powder	15 mL
1 cup	heavy or whipping (35%) cream	250 mL
1	9-inch (23 cm) graham cracker crumb pie crust	1
	Sweetened whipped cream (optional)	

1. Place the pumpkin, cream cheese, sugar, pumpkin pie spice and salt in the Vitamix container. Secure the lid, remove the lid plug and insert the tamper. With the switch on Variable, select speed 1 and turn the machine on. Gradually increase the speed to 10, then flip the switch to High and blend, using the tamper to push the ingredients into the blades, for about 30 seconds or until smooth.

2. Turn the machine off and use a spatula to scrape down the sides of the container. Replace the lid and blend on High for 10 seconds. Scrape the pumpkin mixture into a large bowl. Wash and dry the container.

3. Pour apple juice into a small saucepan and sprinkle gelatin on the surface. Let stand for 5 minutes to soften the gelatin. Place over low heat and whisk until the gelatin melts. Remove from heat and let cool slightly (see tip).

4. Place the cream in the Vitamix container. Secure the lid and remove the lid plug. With the switch on Variable, select speed 1 and turn the machine on. Drizzle the apple juice mixture through the lid opening and blend until incorporated. Gradually increase the speed to 10 and blend for 10 seconds. Turn the machine off and use a spatula to scrape down the sides of the container. Blend for 10 seconds, then scrape, repeating up to three times, just until the cream becomes fluffy. Do not overmix.

5. Scrape the cream mixture into the pumpkin mixture and gently fold the cream into the pumpkin, being careful not to deflate the cream.

6. Scrape the mixture into the pie crust and smooth the top. Refrigerate for at least 8 hours, until set, or tightly wrapped for up to 4 days. Slice and serve while cold. Serve topped with sweetened whipped cream, if desired.

Variation

In place of the graham cracker crust, try a gingersnap crust or even a baked and cooled pastry crust.

Tips

For the most accurate measurements, weigh your dry ingredients. For this recipe, you'll need 220 g brown sugar and 7 g gelatin.

If you can find only larger cans of pumpkin purée, measure out 1 3/4 cups (425 mL) and reserve the remainder for another use.

Do not let the melted gelatin mixture cool for more than a minute. If it starts to set, it will form lumps in the pie.

Mixed Berry Tart in a Hazelnut Crust

Here, a buttery tart crust, speckled with bits of hazelnuts, is topped with creamy filling and adorned with colorful berries. It's a classic summertime dessert, made easier and faster by the Vitamix.

∽∽∽∽∽∽∽∽∽∽∽∽∽∽∽∽∽∽∽∽∽∽∽∽∽∽∽∽∽∽

MAKES 8 SERVINGS

- **11-inch (28 cm) round tart pan with removable bottom, greased and floured**
- **Pastry brush**

1/2 cup	hazelnuts, toasted and skinned (see tip)	125 mL
1/2 cup	cold unsalted butter, cubed	125 mL
1 cup	unbleached all-purpose flour	250 mL
2 tbsp	granulated sugar	30 mL
1/2 tsp	salt	2 mL
1 tbsp	freshly squeezed lemon juice	15 mL
1 tsp	vanilla extract	5 mL
8 oz	brick-style cream cheese, softened and cubed	250 g
3/4 cup	powdered sugar (see page 13)	175 mL
4 oz	strawberries, cut in half lengthwise	125 g
1 cup	raspberries	250 mL
1 cup	blueberries	250 mL
2 tbsp	smooth apricot jam (see tip)	30 mL
1 tbsp	hot water	15 mL

1. Place the hazelnuts in the Vitamix container and secure the lid. With the switch on Variable, select speed 1 and turn the machine on. Quickly increase the speed to 10 and blend for about 5 seconds or until the nuts are finely ground to a powder.

2. Turn the machine off and use a spatula to scrape out the corners of the container. If any chunks of nuts remain, replace the lid and pulse until finely ground. Transfer to a small bowl and set aside.

3. Place the butter, flour, granulated sugar and salt in the container and secure the lid. Select speed 1, turn the machine on and blend for 5 seconds. Turn the machine off and scrape down the sides of the container. Replace the lid and blend for 5 seconds. Continue scraping and blending for 5 seconds at a time until the mixture is creamy and well blended.

4. Turn the machine off and add the ground hazelnuts. Replace the lid and pulse three times, until the nuts are incorporated. Scrape the dough out into a bowl and, if necessary, stir in any clumps of nuts by hand.

5. Place the dough in the prepared pan. Using floured fingers, pat the dough out to the edges of the pan and make a 1/2-inch (1 cm) high rim up the sides of the pan. Refrigerate for 30 minutes.

Tips

For the most accurate measurements, weigh your dry and fresh ingredients. For this recipe, you'll need 60 g hazelnuts, 115 g unbleached flour, 90 g powdered sugar, 125 g raspberries and 74 g blueberries.

To toast and skin hazelnuts, spread the hazelnuts on a rimmed baking sheet and roast in a 350°F (180°C) oven for 10 minutes or until fragrant and toasted. Immediately transfer to a folded kitchen towel, rub the skins from the nuts and let them cool. If some of the hazelnuts stubbornly refuse to give up their skins, return them to the baking sheet and roast for another 5 to 10 minutes, then try again.

Be sure to thoroughly pat berries dry after washing them, to make sure they don't add liquid to the tart.

If your apricot jam has chunks, strain it through a sieve to remove them, then measure the smooth jam; reserve the pieces of fruit for another use.

6. Meanwhile, preheat oven to 350°F (180°C).

7. Bake the pastry shell for 15 to 20 minutes or until lightly browned and firm. Let cool completely in pan on a wire rack. Meanwhile, wash and dry the Vitamix container.

8. Place the lemon juice, vanilla, cream cheese and powdered sugar in the container. Secure the lid, remove the lid plug and insert the tamper. With the switch on Variable, select speed 1 and turn the machine on. Using the tamper to press the ingredients into the blades, gradually increase the speed to 4 and blend for about 10 seconds or until well mixed and creamy.

9. Spread the filling in the cooled tart shell and arrange strawberries, raspberries and blueberries on top.

10. In a cup or small bowl, stir apricot jam with hot water until blended. Using a pastry brush, paint apricot glaze on the fruit and filling. Refrigerate for at least 2 hours, until chilled, or tightly wrapped for up to 3 days. Slice and serve while cold.

Variation

When fresh peaches and apricots are in season, use a sliced peach or 2 sliced apricots to replace the strawberries.

Chocolate Chèvre Pie with Raspberries

This intense, decadent pie has a slight tanginess from the creamy goat cheese and Greek yogurt, and three levels of chocolate in the crust, filling and topping. Fresh raspberries make it gorgeous and add a refreshing juiciness to the chocolate revelry.

MAKES 12 SERVINGS

- Preheat oven to 350°F (180°C)
- 11-inch (28 cm) round tart pan with removable bottom, greased

12 oz	chocolate cream sandwich cookies (23 cookies)	375 g
2 tbsp	melted unsalted butter	30 mL
1/4 cup	plain Greek yogurt	60 mL
1 tsp	vanilla extract	5 mL
12 oz	soft goat cheese (chèvre), at room temperature	375 g
1/2 cup	packed light brown sugar	125 mL
1/2 cup	unsweetened cocoa powder	125 mL
2 cups	raspberries	500 mL
1 oz	semisweet chocolate, melted (see tip)	30 g

Tips

For the most accurate measurements, weigh your dry and fresh ingredients. For this recipe, you'll need 100 g brown sugar, 40 g cocoa and 250 g raspberries.

Melt chocolate in a glass bowl in the microwave on Medium-High (70%) power, or in the top of a double boiler over hot, not boiling water.

Don't try to grind the cookies all at once; adding them one at a time will make nice, even crumbs.

1. Secure the lid of the Vitamix container and remove the lid plug. With the switch on Variable, select speed 4 and turn the machine on. Drop half the cookies, one at a time, through the lid opening, blending to make coarse crumbs. Dump the crumbs into a large bowl and repeat with the remaining cookies.

2. Drizzle butter over crumbs and stir until evenly combined. Press evenly into the prepared pan.

3. Bake in preheated oven for 8 to 10 minutes or until firm to the touch. Let cool completely in pan on a wire rack. Meanwhile, wash the Vitamix container and dry it well.

4. Add the yogurt, vanilla, goat cheese, brown sugar and cocoa to the container and secure the lid. With the switch on Variable, select speed 1 and turn the machine on. Using the tamper to push the ingredients into the blades, gradually increase the speed to 5 and blend for 10 to 15 seconds or until combined.

5. Turn the machine off and use a spatula to scrape down the sides of the container. Replace the lid and blend for 3 to 4 seconds or until the mixture is smooth and well combined.

6. Spread the filling in the cooled tart shell. Arrange berries on filling in a pretty pattern. Drizzle chocolate in a spiral over the berries. Refrigerate for at least 2 hours, until chilled, or tightly wrapped for up to 3 days. Slice and serve while cold.

Variation

Other fruits, such as strawberries, blackberries or even cubed ripe mango, can stand in for the raspberries.

Gluten-Free Crêpes

Use up that almond pulp from your homemade almond milk in a most delicious way. This recipe uses the fresh pulp, still moist from being kneaded in your nut milk bag, so you don't have to dry the pulp in the oven. Serve these crêpes stuffed with soft cheese and fruit, or folded and sprinkled with sugar.

MAKES 6 CRÊPES

- **12-inch (30 cm) nonstick crêpe pan or skillet**
- **Pastry brush**

2	large eggs	2
3/4 cup	Almond Milk (page 212)	175 mL
1/2 cup	almond pulp	125 mL
1/2 tsp	vanilla extract	2 mL
6 tbsp	potato starch	90 mL
1 tsp	granulated sugar	5 mL
1/4 tsp	salt	1 mL
1 tbsp	melted coconut oil or unsalted butter	15 mL
	Canola oil	

Tips

For the most accurate measurements, weigh your dry ingredients. For this recipe, you'll need 148 g almond pulp and 42 g potato starch.

When you make almond milk, save your leftover almond pulp in the freezer. Let it thaw in the refrigerator overnight to make these crêpes.

1. Place the eggs, almond milk, almond pulp, vanilla, potato starch, sugar and salt in the Vitamix container and secure the lid. With the switch on Variable, select speed 1 and turn the machine on. Gradually increase the speed to 5 and blend for 3 to 4 seconds.

2. Turn the machine off and add the coconut oil. Replace the lid and blend for 3 to 4 seconds, until incorporated. Let the batter stand, covered, for 15 minutes to hydrate.

3. Heat the crêpe pan over low heat for about 5 minutes. Using the pastry brush, brush a thin coat of oil over the pan and increase the heat to medium.

4. Blend the crêpe batter by pulsing once. Using a 1/3-cup (75 mL) measure, pour batter onto the hot pan and swirl to coat the bottom of the pan evenly. Cook for about 2 minutes or until the bottom of the crêpe is golden brown and the top is bubbled and firm. Using a rubber spatula, carefully flip the crêpe and cook for 1 to 2 minutes or until golden and set. Invert the pan over a plate to transfer the crêpe and cover loosely with foil or a large pan lid to keep warm. Repeat with the remaining batter, oiling the pan as needed and adjusting the heat as necessary if the crêpes are browning too fast. Serve warm.

Variation

For savory crêpes, omit the vanilla and sugar, and add a pinch more salt. Fill the crêpes with warm chicken and herbs, or warm salmon topped with sour cream.

Buckwheat Crêpes with Ricotta Filling

These crêpes are flecked with the dark gray pigment of buckwheat and have that lovely nutty flavor only buckwheat can provide. Surprisingly, when you grind your own flour, it will be paler in color than the buckwheat flour you purchase at the store.

MAKES 12 CRÊPES

- **Dry grinding container (see tip, page 136)**
- **8-inch (20 cm) crêpe pan or nonstick skillet**
- **Pastry brush**
- **10-cup (2.5 L) casserole dish, buttered**

10 tbsp	buckwheat groats	150 mL
1/2 cup	unbleached all-purpose flour	125 mL
1/2 tsp	salt	2 mL
4	large eggs	4
1 cup	buttermilk	250 mL
3/4 cup	water	175 mL
1/4 cup	unsalted butter, melted	60 mL
	Canola oil or unsalted butter	
3 cups	ricotta cheese	750 mL
1/4 cup	granulated sugar	60 mL
2 tsp	grated lemon zest	10 mL
	Blackberry Lime Coulis (page 54) or jam	

1. Place the buckwheat groats in the dry grinding container and secure the lid. With the switch on Variable, select speed 1 and turn the machine on. Gradually increase the speed to 10 and grind for about 40 seconds or until finely ground.

2. Turn the machine off and add the unbleached flour and salt. Replace the lid and blend for 2 to 3 seconds to mix. Transfer the flour mixture to a large measuring cup or bowl.

3. Place the eggs, buttermilk, water and melted butter in the Vitamix container and secure the lid. Select speed 10 and turn the machine on. Blend for 10 seconds.

4. Turn the machine off and add the flour mixture. Replace the lid and blend on speed 10 for about 10 seconds, just until blended. Turn the machine off and use a spatula to scrape down the sides of the container. Replace the lid and blend for a few seconds to mix. Let the batter stand, covered, for 10 minutes to hydrate.

5. Heat the crêpe pan over low heat for about 5 minutes. Using the pastry brush, brush a thin coat of oil over the pan and increase the heat to medium.

6. Blend the crêpe batter by pulsing once. Using a 1/4-cup (60 mL) measure, pour batter onto the hot pan and swirl to coat the bottom of the pan evenly. Cook for about 2 minutes or until the bottom of the crêpe is golden brown and the top is bubbled and firm. Using a rubber spatula, carefully flip the crêpe and cook for about 30 seconds or until golden and set. Invert the pan over a plate to transfer the crêpe. Repeat with the remaining batter, oiling the pan as needed and adjusting the heat as necessary if the crêpes are browning too fast. Let the crêpes cool completely.

7. Preheat oven 375°F (190°C). In a medium bowl, stir together ricotta, sugar and lemon zest. Measure 1/4 cup (60 mL) of the filling into the center of each crêpe, spreading it across the middle, then roll up the crêpe to make a loose cylinder. Place each rolled crêpe, seam side down, in the prepared casserole dish.

8. Bake for 20 minutes or until heated through. Serve drizzled with Blackberry Lime Coulis or spread with warm jam.

Variation

The sweetened ricotta can be replaced with 4 sautéed sliced apples mixed with a 1/4 cup (60 mL) raisins. Bake as directed in step 8.

Deep, Dark Chocolate Greek Yogurt Pudding

I also call this recipe Emergency Chocolate because it can be made in just a few minutes and delivers a soul-soothing deep chocolate punch. It also delivers some healthful yogurt, so you can feel good about feeding yourself while you indulge.

MAKES 3 SERVINGS

1 cup	plain Greek yogurt	250 mL
1 tsp	vanilla extract	5 mL
4 oz	semisweet chocolate, chopped and melted (see tip, page 166)	125 g

Tips

This pudding is luscious with fat-free, low-fat or full-fat Greek yogurt. Customize it to suit your needs.

Don't use chocolate chips for melting; they are formulated to melt at a higher temperature and hold their shape in a hot cookie.

1. Place the yogurt and vanilla in the Vitamix container. Quickly scrape in the melted chocolate and secure the lid. With the switch on Variable, select speed 1 and turn the machine on. Gradually increase the speed to 10, then turn the machine off.

2. Remove the lid and use a spatula to scrape down the sides of the container. Replace the lid, flip the switch on High and blend for 30 seconds.

3. Transfer the pudding to a bowl or storage container, cover and refrigerate for at least 2 hours, until chilled, or for up to 4 days.

Chocolate Avocado Pudding

Avocado is a fruit, and a creamy, rich one at that. It's just as comfortable in a sweet pudding, like this one, as in guacamole. The Vitamix blends it all to silky perfection.

MAKES 4 SERVINGS		
2	large avocados	2
1/4 cup	unsweetened almond milk	60 mL
1/2 cup	unsweetened cocoa powder	125 mL
1/2 cup	honey (preferably raw) or agave nectar	125 mL
2 tsp	vanilla extract	10 mL

Tips

For the most accurate measurements, weigh your dry and fresh ingredients. For this recipe, you'll need 540 g avocados and 40 g cocoa.

A ripe avocado yields slightly when squeezed. Don't buy an avocado whose stem, or button, has fallen off or whose skin feels loose.

1. Halve the avocados, remove the pits and use a spoon to scoop the flesh out of the shells into the Vitamix container. Add the almond milk, cocoa, honey and vanilla. Secure the lid, remove the lid plug and insert the tamper. With the switch on Variable, select speed 1 and turn the machine on. Using the tamper to push the ingredients into the blades, gradually increase the speed to 5 and blend for about 30 seconds or until creamy.

2. Turn off the machine and use a spatula to scrape down the sides of the container. If necessary, replace the lid and blend for another 15 seconds to make sure all the avocado is smoothly puréed.

3. Transfer the pudding to a bowl or storage container, cover and refrigerate for at least 2 hours, until chilled, or for up to 3 days.

Variation

For an extra-rich pudding with the added flavor of hazelnuts, replace the almond milk with Almond Hazelnut Creamer (page 223).

Raspberry Chocolate Tofu Pudding

For a little protein boost hidden in a dairy-free dessert, give tofu pudding a try. Once chilled, it sets up to a spoonable, spreadable consistency and makes a perfect pairing with berries.

MAKES 6 SERVINGS

- **4-cup (1 L) bowl or six 3/4-cup (175 mL) ramekins**

12 oz	silken tofu	375 g
1/2 cup	agave nectar	125 mL
1 tsp	vanilla extract	5 mL
1/2 tsp	raspberry extract	2 mL
6 oz	semisweet chocolate, chopped and melted (see tip)	175 g
2 cups	raspberries	500 mL

Tips

Melt chocolate in a glass bowl in the microwave on Medium-High (70%) power, or in the top of a double boiler over hot, not boiling water.

Any silken tofu will work, but if you like a firmer pudding, use extra-firm silken tofu.

1. Place the tofu, agave nectar, vanilla and raspberry extract in the Vitamix container. Secure the lid, remove the lid plug and insert the tamper. With the switch on Variable, select speed 1 and turn the machine on. Using the tamper to push the ingredients into the blades, gradually increase the speed to 5 and blend for about 30 seconds or until the tofu is smooth.

2. Turn the machine off and use a spatula to scrape down the sides of the container, making sure all the little bits are stirred in. If necessary, replace the lid and blend for 5 seconds to purée completely.

3. Turn the machine off and pour in the warm melted chocolate. Quickly replace the lid, select speed 1 and turn the machine on. Quickly increase the speed to 5 (it's important to mix the chocolate in before it hardens) and blend for 15 seconds. Turn the machine off and scrape down the container. Continue blending and scraping as needed to mix the chocolate in thoroughly.

4. Scrape half the pudding into the bowl (or into the ramekins, dividing equally) and smooth the top(s). Sprinkle with some of the raspberries. Repeat with the remaining pudding and arrange the remaining berries on top. Refrigerate for at least 1 hour, until chilled, or for up to 4 days.

Variation

For a tropical flavor, replace the raspberries with 2 sliced large bananas, and use coconut extract instead of raspberry.

Blender Chocolate Glaze

This thick, pourable glaze dries to a shiny, deep, dark chocolate finish that will wow your guests. You can make it with dairy or nondairy milk, and it is actually a relatively low-fat way to make your cake spectacular. If making it to frost the Vegan White Cupcakes (page 158), use almond or other nondairy milk.

MAKES ABOUT 1¹/₈ CUPS (280 ML)

1 cup	granulated sugar	250 mL
3 oz	unsweetened chocolate	90 g
²/₃ cup	milk or nondairy milk	150 mL
1 tsp	vanilla extract	5 mL

Tips

Using organic sugar in the glaze will make it vegan, since organic sugar is required to be processed without the use of animal products.

To use this glaze, pour it over a cake or cupcakes and spread gently, then let dry.

1. Place the sugar and chocolate in the Vitamix container and secure the lid. With the switch on Variable, select speed 1 and turn the machine on. Gradually increase the speed to 10 and blend for about 30 seconds or until the chocolate is finely ground.

2. Turn the machine off and use a spatula to scrape the lid, the sides of the container and into the corners at the bottom, moving the ground chocolate to the center.

3. In a small saucepan over medium heat (or in a glass measuring cup in the microwave on High), heat the milk until it just starts to bubble (about 1 minute in the microwave).

4. Pour the hot milk over the chocolate and let stand for 2 minutes. Secure the lid, select speed 1 and turn the machine on. Gradually increase the speed to 10 and blend for 20 seconds. Turn the machine off and scrape down the sides of the container. Continue blending and scraping until the glaze is creamy and thick. Use immediately (see tip).

ICE CREAMS, SORBETS, MILKSHAKES and ICE POPS

TIPS FOR SUCCESS

- Getting comfortable with making ice cream in your Vitamix takes a few tries; it's very easy to under- or overblend, since the machine does things so quickly.
- **Milk Ice Cubes:** To make milk ice cubes, simply fill the trays with whole milk (or 2% milk, for lighter ice cream) and freeze. A standard ice cube tray holds about $1^1/_2$ to 2 cups (375 to 500 mL) milk. Two standard ice cube trays make about 6 cups (1.5 L) cubes.
- If your ice cream or sorbet comes out of the Vitamix with a soft consistency, just transfer it to an airtight container and place in the freezer for 1 hour.
- Store Double Vanilla Ice Cream in the freezer and use it to make the shake recipes in this chapter.
- Ice creams and sorbets made in the Vitamix keep in the freezer, tightly covered, for up to 1 week.
- Standard ice pop molds hold about $^1/_4$ cup (60 mL) apiece, but there are all kinds of variations in size and shape, so you may get fewer or more ice pops than the recipes specify.
- Frozen ice pops can be stored in the freezer for up to 1 month, but if storing them for more than a few days, place the molds or cups in sealable freezer bags to improve the final quality.

Chocolate Ice Cream

Keep a bag of milk ice cubes on hand and you can have fresh, homemade chocolate ice cream in minutes. This creamy blend is a little lighter than most full-fat ice creams, but the fine texture of the mixture makes it seem richer than it is.

MAKES 6 SERVINGS

$^1/_2$ cup	heavy or whipping (35%) cream	125 mL
1 cup	powdered sugar (see page 13)	250 mL
$^1/_2$ cup	unsweetened cocoa powder	125 mL
1 tbsp	vanilla extract	15 mL
4 cups	milk ice cubes (see tip, above)	1 L

1. Place the cream, sugar and cocoa in the Vitamix container. Secure the lid, remove the lid plug and insert the tamper. With the switch on Variable, select speed 1 and turn the machine on. Blend for 30 seconds.

2. Turn the machine off and add the vanilla and ice cubes. Replace the lid and turn the machine on. Gradually increase the speed to 10, then flip the switch to High and, using the tamper to push the cubes into the blades, blend for 30 to 60 seconds or until the sound of the machine changes and it starts to labor, and the ice cream forms 4 mounds (see tip).

3. Serve immediately or transfer to an airtight container and store in the freezer for up to 1 week. Let frozen ice cream soften in the refrigerator for 15 minutes before serving.

Variation

Fudge Swirl Ice Cream: Swirl in some purchased fudge sauce at the end of step 2 and freeze until solid.

Tip

If the ice cream does not form mounds or is not as thick as you'd like, either transfer it to an airtight container and place in the freezer for 1 hour, or keep blending on High and gradually add 1 cup (250 mL) of ice cubes, blending until the sound of the machine changes and the ice cream forms 4 mounds.

Double Vanilla Ice Cream

Vanilla ice cream has the reputation of being "plain." But the pod of an exotic orchid can hardly be considered plain, if you think about it. Adding a double dose will make you fall in love with vanilla all over again.

MAKES 6 SERVINGS		
1	vanilla bean	1
1/2 cup	half-and-half (10%) cream	125 mL
1 cup	powdered sugar (see page 13)	250 mL
1 tsp	vanilla extract	5 mL
4 cups	milk ice cubes (see tip, opposite)	1 L

1. Split the vanilla bean and scrape the seeds into the Vitamix container. Add the cream and sugar. Secure the lid, remove the lid plug and insert the tamper. With the switch on Variable, select speed 1 and turn the machine on. Blend for 30 seconds.

2. Turn the machine off and add the vanilla and ice cubes. Replace the lid and turn the machine on. Gradually increase the speed to 10, then flip the switch to High and, using the tamper to push the cubes into the blades, blend for 30 to 60 seconds or until the sound of the machine changes and it starts to labor, and the ice cream forms 4 mounds (see tip, opposite).

3. Serve immediately or transfer to an airtight container and store in the freezer for up to 1 week. Let frozen ice cream soften in the refrigerator for 15 minutes before serving.

Cherry Vanilla Ice Cream

Frozen cherries have a fantastic texture and flavor in this ice cream, which is almost creamier than other ice creams with more fat. This blend is the best of both worlds, bringing sorbet and ice cream together as one.

MAKES 8 SERVINGS		
1/2 cup	heavy or whipping (35%) cream	125 mL
4 cups	milk ice cubes (see tip, opposite)	1 L
2 cups	frozen dark cherries	500 mL
1/2 cup	powdered sugar (see page 13)	125 mL
1 tbsp	vanilla extract	15 mL

1. Place the cream, ice cubes, cherries, sugar and vanilla in the Vitamix container. Secure the lid, remove the lid plug and insert the tamper. With the switch on Variable, select speed 1 and turn the machine on. Gradually increase the speed to 10, then flip the switch to High and, using the tamper to push the cubes into the blades, blend for 30 to 60 seconds or until the sound of the machine changes and it starts to labor, and the ice cream forms 4 mounds (see tip, opposite).

2. Serve immediately or transfer to an airtight container and store in the freezer for up to 1 week. Let frozen ice cream soften in the refrigerator for 15 minutes before serving.

Variation

Vanilla Banana Ice Cream: Substitute 2 sliced frozen bananas for the cherries.

Apple Pie Ice Cream

Too many "apple pie"–flavored products contain no apples and no pie. This frosty treat, on the other hand, is made of buttery cinnamon apples blended with creamy ice cream.

ᕦᕤᕦᕤᕦᕤᕦᕤᕦᕤᕦᕤᕦᕤᕦᕤᕦᕤᕦᕤᕦᕤᕦᕤᕦᕤᕦᕤᕦᕤᕦᕤᕦᕤᕦᕤ

MAKES 8 SERVINGS

1 tbsp	unsalted butter	15 mL
4	medium apples, peeled and sliced (about 4 cups/1 L)	4
¹/₄ cup	packed light brown sugar	60 mL
1 tbsp	ground cinnamon	15 mL
¹/₄ cup	heavy or whipping (35%) cream	60 mL
1 tsp	vanilla extract	5 mL
4 cups	milk ice cubes (see tip, page 174)	1 L

Tips

Use firm baking apples for this recipe, such as Gala, Fuji, Braeburn or Granny Smith.

Depending on the variety of apple, they may take longer to get very soft in step 1.

Sautéed apples make a fantastic topping for ice cream, pancakes or cake, so try the technique in steps 1 and 2 for other tasty apple dishes.

1. In a large skillet, melt butter over medium heat. Add apples and stir to coat. Increase the heat to medium-high and cook, stirring, for about 5 minutes or until apples are very soft.

2. Reduce heat to low and sprinkle in brown sugar and cinnamon; stir to mix well. Cook, stirring, until the sugar is syrupy. Remove from heat, transfer to a bowl and refrigerate for about 2 hours, until completely cold.

3. Place the cold apple mixture in the Vitamix container and add the cream, vanilla and ice cubes. Secure the lid, remove the lid plug and insert the tamper. With the switch on Variable, select speed 1 and turn the machine on. Gradually increase the speed to 10, using the tamper to push the cubes into the blades, then flip the switch to High and blend for 10 to 20 seconds, pulling the tamper up once the mixture flows around the blades, or until the sound of the machine changes and it starts to labor, and the ice cream forms 4 mounds (see tip, opposite).

4. Serve immediately or transfer to an airtight container and store in the freezer for up to 1 week. Let frozen ice cream soften in the refrigerator for 15 minutes before serving.

Variation

Spiced Pear Ice Cream: Replace the apples with 4 medium pears, peeled and sliced.

Pistachio Gelato

Gelato is Italian ice cream, created in a rainbow of fruit, nut and chocolate flavors. Pistachio gelato is for the pistachio lover, with a pure pistachio base and just enough cream to carry the luscious, nutty goodness. This is a 2-day process, so plan accordingly.

MAKES 4 SERVINGS

- Fine-mesh sieve
- Ice cube tray

3 cups	water	750 mL
3/4 cup	shelled raw pistachios	175 mL
1 cup	whole milk	250 mL
1/2 cup	granulated sugar	125 mL
1/4 cup	half-and-half (10%) cream	60 mL

Tips

Blanching and skinning the nuts is fussy, but it's important to remove the bitter, papery skins; otherwise, your gelato will be bitter.

If the gelato does not form mounds or is not as thick as you'd like, either transfer it to an airtight container and place in the freezer for 1 hour, or keep blending on High and gradually add 1 cup (250 mL) of ice cubes, blending until the sound of the machine changes and the gelato forms 4 mounds.

1. In a small saucepan, bring water to a boil over high heat. Stir in pistachios. Remove from heat and let stand for 2 minutes to blanch the pistachios, then drain well through the sieve.

2. Spread a kitchen towel on the counter and pour the pistachios onto it. Wrap the towel around the nuts and rub the nuts thoroughly, then slip the skins off each nut as you transfer them to a bowl.

3. Place the milk, sugar and pistachios in the Vitamix container and secure the lid. With the switch on Variable, select speed 1 and turn the machine on. Blend for 1 minute or until smooth. Pour into the ice cube tray and freeze for about 3 hours, until solid.

4. Run hot water over the bottom of the ice cube tray and remove the cubes. Transfer to a large sealable freezer bag and freeze for up to 2 weeks.

5. To make gelato, place the cream and the pistachio ice cubes in the Vitamix container. Secure the lid, remove the lid plug and insert the tamper. With the switch on Variable, select speed 1 and turn the machine on. Gradually increase the speed to 10, then flip the switch to High and, using the tamper to push the cubes into the blades, blend for 30 seconds or until the sound of the machine changes and it starts to labor, and the gelato forms 4 mounds (see tip).

6. Serve immediately or transfer to an airtight container and store in the freezer for up to 1 week. Let frozen gelato soften in the refrigerator for 15 minutes before serving.

Variation

Hazelnut Gelato: Substitute hazelnuts for the pistachios.

Peanut Butter Frozen Yogurt

Peanut butter and yogurt, sweetened with honey, make a luscious frozen treat. The earthy sweetness of peanut butter combines with the tangy creaminess of the yogurt for a dessert you'll want to eat often. Try it topped with jammy fruit for a peanut butter and jelly sundae. This is a 2-day process, so plan accordingly.

∾ ∾

MAKES 6 SERVINGS

● **2 ice cube trays**

· ·

2¹/₂ cups	plain yogurt, divided	625 mL
¹/₂ cup	natural peanut butter (store-bought or see recipe, page 20)	125 mL
¹/₂ cup	liquid honey	125 mL
¹/₂ tsp	vanilla extract	2 mL

Tips

You can use fat-free, low-fat or whole milk yogurt for this dessert.

If the frozen yogurt does not form mounds or is not as thick as you'd like, either transfer it to an airtight container and place in the freezer for 1 hour, or keep blending on High and gradually add 1 cup (250 mL) of ice cubes, blending until the sound of the machine changes and the frozen yogurt forms 4 mounds.

1. Place 2 cups (500 mL) yogurt, peanut butter, honey and vanilla in the Vitamix container and secure the lid. With the switch on Variable, select speed 1 and turn the machine on. Quickly increase the speed to 5 and run for 4 seconds, then increase to speed 10 and purée until smooth. Pour into ice cube trays and freeze for about 3 hours, until solid.

2. Run hot water over the bottom of the ice cube trays and remove the cubes. Transfer to a sealable freezer bags and freeze for up to 1 week.

3. To make frozen yogurt, place the remaining yogurt and the peanut butter ice cubes in the Vitamix container. Secure the lid, remove the lid plug and insert the tamper. With the switch on Variable, select speed 1 and turn the machine on. Gradually increase the speed to 10, then flip the switch to High and, using the tamper to push the cubes into the blades, blend for about 1 minute or until the sound of the machine changes and it starts to labor, and the frozen yogurt forms 4 mounds (see tip).

4. Serve immediately or transfer to an airtight container and store in the freezer for up to 1 week. Let frozen yogurt soften in the refrigerator for 15 minutes before serving.

Variation

Make this with any nut butter you choose, from Chocolate Hazelnut Butter (page 22) to Pistachio Butter (page 19).

Mixed Berry Sorbet

If one type of berry is good, then several are fantastic. At least, that's how it works in this easy sorbet. With only three ingredients, you can quickly toss it together for a deceptively sophisticated palate cleanser, snack or dessert.

MAKES 7 SERVINGS		
1/4 cup	unsweetened apple juice	60 mL
1/4 cup	liquid honey	60 mL
1 lb	frozen mixed berries	500 g

Tips

Buy 1-lb (500 mL) bags of frozen fruit and you will be ready to make this sorbet at a moment's notice.

If the sorbet does not form mounds or is not as thick as you'd like, either transfer it to an airtight container and place in the freezer for 1 hour, or keep blending on High and gradually add 1 cup (250 mL) of ice cubes, blending until the sound of the machine changes and the sorbet forms 4 mounds.

1. Place the apple juice, honey and berries in the Vitamix container. Secure the lid, remove the lid plug and insert the tamper. With the switch on Variable, select speed 1 and turn the machine on. Gradually increase the speed to 10, then flip the switch to High and, using the tamper to push the berries into the blades, blend for 30 to 60 seconds or until the sound of the machine changes and it starts to labor, and the sorbet forms 4 mounds (see tip).

2. Serve immediately or transfer to an airtight container and store in the freezer for up to 1 week. Let frozen sorbet soften in the refrigerator for 20 minutes before serving if it is hard to scoop.

Variation

Tropical Sorbet: Substitute a mix of frozen chopped mango, papaya and pineapple for the berries.

Vegan Coconut Sorbet

Nothing could be simpler than this luscious sorbet. Blending the coconut milk with sugar and vanilla, then freezing it in an ice cube tray gives you a dessert on call, ready to be blended to order.

MAKES 4 SERVINGS

- **Ice cube tray**

1	can (14 oz/400 mL) coconut milk (see tip)	1
1 tsp	vanilla extract	5 mL
1/4 cup	granulated sugar	60 mL

Tips

Use full-fat coconut milk; light coconut milk would be too icy.

If the sorbet does not form mounds or is not as thick as you'd like, either transfer it to an airtight container and place in the freezer for 1 hour, or keep blending on High and gradually add 1 cup (250 mL) of ice cubes, blending until the sound of the machine changes and the sorbet forms 4 mounds.

1. Place the coconut milk, vanilla and sugar in the Vitamix container and secure the lid. With the switch on Variable, select speed 1 and turn the machine on. Gradually increase the speed to 10 and blend for 30 seconds. Pour into the ice cube tray and freeze for about 3 hours, until solid.

2. Run hot water over the bottom of the ice cube tray and remove the cubes. Transfer to a sealable freezer bag and freeze for up to 1 week.

3. To make sorbet, place the frozen cubes in the Vitamix container. Secure the lid, remove the lid plug and insert the tamper. With the switch on Variable, select speed 1 and turn the machine on. Gradually increase the speed to 10, then flip the switch to High and, using the tamper to push the cubes into the blades, blend for about 1 minute or until the sound of the machine changes and it starts to labor, and the sorbet forms 4 mounds (see tip).

4. Serve immediately or transfer to an airtight container and store in the freezer for up to 1 week. Let frozen sorbet soften in the refrigerator for 20 minutes before serving if it is hard to scoop.

Variation

Chocolate Coconut Sorbet: Add 1/4 cup (60 mL) unsweetened cocoa powder with the sugar in step 1.

Avocado Açaí Sorbet

Avocado gives the sorbet a rich, creamy texture, remarkably like ice cream but with no dairy. Açaí purée contributes a deep purple color and a tart, exotic flavor that balances the lush avocado perfectly.

MAKES 7 SERVINGS

1/4 cup	water	60 mL
2 tbsp	freshly squeezed lemon juice	30 mL
1	large avocado, halved and pitted	1
4 oz	frozen açaí purée	125 g
1 cup	powdered sugar (see page 13)	250 mL
3 cups	ice cubes	750 mL

Tips

Açaí is sold in a frozen purée form, usually packed in 2-oz (60 g) packets. It's an antioxidant-rich tropical fruit that doesn't travel well in whole form, so the frozen packs allow us to reap the benefits of the delicious exotic fruit in recipes like this one.

Açaí is tart and tangy, so it needs to be balanced with some sweetener.

1. Place the water and lemon juice in the Vitamix container, then scoop in the avocado flesh, discarding the peel. Add the acai purée, sugar and ice cubes. Secure the lid, remove the lid plug and insert the tamper. With the switch on Variable, select speed 1 and turn the machine on. Gradually increase the speed to 10, then flip the switch to High and, using the tamper to push the ice cubes into the blades, blend for 30 to 60 seconds or until the sound of the machine changes and it starts to labor, and the sorbet forms 4 mounds (see tip, page 180).

2. Serve immediately or transfer to an airtight container and store in the freezer for up to 1 week. Let frozen sorbet soften in the refrigerator for 20 minutes before serving if it is hard to scoop.

Variation

Try dragon fruit or other superfruit purées in frozen packets for this sorbet.

Chocolate Cherry Shake

Chocolate and cherries are a delicious flavor combination, and you don't have to tell anyone that they are getting a serving of antioxidant-rich fruit in a decadent shake. Because the only liquid in the mix is chocolate syrup, this is a thick, chocolatey shake, studded with bits of sweet cherry.

MAKES 2 SERVINGS

1/2 cup	chocolate syrup	125 mL
1 cup	frozen sweet cherries	250 mL
2 cups	vanilla ice cream	500 mL

Tip

Measuring ice cream is always an approximation; just stuff as much as you can scoop into a 2-cup (500 mL) measure without melting it and proceed.

1. Place the chocolate syrup, cherries and ice cream in the Vitamix container. Secure the lid, remove the lid plug and insert the tamper. With the switch on Variable, select speed 1 and turn the machine on. Gradually increase the speed to 10, using the tamper to push the ice cream into the blades, and blend for about 30 seconds or until the ice cream is incorporated. (It's okay if there are bits of cherry in the mix.)
2. Pour the shake into chilled glasses and serve immediately.

Variation

Double Chocolate Cherry Shake: Use chocolate ice cream in place of vanilla.

Dulce de Leche Shake

Dulce de leche is Mexican milk caramel, and you will love it in this shake. The thick caramel is an invaluable pantry staple, and even just a dollop or two turns the simplest dessert into a fiesta of flavor.

MAKES 2 SERVINGS

1 cup	milk	250 mL
1/2 cup	dulce de leche	125 mL
2 cups	vanilla ice cream	500 mL

Tip

For even more caramel goodness, swirl a spoonful of dulce de leche into each glass.

1. Place the milk, dulce de leche and ice cream in the Vitamix container. Secure the lid, remove the lid plug and insert the tamper. With the switch on Variable, select speed 1 and turn the machine on. Gradually increase the speed to 10, using the tamper to push the ice cream into the blades, and blend for about 10 seconds or until the ice cream is incorporated and smooth.
2. Pour the shake into chilled glasses and serve immediately.

Variation

Chocolate Dulce de Leche Shake: Use chocolate ice cream in place of vanilla.

Creamy Maple Nut Shake

Maple syrup is a culinary treasure, imbued with deep flavor and natural sweetness. It's wonderful on pancakes, but why stop there? This milkshake is a great way to savor the fantastic combination of maple and walnuts.

MAKES 2 SERVINGS		
³/₄ cup	milk or half-and-half (10%) cream	175 mL
¹/₂ cup	pure maple syrup	125 mL
¹/₄ cup	raw walnut halves	60 mL
2 cups	vanilla ice cream	500 mL

Tip

Maple syrup also goes well with pecans, so you can substitute them for the walnuts in this milkshake.

1. Place the milk, maple syrup, walnuts and ice cream in the Vitamix container. Secure the lid, remove the lid plug and insert the tamper. With the switch on Variable, select speed 1 and turn the machine on. Gradually increase the speed to 10, using the tamper to push the ice cream into the blades, and blend for about 10 seconds or until the ice cream is incorporated and smooth.

2. Pour the shake into chilled glasses and serve immediately.

Blueberry Crumble Shake

Craving a crumble? You could bake a blueberry crumble and top it with frozen yogurt, or you can make this shake, which melds all the crave-worthy flavors of a crumble into a milkshake. Drink your crumble through a straw!

MAKES 2 TO 3 SERVINGS		
¹/₂ cup	milk	125 mL
1 tbsp	pure maple syrup	15 mL
2 cups	frozen blueberries	500 mL
¹/₂ cup	granola	125 mL
2 cups	vanilla frozen yogurt	500 mL

Tip

Frozen berries make this shake a little thicker, but if you have some fresh local berries, feel free to show them off in this recipe.

1. Place the milk, maple syrup, blueberries, granola and frozen yogurt in the Vitamix container. Secure the lid, remove the lid plug and insert the tamper. With the switch on Variable, select speed 1 and turn the machine on. Gradually increase the speed to 10, using the tamper to push the frozen yogurt into the blades, and blend for about 10 seconds or until the frozen yogurt is incorporated and smooth.

2. Pour the shake into chilled glasses and serve immediately.

Variation

Strawberry Crumble Shake: Substitute strawberries for the blueberries, and replace the maple syrup with liquid honey.

Chocolate, Avocado and Cherry Pops

On a hot day, you and your kids want a sweet, cooling treat. These easy ice pops fit the bill, and they are rich and creamy with cashew and avocado, so you can feel good about everybody having a serving of healthful plant foods. You'll need to make the cashew creamer first, so start soaking the cashews the day before.

〰〰〰〰〰〰〰〰〰〰〰〰〰〰〰〰〰〰〰〰〰〰〰〰

MAKES 8 ICE POPS

- **Ice pop molds or 5–oz (150 mL) paper cups and wooden sticks**

1 cup	Cashew Vanilla Creamer (page 224)	250 mL
1	large avocado, halved and pitted	1
1/4 cup	unsweetened cocoa powder	60 mL
1/4 cup	granulated sugar	60 mL
1 tsp	vanilla extract	5 mL
1/2 cup	frozen sweet cherries	125 mL

Tip

Standard ice pop molds hold about 1/4 cup (60 mL) apiece, but there are all kinds of variations in size and shape, so you may get fewer or more than 8 ice pops from this recipe.

1. Place the cashew creamer in the Vitamix container, then scoop in the avocado flesh, discarding the peel. Add the cocoa, sugar and vanilla. Secure the lid, remove the lid plug and insert the tamper. With the switch on Variable, select speed 1 and turn the machine on. Gradually increase the speed to 10, using the tamper to push the ingredients into the blades, and blend for about 20 seconds, just until smooth. Turn the machine off.

2. Finely chop the frozen cherries. Quickly remove the lid from the container, add the cherries and replace the lid. Pulse twice on speed 10 to mix (you don't want to purée the fruit).

3. Pour into the ice pop molds and insert the sticks. Freeze for at least 3 hours, until solid, or for up to 1 month. Unmold ice pops by running warm water over the plastic molds or by tearing off the paper cups.

Variation

Use coconut milk instead of the cashew creamer, for lighter ice pops with a hint of coconut flavor.

Peanut Butter, Chocolate and Banana Pops

Peanut butter and chocolate is a combo that works just about anywhere you put it. These ice pops are delectable and rich, but actually deliver a bit of protein and fruit along with the fun.

- **Ice pop molds or 5-oz (150 mL) paper cups and wooden sticks**

1 cup	plain yogurt	250 mL
1/2 cup	natural peanut butter (store-bought or see recipe, page 20)	125 mL
1 tsp	vanilla extract	5 mL
2	large bananas	2
1/4 cup	packed light brown sugar	60 mL
1/4 cup	unsweetened cocoa powder	60 mL

Tip

Save your overripe bananas for this; they purée perfectly into ice pops.

1. Place the yogurt, peanut butter, vanilla, bananas, sugar and cocoa in the Vitamix container. Secure the lid, remove the lid plug and insert the tamper. With the switch on Variable, select speed 1 and turn the machine on. Gradually increase the speed to 10, using the tamper to push the ingredients into the blades, and blend for about 20 seconds or until smooth.

2. Pour into the ice pop molds and insert the sticks. Freeze for at least 3 hours, until solid, or for up to 1 month. Unmold ice pops by running warm water over the plastic molds or by tearing off the paper cups.

Variation

Almond, Chocolate and Banana Pops: Use homemade Almond Butter (page 18) and add 1/2 tsp (2 mL) almond extract.

Strawberry, Banana and Green Tea Pops

Drink your tea truly iced in this frozen treat. The strawberries contribute tart sweetness, and the creamy bananas feel like ice cream in your mouth.

∽∾∽∾∽∾∽∾∽∾∽∾∽∾∽∾∽∾∽∾∽∾∽∾∽∾∽∾∽∾∽∾∽∾∽∾

MAKES 10 ICE POPS

- **Ice pop molds or 5–oz (150 mL) paper cups and wooden sticks**

1/2 cup	brewed green tea, cooled	125 mL
1/4 cup	liquid honey	60 mL
1	large banana	1
2 cups	frozen strawberries	500 mL

Tip

You can use fresh strawberries in this recipe, but the blended mixture will not be thick enough to insert the sticks into the pops right away. After pouring the mixture into the ice pop molds, freeze the ice pops for 30 minutes before inserting the sticks.

1. Place the green tea, honey, banana and strawberries in the Vitamix container. Secure the lid, remove the lid plug and insert the tamper. With the switch on Variable, select speed 1 and turn the machine on. Gradually increase the speed to 10, using the tamper to push the ingredients into the blades, and blend for about 30 seconds or until smooth.

2. Pour into the ice pop molds and insert the sticks. Freeze for at least 3 hours, until solid, or for up to 1 month. Unmold ice pops by running warm water over the plastic molds or by tearing off the paper cups.

Variation

Rosehip Strawberry Pops: Use brewed rosehip tea instead of green tea.

Orange Almond Cream Pops

In these colorful pops, freshly made almond milk is poured into the mold, then a sweet orange purée is poured down the side, for two different flavors in the finished pop.

● **Ice pop molds or 5-oz (150 mL) paper cups and wooden sticks**

ALMOND MILK

¹/₄ cup	raw almonds	60 mL
	Water	
¹/₄ tsp	vanilla extract	1 mL
¹/₄ cup	granulated sugar	60 mL

ORANGE MIXTURE

2	large oranges, peeled and seeded	2
¹/₄ cup	granulated sugar	60 mL

Tips

Buy seedless oranges and save time removing the seeds.

If you are crafty, you can set up your molds to freeze the almond mixture on a slant, so that when you add the orange mixture, you have two clearly divided flavors in each pop.

1. *Almond Milk:* Place almonds in a medium bowl and add ³/₄ cup (175 mL) cool water. Let soak in the refrigerator overnight. Drain and rinse.

2. Place 1 cup (250 mL) fresh water, the drained almonds, vanilla and sugar in the Vitamix container and secure the lid. With the switch on Variable, select speed 1 and turn the machine on. Gradually increase the speed to 10, then flip the switch to High and blend for 1 minute or until very creamy and smooth.

3. Pour the almond mixture into the ice pop molds, dividing equally. Set aside. Rinse the Vitamix container.

4. *Orange Mixture:* Place the oranges and sugar in the container and secure the lid. With the switch on Variable, select speed 1 and turn the machine on. Gradually increase the speed to 10, then flip the switch to High and blend for about 40 seconds or until completely liquefied.

5. Pour the orange mixture down the side of each ice pop cup so that it doesn't mix with the almond mixture. Freeze for 30 minutes, then insert the sticks. Freeze for at least 3 hours, until solid, or for up to 1 month. Unmold ice pops by running warm water over the plastic molds or by tearing off the paper cups.

Variation

Orange Cashew Cream Pops: Replace the almonds with raw cashews.

Piña Colada Pops

Because coconut is so luscious, these ice pops are almost like ice cream bars laced with brilliant pineapple.

∾ ∾

MAKES 16 ICE POPS

- **Ice pop molds or 5-oz (150 mL) paper cups and wooden sticks**

1	can (14 oz/398 mL) crushed pineapple, with juice	1
¹/₄ cup	granulated sugar, divided	60 mL
1 cup	coconut milk	250 mL
¹/₂ tsp	coconut extract	2 mL

Tip

If you want to use fresh pineapple, finely chop it to make 1¹/₂ cups (375 mL) and add any juice from the cutting board.

1. Place the pineapple and 2 tbsp (30 mL) sugar in the Vitamix container and secure the lid. With the switch on Variable, select speed 1 and turn the machine on. Blend for about 30 seconds, until smooth.

2. Pour the pineapple mixture into the ice pop molds, dividing equally. Freeze for 20 minutes, placing the molds on a slant, if possible. Rinse the Vitamix container.

3. Place the coconut milk, coconut extract and the remaining sugar in the container and secure the lid. With the switch on Variable, select speed 1 and turn the machine on. Gradually increase the speed to 10, then flip the switch to High and blend for 3 to 4 seconds.

4. Pour 1 tbsp (15 mL) of the coconut mixture on top of the pineapple layer in each cup, then insert the sticks. Freeze for at least 3 hours, until solid, or for up to 1 month. Unmold ice pops by running warm water over the plastic molds or by tearing off the paper cups.

Variation

Mango Colada Pops: Replace the pineapple with 1¹/₂ cups (375 mL) chopped mango and 1 tbsp (15 mL) orange juice.

TRUFFLES and ENERGY BALLS

TIPS FOR SUCCESS

- The truffle and energy ball recipes call for a #70 scoop, in which a level scoop is $1/2$ oz (15 g), or about 1 tbsp (15 mL). If you don't have a scoop, you can use a tablespoon or a melon baller, or just go free-form.
- To make a shiny, snappy coating out of chocolate, you have to temper it. But for truffles that are both easy and beautiful, you can simply coat them in untempered chocolate, then cover any imperfections with unsweetened cocoa powder or powdered sugar, as instructed in the recipes.
- If you prefer, you can skip the step of coating the truffles in melted chocolate and simply roll them in unsweetened cocoa powder or powdered sugar.
- Energy balls rely on the stickiness of dates and other dried fruit to hold them together. If your mixture is too dry, try drizzling in a little water or melted coconut oil.
- While it is best to keep energy balls in the refrigerator, it is perfectly fine to transfer a few to a sandwich bag to carry with you; they will be fine at room temperature for a couple of days.

Milk Chocolate and Dulce de Leche Truffles

We should all be very grateful to Mexico, which has given us many culinary treasures. Not the least of them is dulce de leche, a creamy milk-based caramel. Available in cans and jars, it allows you to skip the process of making your own caramel and still add the distinctive burnt sugar and cream flavor to desserts.

∽∾

MAKES 16 TRUFFLES

- **#70 scoop (see tip, page 189)**
- **Baking sheet, lined with parchment paper**

5 oz	milk chocolate, coarsely chopped	150 g
1/4 cup	heavy or whipping (35%) cream	60 mL
1/4 cup	dulce de leche	60 mL

COATING

4 oz	milk or semisweet chocolate	125 g
1/4 cup	unsweetened cocoa powder or powdered sugar (see page 13)	60 mL

1. Place the milk chocolate in the Vitamix container and secure the lid. With the switch on Variable, select speed 1 and turn the machine on. Gradually increase the speed to 5 and blend for 5 to 10 seconds or until the chocolate is finely chopped. Turn the machine off and use a spatula to scrape the chocolate toward the center of the container.

2. In a small saucepan, bring cream to a boil over medium heat, stirring constantly.

3. Pour the cream over the chocolate and replace the lid. Select speed 1 and turn the machine on. Gradually increase the speed to 3 and blend for 10 to 20 seconds or until the mixture at the bottom of the container looks creamy but there are a few bits of chocolate sticking to the sides. Turn the machine off and scrape down the sides of the container. Continue blending and scraping until creamy and smooth.

4. Turn the machine off and add the dulce de leche. Replace the lid and blend on speed 3 for about 10 seconds or until incorporated.

5. Transfer the mixture to a medium bowl, cover and refrigerate for about 3 hours, until cold and set.

6. Using the scoop, scoop out portions of truffle filling. Roll each portion into a ball and place on prepared baking sheet. Refrigerate for about 2 hours, until firm.

7. *Coating:* Place chocolate in a heatproof bowl set over a saucepan of hot, not boiling water and melt, stirring until smooth. Remove from heat.

8. Sift cocoa into a medium bowl. Using a fork, dip each truffle in melted chocolate, gently tapping the fork to let excess chocolate fall back into the bowl (see tip, page 189). Roll each ball in cocoa, shaking off excess, then return to the baking sheet and refrigerate for 1 to 2 hours or until the chocolate is set.

9. Serve immediately or store in an airtight container in the refrigerator for up to 2 weeks.

Variation

If you can find cajeta, a Mexican milk caramel made with goat milk, substitute that for the dulce de leche, for a subtle tanginess.

Tip

Instead of heating the cream on the stovetop, you can heat it to a boil in a microwave-safe ramekin or measuring cup on Medium (50%) power.

Deep, Dark Vanilla Truffles

These bite-size confections are dense and luscious, a dark chocolate lover's dream come true. With just enough cream to carry intense chocolate across your tongue, truffles are perfect as a small dessert, or as a pick-me-up at any time of the day.

∽∽ ∽∽ ∽∽ ∽∽ ∽∽ ∽∽ ∽∽ ∽∽ ∽∽ ∽∽ ∽∽ ∽∽ ∽∽ ∽∽ ∽∽ ∽∽ ∽∽ ∽∽

MAKES 16 TRUFFLES

- **#70 scoop (see tip, page 189)**
- **Baking sheet, lined with parchment paper**

4 oz	semisweet chocolate, coarsely chopped	125 g
1/4 cup	heavy or whipping (35%) cream	60 mL
1 tbsp	unsalted butter	15 mL
1 tbsp	vanilla extract	15 mL
2 tsp	light (white or golden) corn syrup	10 mL

COATING

4 oz	semisweet chocolate, chopped	125 g
1/4 cup	unsweetened cocoa powder	60 mL

1. Place the chocolate in the Vitamix container. Secure the lid. With the switch on Variable, select speed 1 and turn the machine on. Gradually increase the speed to 5 and blend for 5 to 10 seconds or until the chocolate is finely chopped. Turn the machine off and use a spatula to scrape the chocolate toward the center of the container.

2. In a small saucepan, combine cream, butter, vanilla and corn syrup. Bring to a boil over medium heat, stirring constantly.

3. Pour the cream mixture over the chocolate and replace the lid. Select speed 1 and turn the machine on. Gradually increase the speed to 3 and blend for 10 to 20 seconds or until the mixture at the bottom of the container looks creamy but there are a few bits of chocolate sticking to the sides. Turn the machine off and scrape down the sides of the container. Continue blending and scraping until creamy and smooth.

4. Transfer the mixture to a medium bowl, cover and refrigerate for about 3 hours, until cold and set.

5. Using the scoop, scoop out portions of truffle filling. Roll each portion into a ball and place on prepared baking sheet. Refrigerate for about 2 hours, until firm.

6. *Coating:* Place chocolate in a heatproof bowl set over a saucepan of hot, not boiling water and melt, stirring until smooth. Remove from heat.

7. Sift cocoa into a medium bowl. Using a fork, dip each truffle in melted chocolate, gently tapping the fork to let excess chocolate fall back into the bowl (see tip, page 189). Roll each ball in cocoa, shaking off excess, then return to the baking sheet and refrigerate for 1 to 2 hours or until the chocolate is set.

8. Serve immediately or store in an airtight container in the refrigerator for up to 2 weeks.

Variation

Other extracts make delicious truffles as well. Substitute raspberry, almond or coffee extract for the vanilla to play with those flavors.

Tip

Semisweet chocolate is any chocolate with over 60% cacao solids, and there are bars ranging all the way up to 90%. When you select your chocolate, remember that the more cacao there is, the less sugar there is, so a very high-cacao chocolate will make a truffle that is barely sweet.

Brandied Cherry Truffles

Chocolate on its own is fantastic, but add liquor and fruit, and it cannot be denied. Here, thirsty dried cherries soak in brandy before being ensconced in a creamy chocolate truffle matrix. If you are avoiding alcohol, soak the fruit in cherry or pomegranate juice instead.

MAKES 30 TRUFFLES

- **Fine-mesh sieve**
- **#70 scoop (see tip, page 189)**
- **Baking sheet, lined with parchment paper**

1/2 cup	dried sweet cherries	125 mL
1/2 cup	brandy (approx.)	125 mL
8 oz	semisweet chocolate, coarsely chopped	250 g
1/2 cup	heavy or whipping (35%) cream	125 mL
2 tbsp	unsalted butter	30 mL
1 tbsp	light (white or golden) corn syrup	15 mL

COATING

12 oz	semisweet chocolate, chopped	375 g
1/2 cup	unsweetened cocoa powder	125 mL

1. Place cherries in a small bowl and add enough brandy to cover. Cover and let soak at room temperature overnight.

2. Drain cherries through the sieve into a bowl, pressing to extract as much liquid as possible. Measure 1/4 cup (60 mL) brandy and set aside (reserve any extra for another use). Finely chop the cherries and set aside separately.

3. Place the chocolate in the Vitamix container. Secure the lid. With the switch on Variable, select speed 1 and turn the machine on. Gradually increase the speed to 5 and blend for 5 to 10 seconds or until the chocolate is finely chopped. Turn the machine off and use a spatula to scrape the chocolate toward the center of the container.

4. In a small saucepan, combine cream, butter, corn syrup and the reserved brandy. Bring to a boil over medium heat, stirring constantly.

5. Pour the cream mixture over the chocolate in the container and replace the lid. Select speed 1 and turn the machine on. Gradually increase the speed to 3 and blend for 10 to 20 seconds or until the mixture at the bottom of the container looks creamy but there are a few bits of chocolate sticking to the sides. Turn the machine off and scrape down the sides of the container. Continue blending and scraping until creamy and smooth.

6. Transfer the mixture to a medium bowl and stir in cherries. Cover and refrigerate for about 3 hours, until cold and set.

7. Using the scoop, scoop out portions of truffle filling. Roll each portion into a ball and place on prepared baking sheet. Refrigerate for about 2 hours, until firm.

8. *Coating:* Place chocolate in a heatproof bowl set over a saucepan of hot, not boiling water and melt, stirring until smooth. Remove from heat.

9. Sift cocoa into a medium bowl. Using a fork, dip each truffle in melted chocolate, gently tapping the fork to let excess chocolate fall back into the bowl (see tip, page 189). Roll each ball in cocoa, shaking off excess, then return to the baking sheet and refrigerate for 1 to 2 hours or until the chocolate is set.

10. Serve immediately or store in an airtight container in the refrigerator for up to 2 weeks.

Variation

For a fall favorite, substitute dried cranberries for the cherries and soak them in bourbon.

Matcha Almond Butter Energy Bars

Matcha is a powdered green tea celebrated for its high antioxidant content and energizing qualities. It will add a pleasant boost to these simple squares.

∿∿∿∿∿∿∿∿∿∿∿∿∿∿∿∿∿∿∿∿∿∿∿∿∿∿∿∿∿∿

MAKES 8 BARS

- **6-inch (15 cm) square of waxed paper, parchment paper or plastic wrap**

1 cup	pitted Medjool dates	250 mL
1/4 cup	quick-cooking rolled oats, divided	60 mL
1 tsp	matcha tea	5 mL
2 tbsp	almond butter	30 mL
1/2 tsp	almond extract	2 mL

1. Place the dates, 2 tbsp (30 mL) oats, matcha, almond butter and almond extract in the Vitamix container. Secure the lid, remove the lid plug and insert the tamper. With the switch on Variable, select speed 1 and turn the machine on. Using the tamper to push the ingredients into the blades, gradually increase the speed to 5 and blend for 30 seconds. Turn the machine off and use a spatula to scrape down the sides of the container. Continue blending for 30 seconds, then scraping, until the mixture is coarsely blended.

2. Place the waxed paper on a cutting board and sprinkle with 1 tbsp (15 mL) oats. Scrape the date mixture onto the oats. Using damp hands, press the mixture into a 4-inch (10 cm) square. Sprinkle the remaining oats on top and press to adhere. Cut into 8 bars.

3. Serve immediately or store, tightly wrapped, in the refrigerator for up to 1 month.

Apple Pie Energy Balls

Apples and cinnamon combine like the flavor all-stars they are to make these energizing little snacks taste like a favorite dessert.

∿∿∿∿∿∿∿∿∿∿∿∿∿∿∿∿∿∿∿∿∿∿∿∿∿∿∿∿∿∿

MAKES 9 BALLS

- **#70 scoop (see tip, page 189)**

2 tbsp	agave nectar	30 mL
2 tbsp	almond butter	30 mL
1 cup	dried apple slices	250 mL
2 tbsp	chia seeds, divided	30 mL
1 tsp	ground cinnamon	5 mL

1. Place the agave nectar, almond butter, apples, 1 tbsp (15 mL) chia seeds and cinnamon in the Vitamix container. Secure the lid, remove the lid plug and insert the tamper. With the switch on Variable, select speed 1 and turn the machine on. Blend for 30 to 40 seconds, using the tamper to push the ingredients into the blades. Gradually increase the speed to 4 or 5, making sure the mixture stays engaged with the blades and blending until a sticky ball is moving freely around the blades.

2. Scrape the apple mixture into a medium bowl. Dampen the scoop and scoop out 9 portions of the mixture, rolling each portion into a ball.

3. Place the remaining chia seeds in another medium bowl. Roll the balls in chia seeds, then place in an airtight container.

4. Serve immediately or store, tightly covered, in the refrigerator for up to 1 month.

Cacao Nib, Prune and Coconut Energy Balls

Cacao nibs are the raw beans that cocoa and chocolate are made from. They provide both a chocolate flavor and a gentle crunchiness to these energy balls. They also give you a mild caffeine boost, for a bit of energy as you make your way through your workout.

MAKES 8 BALLS

● **#70 scoop (see tip, page 189)**

1/2 cup	unsweetened shredded coconut, divided	125 mL
2 tbsp	coconut oil	30 mL
1 tsp	vanilla extract	5 mL
1/2 tsp	coconut extract	2 mL
1 cup	pitted prunes	250 mL
1/4 cup	quick-cooking rolled oats	60 mL
2 tbsp	cacao nibs	30 mL

Tip

Buy the moistest, softest pitted prunes you can find. If your prunes are flexible but not plump, soak them overnight in cool water, then drain and pat dry.

1. Place 2 tbsp (30 mL) coconut in a medium bowl and set aside.

2. Place the coconut oil, vanilla, coconut extract, prunes, oats, cacao nibs and the remaining coconut in the Vitamix container. Secure the lid, remove the lid plug and insert the tamper. With the switch on Variable, select speed 1 and turn the machine on. Using the tamper to push the ingredients into the blades, gradually increase the speed to 5 and blend for 30 seconds. Turn the machine off and use a spatula to scrape down the sides of the container. Continue blending for 30 seconds, then scraping, until the mixture is coarsely blended.

3. Scrape the prune mixture into another medium bowl. Dampen the scoop and scoop out 8 portions of the mixture, rolling each portion into a ball. Roll the balls in the reserved coconut, then place in an airtight container.

4. Serve immediately or store, tightly covered, in the refrigerator for up to 1 month.

Variation

For a mocha version, add 1 tbsp (15 mL) coffee beans with the cacao nibs.

Chocolate Pecan Pie Energy Balls

Just because you are out on the trail doesn't mean you can't have a treat that tastes like pie. Hints of molasses and maple give the date purée a caramel flavor, and pecans will remind you of a favorite Thanksgiving treat.

MAKES 12 BALLS

- **#70 scoop (see tip, page 189)**

1/2 cup	raw pecan halves	125 mL
1/4 cup	blanched almonds (see tip)	60 mL
1 tbsp	pure maple syrup or liquid honey	15 mL
1 tsp	light (fancy) molasses	5 mL
1 cup	pitted Medjool dates	250 mL
1/4 cup	unsweetened cocoa powder, divided	60 mL
Pinch	salt	Pinch

Tips

For the blanched almonds, you can use either whole or slivered almonds. If using whole, measure out a heaping 1/4 cup (60 mL); if using slivered, measure out a level 1/4 cup (60 mL).

If your fruit and nuts are flying up out of the blades, you are going too fast. Reduce the speed and use the tamper until the ingredients are minced and sticking together.

1. Place the pecans and almonds in the Vitamix container and secure the lid. With the switch on Variable, select speed 1 and turn the machine on. Gradually increase the speed to 7 and blend for 4 to 6 seconds or until the nuts are minced.

2. Turn the machine off and use a spatula to scrape the nuts from the corners of the container. Add the maple syrup, molasses, dates, 2 tbsp (30 mL) cocoa and salt. Replace the lid, remove the lid plug and insert the tamper. Select speed 1 and turn the machine on. Blend, using the tamper to push the ingredients into the blades. Very gradually, as the dates are chopped into tiny pieces, increase the speed to 3 or 4, making sure the mixture stays engaged with the blades. Turn the machine off and scrape down the sides of the container. Continue blending and scraping until a sticky ball is moving freely around the blades.

3. Scrape the nut mixture into a medium bowl. Dampen the scoop and scoop out 12 portions of the mixture, rolling each portion into a ball.

4. Place the remaining cocoa in another medium bowl. Roll the balls in cocoa, then place in an airtight container.

5. Serve immediately or store, tightly covered, in the refrigerator for up to 1 month.

Variation

To make these extra-chocolatey, add 2 tbsp (30 mL) mini chocolate chips at the end of step 2 and pulse to mix in.

Cinnamon Nut Energy Balls

Cinnamon is a perennial favorite flavor, and it has a healing side benefit of helping balance blood sugar. These high-energy, high-fiber tidbits are rolled in a crunchy coating of Sucanat and cinnamon, so you get even more cinnamon goodness.

MAKES 18 BALLS		

● **#70 scoop (see tip, page 189)**

1/2 cup	blanched almonds (see tip)	125 mL
1/2 cup	unsweetened shredded coconut	125 mL
1/4 cup	raw walnut halves	60 mL
1 cup	pitted Medjool dates	250 mL
1/4 cup	tahini	60 mL
1 tbsp	ground cinnamon	15 mL
1/4 tsp	fine-grain sea salt	1 mL

COATING

| 1/4 cup | Sucanat | 60 mL |
| 2 tsp | ground cinnamon | 10 mL |

Tips

For the blanched almonds, you can use either whole or slivered almonds. If using whole, measure out a heaping 1/2 cup (125 mL); if using slivered, measure out a level 1/2 cup (125 mL).

Sucanat is a raw, unrefined, uncrystallized cane juice product that looks like powdery brown sugar. It sometimes goes by the name rapadura. Coconut sugar can also be used.

1. Place the almonds, coconut and walnuts in the Vitamix container and secure the lid. With the switch on Variable, select speed 1 and turn the machine on. Gradually increase the speed to 5 and blend for 4 to 6 seconds or until the nuts are minced.

2. Turn the machine off and add the dates, tahini, cinnamon and salt. Replace the lid, remove the lid plug and insert the tamper. Select speed 1 and turn the machine on. Using the tamper to push the ingredients into the blades, gradually increase the speed to 10 and blend for about 1 minute to a thick purée.

3. Scrape the nut mixture into a medium bowl. Dampen the scoop and scoop out 18 portions of the mixture, rolling each portion into a ball.

4. *Coating:* In another medium bowl, combine Sucanat and cinnamon. Roll the balls in cinnamon mixture, then place in an airtight container.

5. Serve immediately or store, tightly covered, in the refrigerator for up to 1 month.

Variation

Instead of almonds, try peanuts.

Blueberry Lemon Energy Balls

Blueberries are beloved because they taste like summer, and because they deliver remarkable amounts of antioxidants, especially the anthocyanins that protect your eyes. Adding dried blueberries to these tangy energy balls is a great way to take our purple berries out for a spin.

MAKES 10 BALLS

- **#70 scoop (see tip, page 189)**

$1/2$ cup	pitted Medjool dates	125 mL
$1/2$ cup	dried blueberries	125 mL
$1/4$ cup	raw cashews	60 mL
1 tbsp	grated lemon zest, divided	15 mL
$1/2$ tsp	vanilla extract	2 mL

Tip

Look for dried blueberries that have been sweetened with apple juice, a natural alternative to the sugar that coats some dried fruits. The apple juice keeps them moist.

1. Place the dates, blueberries, cashews, $1/2$ tsp (2 mL) lemon zest and vanilla in the Vitamix container. Secure the lid, remove the lid plug and insert the tamper. With the switch on Variable, select speed 1 and turn the machine on. Blend, using the tamper to push the ingredients into the blades. Very gradually, as the dates are chopped into tiny pieces, increase the speed to 4 or 5, making sure the mixture stays engaged with the blades. Turn the machine off and scrape down the sides of the container. Continue blending and scraping to a thick purée, about 1 to 2 minutes total.

2. Scrape the date mixture into a medium bowl. Dampen the scoop and scoop out 10 portions of the mixture, rolling each portion into a ball.

3. Place the remaining lemon zest in another medium bowl. Roll the balls in lemon zest, then place in an airtight container.

4. Serve immediately or store, tightly covered, in the refrigerator for up to 1 month.

Variation

Try soft dried strawberries in place of blueberries, for another summery flavor.

Mango Coconut Energy Balls

Taste the tropics with a combo of sweet-tart dried mangos and chewy sweet coconut. When your energy snack looks like a snowball, you will be ready to run a mile to get one.

∾ ∾

MAKES 12 BALLS

- **#70 scoop (see tip, page 189)**

3/4 cup	unsweetened shredded coconut, divided	175 mL
1 tbsp	water	15 mL
1 tbsp	melted coconut oil	15 mL
1 cup	soft dried mango slices	250 mL
1/2 cup	pitted Medjool dates	125 mL

Tip
Buy unsweetened coconut unless you want your energy balls to taste like candy.

1. Place 1/2 cup (125 mL) coconut in the Vitamix container and secure the lid. With the switch on Variable, select speed 5. Pulse four or five times, until the coconut is finely ground.

2. Remove the lid and add the water, coconut oil, mangos and dates. Replace the lid, remove the lid plug and insert the tamper. Select speed 1 and turn the machine on. Quickly increase the speed to 10, then flip the switch to High and, using the tamper to push the ingredients into the blades, blend for about 1 minute or until the mixture is sticky and thick, with some chunks of mango and coconut.

3. Scrape the coconut mixture into a medium bowl. Dampen the scoop and scoop out 12 portions of the mixture, rolling each portion into a ball.

4. Place the remaining coconut in another medium bowl. Roll the balls in coconut, then place in an airtight container.

5. Serve immediately or store, tightly covered, in the refrigerator for up to 1 month.

Variation
Substitute soft dried papaya slices for the mango.

BABY FOOD

TIPS FOR SUCCESS

- For the first 6 months, breast milk is the optimum food for your baby. At 6 months, or as recommended by your pediatrician, start introducing single-ingredient purées. Wait a few days after introducing one new food before trying another, so that you can track any reactions.
- In these recipes, a serving of baby food is about $1/4$ cup (60 mL). This is a general recommendation; your baby's needs will change with age and weight.
- Babies need to be exposed to a new food or texture 6 to 10 times to become familiar with it. If your baby spits out peas or lentils the first 5 times, keep trying. You are building your child's palate for a lifetime.
- When making baby food, don't add salt or sweeteners. Your baby doesn't need them.
- Your baby may prefer a thinner or thicker consistency of baby food. These recipes are on the thicker end of the spectrum, so feel free to stir in some breast milk or water to thin them out.
- Processed baby food may be easy and convenient, but freshly made baby food will have more nutrients because it was just made and wasn't pasteurized under high heat.
- When shopping for baby food ingredients, choose organic foods when possible. Your baby's development is too important to expose her to pesticides and herbicides in food.
- When preparing baby food, be extra-careful to prevent bacterial contamination. Wash and sanitize the cutting board, knives and all food contact surfaces. Take the time to soak produce in cold water for 5 minutes, then thoroughly swish and rinse. Rinse whole grains, too.

Leafy Greens

Use this recipe as a template for making any leafy green into an easy baby food. Pick one of the greens on the list and make a spoonable purée out of it. Greens are packed with important minerals, vitamin A, vitamin C and even some calcium and protein.

∾ ∾

MAKES ABOUT 2 CUPS (500 ML)

- Ice cube trays or muffin pan, lined with paper or silicone liners

. . . .

PICK ONE

3 cups	lightly packed chopped cabbage	750 mL
	or	
6 cups	lightly packed trimmed kale leaves	1.5 L
	or	
4 cups	lightly packed spinach leaves	1 L

Tip

Introduce green vegetables at 6 months or according to your pediatrician's recommendations. Studies show that lifelong taste preferences are formed at this age, and you will be helping your baby develop a taste for vegetables.

1. In a large skillet with a lid, combine leafy greens and ½ cup (125 mL) water. Bring to a boil over medium-high heat. Reduce heat to medium-low, cover and boil gently for 5 minutes for cabbage and kale, or 2 minutes for spinach. Uncover and check to make sure the greens are very soft. If not, cover and boil gently until very soft.

2. Transfer the greens and cooking liquid to the Vitamix container and secure the lid. With the switch on Variable, select speed 1 and turn the machine on. Gradually increase the speed to 10, then flip the switch to High and blend for about 30 seconds or until very smooth. Turn the machine off. If the purée is very thick, add water, a little bit at a time, and blend to the desired consistency.

3. Let cool and serve immediately, store in an airtight container in the refrigerator for up to 24 hours or transfer to ice cube trays or prepared muffin pan in appropriate portions and freeze until solid. Once frozen, transfer to airtight containers or sealable freezer bags and store in the freezer for up to 2 months. Thaw a day's worth of cubes in the refrigerator for 4 hours.

Variation

If your baby balks at single-ingredient green purées, steam 2 peeled carrots and add them to the greens before blending, to sweeten the mix. If your baby accepts this, gradually decrease the amount of carrot in each batch.

Root Veggies

This recipe is a template for making naturally sweet, creamy root vegetable purées. Your baby will love the mild, digestible roots as a side or stirred into a meat or bean purée. Pick one vegetable and keep it simple.

- **Ice cube trays or muffin pan, lined with paper or silicone liners**

PICK ONE

2 cups	chopped peeled carrots	500 mL
	or	
2 cups	chopped peeled parsnips	500 mL
	or	
3 cups	chopped peeled sweet potato	750 mL
	or	
2 cups	chopped peeled turnips	500 mL
	or	
2 cups	chopped peeled beets	500 mL

Tip

Use a sharp paring knife to peel beets or turnips — it's easier than using a vegetable peeler.

1. In a medium saucepan, combine root vegetables and 1 cup (250 mL) water. Bring to a boil over medium-high heat. Reduce heat to medium-low, cover and boil gently for 15 to 20 minutes (25 minutes for beets) or until the vegetables are very soft and falling apart.

2. Transfer the vegetables and cooking liquid to the Vitamix container. Secure the lid, remove the lid plug and insert the tamper. With the switch on Variable, select speed 1 and turn the machine on. Using the tamper to push the vegetables into the blades, gradually increase the speed to 10 and blend until very smooth. Turn the machine off. If the purée is very thick, add water, a little bit at a time, and blend to the desired consistency.

3. Let cool and serve immediately, store in an airtight container in the refrigerator for up to 24 hours or transfer to ice cube trays or prepared muffin pan in appropriate portions and freeze until solid. Once frozen, transfer to airtight containers or sealable freezer bags and store in the freezer for up to 2 months. Thaw a day's worth of cubes in the refrigerator for 4 hours.

Variation

Branch out with other roots and introduce your baby to rutabaga, daikon and taro.

Apple Oat Porridge

Dates and apple add even more fiber to healthful whole-grain steel-cut oats, with natural sweetness to make this porridge taste delicious to your baby.

∽ ∽

MAKES ABOUT 2¹/₂ CUPS (625 ML)

- **Ice cube trays or muffin pan, lined with paper or silicone liners**

2	large pitted Medjool dates	2
1	large apple, chopped	1
¹/₂ cup	steel-cut oats	125 mL
2 cups	water	500 mL

Tip

Leave the skin on the apple: it's very nutritious, and your Vitamix will make it invisible and soft enough for baby to eat.

1. In a small saucepan, combine dates, apple, oats and water. Bring to a boil over medium-high heat, stirring occasionally. Reduce heat to medium-low, cover and boil gently for 25 minutes, stirring every 10 minutes, until very soft and creamy.

2. Transfer the oat mixture to the Vitamix container and secure the lid. With the switch on Variable, select speed 1 and turn the machine on. Gradually increase the speed to 10, then flip the switch to High and blend for about 40 seconds or until very smooth.

3. Let cool and serve immediately, store in an airtight container in the refrigerator for up to 24 hours or transfer to ice cube trays or prepared muffin pan in appropriate portions and freeze until solid. Once frozen, transfer to airtight containers or sealable freezer bags and store in the freezer for up to 2 months. Thaw a day's worth of cubes in the refrigerator for 4 hours.

Variation

Try this recipe with another fruit, such as a pear, peach or plum, in place of the apple.

Carrot and Cinnamon Oats

Your baby will start a lifelong relationship with cinnamon when you feed him this creamy breakfast. Just a tiny bit is enough to give him an introduction to his first spice. As it becomes familiar, you can increase the amount and see how it goes.

MAKES ABOUT 2¹/₂ CUPS (625 ML)

- **Ice cube trays or muffin pan, lined with paper or silicone liners**

4	large pitted prunes	4
1 cup	sliced carrots	250 mL
¹/₂ cup	steel-cut oats	125 mL
¹/₄ tsp	ground cinnamon	1 mL
2 cups	water	500 mL

Tip

If your baby is constipated, prunes are a gentle and natural way to help relieve his discomfort. Try soaking prunes in boiling water, then purée them in the Vitamix to serve solo.

1. In a small saucepan, combine prunes, carrots, oats, cinnamon and water. Bring to a boil over medium-high heat, stirring occasionally. Reduce heat to medium-low, cover and boil gently for 25 minutes, stirring every 10 minutes, until very soft and creamy.

2. Transfer the oat mixture to the Vitamix container and secure the lid. With the switch on Variable, select speed 1 and turn the machine on. Gradually increase the speed to 10, then flip the switch to High and blend for about 40 seconds or until very smooth.

3. Let cool and serve immediately, store in an airtight container in the refrigerator for up to 24 hours or transfer to ice cube trays or prepared muffin pan in appropriate portions and freeze until solid. Once frozen, transfer to airtight containers or sealable freezer bags and store in the freezer for up to 2 months. Thaw a day's worth of cubes in the refrigerator for 4 hours.

Variation

Creamy Millet Cereal: Substitute millet for the oats and cook for 5 minutes longer.

Kale, Corn and Carrots

When health authorities tell you to eat the rainbow, they mean to seek out an assortment of colors so that you get a balanced array of nutrients from vegetables. In this recipe you can feed your baby three colors at once.

MAKES ABOUT 2 CUPS (500 ML)

- **Ice cube trays or muffin pan, lined with paper or silicone liners**

3 cups	lightly packed trimmed kale leaves	750 mL
1 cup	sliced carrots	250 mL
1/2 cup	corn kernels	125 mL
1 cup	water (approx.)	250 mL

Tip

To use fresh sweet corn, figure that an average ear of corn will yield about 1/2 cup (125 mL) kernels.

1. In a small saucepan, combine kale, carrots, corn and water. Bring to a boil over medium-high heat, stirring occasionally. Reduce heat to medium-low, cover and simmer for 10 minutes or until vegetables are soft.

2. Transfer the vegetables and cooking liquid to the Vitamix container and secure the lid. With the switch on Variable, select speed 1 and turn the machine on. Gradually increase the speed to 10, then flip the switch to High and blend for 40 seconds or until smooth. If the purée is very thick, add water, a little bit at a time, and blend to the desired consistency.

3. Let cool and serve immediately, store in an airtight container in the refrigerator for up to 24 hours or transfer to ice cube trays or prepared muffin pan in appropriate portions and freeze until solid. Once frozen, transfer to airtight containers or sealable freezer bags and store in the freezer for up to 2 months. Thaw a day's worth of cubes in the refrigerator for 4 hours.

Variation

For a different yellow vegetable, substitute chopped yellow summer squash for the corn.

Sweet Potatoes and Bananas

This orange purée is sure to be a hit with your baby, with the roasted bananas giving the sweet potatoes an extra hint of sweetness.

∽ ∽

MAKES ABOUT 2 CUPS (500 ML)

- **Preheat oven to 400°F (200°C)**
- **2 baking sheets**
- **Ice cube trays or muffin pan, lined with paper or silicone liners**

1	medium sweet potato (about 9 oz/270 g)	1
1 tsp	canola oil	5 mL
2	bananas, peeled	2

Tip

Roasting the banana is recommended to make sure any bacteria are killed, keeping your baby safe. It's also delicious.

1. Pierce sweet potato three times with a fork and place on a baking sheet. Roast in preheated oven for about 25 minutes or until tender when pierced with a knife. Let cool on pan on a wire rack until cool enough to handle, then strip off and discard skin.

2. Meanwhile, spread canola oil on another baking sheet and place bananas on top. Roast for about 16 minutes, flipping the bananas over halfway through, until soft and browned. Let cool on pan on a wire rack.

3. Place the sweet potato and bananas in the Vitamix container and secure the lid. With the switch on Variable, select speed 1 and turn the machine on. Gradually increase the speed to 10, then flip the switch to High and blend for 40 seconds or until smooth.

4. Let cool and serve immediately, store in an airtight container in the refrigerator for up to 24 hours or transfer to ice cube trays or prepared muffin pan in appropriate portions and freeze until solid. Once frozen, transfer to airtight containers or sealable freezer bags and store in the freezer for up to 2 months. Thaw a day's worth of cubes in the refrigerator for 4 hours.

Variation

There are many fun varieties of sweet potatoes available, ranging from deep orange to yellow, white and even purple. Try them all.

Red Lentils and Carrots

Introduce your baby to a mild, easy legume, and she will develop a taste for one of the most healthful foods out there. Red lentils fit the bill, and cook quickly.

∾ ∾

MAKES ABOUT 2³/₄ CUPS (675 ML)

- **Ice cube trays or muffin pan, lined with paper or silicone liners**

. . . .

2	large carrots, chopped	2
1/2 cup	dried red lentils	125 mL
2 cups	water (approx.)	500 mL

Tip

Red lentils are fantastic for the whole family. Make a double batch of this and use half to make a simple hummus: just stir in 2 tbsp (30 mL) each of tahini and lemon juice and season to taste with salt.

1. In a small saucepan, combine carrots, lentils and water. Bring to a boil over medium-high heat, stirring occasionally. Reduce heat to medium-low, cover and boil gently for 25 minutes, stirring every 10 minutes, until lentils are falling-apart tender.

2. Transfer the lentil mixture to the Vitamix container and secure the lid. With the switch on Variable, select speed 1 and turn the machine on. Gradually increase the speed to 10, then flip the switch to High and blend for 40 seconds or until smooth. If the purée is very thick, add water, a little bit at a time, and blend to the desired consistency.

3. Let cool and serve immediately, store in an airtight container in the refrigerator for up to 24 hours or transfer to ice cube trays or prepared muffin pan in appropriate portions and freeze until solid. Once frozen, transfer to airtight containers or sealable freezer bags and store in the freezer for up to 2 months. Thaw a day's worth of cubes in the refrigerator for 4 hours.

Variation

Small green lentils are also excellent in this recipe.

Chickpeas and Quinoa

Two high-protein plant foods, chickpeas and quinoa, give you plenty of fiber and nutrition for an affordable price. Your baby needs to be introduced to the flavors of these healthy foods, to help build a lifetime of healthful eating habits.

MAKES ABOUT 2 CUPS (500 ML)

- **Ice cube trays or muffin pan, lined with paper or silicone liners**

1/4 cup	dried chickpeas	60 mL
	Water	
1/4 cup	white quinoa, rinsed	60 mL

Tip

Soak the chickpeas in the refrigerator overnight, especially in the summer, when sitting out at room temperature can cause them to ferment.

1. Rinse chickpeas and place in a bowl with 1 cup (250 mL) cool water. Let soak overnight in the refrigerator or at room temperature, then drain.

2. In a small saucepan, combine soaked chickpeas and 3 cups (750 mL) fresh water. Bring to a boil over medium-high heat, stirring occasionally. Reduce heat to medium-low, cover and simmer for 45 minutes, adjusting heat as necessary to keep the water at a simmer, until chickpeas are soft.

3. Stir in quinoa, increase heat to medium-high and return to a boil. Cover, reduce heat to low and simmer for 20 minutes or until quinoa is tender.

4. Transfer the chickpea mixture to the Vitamix container and secure the lid. With the switch on Variable, select speed 1 and turn the machine on. Gradually increase the speed to 10, then flip the switch to High and blend for 1 minute or until smooth. Turn the machine off. If the purée is very thick, add water, a little bit at a time, and blend to the desired consistency.

5. Let cool and serve immediately, store in an airtight container in the refrigerator for up to 24 hours or transfer to ice cube trays or prepared muffin pan in appropriate portions and freeze until solid. Once frozen, transfer to airtight containers or sealable freezer bags and store in the freezer for up to 2 months. Thaw a day's worth of cubes in the refrigerator for 4 hours.

Variation

White beans make a nice substitute for chickpeas; they are mild in flavor and pale in color.

Chicken and Spinach

Combine chicken and spinach for a hearty, vegetable-rich meal for your growing baby.

◎◎◎◎◎◎◎◎◎◎◎◎◎◎◎◎◎◎◎◎◎◎◎◎◎◎◎◎◎◎

MAKES 2 CUPS (500 ML)

- **Ice cube trays or muffin pan, lined with paper or silicone liners**

8 oz	boneless skinless chicken breast, cut into 1-inch (2.5 cm) cubes (1½ cups/375 mL)	250 g
1	stalk celery, chopped	1
1½ cups	water (approx.)	375 mL
2 cups	lightly packed spinach leaves	500 mL

Tip

Don't bother to chop the spinach; just wash it well and add it to the pot. The Vitamix will take care of it.

1. In a small saucepan, combine chicken, celery and water. Bring to a boil over medium-high heat, stirring occasionally. Reduce heat to low, cover and simmer for 15 minutes or until chicken is no longer pink inside. Stir in spinach, cover and simmer for 5 minutes or until spinach is soft.

2. Transfer the chicken mixture to the Vitamix container and secure the lid. With the switch on Variable, select speed 1 and turn the machine on. Gradually increase the speed to 10, then flip the switch to High and blend for 1 minute or until velvety smooth. Turn the machine off. If the purée is very thick, add water, a little bit at a time, and blend to the desired consistency.

3. Let cool and serve immediately, store in an airtight container in the refrigerator for up to 24 hours or transfer to ice cube trays or prepared muffin pan in appropriate portions and freeze until solid. Once frozen, transfer to airtight containers or sealable freezer bags and store in the freezer for up to 2 months. Thaw a day's worth of cubes in the refrigerator for 4 hours.

Variation

Introduce your baby to Swiss chard or arugula by substituting a few leaves for the spinach, then gradually increase with each batch.

Chicken Stew

This stew is a complete meal in one bowl, with protein, vegetables and a whole grain in a convenient purée.

෴ ෴ ෴ ෴ ෴ ෴ ෴ ෴ ෴ ෴ ෴ ෴ ෴ ෴ ෴ ෴ ෴ ෴ ෴

MAKES 2 CUPS (500 ML)

- **Ice cube trays or muffin pan, lined with paper or silicone liners**

. . . .

1	small carrot, chopped	1
1	stalk celery, chopped	1
1 tbsp	millet	15 mL
2 1/2 cups	water	625 mL
4 oz	boneless skinless chicken breast, cut into 1-inch (2.5 cm) cubes (3/4 cup/175 mL)	125 g

Tip

When purchasing the chicken breast for this recipe, look for a package that contains an 8-oz (250 g) piece. It will be easy to cut the piece in half and use the other half for another recipe.

1. In a small pot, combine carrot, celery, millet and water. Bring to a boil over medium-high heat, stirring occasionally. Reduce heat to medium-low, cover and boil gently for 10 minutes. Stir in chicken, reduce heat to low, cover and simmer for 10 minutes or until chicken is no longer pink inside and vegetables are very soft.

2. Transfer the chicken mixture to the Vitamix container and secure the lid. With the switch on Variable, select speed 1 and turn the machine on. Gradually increase the speed to 7 as the food engages with the blades. Once on speed 7, blend for 30 seconds.

3. Turn the machine off and use a spatula to scrape down the sides of the container. Replace the lid and blend for about 10 seconds or until very smooth.

4. Let cool and serve immediately or transfer to ice cube trays or prepared muffin pan in appropriate portions and freeze until solid. Once frozen, transfer to airtight containers or sealable freezer bags and store in the freezer for up to 2 months. Thaw a day's worth of cubes in the refrigerator for 4 hours.

Variation

Feed your baby some nourishing salmon by substituting wild-caught salmon for the chicken. Cook for only 5 minutes after adding the salmon, then purée.

Turkey, Potato and Green Bean Stew

Turkey is a mild-tasting, high-protein food for your baby. This stew has green beans and potato, just like the Thanksgiving meals your baby will love later on.

∽◌∽

MAKES ABOUT 2 CUPS (500 ML)

- **Ice cube trays or muffin pan, lined with paper or silicone liners**

. . . .

3/4 cup	trimmed green beans	175 mL
3/4 cup	cubed peeled potato	175 mL
4 oz	boneless skinless turkey breast, cut into 1-inch (2.5 cm) cubes (3/4 cup/175 mL)	125 g
1 1/2 cups	water (approx.)	375 mL

Tip

Buy a turkey breast cutlet and divide it into 4-oz (125 g) portions to use for this recipe. Freeze the remaining portions until you need another batch.

1. In a small saucepan, combine green beans, potato, turkey and water. Bring to a boil over medium-high heat, stirring occasionally. Reduce heat to low, cover and simmer for 15 minutes or until turkey is no longer pink inside and vegetables are very soft.

2. Transfer the turkey mixture to the Vitamix container and secure the lid. With the switch on Variable, select speed 1 and turn the machine on. Gradually increase the speed to 10, then flip the switch to High and blend for 1 minute or until velvety smooth. Turn the machine off. If the purée is very thick, add water, a little bit at a time, and blend to the desired consistency.

3. Let cool and serve immediately or transfer to ice cube trays or prepared muffin pan in appropriate portions and freeze until solid. Once frozen, transfer to airtight containers or sealable freezer bags and store in the freezer for up to 2 months. Thaw a day's worth of cubes in the refrigerator for 4 hours.

Variation

For a little more vitamin A, and to add a little color to the stew, substitute sweet potato for the potato.

NONDAIRY MILKS

TIPS FOR SUCCESS

- Many nuts, seeds, beans and grains can be made into milk. I selected those that make a whiter milk, since that is familiar. But if you don't care about color, you can make milk from green pistachios or pumpkin seeds, or black beans, for different tints and flavors in the finished milk. Chickpeas and some other beans are too starchy and gelatinous to strain well.
- **To strain milk:** If you wish to strain your milk after blending it, place a nut milk straining bag in a colander, or place a fine-mesh sieve lined with cheesecloth over a large bowl. Pour the milk through the bag or sieve. Squeeze the bag, or press with a rubber spatula through the sieve, to extract the milk.
- There are many benefits to drinking nut, grain and seed milks, but if you are looking for protein, soy milk is the all-time champion. A cup (250 mL) of soy milk ranges from 7 to 10 grams of protein — even more if you use less water.
- To use nondairy milks in baking, it is helpful to acidulate them. Add 1 tbsp (15 mL) apple cider vinegar or lemon juice to each cup (250 mL) of nondairy milk and let stand for a few minutes. This makes a good stand-in for buttermilk and also helps to activate baking soda, which needs an acid to work.
- The great thing about making your own nondairy milks is that you control the thickness: simply add less water for a thicker, more concentrated milk or more water for a thinner milk.

Almond Milk

Almond milk, with its bright white color and creamy, neutral taste, is probably the most popular nondairy milk these days. It stands in for dairy milks very successfully in both sweet and savory applications. Making your own means you can leave out the stabilizers and emulsifiers.

MAKES ABOUT 4 CUPS (1 L), OR 3½ CUPS (875 ML) IF STRAINED

1 cup	whole raw almonds	250 mL
	Water	
2	pitted Medjool dates (optional)	2
1 tsp	vanilla extract (optional)	5 mL

Tips

If desired, you can use blanched whole almonds or slivered almonds, which have had the skin removed. You can also soak the whole almonds in boiling water, then, when cool enough to handle, squeeze each one to loosen and slip the skin off. If you don't mind a slightly darker color, just use whole, skin-on almonds.

You can use ¼ cup (60 mL) brown rice syrup in place of the dates, if you prefer.

Go unsweetened, for a clean almond taste, or use your favorite sweetener. Sugar is very sweet and neutral-tasting, while pure maple syrup or dark agave nectar will produce a stronger flavor.

If you choose to strain the milk, you should have about ½ to ¾ cup (125 to 175 mL) of nut pulp left over. Save it for another use, such as a facial, or dry it out to use as flour (see Making Almond Flour, at right).

Almond milk will settle in the refrigerator and will need to be shaken to remix the solids and liquids. Taking the step of stabilizing the milk, as in step 3, helps it to stay mixed longer.

1. Place almonds in a medium bowl and add enough cool water to cover. Let soak at room temperature overnight. Drain.

2. Place 3 cups (750 mL) fresh water, the drained almonds, dates (if using) and vanilla (if using) in the Vitamix container and secure the lid. With the switch on Variable, select speed 1 and turn the machine on. Gradually increase the speed to 10, then flip the switch to High and blend for 2 to 3 minutes or until completely smooth.

3. If desired, strain the milk (see tip, page 211), then, to stabilize it, pour it into a medium pot over medium heat and heat, stirring constantly, to 160°F (71°C). (It will thicken slightly.)

4. Use immediately or let cool completely, then pour into jars and store in the refrigerator for up to 1 week. Shake well before serving.

Making Almond Flour

To dry the leftover nut pulp for flour, preheat the oven to 170°F (80°C) if your oven goes that low, or 200°F (100°C) if that is the lowest setting. Line a baking sheet with parchment paper and spread the pulp on the parchment. Put the pan in the oven, leaving the door ajar. Bake for 2 hours, then check the moisture level of the pulp by squeezing a few handfuls. If it still feels damp, put it back in for up to 1 hour. When the pulp is dry, let it cool in the pan on a wire rack, then transfer it to the Vitamix and secure the lid. With the switch on Variable, select speed 1 and turn the machine on. Quickly increase the speed to 10 and process for 20 seconds, just until powdery.

Cashew Milk

Cashew milk is one of the richest, creamiest milks out there, depending on how much water you use. There's no need to strain cashew milk; just shake it well.

MAKES ABOUT 5 CUPS (1.25 L)

1 cup	raw cashews	250 mL
	Water	
1/4 cup	brown rice syrup or liquid honey (optional)	60 mL
1/2 tsp	vanilla extract (optional)	2 mL
Pinch	salt (optional)	Pinch

Tips

For a more stable milk, use boiling water in step 2 or heat the finished milk to 160°F (71°C) in a pot on the stove, stirring constantly. If you want a raw milk, use cold water and don't cook it.

Buy broken raw cashew pieces for making milks; they are usually quite a bit less expensive.

This is about as rich as 2% milk. For a mouthfeel more like whole milk, use 3 cups (750 mL) water in step 2.

1. Place cashews in a medium bowl and add enough cool water to cover. Let soak at room temperature overnight. Drain.

2. Place 4 cups (1 L) fresh water and the drained cashews in the Vitamix container and secure the lid. With the switch on Variable, select speed 1 and turn the machine on. Gradually increase the speed to 10, then flip the switch to High and blend for 45 to 60 seconds or until completely smooth.

3. Turn the machine off and add the brown rice syrup, vanilla and/or salt (if using). Replace the lid and blend for a few seconds, until incorporated.

4. Use immediately or pour into jars and store in the refrigerator for up to 1 week. Shake well before serving.

Golden Almond Cashew Milk

Golden milk is a comforting and healing beverage that is good for colds, aches and pains, and brain health. The addition of black pepper makes the turmeric measurably more potent, and contributes a peppery kick. If you make a habit of drinking golden milk, you'll join the ranks of the centenarians of Okinawa, who drink it daily.

MAKES ABOUT 4 CUPS (1 L), OR 3¹/₂ CUPS (875 ML) IF STRAINED

³/₄ cup	blanched almonds (see tip)	175 mL
¹/₄ cup	raw cashews	60 mL
3 cups	cool water	750 mL
6	slices fresh turmeric (or 1¹/₂ tsp/7 mL ground turmeric)	6
1 tsp	whole black peppercorns	5 mL
3 tbsp	grated palm sugar, Manuka honey or royal jelly (see tips)	45 mL
1 tbsp	rose water	15 mL

Tips

For the blanched almonds, you can use either whole or slivered almonds. If using whole, measure out a heaping ³/₄ cup (175 mL); if using slivered, measure out a level ³/₄ cup (175 mL).

You can play with the amount of turmeric and pepper you use, to suit your taste.

Manuka honey is a variety of honey from Australia that has measurable antibiotic and antioxidant properties, so it is a good addition to your golden milk during cold season. If you cannot find it, you can use any honey in this recipe.

Royal jelly is the special, concentrated honey that is served to the queen bee. It is higher in many nutrients and is considered very energizing.

Almond milk will settle in the refrigerator and will need to be shaken to remix the solids and liquids. Taking the step of stabilizing the milk, as in step 5, helps it to stay mixed longer.

1. In a bowl, combine almonds, cashews and water. Let soak at room temperature overnight.

2. Transfer the nuts and soaking water to the Vitamix container and secure the lid. With the switch on Variable, select speed 1 and turn the machine on. Gradually increase the speed to 10, then flip the switch to High and blend for 2 to 3 minutes or until smooth.

3. If desired, strain the milk (see tip, page 211), then pour it back into the Vitamix container.

4. Add the turmeric, peppercorns, sugar and rose water to the container and secure the lid. With the switch on Variable, select speed 1 and turn the machine on. Gradually increase the speed to 10, then flip the switch to High and blend for 1 minute, until smooth.

5. To stabilize the milk, pour it into a medium pot over medium heat and heat, stirring constantly, to 160°F (71°C). (It will thicken slightly.)

6. Serve warm or pour into jars and let cool completely, then cover and store in the refrigerator for up to 1 week.

Coconut Milk

This coconut milk is midway between the type in a can and the kind sold as a beverage. It has the benefit of being incredibly easy to make, especially compared to cracking open a whole coconut and making milk from that. The sweet, pure white milk is really delicious without any additional sweetener.

MAKES ABOUT 1¹/₂ CUPS (375 ML)

1 cup	unsweetened shredded coconut	250 mL
	Cool water	
2 cups	boiling water	500 mL
1 to 2 tbsp	raw sugar, agave nectar or brown rice syrup (optional)	15 to 30 mL

Tip

Keep unsweetened shredded coconut in the pantry so you will always be ready to make this milk.

1. Place coconut in a jar or bowl and add enough cool water to cover by 1 inch (2.5 cm). Let soak for at least 3 hours at room temperature or for up to 3 days in the refrigerator. Drain.

2. Place the boiling water, drained coconut and sugar to taste (if using) in the Vitamix container and secure the lid. With the switch on Variable, select speed 1 and turn the machine on. Gradually increase the speed to 10, then flip the switch to High and blend for 3 minutes or until completely smooth.

3. If desired, strain the milk (see tip, page 211).

4. Use immediately or pour into jars and store in the refrigerator for up to 1 week. Shake well before serving.

Variation

For a spicy Indian-inspired beverage, add 1 tbsp (15 mL) Chai Spice Mix (see the recipe for Chai Russians, page 281) to the mixture after straining, and blend again for 30 seconds.

Vanilla Soy Milk

Soy milk has the most protein of all the nondairy milks, and if you make it with less water, it will be even higher in protein. When you make your own, you can skip the additives and stabilizers. It's silky and rich-tasting, and the vanilla covers the hint of beany taste.

MAKES ABOUT 7 CUPS (1.75 L)

- **Large strainer**
- **Nut milk straining bag or cheesecloth**

1 cup	dried soybeans	250 mL
	Water	
1/2 cup	brown rice syrup (approx.)	125 mL
1/2 tsp	vanilla extract (approx.)	2 mL
Pinch	salt	Pinch

1. Place soybeans in a medium bowl and add enough cool water to cover by 2 inches (5 cm). Let soak at room temperature overnight. Drain and rinse.

2. Place 4 cups (1 L) fresh water and the drained beans in the Vitamix container and secure the lid. With the switch on Variable, select speed 1 and turn the machine on. Gradually increase the speed to 10, then flip the switch to High and blend for 1 minute or until smooth.

3. Transfer the milk to a large pot and stir in 4 cups (1 L) water. Bring to a boil over high heat (be careful: it will foam up and boil over easily). Reduce heat and simmer, stirring often, for 20 minutes. As it simmers, a thick foam will form on top; use a slotted spoon to skim off the foam a couple of times.

4. Meanwhile, place a large bowl or pot in the sink and set the strainer in the bowl. Put the nut milk bag in the strainer, or line the strainer with cheesecloth.

5. Remove the milk from the heat and skim off the foam one last time. Pour about 2 cups (500 mL) at a time into the bag or cheesecloth. Using a rubber spatula, stir the draining milk to speed the draining. If your bag is getting full, scrape the pulp to the side, if you can, and pour in the rest of the milk a little at a time as it drains. Stir and press the pulp until it is pretty thick, then pull up the bag or cloth around the pulp and twist to make a bundle. Press on the pulp through the fabric to extract as much milk as you can.

6. Stir rice syrup, vanilla and salt into the warm soy milk. Taste and add more rice syrup or vanilla as desired, stirring to mix well.

7. Pour into jars and let cool completely. Use immediately or cover and store in the refrigerator for up to 1 week. Shake well before serving.

Variation

Add 2 tsp (10 mL) pumpkin pie spice with the vanilla, for a pumpkin pie–scented milk.

Tips

Always buy organic soybeans — they are free of pesticides and herbicides, and are non-GMO.

If desired, save the pulp (okara) for a facial mask (see page 297) or another use.

Sesame Maple Soy Milk

On their own, sesame seeds are too oily to make a good milk, but added to soy milk, they boost the calcium content and add a nutty flavor. I use brown sesame seeds, which are unhulled, because the Vitamix can power through the nutritious hulls with no problem.

〜〜〜〜〜〜〜〜〜〜〜〜〜〜〜〜〜〜〜〜〜〜〜〜〜〜〜〜〜

MAKES ABOUT 7¹/₂ CUPS (1.875 L)

- **Large strainer**
- **Nut milk straining bag or cheesecloth**

. . . .

1 cup	dried soybeans	250 mL
	Water	
¹/₂ cup	brown sesame seeds	125 mL
¹/₂ cup	pure maple syrup (approx.)	125 mL
Pinch	salt	Pinch

1. Place soybeans in a medium bowl and add enough cool water to cover by 2 inches (5 cm). Let soak at room temperature overnight. Drain and rinse.

2. Meanwhile, in a 2-cup (500 mL) measuring cup or bowl, combine sesame seeds and 1 cup (250 mL) water. Let soak for at least 1 hour at room temperature or for up to 2 days in the refrigerator.

3. Place 3 cups (750 mL) water, the drained beans and sesame seeds with soaking water in the Vitamix container and secure the lid. With the switch on Variable, select speed 1 and turn the machine on. Gradually increase the speed to 10, then flip the switch to High and blend for 1 minute or until smooth.

4. Transfer the milk to a large pot and stir in 4 cups (1 L) water. Bring to a boil over high heat (be careful: it will foam up and boil over easily). Reduce heat and simmer, stirring often, for 20 minutes. As it simmers, a thick foam will form on top; use a slotted spoon to skim off the foam a couple of times.

5. Meanwhile, place a large bowl or pot in the sink and set the strainer in the bowl. Put the nut milk bag in the strainer, or line the strainer with cheesecloth.

6. Remove the milk from the heat and skim off the foam one last time. Pour about 2 cups (500 mL) at a time into the bag or cheesecloth. Using a rubber spatula, stir the draining milk to speed the draining. If your bag or cloth is getting full, scrape the pulp to the side, if you can, and pour in the rest of the milk a little at a time as it drains. Stir and press the pulp until it is pretty thick, then pull up the bag or cloth around the pulp and twist to make a bundle. Press on the pulp through the fabric to extract as much milk as you can.

7. Stir maple syrup and salt into the warm soy milk. Taste and add more maple syrup as desired, stirring to mix well.

8. Pour into jars and let cool completely. Use immediately or cover and store in the refrigerator for up to 1 week. Shake well before serving.

Variation

Sunflower seeds can stand in for the sesame seeds.

Tips

Always use a dark (grade B) maple syrup, which has the most flavor.

If desired, save the pulp (okara) for a facial mask (see page 297) or another use.

Barley Milk with Apple

If you are using barley only to make soup, you are missing out. Stock up on this healthful grain and use it in salads, pilafs and this milk. Barley is rich in the beta-glucans starch that lowers cholesterol. It also contains a little bit of gluten, so it's not appropriate for people with celiac disease or gluten intolerance.

∿∿∿∿∿∿∿∿∿∿∿∿∿∿∿∿∿∿∿∿∿∿∿∿∿∿∿∿∿

MAKES ABOUT 7 CUPS (1.75 L)

6 cups	water, divided	1.5 L
1/4 cup	pearl barley	60 mL
1	medium apple, cut into large chunks	1
Pinch	salt	Pinch
2 tbsp	granulated sugar (optional)	30 mL

Tip

For a healthy dose of minerals and vitamins, try making this milk with hulled or "naked" barley that has not been pearled, a process that removes the bran. It will take closer to an hour to cook; check and replenish the water as needed.

1. In a small saucepan, bring 2 cups (500 mL) water to a boil over high heat. Add barley, apple and salt; return to a boil. Reduce heat to low, cover and simmer for 30 minutes or until tender. Remove from heat, uncover and let cool slightly.

2. Transfer the barley mixture to the Vitamix container and add the remaining water and the sugar (if using). Secure the lid. With the switch on Variable, select speed 1 and turn the machine on. Gradually increase the speed to 10, then flip the switch to High and blend for 1 minute or until smooth.

3. Pour into jars and let cool completely. Use immediately or cover and store in the refrigerator for up to 1 week. Shake well before serving.

Variation

Try using a pear in place of the apple, for a delicate pear flavor.

Vanilla Flax Milk

Flax is an amazing little seed, loaded with essential fatty acids and lignans, a special kind of fiber that reduces cholesterol and inflammation. Making milk from flax means leaving some of the healthy fiber behind after straining, so be sure to use that miracle fiber in a baked good or skin treatment.

MAKES ABOUT 6 CUPS (1.5 L)

1 cup	golden flax seeds	250 mL
7 cups	water, divided	1.75 L
1/2 cup	granulated sugar or pure maple syrup	125 mL
1 1/2 tsp	vanilla extract	7 mL

Tips

Brown or golden flax seeds both work in this recipe, but the lighter-colored golden flax seeds make a whiter milk.

Adding all the water in step 2 may cause an overflow while blending so it's best to thin as desired after blending.

1. In a jar or bowl, combine flax seeds and 2 cups (500 mL) water. Cover and let soak in the refrigerator overnight.

2. Place 4 cups (1 L) water and the flax mixture in the Vitamix container and secure the lid. With the switch on Variable, select speed 1 and turn the machine on. Gradually increase the speed to 10, then flip the switch to High and blend for 1 minute or until smooth.

3. If desired, strain the milk (see tip, page 211), then whisk in the remaining water, sugar and vanilla until blended.

4. Use immediately or pour into jars and store in the refrigerator for up to 1 week. Shake well before serving. If the milk seems too thick, add a little water and shake to mix.

Variation

Whisk in 2 tsp (10 mL) pumpkin pie spice, for a seasonal treat.

Sunny Vanilla Millet Milk

The sunny yellow tint of millet lends itself to a pairing with another golden food, the health-promoting turmeric root.

MAKES ABOUT 3 CUPS (750 ML)

1/4 cup	millet	60 mL
3 cups	water, divided	750 mL
1/4 tsp	ground turmeric	1 mL
2 tbsp	liquid honey	30 mL
1 tsp	vanilla extract	5 mL

Tips

For raw foodists, soaking will be the preferred method, and millet is soft enough to blend to a creamy milk in the Vitamix after soaking. If you want a slightly sweeter milk, and want it within the hour, use the cooking method.

Turmeric is a potent protector, and studies link regular consumption of the bright yellow spice with lower rates of Alzheimer's disease, reduced aches and pains, and a healthy liver.

1. To soak the millet, place it in a bowl and add 1½ cups (375 mL) water; let soak at room temperature for at least 8 hours or overnight. Alternatively, to cook the millet, in a small saucepan, combine millet and 1½ cups (375 mL) water; bring to a boil over medium-high heat. Reduce heat to low, cover and simmer for 20 minutes or until tender.

2. Transfer the millet with its soaking or cooking water to the Vitamix container and add the remaining water. Secure the lid. With the switch on Variable, select speed 1 and turn the machine on. Gradually increase the speed to 10, then flip the switch to High and blend for 1 minute.

3. Turn the machine off and add the turmeric, honey and vanilla. Replace the lid. With the switch on Variable, select speed 1 and turn the machine on. Gradually increase the speed to 10 and blend for 5 seconds or until well mixed.

4. Use immediately or pour into jars and store in the refrigerator for up to 1 week. Shake well before serving.

Variation

If you have access to fresh turmeric, use a heaping teaspoon (5 mL) of minced fresh turmeric in place of ground.

Chocolate Millet Milk

Millet is one of the most underappreciated grains. Mild, sweet and gluten-free, it is a tiny powerhouse that can be ground for flour or cooked like rice. It also makes a light, lean milk that will remind you of rice milk in texture.

MAKES ABOUT 4 CUPS (1 L)

1/4 cup	millet	60 mL
4 cups	water, divided	1 L
4	large pitted Medjool dates	4
4 tsp	unsweetened cocoa powder	20 mL
1/4 tsp	vanilla extract	1 mL

1. To soak the millet, place it in a bowl and add 2 cups (500 mL) water; let soak at room temperature for at least 8 hours or overnight. Alternatively, to cook the millet, in a small saucepan, combine millet and 2 cups (500 mL) water; bring to a boil over medium-high heat. Reduce heat to low, cover and simmer for 20 minutes or until tender.

2. Transfer the millet with its soaking or cooking water to the Vitamix container and add the remaining water, dates, cocoa and vanilla. Secure the lid. With the switch on Variable, select speed 1 and turn the machine on. Gradually increase the speed to 10, then flip the switch to High and blend for 2 minutes or until completely smooth.

3. Use immediately or pour into jars and store in the refrigerator for up to 1 week. Shake well before serving.

Variation

Sweeten your milk with 2 tbsp (30 mL) packed light brown sugar (in addition to the dates), for a sweeter chocolate milk.

Vanilla Brown Rice Milk

This is a great way to use up leftover brown rice. You can cook up a big batch of brown rice to use for lunches and dinners, and use some of it to make this milk.

MAKES ABOUT 5 CUPS (1.25 L)

4 cups	water	1 L
1 cup	cooked brown rice	250 mL
2 tbsp	brown rice syrup	30 mL
1 tsp	vanilla extract	5 mL
Pinch	salt (optional)	Pinch

1. Place the water, brown rice, brown rice syrup, vanilla and salt (if using) in the Vitamix container and secure the lid. With the switch on Variable, select speed 1 and turn the machine on. Gradually increase the speed to 10, then flip the switch to High and blend for 1 minute or until smooth. Turn the machine off.

2. Use immediately or pour into jars and store in the refrigerator for up to 1 week. Shake well before serving.

Variation

Use a whole grain rice blend, with red, black and other kinds of rice mixed with brown, for a nuttier, slightly more beige milk.

Horchata

If you've ever tried horchata at a Mexican restaurant, you know how refreshing and tasty it is over ice. This version is beefed up with almonds and brown rice, rather than the plain white rice most cooks use. Once you have a jar of horchata in the fridge, you may find yourself pouring it over cereal or into coffee and tea.

MAKES ABOUT 8 CUPS (2 L)

1/2 cup	blanched almonds (see tip)	125 mL
	Water	
1 cup	brown rice	250 mL
6 tbsp	granulated sugar	90 mL
2 tsp	ground cinnamon	10 mL
Pinch	salt	Pinch

Tips

For the blanched almonds, you can use either whole or slivered almonds. If using whole, measure out a heaping 1/2 cup (125 mL); if using slivered, measure out a level 1/2 cup (125 mL).

Soak the brown rice overnight too, then drain off the water before cooking, and you will decrease the amount of arsenic in the grain. Trace amounts of arsenic have been found in the bran of brown rice, originating in the soil where it was grown. Arsenic levels are highest in rice grown in the American South and lower in the western states and overseas. Soaking removes a good part of it.

For a thinner milk, add more water to taste in step 3.

1. Place almonds in a medium bowl and add enough cool water to cover. Let soak at room temperature overnight. Drain.

2. In a small saucepan, bring 2 cups (500 mL) water to a boil over high heat. Stir in rice and return to a boil. Reduce heat to low, cover and simmer for about 40 minutes or until the water is absorbed and the rice is tender.

3. Place 6 cups (1.5 L) water, the drained almonds, rice, sugar, cinnamon and salt in the Vitamix container and secure the lid. With the switch on Variable, select speed 1 and turn the machine on. Gradually increase the speed to 10, then flip the switch to High and blend for 2 to 3 minutes or until smooth.

4. Pour into jars and let cool completely. Use immediately or cover and store in the refrigerator for up to 1 week. Shake well before serving.

Variations

Use white rice for a more traditional taste, cooking it for about 20 minutes in step 2.

If you like cinnamon, add another 1 tsp (5 mL).

Almond Hazelnut Creamer

Almonds make a pretty neutral milk, but with a boost of hazelnuts and almond extract, this rich creamer becomes a dense, nutty celebration. Take a jar to work, and you will be the envy of the coffee-drinking crowd.

MAKES ABOUT 2¹/₂ CUPS (625 ML)

³/₄ cup	blanched almonds (see tip)	175 mL
¹/₄ cup	skinned toasted hazelnuts (see tip)	60 mL
	Water	
2 tbsp	agave nectar	30 mL
¹/₄ tsp	almond extract	1 mL
Pinch	salt (optional)	Pinch

Tips

For the blanched almonds, you can use either whole or slivered almonds. If using whole, measure out a heaping ³/₄ cup (175 mL); if using slivered, measure out a level ³/₄ cup (175 mL).

To toast and skin hazelnuts, spread the hazelnuts on a rimmed baking sheet and roast in a 350°F (180°C) oven for 10 minutes or until fragrant and toasted. Immediately transfer to a folded kitchen towel, rub the skins from the nuts and let them cool. If some of the hazelnuts stubbornly refuse to give up their skins, return them to the baking sheet and roast for another 5 to 10 minutes, then try again.

Almond creamer will settle in the refrigerator and will need to be shaken to remix the solids and liquids. Taking the step of stabilizing the creamer, as in step 3, helps it to stay mixed longer.

1. Place almonds and hazelnuts in a medium bowl and add enough cool water to cover. Let soak at room temperature overnight. Drain.

2. Place 1¹/₂ cups (375 mL) water, the drained nuts, agave nectar, almond extract and salt (if using) in the Vitamix container and secure the lid. With the switch on Variable, select speed 1 and turn the machine on. Gradually increase the speed to 10, then flip the switch to High and blend for 1 minute or until smooth.

3. To stabilize the creamer, pour it into a medium pot over medium heat and heat, stirring constantly, to 160°F (71°C). (It will thicken slightly.)

4. Pour into jars and let cool completely, then cover and store in the refrigerator for up to 1 week. Shake well before using.

Variation

Honey is delicious in place of the agave nectar, or you can experiment with any other sweetener.

Cashew Vanilla Creamer

If you like to put cream in your coffee or tea, you will love this creamer. It's rich and creamy, and holds its own in a cup of strong brew. Raw cashews are the perfect base for a creamer, turning your morning cup into a real treat.

MAKES ABOUT 2 CUPS (500 ML)

1 cup	raw cashews	250 mL
	Water	
4	large pitted Medjool dates	4
1 tsp	vanilla extract	5 mL
	Liquid honey or granulated sugar (optional)	

Tips

You can soak and drain cashews for this recipe, then freeze them. To make the milk, just use hot water and let stand for a minute before blending.

You can use 2 tbsp (30 mL) liquid honey in place of the dates, if you prefer.

1. Place cashews in a medium bowl and add enough cool water to cover. Let soak at room temperature overnight. Drain.

2. Place 1 cup (250 mL) water, the drained cashews, dates and vanilla in the Vitamix container and secure the lid. With the switch on Variable, select speed 1 and turn the machine on. Gradually increase the speed to 5 and blend for 1 minute or until smooth. Flip the switch to High and blend for 1 to 2 minutes to make it really creamy.

3. Turn the machine off and taste the creamer. If you want it sweeter, add honey or sugar to taste, then replace the lid and blend until incorporated.

4. Use immediately or pour into jars and store in the refrigerator for up to 1 week. Shake well before using.

Variation

If you are into flavored creamers, your options are as wide as the selection of extracts at your grocery store. Almond extract, coconut extract and even buttered rum flavors can replace or pair with vanilla for an even more exotic taste.

Mixed Berry Probiotic Blast (page 228)

Aloe Papaya Walnut Skin Booster (page 244)

Goji and Raspberry Smoothie Bowl
with Muesli Topping (page 250)

Triple-Green Shrub (page 266)

Beet Berry Hibiscus Tea (page 268) and
Strawberry Kombucha Sipper (page 272)

Lemon Thyme Vodka Slushy (page 279)

Bloody Mary Slushy (page 280)

Cucumber Tea Tree Mask
for Breakouts (page 299)

SMOOTHIES

Blueberry Green Smoothie

This smoothie is the perfect place to hide healthy greens, in the guise of a tasty shake. This combo is great for supporting eye health, with antioxidants and vitamins that protect vision and overall immunity.

MAKES 2 SERVINGS

1 cup	coconut kefir or coconut water	250 mL
1/4 cup	large-flake (old-fashioned) rolled oats	60 mL
1	large frozen banana	1
1 1/2 cups	frozen blueberries	375 mL
4 oz	fresh spinach or kale leaves or other dark leafy greens	125 g

Tip

Spinach is the mildest in flavor, so if you are new to greens in your smoothie, start with spinach and work your way up to kale.

1. Place the kefir, oats, banana, blueberries and greens in the Vitamix container. Secure the lid, remove the lid plug and insert the tamper. With the switch on Variable, select speed 1 and turn the machine on. Gradually increase the speed to 10, using the tamper to push the ingredients into the blades, then flip the switch to High and blend for about 20 seconds or to the desired consistency. Serve immediately.

Variation

For a more filling smoothie, use dairy kefir and throw in some ice cubes so it won't be too thick.

Beat the Blues Smoothie

We all love basil in pesto, but did you know that fresh basil helps to fight depression? Your brain needs the good fats that are in the chia seeds in this smoothie too.

MAKES 2 SERVINGS		
1 cup	plain yogurt	250 mL
2 tbsp	chia seeds	30 mL
2 cups	frozen blueberries	500 mL
2 cups	lightly packed fresh spinach leaves	500 mL
1/2 cup	lightly packed fresh basil	125 mL
1/2 cup	ice cubes	125 mL

Tip

When fresh basil is in season, make this smoothie a regular feature of your morning routine.

1. Place the yogurt, chia seeds, blueberries, spinach, basil and ice cubes in the Vitamix container. Secure the lid, remove the lid plug and insert the tamper. With the switch on Variable, select speed 1 and turn the machine on. Gradually increase the speed to 10, using the tamper to push the ingredients into the blades, then flip the switch to High and blend for about 20 seconds or to the desired consistency. Serve immediately.

Variation

If you don't have chia seeds, substitute flax seeds or hemp seeds.

Strawberry Banana Smoothie

This thick, vibrantly pink-tinted smoothie is a great starter smoothie for kids and adults alike.

MAKES 2 SERVINGS		
1/2 cup	milk	125 mL
1 cup	plain Greek yogurt	250 mL
1/2 tsp	vanilla extract	2 mL
1	large frozen banana	1
2 cups	frozen strawberries	500 mL

Tip

The only sweetener is the banana, so if you want a little more sweetness, add 1 tbsp (15 mL) honey.

1. Place the milk, yogurt, vanilla, banana and strawberries in the Vitamix container. Secure the lid, remove the lid plug and insert the tamper. With the switch on Variable, select speed 1 and turn the machine on. Gradually increase the speed to 10, using the tamper to push the ingredients into the blades, then flip the switch to High and blend for about 20 seconds or to the desired consistency. Serve immediately.

Variation

Substitute other frozen berries, such as raspberries or blueberries.

Mixed Berry Probiotic Blast

Probiotics are the good bacteria in fermented foods like kefir and yogurt. They help to populate your gut with immune-boosting, supportive microorganisms. Adding a prebiotic like oats, a fiber-rich food that probiotic bacteria love, helps your good bacteria thrive.

MAKES 2 SERVINGS		
1 cup	plain kefir	250 mL
1/2 tsp	vanilla extract	2 mL
1/4 cup	large-flake (old-fashioned) rolled oats	60 mL
1	large frozen banana	1
2 cups	frozen mixed berries	500 mL

Tip

Frozen berries make the smoothie thicker and more like a milkshake, but if you have fresh ones, go ahead and celebrate the season by using them.

1. Place the kefir, vanilla, oats, banana and berries in the Vitamix container. Secure the lid, remove the lid plug and insert the tamper. With the switch on Variable, select speed 1 and turn the machine on. Gradually increase the speed to 10, using the tamper to push the ingredients into the blades, then flip the switch to High and blend for about 20 seconds or to the desired consistency. Serve immediately.

Variation

Other berries, or even frozen peaches, are delicious in this smoothie.

Cherry Pomegranate Antioxidant Smoothie

Red fruits are great sources of antioxidants, and cherries and pomegranate are delicious delivery systems for protective phytochemicals.

MAKES 2 SERVINGS		
1 cup	plain Greek yogurt	250 mL
1/2 cup	unsweetened pomegranate juice	125 mL
2 tbsp	chia seeds	30 mL
2 cups	frozen sweet cherries	500 mL

Tip

Pomegranate juice comes in all sorts of blends, with added juices like blueberry or açaí, which are also nice in this smoothie. Just make sure you don't buy one with added sugar.

1. Place the yogurt, pomegranate juice, chia seeds and cherries in the Vitamix container. Secure the lid, remove the lid plug and insert the tamper. With the switch on Variable, select speed 1 and turn the machine on. Gradually increase the speed to 10, using the tamper to push the ingredients into the blades, then flip the switch to High and blend for about 20 seconds or to the desired consistency. Serve immediately.

Peanut Butter and Jelly Smoothie

The favorite flavor combo of peanut butter and jelly makes this simple smoothie soothingly familiar.

MAKES 2 SERVINGS		
1 cup	plain yogurt	250 mL
2 tbsp	natural peanut butter (store-bought or see recipe, page 20)	30 mL
1	large frozen banana	1
1 cup	frozen red grapes	250 mL

Tip

When you have too many grapes to eat within a day or two, freeze them for this smoothie.

1. Place the yogurt, peanut butter, banana and grapes in the Vitamix container. Secure the lid, remove the lid plug and insert the tamper. With the switch on Variable, select speed 1 and turn the machine on. Gradually increase the speed to 10, using the tamper to push the ingredients into the blades, then flip the switch to High and blend for about 20 seconds or to the desired consistency. Serve immediately.

Variation

Almond or other nut butters can stand in for the peanut butter.

Power Peach

Sweet peaches and banana create a soothing backdrop for sprightly parsley and hemp and chia seeds. Parsley is more than just a garnish; it's a potent anticancer, antioxidant green with plenty of vitamins C, A and K to promote optimum well-being.

MAKES 2 SERVINGS		
1 cup	unsweetened soy or almond milk	250 mL
2 tbsp	hemp seeds	30 mL
1 tbsp	chia seeds	15 mL
1	large frozen banana	1
1 cup	frozen peach slices	250 mL
1 cup	lightly packed parsley stems and leaves	250 mL

Tip

Save parsley stems when you are cooking, and you can purée them in your super-powerful blender to make this yummy smoothie.

1. Place the milk, hemp seeds, chia seeds, banana, peaches and parsley in the Vitamix container. Secure the lid, remove the lid plug and insert the tamper. With the switch on Variable, select speed 1 and turn the machine on. Gradually increase the speed to 10, using the tamper to push the ingredients into the blades, then flip the switch to High and blend for about 20 seconds or to the desired consistency. Serve immediately.

Variation

If parsley seems a little too peppery for your palate, try this smoothie with spinach, then work up to half parsley to see how you like it.

Peach Raspberry Blush

This is the taste of summer, with ripe peaches and raspberries singing a chorus. Studies show that the phenolic compounds in peaches help prevent inflammation and diabetes, so you can feel "peachy."

MAKES 2 SERVINGS		
1 cup	unsweetened almond milk	250 mL
1	medium tangerine (or $1/2$ orange), peeled and seeded	1
1 cup	frozen peach slices	250 mL
1 cup	frozen raspberries	250 mL

Tip

Instead of buying orange juice, just buy oranges and make juices and smoothies with them in your Vitamix.

1. Place the almond milk, tangerine, peaches and raspberries in the Vitamix container. Secure the lid, remove the lid plug and insert the tamper. With the switch on Variable, select speed 1 and turn the machine on. Gradually increase the speed to 10, using the tamper to push the ingredients into the blades, then flip the switch to High and blend for about 20 seconds or to the desired consistency. Serve immediately.

Variation

Apricot slices can be substituted for the peaches, and are also delicious in this smoothie.

Honeydew and Kiwi Greenie

Add some color to your morning with this fruity green smoothie. Spirulina is a dried algae that is a concentrated source of protein and minerals, and it adds a deep emerald color to the smoothie.

MAKES 2 SERVINGS		
1 cup	plain kefir	250 mL
1	medium kiwifruit, peeled	1
2 cups	cubed honeydew melon	500 mL
1 tsp	spirulina powder	5 mL
1	large frozen banana	1

Tip

Peel, seed and cube a whole melon at the beginning of the week and keep it in a storage tub. Then you can have a melon smoothie twice, or simply eat the rest of the melon as a healthy snack. You'll need about half a 2-lb (1 kg) melon to get 2 cups (500 mL) cubes.

1. Place the kefir, kiwi, honeydew, spirulina and banana in the Vitamix container. Secure the lid, remove the lid plug and insert the tamper. With the switch on Variable, select speed 1 and turn the machine on. Gradually increase the speed to 10, using the tamper to push the ingredients into the blades, then flip the switch to High and blend for about 20 seconds or to the desired consistency. Serve immediately.

Variation

It won't be as pretty and green, but cantaloupe can stand in for honeydew in this smoothie.

Tropical Dream

Pretend you are lying on a white sand beach, where coconuts and pineapples are ripening in the sun. This tasty smoothie tastes like the tropics, with a creamy tofu base to give you a sustaining meal.

⋙⋘⋙⋘⋙⋘⋙⋘⋙⋘⋙⋘⋙⋘⋙⋘⋙⋘⋙⋘⋙⋘⋙⋘⋙⋘⋙⋘⋙⋘

MAKES 2 SERVINGS		
1 cup	coconut water	250 mL
5 oz	firm silken tofu	150 g
4	large pitted Medjool dates	4
2 tbsp	hemp seeds	30 mL
1 cup	frozen pineapple cubes	250 mL

Tip

Once you open the package of tofu, save the remaining half in a storage tub with water to cover. Then you are ready to use the rest in a smoothie like this one.

1. Place the coconut water, tofu, dates, hemp seeds and pineapple in the Vitamix container. Secure the lid, remove the lid plug and insert the tamper. With the switch on Variable, select speed 1 and turn the machine on. Gradually increase the speed to 10, using the tamper to push the ingredients into the blades, then flip the switch to High and blend for about 20 seconds or to the desired consistency. Serve immediately.

Variation

Coconut kefir or kombucha can stand in for the coconut water, and will add probiotics.

Orange Beet Cream Smoothie

If you think you don't like beets, try this yummy smoothie with golden beets sandwiched between orange, pineapple and vanilla soy milk. Beets are good for your heart and circulation, so when you combine them with essential fats and fiber from flax, you have a great pre-workout drink.

⋙⋘⋙⋘⋙⋘⋙⋘⋙⋘⋙⋘⋙⋘⋙⋘⋙⋘⋙⋘⋙⋘⋙⋘⋙⋘⋙⋘⋙⋘

MAKES 2 SERVINGS		
3/4 cup	vanilla soy milk	175 mL
1	large orange, peeled and seeded	1
3/4 cup	chopped yellow beet	175 mL
2 tbsp	golden flax seeds	30 mL
1/2 cup	frozen pineapple cubes	125 mL

Tip

You can buy frozen cubed pineapple, or you can drain canned pineapple and freeze the cubes for use in this smoothie.

1. Place the soy milk, orange, beet, flax seeds and pineapple in the Vitamix container. Secure the lid, remove the lid plug and insert the tamper. With the switch on Variable, select speed 1 and turn the machine on. Gradually increase the speed to 10, using the tamper to push the ingredients into the blades, then flip the switch to High and blend for about 20 seconds or to the desired consistency. Serve immediately.

Variation

Any vanilla-flavored nondairy milk is great in this recipe, and vanilla yogurt would also be delicious.

Thai Stinger

If you love the local Thai place and enjoy a hint of chile heat, this is the smoothie for you. With a base of high-protein tofu and luscious papaya, it is spiked with healthy herbs and turmeric, as well as a bit of red chile kick. Eating hot chiles has been shown to increase your metabolism, making you burn a few more calories, without doing anything but enjoy.

∽∾

MAKES 2 SERVINGS

1/2 cup	coconut water	125 mL
3 oz	firm silken tofu	90 g
1/2	medium cucumber	1/2
1/4 cup	lightly packed holy basil (see tip)	60 mL
1	slice gingerroot	1
1	slice fresh turmeric	1
1/2	medium red chile pepper (or to taste)	1/2
2 cups	frozen papaya cubes	500 mL

Tips

Buy aseptic (Tetra) packs of silken tofu that don't need to be refrigerated, so you can have them handy for smoothies like this one.

Holy basil is the favored variety in Thailand, and it gives the smoothie a faint licorice-basil flavor. It is lauded as an antioxidant-rich, health-promoting herb in its own right. If you can't find holy basil, you can use another variety of basil or substitute mint.

1. Place the coconut water, tofu, cucumber, basil, ginger, turmeric, chile and papaya in the Vitamix container. Secure the lid, remove the lid plug and insert the tamper. With the switch on Variable, select speed 1 and turn the machine on. Gradually increase the speed to 10, using the tamper to push the ingredients into the blades, then flip the switch to High and blend for about 20 seconds or to the desired consistency. Serve immediately.

Variation

Try this with frozen pineapple instead of papaya.

Scarlet Beet Kefir Smoothie

Beets are the darlings of the athletic world now that we know that they contain nitric oxide, which relaxes the circulatory system enough to make your body perform better. They're also incredibly good for your heart. Add some berries and energizing royal jelly, and you are ready to run.

MAKES 2 SERVINGS		
1 cup	plain kefir	250 mL
1 tsp	freshly squeezed lemon juice	5 mL
1 tsp	royal jelly or honey	5 mL
1/2 cup	cubed beet	125 mL
2 tbsp	hemp seeds	30 mL
1 cup	frozen strawberries	250 mL
1 cup	ice cubes	250 mL

1. Place the kefir, lemon juice, royal jelly, beet, hemp seeds, strawberries and ice cubes in the Vitamix container.

Secure the lid, remove the lid plug and insert the tamper. With the switch on Variable, select speed 1 and turn the machine on. Gradually increase the speed to 10, using the tamper to push the ingredients into the blades, then flip the switch to High and blend for about 20 seconds or to the desired consistency. Serve immediately.

Variation

Hemp seeds add protein and good fats, but you can always swap in another seed, like sunflower or sesame, for a different flavor.

Creamy Green Booster

The light sweetness of electrolyte-rich coconut water, combined with creamy banana, balances the slight pepperiness of parsley and kale. Boost your immunity with the vitamin C from kiwi, and soothe your mind with brain-boosting fats from avocado, all while sipping a tasty smoothie.

MAKES 2 SERVINGS		
2 cups	coconut water	500 mL
1	medium kiwifruit, peeled	1
1/4	large avocado	1/4
1	large frozen banana	1
2	leaves kale	2
1/4 cup	lightly packed parsley stems and leaves	60 mL

1. Place the coconut water, kiwi, avocado, banana, kale and parsley in the Vitamix container. Secure the lid, remove the lid plug and insert the tamper. With the switch on Variable, select speed 1 and turn the machine on. Gradually increase the speed to 10, using the tamper to push the ingredients into the blades, then flip the switch to High and blend for about 20 seconds or to the desired consistency. Serve immediately.

Tip

Save parsley stems when you are cooking, and use them up in this smoothie.

Variation

Try coconut kefir in place of the coconut water for a probiotic boost.

Creamy Green Meal-in-a-Glass

The combo of avocado and kale makes this green smoothie a nutrition superstar. Avocados contain monounsaturated fats that help you absorb the nutrients from other foods, especially beta-carotene to protect your eyes. And all the fiber will fill you up.

MAKES 2 SERVINGS		
1/4 cup	coconut water	60 mL
1/2	medium avocado	1/2
1/2	medium lime, peeled	1/2
1 cup	frozen grapes	250 mL
4	leaves kale	4
1 cup	ice cubes	250 mL

Tips

To keep the other half of the avocado from turning brown, rub the cut surface with lime juice and wrap tightly with plastic wrap. Use in another recipe within a day.

You can always use a lemon instead of a lime, or try another leafy green. Far better to use up the greens you have than to have them go to waste.

1. Place the coconut water, avocado, lime, grapes, kale and ice cubes in the Vitamix container. Secure the lid, remove the lid plug and insert the tamper. With the switch on Variable, select speed 1 and turn the machine on. Gradually increase the speed to 10, using the tamper to push the ingredients into the blades, then flip the switch to High and blend for about 20 seconds or to the desired consistency. Serve immediately.

Tangy Tummy Pleaser

If you may have overindulged last night, or eaten a combination of foods that don't agree with you, soothe that rumbly tummy with this smoothie. Cucumber nourishes and hydrates, kefir and cider vinegar bring good bacteria to help with digestion, and fresh ginger has long been recommended to settle your stomach.

MAKES 2 SERVINGS

1/2 cup	coconut kefir	125 mL
1 tsp	apple cider vinegar	5 mL
1	medium cucumber (unpeeled), quartered	1
2	slices gingerroot	2
1	large frozen banana	1

Tips

If you can't find coconut kefir, make this with kombucha so you will still get some good probiotics for your belly.

Slice and freeze ginger when you have a surplus, and you will have it on hand to throw into a smoothie, juice, sauce or stir-fry.

1. Place the kefir, vinegar, cucumber, ginger and banana in the Vitamix container. Secure the lid, remove the lid plug and insert the tamper. With the switch on Variable, select speed 1 and turn the machine on. Gradually increase the speed to 10, using the tamper to push the ingredients into the blades, then flip the switch to High and blend for about 20 seconds or to the desired consistency. Serve immediately.

Summer Oatmeal Smoothie

A steaming bowl of healthy oatmeal is perfect in the colder months, but in summer, not so much. In this smoothie, you can reap the benefits of oats in a cold and sippable form. Oats are full of filling fiber, to make your breakfast last a little longer, and also lower your cholesterol levels.

MAKES 2 SERVINGS		
1¹/₂ cups	coconut water	375 mL
2 tsp	freshly squeezed lemon juice	10 mL
¹/₄ cup	slivered almonds	60 mL
¹/₄ cup	large-flake (old-fashioned) rolled oats	60 mL
2	slices gingerroot	2
2 cups	frozen blueberries	500 mL

Tip

Make sure you run the Vitamix long enough to finely grind the ginger, to get that warming, spicy flavor throughout.

1. Place the coconut water, lemon juice, almonds, oats, ginger and blueberries in the Vitamix container. Secure the lid, remove the lid plug and insert the tamper. With the switch on Variable, select speed 1 and turn the machine on. Gradually increase the speed to 10, using the tamper to push the ingredients into the blades, then flip the switch to High and blend for about 20 seconds or to the desired consistency. Serve immediately.

Variations

Try other rolled grains, such as barley or quinoa, for a different flavor.

Blueberries are perfect in this, but other frozen berries work well, too.

Porridge Smoothie

If you are looking for a filling, fiber-rich breakfast, this smoothie is for you. Oats and prunes deliver all the fiber you would get in a bowl of oatmeal, in the guise of a frosty shake.

MAKES 2 SERVINGS		
1¹/₂ cups	plain yogurt	375 mL
1 tbsp	honey	15 mL
4	pitted medium prunes	4
¹/₄ cup	large-flake (old-fashioned) rolled oats	60 mL
¹/₂ tsp	ground cinnamon	2 mL
1 cup	ice cubes	250 mL

Tip

Make sure to buy soft, moist prunes, and keep them tightly wrapped so they won't dry out. They'll be much easier to purée that way.

1. Place the yogurt, honey, prunes, oats, cinnamon and ice cubes in the Vitamix container. Secure the lid, remove the lid plug and insert the tamper. With the switch on Variable, select speed 1 and turn the machine on. Gradually increase the speed to 10, using the tamper to push the ingredients into the blades, then flip the switch to High and blend for about 20 seconds or to the desired consistency. Serve immediately.

Variation

You can use dates instead of prunes, if you have them handy. Both are full of fiber and concentrated fruit nutrition.

Green Papaya Protein Smoothie

After a workout or before a long day, you need a boost of protein, as well as the nourishment of a mess of green spinach. Papaya delivers tons of vitamin C and antioxidants, as well as fruity flavor.

MAKES 2 SERVINGS		
1 cup	unsweetened almond milk	250 mL
1/4 cup	large-flake (old-fashioned) rolled oats	60 mL
2 tbsp	almond butter	30 mL
2 tbsp	royal jelly or honey	30 mL
1 1/2 cups	frozen papaya cubes	375 mL
4 cups	lightly packed fresh spinach leaves	1 L
1 cup	ice cubes	250 mL

Tips

Using your own freshly made almond milk and almond butter makes this smoothie extra fresh and affordable. See the recipes on pages 212 and 18.

Royal jelly is the special honey reserved for the queen bee. It contains concentrated vitamins and minerals, and is recommended for longevity, energy and women's health.

1. Place the almond milk, oats, almond butter, royal jelly, papaya, spinach and ice cubes in the Vitamix container. Secure the lid, remove the lid plug and insert the tamper. With the switch on Variable, select speed 1 and turn the machine on. Gradually increase the speed to 10, using the tamper to push the ingredients into the blades, then flip the switch to High and blend for about 20 seconds or to the desired consistency. Serve immediately.

Variations

You can use any other milk in place of the almond milk.

Substitute another nut butter for the almond butter.

Green Almond Protein Smoothie

Did you know that spinach is actually a good source of protein, considering how low-calorie it is? The spinach in this smoothie adds 3 grams of protein and only 21 calories. The almond butter adds 4 grams of protein and 200 calories. Almond butter is also very nutrient-dense, with good fats, calcium and iron. If you want more protein still, use yogurt, which has 13 grams of protein per cup (250 mL).

MAKES 2 SERVINGS

1 cup	coconut water, unsweetened almond milk or plain yogurt	250 mL
1/4 tsp	almond extract	1 mL
2 tbsp	almond butter	30 mL
1	large frozen banana	1
2 cups	frozen strawberries	500 mL
3 cups	lightly packed fresh spinach leaves	750 mL

Tip

If you make your own almond milk and almond butter, you will have the best flavor and freshness, and will save money in the bargain. See the recipes on pages 212 and 18.

1. Place the coconut water, almond extract, almond butter, banana, strawberries and spinach in the Vitamix container. Secure the lid, remove the lid plug and insert the tamper. With the switch on Variable, select speed 1 and turn the machine on. Gradually increase the speed to 10, using the tamper to push the ingredients into the blades, then flip the switch to High and blend for about 20 seconds or to the desired consistency. Serve immediately.

Variation

In a pinch, peanut butter or another nut butter can fill in for the almond butter.

Chocolate Almond Buzz

Sometimes you need an energy boost. Why not enjoy the lush flavor of chocolate and get a little caffeine along with the rush of antioxidants and brain-protecting chemicals?

MAKES 2 SERVINGS		
1 cup	unsweetened almond milk	250 mL
1 tbsp	honey or royal jelly (optional)	15 mL
1 tsp	vanilla extract	5 mL
1/4 cup	unsweetened cocoa powder	60 mL
1	large frozen banana	1
2 cups	lightly packed fresh spinach leaves	500 mL
1 cup	ice cubes	250 mL

Tip

If you make your own fresh almond milk (page 212), you may be sweetening it with dates or another sweetener, so you may not need the added sweetness of honey in this smoothie.

1. Place the almond milk, honey (if using), vanilla, cocoa, banana, spinach and ice cubes in the Vitamix container. Secure the lid, remove the lid plug and insert the tamper. With the switch on Variable, select speed 1 and turn the machine on. Gradually increase the speed to 10, using the tamper to push the ingredients into the blades, then flip the switch to High and blend for about 20 seconds or to the desired consistency. Serve immediately.

Variation

Other nondairy or dairy milks can step in for almond milk, according to your preferences.

Jet Fuel

Start your engines at the first meal of the day, or serve this as a mid-afternoon slump-busting snack. Red chiles give you the metabolism boost of capsaicin and awaken your sleepy taste buds.

MAKES 2 SERVINGS		
1 cup	unsweetened almond milk	250 mL
1	medium red chile pepper (see tip)	1
1 cup	frozen mango cubes	250 mL
1 cup	frozen strawberries	250 mL
1/2 cup	ice cubes	125 mL

Tip

If you want more heat from a chile, leave the seeds and membranes in. For more of the flavor and a little less of the heat, remove the seeds and membranes.

1. Place the almond milk, chile, mango, strawberries and ice cubes in the Vitamix container. Secure the lid, remove the lid plug and insert the tamper. With the switch on Variable, select speed 1 and turn the machine on. Gradually increase the speed to 10, using the tamper to push the ingredients into the blades, then flip the switch to High and blend for about 20 seconds or to the desired consistency. Serve immediately.

Variation

The mango can be replaced with papaya or even peaches, if you have some handy.

Melon Multitasker

Fuel up for your busy day with bright orange cantaloupe, full of vitamin C to protect you from sun damage and reduce inflammation. A one-two punch of red chile and matcha tea will provide gentle, long-lasting energy.

∽∾ ∽∾

MAKES 2 SERVINGS

1/2 cup	unsweetened almond milk	125 mL
2 cups	cubed cantaloupe	500 mL
1	slice gingerroot	1
1/2	medium red chile pepper (see tip, page 239)	1/2
1/2 tsp	matcha powder	2 mL
1 cup	ice cubes	250 mL

Tip

Buy a big cantaloupe, serve half for breakfast and save half for making smoothies like this one. It's one of the less expensive fruits in the summertime.

1. Place the almond milk, cantaloupe, ginger, chile, matcha and ice cubes in the Vitamix container. Secure the lid, remove the lid plug and insert the tamper. With the switch on Variable, select speed 1 and turn the machine on. Gradually increase the speed to 10, using the tamper to push the ingredients into the blades, then flip the switch to High and blend for about 20 seconds or to the desired consistency. Serve immediately.

Variation

Honeydew can stand in for cantaloupe in a pinch, for a much greener smoothie.

Matcha Latte Smoothie

Now that coffee shops offer matcha lattes, we've all had a chance to learn to love the sweet, vegetal flavor of powdered green tea. Matcha is a great source of antioxidants and theine, a slightly different form of caffeine from the kind in coffee. Tea is associated with calm energy, and is recommended for weight loss.

MAKES 2 SERVINGS

1/2 cup	coconut milk	125 mL
2 tbsp	honey	30 mL
1/2	medium avocado	1/2
1/2 tsp	matcha powder	2 mL
1 cup	ice cubes	250 mL

Tips

When you open up a can of coconut milk, whisk well, then take out the 1/2 cup (125 mL) you need for this recipe. Divide the remainder into 1/2-cup (125 mL) portions and freeze. You will have conveniently sized portions to add to smoothies, curries, soups and other dishes.

For a little more matcha flavor, try adding another 1/4 tsp (1 mL) to the mix.

1. Place the coconut milk, honey, avocado, matcha and ice cubes in the Vitamix container. Secure the lid, remove the lid plug and insert the tamper. With the switch on Variable, select speed 1 and turn the machine on. Gradually increase the speed to 10, using the tamper to push the ingredients into the blades, then flip the switch to High and blend for about 20 seconds or to the desired consistency. Serve immediately.

Almond Chai Smoothie

Of course chai spices are delicious, with warming cinnamon and fragrant cardamom in the blend. But they are also health-promoting, with cinnamon working to help stabilize blood sugar and ginger working to boost immunity.

MAKES 2 SERVINGS

1 cup	cold brewed chai tea	250 mL
1/2 cup	unsweetened almond milk	125 mL
1 tbsp	honey	15 mL
1/4 tsp	ground cinnamon	1 mL
1/4 tsp	ground ginger	1 mL
1/8 tsp	ground turmeric	0.5 mL
1 cup	frozen mango cubes	250 mL
1 cup	ice cubes	250 mL

Tips

Buy a chai tea bag for this, or use a chai spice mix with black tea. If you want to avoid caffeine, there are decaf and herbal chai teas, too.

If you want to use prebrewed, boxed chai tea, it's usually quite sweet, so skip the honey in the recipe.

1. Place the tea, almond milk, honey, cinnamon, ginger, turmeric, mango and ice cubes in the Vitamix container. Secure the lid, remove the lid plug and insert the tamper. With the switch on Variable, select speed 1 and turn the machine on. Gradually increase the speed to 10, using the tamper to push the ingredients into the blades, then flip the switch to High and blend for about 20 seconds or to the desired consistency. Serve immediately.

Hi-Pro Hemp Smoothie

Black tea is just green tea that has been oxidized in processing, which gives it deep flavor and boosts some of the antioxidants. Here, creamy soy milk and puréed hemp seeds give it some luscious creaminess, as well as amping up the protein levels.

MAKES 2 SERVINGS		
1/2 cup	cold brewed black tea	125 mL
1/2 cup	cold vanilla soy milk	125 mL
1/4 cup	hemp seeds	60 mL
2 cups	lightly packed fresh spinach leaves	500 mL
1 cup	ice cubes	250 mL

Tip

If you plan ahead and make the tea the night before, you can keep it in the refrigerator overnight. That way, all your ingredients will be nice and cold for a thick, creamy smoothie.

1. Place the tea, soy milk, hemp seeds, spinach and ice cubes in the Vitamix container. Secure the lid, remove the lid plug and insert the tamper. With the switch on Variable, select speed 1 and turn the machine on. Gradually increase the speed to 10, using the tamper to push the ingredients into the blades, then flip the switch to High and blend for about 20 seconds or to the desired consistency. Serve immediately.

Variation

Once you enter the world of tea, the options are endless. Green tea, jasmine tea, oolong tea or any of your favorites can make a tasty replacement for the black tea in this smoothie.

Aloe Papaya Walnut Skin Booster

Skin care starts on the inside, with a diet rich in skin-loving nutrients. Papaya protects with a rush of antioxidants and vitamin A, while aloe soothes. Walnuts give your thirsty skin a boost of good fats.

MAKES 2 SERVINGS		
1 cup	plain kefir	250 mL
1 tbsp	aloe vera juice	15 mL
1 tbsp	freshly squeezed lemon juice	15 mL
3 cups	cubed papaya	750 mL
1/4 cup	raw walnuts	60 mL

Tips

You'll need about one-quarter of a 3-lb (1.5 kg) papaya to make 3 cups (750 mL) cubes.

Save the peel of the papaya and rub it on your face for a quick exfoliation.

1. Place the kefir, aloe vera juice, lemon juice, papaya and walnuts in the Vitamix container. Secure the lid, remove the lid plug and insert the tamper. With the switch on Variable, select speed 1 and turn the machine on. Gradually increase the speed to 10, using the tamper to push the ingredients into the blades, then flip the switch to High and blend for about 20 seconds or to the desired consistency. Serve immediately.

Variation

In a pinch, mangos can stand in for papaya in this smoothie.

Tropical Sun-Kissed Skin Smoothie

Dreaming of sunny beaches? Make this fruity smoothie, and make your skin happy at the same time. Coconut contains anti-inflammatory capric and caprylic acids, which prevent inflammation. Add fruits rich in vitamin C and enzymes, and the powerful antioxidants in turmeric, and you have a delicious drink to prevent damage from the inside out.

MAKES 2 SERVINGS		
1/2 cup	coconut milk	125 mL
1/2 cup	coconut water	125 mL
1/2 tsp	ground turmeric	2 mL
1/4 tsp	ground allspice	1 mL
1 cup	frozen papaya cubes	250 mL
1 cup	frozen pineapple cubes	250 mL

Tip

If you can find fresh turmeric, use 2 or 3 slices of the root instead of the ground turmeric.

1. Place the coconut milk, coconut water, turmeric, allspice, papaya and pineapple in the Vitamix container. Secure the lid, remove the lid plug and insert the tamper. With the switch on Variable, select speed 1 and turn the machine on. Gradually increase the speed to 10, using the tamper to push the ingredients into the blades, then flip the switch to High and blend for about 20 seconds or to the desired consistency. Serve immediately.

Variation

For a richer drink, use all coconut milk and add 1/2 cup (125 mL) ice cubes. For a leaner one, use all coconut water.

Tropical Green Smoother

For beautiful skin, you need to maintain a healthy population of probiotics. Kefir is a tasty and creamy way to get your good bacteria, while the avocado soothes your skin with essential fats and the fiber that the bacteria need to flourish.

MAKES 2 TO 4 SERVINGS		
1 cup	plain kefir	250 mL
1	medium avocado, halved and pitted	1
1	large frozen banana	1
3 cups	frozen papaya cubes	750 mL
4 cups	lightly packed fresh spinach leaves	1 L

Tip

This recipe uses a whole 4-oz (125 g) bag of salad spinach, so you can shop accordingly and have plenty of bags on hand.

1. Place the kefir, avocado, banana, papaya and spinach in the Vitamix container. Secure the lid, remove the lid plug and insert the tamper. With the switch on Variable, select speed 1 and turn the machine on. Gradually increase the speed to 10, using the tamper to push the ingredients into the blades, then flip the switch to High and blend for about 20 seconds or to the desired consistency. Serve immediately.

Variation

You can always substitute yogurt for kefir in a pinch. It's good to eat a variety of probiotic foods, so don't just limit yourself to one or the other.

Green Face Cleaner Smoothie

If you want great skin, feed it leafy greens, which are packed with vitamins A and C, and iron to help rebuild collagen. Turmeric is a powerful antioxidant and speeds healing.

MAKES 2 SERVINGS		
1 cup	unsweetened almond milk	250 mL
2 cups	cubed pineapple	500 mL
3	slices gingerroot	3
2	slices fresh turmeric	2
4 cup	lightly packed fresh spinach leaves	1 L

Tip

Look for fresh turmeric in natural foods stores and some well-stocked supermarkets, or seek it out in Indian groceries. It freezes well, sliced and tightly wrapped.

1. Place the almond milk, pineapple, ginger, turmeric and spinach in the Vitamix container. Secure the lid, remove the lid plug and insert the tamper. With the switch on Variable, select speed 1 and turn the machine on. Gradually increase the speed to 10, using the tamper to push the ingredients into the blades, then flip the switch to High and blend for about 20 seconds or to the desired consistency. Serve immediately.

Variation

In place of the spinach, try hearty greens like Swiss chard or kale for even more green power.

Clear Skin Quickie

Give your skin a boost with the healthy fats of avocado and the cell-protecting vitamin C in kiwi. Kiwi seeds contain essential fatty acids, for even more benefits.

MAKES 2 SERVINGS		
3/4 cup	plain kefir	175 mL
1	medium avocado, halved and pitted	1
2	medium kiwifruit, peeled	2
1	large frozen banana	1
4 cups	lightly packed fresh spinach leaves	1 L

Tip

Kiwis are like any soft fruit: if they are very firm, they are not ripe. Let them sit on the windowsill until they give slightly to a gentle squeeze. Then they will be sweet and tender.

1. Place the kefir, avocado, kiwi, banana and spinach in the Vitamix container. Secure the lid, remove the lid plug and insert the tamper. With the switch on Variable, select speed 1 and turn the machine on. Gradually increase the speed to 10, using the tamper to push the ingredients into the blades, then flip the switch to High and blend for about 20 seconds or to the desired consistency. Serve immediately.

Variation

Try this one with 3 cups (750 mL) trimmed kale leaves instead of spinach, for a super-green experience.

Pumpkin Pie Skin Saver

Pumpkin is a great source of powerful vitamin A, which both hampers skin aging by boosting collagen production and fights acne. Drinks and foods flavored like pumpkin pie are all the rage, and it's far better to enjoy real pumpkin and real spice.

MAKES 2 SERVINGS		
1 cup	plain yogurt	250 mL
1/2 cup	unsweetened pumpkin purée (canned or fresh)	125 mL
1 tbsp	honey or royal jelly	15 mL
1/2 tsp	vanilla extract	2 mL
1 tbsp	golden flax seeds	15 mL
1/2 tsp	pumpkin pie spice	2 mL
1/2 cup	ice cubes	125 mL

1. Place the yogurt, pumpkin, honey, vanilla, flax seeds, pumpkin pie spice and ice cubes in the Vitamix container. Secure the lid, remove the lid plug and insert the tamper. With the switch on Variable, select speed 1 and turn the machine on. Gradually increase the speed to 10, using the tamper to push the ingredients into the blades, then flip the switch to High and blend for about 20 seconds or to the desired consistency. Serve immediately.

Variation

Bake a winter squash or sweet potato to use in this smoothie, for a sweeter flavor than canned pumpkin.

SMOOTHIE BOWLS and PARFAITS

TIPS FOR SUCCESS

- If your Vitamix has a Smoothie function, feel free to use it instead of following the blending instructions in the recipes.
- A smoothie bowl is a thick smoothie topped with some solid food, and you're meant to eat it with a spoon. It's for those days when you don't want your breakfast through a straw.
- It's important that your smoothie base is thick enough to hold the toppings afloat. If it seems too thin, add a handful of ice cubes and blend again.
- The key to a beautiful smoothie bowl is the careful composition of the toppings. Some of these are as simple as a sprinkle of granola; others have several components. When placing your toppings on the bowls, put contrasting colors beside each other, and arrange them in rows or quadrants to draw the eye.

Plum Berry Smoothie with Honey Nut O's

Kids love oaty-o cereals, and so do many adults. Instead of pouring boring old milk on your cereal, try floating cereal on this fruity smoothie purée, and add some crunchy almonds.

MAKES 2 SERVINGS		
1 cup	unsweetened almond milk	250 mL
1	large plum, pitted	1
1/2 cup	frozen raspberries	125 mL
1	large frozen banana	1
1 1/2 cups	honey nut oat cereal o's	375 mL
1/4 cup	toasted slivered almonds (optional)	60 mL

1. Place the almond milk, plum, raspberries and banana in the Vitamix container. Secure the lid, remove the lid plug and insert the tamper. With the switch on Variable, select speed 1 and turn the machine on. Gradually increase the speed to 10, using the tamper to push the ingredients into the blades, then flip the switch to High and blend for 10 to 20 seconds or to the desired consistency.

2. Pour into wide bowls and top with cereal and slivered almonds (if using). Serve immediately.

Variation

If you have another favorite cereal, you can use it instead of the honey nut o's.

Date Shake with Ginger Granola

Date shakes may be the original smoothie, emerging as a featured treat in California in the 1960s as a way to enjoy the local dates and cool off on a hot day. Dates are such a healthful natural sweetener, we still rely on them in smoothies and energy bars for a quick burst of fruit sweetness.

MAKES 2 SERVINGS		
1 cup	plain yogurt	250 mL
6	large pitted Medjool dates	6
1	large frozen banana	1
1 cup	ice cubes	250 mL
1 cup	ginger granola	250 mL
1	small mango, sliced	1
1	small kiwifruit, peeled and sliced	1

Tip
Buy the moistest, softest dates you can find.

1. Place the yogurt, dates, banana and ice cubes in the Vitamix container. Secure the lid, remove the lid plug and insert the tamper. With the switch on Variable, select speed 1 and turn the machine on. Gradually increase the speed to 10, using the tamper to push the ingredients into the blades, then flip the switch to High and blend for 10 to 20 seconds or to the desired consistency.

2. Pour into wide bowls and top with granola, mango and kiwi. Serve immediately.

Variation

If peaches are in season, use 2 small ripe peaches instead of the mango.

Banana Cinnamon Tofu Smoothie Bowl Topped with Granola

This is the most basic of smoothie bowls — just a simple smoothie with hidden greens, spiked with cinnamon. Topped with crunchy cinnamon raisin granola, it's like having a healthful and nourishing ice cream parfait for breakfast.

∽∽ ∽∽

MAKES 1 SERVING

1/2 cup	unsweetened almond milk	125 mL
3 oz	firm silken tofu	90 g
1/2 tsp	ground cinnamon	2 mL
1	large frozen banana	1
1 cup	lightly packed fresh spinach leaves	250 mL
1/2 cup	ice cubes	125 mL
1/2 cup	cinnamon raisin granola	125 mL

Tip

Keep aseptic (Tetra) boxes of silken tofu in the pantry, so you will always be ready to add a protein boost to smoothies like this one. This recipe only uses one-quarter of the package. Save the rest in a storage container with cold water to cover, and use it up by making a Thai Stinger smoothie (page 232) or Tropical Dream smoothie (page 231).

1. Place the almond milk, tofu, cinnamon, banana, spinach and ice cubes in the Vitamix container. Secure the lid, remove the lid plug and insert the tamper. With the switch on Variable, select speed 1 and turn the machine on. Gradually increase the speed to 10, using the tamper to push the ingredients into the blades, then flip the switch to High and blend for 10 to 20 seconds or to the desired consistency.

2. Pour into a wide bowl and top with granola. Serve immediately.

Goji and Raspberry Smoothie Bowl with Muesli Topping

Goji berries look like little red raisins, but they are not like any other fruit. They are the highest-protein fruit and contain all eight essential amino acids. They are also high in vitamin C, carotenoids and iron, and contain 21 trace minerals. They are not sweet like raisins, so using them in a smoothie bowl is a great way to blend them with other fruit for flavor.

MAKES 2 SERVINGS		
1 cup	unsweetened almond milk	250 mL
1/4 cup	dried goji berries, soaked and drained (see tip)	60 mL
1	large frozen banana	1
1 cup	frozen raspberries	250 mL
1	large kiwifruit, peeled and sliced	1
1/2 cup	muesli	125 mL
1/4 cup	chopped raw walnuts	60 mL

Tips

To soak dried goji berries, place them in a medium bowl and add enough cool water to cover by 1 inch (2.5 cm). Let stand for 1 hour (more if the goji berries are very firm). Drain before using. Be sure to drink the soaking liquid, as it contains flavor and nutrients.

Kiwis are a popular topping for smoothie bowls because they are so pretty when sliced. Try fanning the slices across the top of the smoothie in rows or a circle, then sprinkling muesli and walnuts in the spaces.

1. Place the almond milk, goji berries, banana and raspberries in the Vitamix container. Secure the lid, remove the lid plug and insert the tamper. With the switch on Variable, select speed 1 and turn the machine on. Gradually increase the speed to 10, using the tamper to push the ingredients into the blades, then flip the switch to High and blend for 10 to 20 seconds or to the desired consistency.

2. Pour into wide bowls and top with kiwi, muesli and walnuts. Serve immediately.

Variation

Substitute 1/2 cup (125 mL) mashed cooked sweet potato for the banana for an orange-colored, less-sweet smoothie base.

Açaí Smoothie Bowl with Quinoa and Pumpkin Seeds

Little frozen packets of açaí make it easy to enjoy this tropical superfruit in a smoothie or smoothie bowl. Don't bother to defrost, just toss the frozen purée right into your Vitamix.

MAKES 1 SERVING

1/2 cup	coconut water	125 mL
2	medium dates, pitted	2
1 tbsp	dried goji berries, soaked and drained (see tip, opposite)	15 mL
1/2 tsp	matcha powder	2 mL
7 oz	frozen açaí purée	210 g
1	large frozen banana	1
1	kiwifruit, peeled and sliced	1
1/2 cup	cooked quinoa (see tip), chilled	125 mL
2 tbsp	toasted green pumpkin seeds (pepitas)	30 mL
	Additional dried goji berries	

Tips

Quinoa is a versatile whole grain, rich in protein, calcium, fiber and other nutrients. To cook quinoa, bring 1 1/2 cups (375 mL) water to a boil in a small saucepan, add 1 cup (250 mL) quinoa and return to the boil, then cover the pot and reduce the heat to low. Cook for 14 to 15 minutes, or until tender, then fluff the quinoa with a fork. Makes about 2 1/2 cups (625 mL).

Toast pumpkin seeds in a large skillet over medium-high heat, swirling until they start to pop and smell toasty, about 3 minutes. Immediately transfer to a bowl and let cool completely before use.

1. Place the coconut water, dates, goji berries, matcha, açaí and banana in the Vitamix container. Secure the lid, remove the lid plug and insert the tamper. With the switch on Variable, select speed 1 and turn the machine on. Gradually increase the speed to 10, using the tamper to push the ingredients into the blades, then flip the switch to High and blend for 10 to 20 seconds or to the desired consistency.

2. Pour into a wide bowl and top with kiwi, quinoa, pumpkin seeds and additional goji berries. Serve immediately.

Variation

Use leftover cooked brown rice in place of the quinoa, for a yummy variation.

Green Smoothie Bowl with Berries, Bananas, Nuts and Flax

This creamy green smoothie is a perfect canvas for raspberries, blueberries, crunchy walnuts and flax. Get creative and make a pretty picture, then eat it.

1 cup	plain kefir	250 mL
1	large frozen banana	1
1/2 cup	frozen blueberries	125 mL
3 cups	lightly packed fresh spinach leaves	750 mL
1/2 cup	chopped raw walnuts	125 mL
2 tbsp	golden flax seeds	30 mL
1/2 cup	fresh blueberries	125 mL
1/2 cup	fresh raspberries	125 mL

Tip

Whole flax seeds are lovely, and golden flax seeds have a pretty yellow color. If you can only find brown flax seeds, use those instead.

1. Place the kefir, banana, frozen blueberries and spinach in the Vitamix container. Secure the lid, remove the lid plug and insert the tamper. With the switch on Variable, select speed 1 and turn the machine on. Gradually increase the speed to 10, using the tamper to push the ingredients into the blades, then flip the switch to High and blend for 10 to 20 seconds or to the desired consistency.

2. Pour into wide bowls and top with rows of walnuts, flax seeds, fresh blueberries and raspberries. Serve immediately.

Variation

Use plain yogurt instead of kefir, for a slightly thicker smoothie bowl base.

Sweet Potato Spice Smoothie Bowl with Quinoa and Sesame

In fall and winter, sweet potatoes and apples are in season, and eating in season is a good way to feel more balanced. This yummy bowl, topped with sweetened quinoa, will remind you of sweet potato pie.

MAKES 1 SERVING		
1	medium apple	1
1/2 cup	cooked quinoa (see tip, page 251), chilled	125 mL
1 tbsp	toasted sesame seeds (see tip, page 21)	15 mL
1 tsp	liquid honey	5 mL
1/2 cup	unsweetened almond milk	125 mL
1/2 cup	mashed sweet potato	125 mL
1/2 tsp	ground cinnamon	2 mL
1/4 tsp	ground allspice	1 mL

Tip

Whenever you are baking, put a sweet potato in the oven to roast. Pierce it a couple of times with a fork, wrap it loosely in foil or put it in a bread pan, and slide it alongside your other food. Depending on the size of the sweet potato and the temperature you're baking at, it should be soft and sweet in about 30 minutes. Let it cool, peel and mash it, and refrigerate in an airtight container until you need some for a smoothie or a baking recipe.

1. Cut apple lengthwise into quarters and cut out core. Cut 4 thin slices from one quarter and set aside for topping.

2. In a small bowl, combine quinoa, sesame seeds and honey. Set aside.

3. Place the almond milk, sweet potato, cinnamon, allspice and the remaining apple in the Vitamix container. Secure the lid, remove the lid plug and insert the tamper. With the switch on Variable, select speed 1 and turn the machine on. Gradually increase the speed to 10, using the tamper to push the ingredients into the blades, then flip the switch to High and blend for 10 to 20 seconds or to the desired consistency.

4. Pour into a wide bowl and pile the quinoa mixture in the middle, then garnish with the reserved apple slices.

Variation

You can use canned pumpkin purée (not pie filling) in place of the sweet potato, but the smoothie will be less sweet.

Peanut Butter and Honey Smoothie with Cocoa Granola

Skip the toast — you can have your peanut butter and honey in a cool and crunchy smoothie bowl. Cocoa granola and sweet red cherries make a pretty topping.

∽∾ ∽∾

MAKES 2 SERVINGS

1 cup	plain yogurt	250 mL
2 tbsp	honey (optional)	30 mL
1/4 cup	natural peanut butter (store-bought or see recipe, page 20)	60 mL
1 tbsp	chia seeds	15 mL
1	large frozen banana	1
1 cup	cocoa granola	250 mL
1 cup	pitted fresh or thawed frozen sweet cherries	250 mL

Tip

Frozen dark sweet cherries are always available, so keep them in the freezer for this and the Cherry Vanilla Ice Cream (page 175).

1. Place the yogurt, honey (if using), peanut butter, chia seeds and banana in the Vitamix container. Secure the lid, remove the lid plug and insert the tamper. With the switch on Variable, select speed 1 and turn the machine on. Gradually increase the speed to 10, using the tamper to push the ingredients into the blades, then flip the switch to High and blend for 10 to 20 seconds or to the desired consistency.

2. Pour into wide bowls and top with granola and cherries. Serve immediately.

Variation

Make this with homemade almond butter (page 18) for a different flavor.

Mocha Cacao Smoothie with Vanilla Wafers

If you like to start the day with a cup of strong coffee, this smoothie bowl will replace it, all while delivering a breakfast rich in protein, fiber and antioxidants.

MAKES 2 SERVINGS

3 tbsp	granulated sugar	45 mL
2 tbsp	cacao nibs	30 mL
1 tbsp	coffee beans	15 mL
1 cup	plain Greek yogurt	250 mL
1/2 tsp	vanilla extract	2 mL
8	milk ice cubes (see tip, page 174)	8
4	large strawberries, thinly sliced	4
1	large banana, sliced	1
8	vanilla wafers (or to taste)	8

Tips

Cacao nibs and coffee beans both deliver a good dose of caffeine, so if you are sensitive to caffeine, this may not be the bowl for you. For slightly less of a boost, you can use decaffeinated coffee beans.

At the end of step 2, if you turn the blender off and hear the sound of ice cubes falling onto the blades, the smoothie isn't ready; blend again for 5 seconds.

1. Place the sugar, cacao nibs and coffee beans in the Vitamix container and secure the lid. With the switch on Variable, select speed 1 and turn the machine on. Gradually increase the speed to 10 and grind for about 20 seconds to a fine powder.

2. Turn the machine off and scrape the powder from the corners of the container. Add the yogurt, vanilla and milk ice cubes. Replace the lid, remove the lid plug and insert the tamper. With the switch on Variable, select speed 1 and turn the machine on. Gradually increase the speed to 10, using the tamper to push the ingredients into the blades, then flip the switch to High and blend for about 30 seconds or until smooth.

3. Pour into wide bowls and top with strawberries and banana. Arrange the vanilla wafers along the rim of the bowl for dipping in the smoothie.

Chocolate, Avocado and Spiced Quinoa Parfaits

This breakfast looks and tastes like a fancy dessert, all the while bursting with nourishing whole foods. The only sweetener is the banana, unless you opt for a little honey, but your taste buds will believe you are reveling in chocolate mousse.

MAKES 1 SERVING

1/2 cup	cooked quinoa (see tip, page 251), chilled	125 mL
2 tbsp	currants	30 mL
1/2 tsp	ground cinnamon	2 mL
1/2 cup	coconut milk or unsweetened almond milk	125 mL
1/2 tsp	vanilla extract	2 mL
1 1/2 tsp	unsweetened cocoa powder	7 mL
1/2	medium avocado	1/2
1	large frozen banana	1
	Liquid honey (optional)	

Tip

Save the rest of the avocado to make Creamy Green Meal-in-a-Glass (page 234).

1. In a small bowl, combine quinoa, currants and cinnamon. Set aside.
2. Place the coconut milk, vanilla, cocoa, avocado and banana in the Vitamix container. Secure the lid, remove the lid plug and insert the tamper. With the switch on Variable, select speed 1 and turn the machine on. Gradually increase the speed to 10, using the tamper to push the ingredients into the blades, then flip the switch to High and blend for 10 to 20 seconds or to the desired consistency.
3. Spoon half the smoothie into a tall 16-oz (500 mL) glass and top with half the quinoa mixture, then repeat the layers. Drizzle with honey, if desired. Serve immediately.

Variation

If you don't have cooked quinoa, use a good granola in its place.

WHOLE JUICES and BLENDS

Cranberry Crush

Cranberries are so full of antioxidants, vitamin C and fiber, it is a shame to relegate them to being eaten in sauce once or twice a year. This refreshing drink should be as popular as all those pumpkin-spiced drinks, all year round.

MAKES 2 SERVINGS

$1^1/_2$ cups	fresh unsweetened apple cider (see tip)	375 mL
2 tbsp	pure maple syrup	30 mL
1 cup	cranberries	250 mL

Tip

Fresh apple cider is available only in the fall, and it is usually unfiltered. The rest of the year, look for bottled apple cider and add $1/2$ tsp (2 mL) apple cider vinegar.

1. Place the cider, maple syrup and cranberries in the Vitamix container. Secure the lid, remove the lid plug and insert the tamper. With the switch on Variable, select speed 1 and turn the machine on. Gradually increase the speed to 10, using the tamper to push the ingredients into the blades, then flip the switch to High and blend for about 1 minute or until there are no visible bits. Serve immediately.

Variation

Replace the apple cider with unsweetened pomegranate or cranberry juice.

Berry Mint Jazz

Kiwifruit are even higher in vitamin C than oranges, ounce for ounce, and have their own array of protective antioxidants and carotenoids. Kiwi tastes a bit like strawberry and makes a great flavor combo with blackberries.

MAKES 2 SERVINGS		
1¹/₂ cups	coconut water	375 mL
1	kiwifruit, peeled	1
1	small apple, quartered and cored	1
¹/₂ cup	blackberries	125 mL
¹/₄ cup	lightly packed fresh mint stems and leaves	60 mL

Tip

Peel kiwifruit with a sharp paring knife, stripping the soft skin from the flesh. When kiwis are very soft, you can halve them stem to tip and use a spoon to scoop out the flesh.

1. Place the coconut water, kiwi, apple, blackberries and mint in the Vitamix container. Secure the lid, remove the lid plug and insert the tamper. With the switch on Variable, select speed 1 and turn the machine on. Gradually increase the speed to 10, using the tamper to push the ingredients into the blades, then flip the switch to High and blend for about 1 minute or until there are no visible bits. Serve immediately.

Variation

For a sophisticated version of this jazzy juice, use fresh basil instead of mint.

Vision Quest

Blueberries contain anthocyanins, which protect the retina from both oxygen and sun damage. Women who consume carrots twice a week or more have significantly lower rates of glaucoma. Put them with antioxidant-rich kale, and you have a cocktail for protecting your vision.

MAKES 2 SERVINGS		
1 cup	coconut water	250 mL
1 cup	blueberries	250 mL
1	large carrot, cut into chunks	1
1	leaf kale	1

Tip

Frozen blueberries are a bargain, and the valuable nutrients are retained in the frozen fruit. Both frozen and fresh work equally well in this juice.

1. Place the coconut water, blueberries, carrot and kale in the Vitamix container. Secure the lid, remove the lid plug and insert the tamper. With the switch on Variable, select speed 1 and turn the machine on. Gradually increase the speed to 10, using the tamper to push the ingredients into the blades, then flip the switch to High and blend for about 1 minute or until there are no visible bits. Serve immediately.

Variation

Blackberries are brilliant purple berries that are also rich in antioxidants, so try them in this juice in place of the blueberries.

Apple Grape Juice

This is a great starter juice, and is a good choice for kids who want something familiar. Sweet red grapes are rich in antioxidants and vitamin C, and apple peels contain potent heart-protective compounds. Sparkling water gives the drink a little lift, like a really good-for-you soda.

MAKES 2 SERVINGS

1 cup	sparkling water	250 mL
1/2	medium lemon, peeled and seeded	1/2
1 cup	red grapes	250 mL
1	small apple, quartered and cored	1

Tip

If you want to keep the water as fizzy as possible, add it after puréeing all the fruit and blend for 1 second on speed 6.

1. Place the water, lemon, grapes and apple in the Vitamix container. Secure the lid, remove the lid plug and insert the tamper. With the switch on Variable, select speed 1 and turn the machine on. Gradually increase the speed to 10, using the tamper to push the ingredients into the blades, then flip the switch to High and blend for about 1 minute or until there are no visible bits. Serve immediately.

Variation

Use an unsweetened flavored sparkling water, like lemon, lime or coconut, for more flavor.

Cantaloupe, Lime and Ginger

Cantaloupes are so juicy and sweet, they make a fantastic juice. A cup (250 mL) of cantaloupe provides a day's worth of vitamin A and vitamin C, so you'll be ahead of the game.

MAKES 2 SERVINGS

1 cup	cubed cantaloupe	250 mL
1/2	lime, peeled	1/2
2	slices gingerroot	2
1 cup	ice cubes	250 mL

Tip

Buy a big cantaloupe and cut it up for use all week in juices, fruit salads and soups.

1. Place the cantaloupe, lime, ginger and ice cubes in the Vitamix container. Secure the lid, remove the lid plug and insert the tamper. With the switch on Variable, select speed 1 and turn the machine on. Gradually increase the speed to 10, using the tamper to push the ingredients into the blades, then flip the switch to High and blend for about 1 minute or until there are no visible bits. Serve immediately.

Variation

There are many delicious varieties of melon, including muskmelons, French breakfast melons, Charentais melons and Galia melons. All would make delicious variations of this juice.

Watermelon Agave Aqua Fresca

We know that watermelons are sweet and refreshing, but did you know they are also really good for your heart health? Watermelon contains nitric acid, which improves blood flow, and lycopene, a carotenoid known to protect the heart and prostate. Adding a little chile is also good for the heart and makes this a perfect drink to pair with guacamole.

MAKES 2 SERVINGS		
2 cups	cubed watermelon	500 mL
1 tbsp	agave nectar	15 mL
1/2	medium red chile pepper (or to taste)	1/2
1 cup	ice cubes	250 mL

Tip

Watermelon seeds are not only safe to eat, but contain iron and zinc.

1. Place the watermelon, agave nectar, chile and ice cubes in the Vitamix container. Secure the lid, remove the lid plug and insert the tamper. With the switch on Variable, select speed 1 and turn the machine on. Gradually increase the speed to 10, using the tamper to push the ingredients into the blades, then flip the switch to High and blend for about 1 minute or until there are no visible bits. Serve immediately.

Variation

Try this with honey instead of agave, for a hint of honey flavor.

Heart Healer

In studies, people who drink orange juice have been shown to have lower rates of cardiovascular disease, a finding attributed to the folate, potassium and vitamin C in oranges. Add some anti-inflammatory turmeric and cayenne, and you have a big glass of heart health.

MAKES 2 SERVINGS		
1 cup	water	250 mL
1	large orange, peeled and seeded	1
6	slices fresh turmeric (or 1 1/2 tsp/7 mL ground turmeric)	6
1/8 tsp	cayenne pepper	0.5 mL

Tips

Ground turmeric is much more concentrated than fresh, so a small amount goes a long way.

If the juice is too spicy for your taste, just reblend it with another orange.

1. Place the water, orange, turmeric and cayenne in the Vitamix container. Secure the lid, remove the lid plug and insert the tamper. With the switch on Variable, select speed 1 and turn the machine on. Gradually increase the speed to 10, using the tamper to push the ingredients into the blades, then flip the switch to High and blend for about 1 minute or until there are no visible bits. Serve immediately.

Grapefruit Zinger

Celebrate citrus with this spicy cocktail. Ginger is a soothing digestive aid and warms the body, and cayenne is good for your circulation.

∽◡∽ ◡∽

MAKES 2 SERVINGS		
1	large grapefruit, peeled and seeded	1
1	large orange, peeled and seeded	1
2	slices gingerroot	2
1/4 tsp	cayenne pepper	1 mL
1 cup	ice cubes	250 mL

Tips

If you are on any kind of blood thinner or heart medication, make sure grapefruit is not on your list of foods to avoid.

Grapefruits range from deep red to white in color. Mix it up and try red one day, pink the next.

1. Place the grapefruit, orange, ginger, cayenne and ice cubes in the Vitamix container. Secure the lid, remove the lid plug and insert the tamper. With the switch on Variable, select speed 1 and turn the machine on. Gradually increase the speed to 10, using the tamper to push the ingredients into the blades, then flip the switch to High and blend for about 1 minute or until there are no visible bits. Serve immediately.

Lemon Turmeric Drink

This drink relies on the electrolyte-rich base of coconut water to carry some soothing and healing spices. It's great after a workout or before a big meal.

∽◡∽ ◡∽

MAKES 2 SERVINGS		
1 1/2 cups	coconut water	375 mL
1	large lemon, peeled and seeded	1
2	slices fresh turmeric (or 1/4 tsp/1 mL ground turmeric)	2
1/2 tsp	ground cinnamon	2 mL

Tip

Don't buy coconut water in metal cans — it will taste tinny. Aseptic (Tetra) boxes are the way to go.

1. Place the coconut water, lemon, turmeric and cinnamon in the Vitamix container. Secure the lid, remove the lid plug and insert the tamper. With the switch on Variable, select speed 1 and turn the machine on. Gradually increase the speed to 10, using the tamper to push the ingredients into the blades, then flip the switch to High and blend for about 1 minute or until there are no visible bits. Serve immediately.

Variation

Add 1/8 tsp (0.5 mL) black pepper to help make the protective chemicals in the turmeric more available and effective.

Jasmine Lemonade

Jasmine tea is made by layering jasmine flowers between the tea leaves so that the fresh flowers perfume the tea. It's all about the scent, so take a moment to enjoy the floral notes in your juice as you lift it to your lips.

MAKES 2 SERVINGS		
1 cup	boiling water	250 mL
1 tsp	loose-leaf jasmine tea (or 1 tea bag)	5 mL
1 tbsp	agave nectar (or to taste)	15 mL
1	large lemon, peeled and seeded	1
1	large orange, peeled and seeded	1
1	small apple, quartered and cored	1

Tip

Buy jasmine green tea or jasmine oolong tea, depending on your taste. There is a little more caffeine in black tea than green.

1. In a teapot or a heatproof measuring cup, steep tea in boiling water for 5 minutes. Remove tea and let the infusion cool completely.
2. Place the cooled tea, agave nectar, lemon, orange and apple in the Vitamix container. Secure the lid, remove the lid plug and insert the tamper. With the switch on Variable, select speed 1 and turn the machine on. Gradually increase the speed to 10, using the tamper to push the ingredients into the blades, then flip the switch to High and blend for about 1 minute or until there are no visible bits. Serve immediately.

Variation

Use a floral honey in place of the agave nectar, for an even more flowery flavor.

Green Ginger Lemonade

Cucumber and spinach are really good for your skin, so make this refreshing drink to keep your skin glowing.

MAKES 2 SERVINGS		
1/2	medium cucumber, cut into chunks	1/2
1/2	large lemon, peeled and seeded	1/2
1	small pear, quartered and cored	1
2	slices gingerroot	2
1 cup	lightly packed fresh spinach leaves	250 mL
1 cup	ice cubes	250 mL

Tip

Always buy unwaxed organic cucumbers so you can get the benefits of the nutritious skin.

1. Place the cucumber, lemon, pear, ginger, spinach and ice cubes in the Vitamix container. Secure the lid, remove the lid plug and insert the tamper. With the switch on Variable, select speed 1 and turn the machine on. Gradually increase the speed to 10, using the tamper to push the ingredients into the blades, then flip the switch to High and blend for about 1 minute or until there are no visible bits. Serve immediately.

Variation

Try kale instead of spinach, for a deeper green taste.

Tomato Lemonade

Tomatoes are botanically classified as a fruit, and they make a delicious fruity juice when blended with apples and lemons. Call it pink lemonade and enjoy it — it delivers protective lycopene and vitamin C.

MAKES 2 SERVINGS		
3	medium tomatoes, cored	3
2	large lemons, peeled and seeded	2
2	small apples, quartered and cored	2

Tip

Use a rasp grater, such as a Microplane, to remove the zest from the lemon before peeling it. Store the zest in a small jar or bag in the refrigerator for up to 3 days or in the freezer for up to 3 months.

1. Place the tomatoes, lemons and apples in the Vitamix container. Secure the lid, remove the lid plug and insert the tamper. With the switch on Variable, select speed 1 and turn the machine on. Gradually increase the speed to 10, using the tamper to push the ingredients into the blades, then flip the switch to High and blend for about 1 minute or until there are no visible bits. Serve immediately.

Variation

Try this with pears in place of apples for a slightly sweeter, milder taste.

Basil Kale Limeade

Basil is not just the essential herb for spaghetti sauce, it's a delicious addition to a juice like this one. Like other green leaves, it is high in flavonoids, which protect your body. It is also uniquely blessed with antibacterial compounds.

MAKES 2 SERVINGS		
1 cup	coconut water	250 mL
1/2	large lime, peeled	1/2
1	leaf kale	1
1/4 cup	lightly packed fresh basil	60 mL

Tip

Basil doesn't like being kept for long in the refrigerator. Keep it in a jar with the stems in water, like a bouquet, with a large plastic bag over the top, on the counter or in the fridge for up to 3 days.

1. Place the coconut water, lime, kale and basil in the Vitamix container. Secure the lid, remove the lid plug and insert the tamper. With the switch on Variable, select speed 1 and turn the machine on. Gradually increase the speed to 10, using the tamper to push the ingredients into the blades, then flip the switch to High and blend for about 1 minute or until there are no visible bits. Serve immediately.

Variation

Thai basil will give this drink a Thai feel, and it would be a perfect pairing with pad Thai and tom yum.

Greens and Orange Juice

To fully absorb the iron in greens, make sure to consume them with foods high in vitamin C. This juice gives you a one-two punch of plant nutrition, combined in a way that allows you to absorb the nutrients.

MAKES 2 SERVINGS		
1 cup	water	250 mL
1	large orange, peeled and seeded	1
3	slices gingerroot	3
1	large leaf kale	1

Tip

Use a rasp grater, such as a Microplane, to remove the zest from the orange before peeling it. Store the zest in a small jar or bag in the refrigerator for up to 3 days or in the freezer for up to 3 months.

1. Place the water, orange, ginger and kale in the Vitamix container. Secure the lid, remove the lid plug and insert the tamper. With the switch on Variable, select speed 1 and turn the machine on. Gradually increase the speed to 10, using the tamper to push the ingredients into the blades, then flip the switch to High and blend for about 1 minute or until there are no visible bits. Serve immediately.

Variation

For a milder juice, substitute 1 cup (250 mL) packed spinach leaves for the kale.

Green Power

Eating your greens is so much easier now that you can blend them and sip them through a straw. Kale contains many healthful compounds, including glucosinolates, which help detox the body at a cellular level.

MAKES 2 SERVINGS		
1 cup	coconut water or coconut kefir	250 mL
1/2	medium lime, peeled	1/2
1	medium green apple, quartered and cored	1
1	stalk celery, cut into chunks	1
1	leaf kale	1

Tip

Celery juice is good for headaches, so if you feel one coming on, make this juice with 4 celery stalks.

1. Place the coconut water, lime, apple, celery and kale in the Vitamix container. Secure the lid, remove the lid plug and insert the tamper. With the switch on Variable, select speed 1 and turn the machine on. Gradually increase the speed to 10, using the tamper to push the ingredients into the blades, then flip the switch to High and blend for about 1 minute or until there are no visible bits. Serve immediately.

Variation

Try a collard green leaf instead of kale, for a different kind of green nutrition.

Triple-Green Shrub

If one kind of green is good, three is better. This is a juice for grownups, all green and, if you use water, not sweet at all.

MAKES 2 SERVINGS

1 cup	coconut water or water	250 mL
1 tbsp	apple cider vinegar	15 mL
2	leaves kale	2
1 cup	lightly packed fresh spinach leaves	250 mL
1/2 cup	lightly packed fresh parsley (see tip)	125 mL

Tip

You can use parsley stems in this juice and save the leaves for cooking, if you have a plan to use them up.

1. Place the coconut water, vinegar, kale, spinach and parsley in the Vitamix container. Secure the lid, remove the lid plug and insert the tamper. With the switch on Variable, select speed 1 and turn the machine on. Gradually increase the speed to 10, using the tamper to push the ingredients into the blades, then flip the switch to High and blend for about 1 minute or until there are no visible bits. Serve immediately.

Variation

Substitute arugula for the spinach, for a more peppery juice.

Warming Greens Juice

Did you know that consuming hot chiles actually boosts your metabolism? Hot peppers increase thermogenesis (heat production) for 20 minutes after you eat them. They are also rich in vitamin C and antioxidants.

MAKES 2 SERVINGS

1 cup	water	250 mL
1/2	medium lime, peeled	1/2
1	small apple, quartered and cored	1
1	large red chile pepper, seeded	1
1	leaf kale	1

Tip

Whole chiles freeze well. Buy them in late summer at a farmers' market, wash and dry them, then freeze them on a baking sheet. Once solid, transfer to an airtight container and store in the freezer for up to 4 months.

1. Place the water, lime, apple, chile and kale in the Vitamix container. Secure the lid, remove the lid plug and insert the tamper. With the switch on Variable, select speed 1 and turn the machine on. Gradually increase the speed to 10, using the tamper to push the ingredients into the blades, then flip the switch to High and blend for about 1 minute or until there are no visible bits. Serve immediately.

Variation

If you have a high heat tolerance, try this with 2 chiles.

Green Energy Cocktail

Blend some cool green tea with leafy green vegetables and green apple, and you have a drink that energizes. Green juices give you a quick nutritive boost, while a little bit of caffeine in the green tea sharpens your mind.

MAKES 2 SERVINGS

1 cup	brewed green tea, cooled	250 mL
1/2 tsp	freshly squeezed lemon juice	2 mL
1	small green apple, quartered and cored	1
2	leaves kale	2
2 cups	lightly packed fresh spinach leaves	500 mL

Tip

Keep brewed green tea in the refrigerator so you always have a good base for an energizing green juice.

1. Place the tea, lemon juice, apple, kale and spinach in the Vitamix container. Secure the lid, remove the lid plug and insert the tamper. With the switch on Variable, select speed 1 and turn the machine on. Gradually increase the speed to 10, using the tamper to push the ingredients into the blades, then flip the switch to High and blend for about 1 minute or until there are no visible bits. Serve immediately.

Variation

Flavored teas add extra interest to this juice. Try green tea flavored with pomegranate, lemon or jasmine for fun variations.

Red Antioxidant Rush

This juice is a medley of superfood superstars, all of which have the bright colors that assure you they are rich in antioxidants.

MAKES 2 SERVINGS

1 cup	coconut water or water	250 mL
2 tsp	apple cider vinegar (optional)	10 mL
1	large orange, peeled and seeded	1
1	large carrot, cut into chunks	1
1/2	medium beet, cut into cubes	1/2
1	leaf kale	1
1/2 cup	sliced red cabbage	125 mL

Tip

Use up a wedge of red cabbage in salads, slaws and juices like this one.

1. Place the coconut water, vinegar (if using), orange, carrot, beet, kale and cabbage in the Vitamix container. Secure the lid, remove the lid plug and insert the tamper. With the switch on Variable, select speed 1 and turn the machine on. Gradually increase the speed to 10, using the tamper to push the ingredients into the blades, then flip the switch to High and blend for about 1 minute or until there are no visible bits. Serve immediately.

Variation

Substitute a grapefruit for the orange and omit the apple cider vinegar.

Beet Berry Hibiscus Tea

Hibiscus tea is made from the deep red blooms of the hibiscus plant. It is very rich in vitamin C and has a sour, citrusy flavor that goes well with both beets and strawberries.

MAKES 2 SERVINGS

1 cup	boiling water	250 mL
1 tsp	loose-leaf hibiscus tea (or 1 tea bag)	5 mL
1 cup	frozen strawberries	250 mL
1/2	medium beet, cut into cubes	1/2

Tip

Brew the tea the day before and refrigerate it for a nice cold juice.

1. In a teapot or a heatproof measuring cup, steep tea in boiling water for 5 minutes. Remove tea and let the infusion cool completely.
2. Place the cooled tea, strawberries and beet in the Vitamix container. Secure the lid, remove the lid plug and insert the tamper. With the switch on Variable, select speed 1 and turn the machine on. Gradually increase the speed to 10, using the tamper to push the ingredients into the blades, then flip the switch to High and blend for about 1 minute or until there are no visible bits. Serve immediately.

Variation

Rosehip tea would be another bright red, high-C tea to use in this juice.

Winter Wakeup

Brilliant red beets contain folate, an important B vitamin, and lots of iron — both things women need. Cranberries and an orange add plenty of vitamin C to keep you healthy all winter long.

MAKES 2 SERVINGS

1/2 cup	water	125 mL
1	large orange, peeled and seeded	1
1/2 cup	cranberries	125 mL
1/2	medium beet, cubed	1/2
1/2 tsp	ground cinnamon	2 mL
1/2 cup	ice cubes	125 mL

Tip

Cinnamon is a warming spice and also aids in maintaining blood sugar balance. For a spicier drink, you can use up to double the amount of cinnamon.

1. Place the water, orange, cranberries, beet, cinnamon and ice cubes in the Vitamix container. Secure the lid, remove the lid plug and insert the tamper. With the switch on Variable, select speed 1 and turn the machine on. Gradually increase the speed to 10, using the tamper to push the ingredients into the blades, then flip the switch to High and blend for about 1 minute or until there are no visible bits. Serve immediately.

Carrot, Apple and Ginger

Ginger has long been prescribed to help with digestion and calm an upset stomach. It's also a potent antioxidant, and pairing it with antioxidant-rich carrots is both protective and delicious.

MAKES 2 SERVINGS		
1/2 cup	water or coconut water	125 mL
1	small apple, quartered and cored	1
2	slices gingerroot	2
1	large carrot, cut into chunks	1
1 cup	ice cubes	250 mL

Tip

If your ginger is very young, with papery skin, you don't have to peel it.

1. Place the water, apple, ginger, carrot and ice cubes in the Vitamix container. Secure the lid, remove the lid plug and insert the tamper. With the switch on Variable, select speed 1 and turn the machine on. Gradually increase the speed to 10, using the tamper to push the ingredients into the blades, then flip the switch to High and blend for about 1 minute or until there are no visible bits. Serve immediately.

Variation

Try this with maple water, for a hint of maple flavor.

Carrot, Kale and Apple

Carrots are famously high in vitamin A and beta-carotene, and help protect your heart. Kale is famed for its anticancer properties. Together, they make a very healthful drink.

MAKES 2 SERVINGS		
1 1/4 cups	coconut water	300 mL
1	small apple, quartered and cored	1
1	large carrot, cut into chunks	1
2	leaves kale	2

Tip

If drinking kale juice is new to you, save the stems for stir-fries or other uses, as they are a bit more bitter than the leaves.

1. Place the coconut water, apple, carrot and kale in the Vitamix container. Secure the lid, remove the lid plug and insert the tamper. With the switch on Variable, select speed 1 and turn the machine on. Gradually increase the speed to 10, using the tamper to push the ingredients into the blades, then flip the switch to High and blend for about 1 minute or until there are no visible bits. Serve immediately.

Variation

Substitute 2 more carrots for the apple, for a carrot and kale special.

Orange Carrot Juice

This basic juice is nearly instant, with brilliant orange and carrot to give you a boost. Adding a bit of lemon brings out the sweetness of the other ingredients and adds even more vitamin C.

MAKES 2 SERVINGS		
1 cup	water	250 mL
1	large orange, peeled and seeded	1
1/4	large lemon, peeled and seeded	1/4
1	large carrot, cut into chunks	1

Tip

Always remove the seeds from citrus fruits before juicing. The seeds are bitter and contain trace amounts of cyanide compounds.

1. Place the water, orange, lemon and carrot in the Vitamix container. Secure the lid, remove the lid plug and insert the tamper. With the switch on Variable, select speed 1 and turn the machine on. Gradually increase the speed to 10, using the tamper to push the ingredients into the blades, then flip the switch to High and blend for about 1 minute or until there are no visible bits. Serve immediately.

Sweet Potato Curry Juice

Sweet potatoes are a great source of vitamin A. Puréed sweet potato makes a surprisingly creamy, sweet juice. Fresh turmeric is fantastically health-protective and is associated with lower rates of Alzheimer's disease and inflammation.

MAKES 2 SERVINGS		
1 cup	water	250 mL
12 oz	sweet potato, cut into cubes (about 3 cups/750 mL)	375 g
1/2	lemon, peeled and seeded	1/2
6	slices fresh turmeric (or 1 1/2 tsp/7 mL ground turmeric)	6
2	slices gingerroot	2
1/2	small red chile pepper, seeded	1/2
	Honey (optional)	

Tip

Look for fresh turmeric in Indian markets, well-stocked grocery stores and natural foods stores. It looks like gingerroot, but is usually a little thinner.

1. Place the water, sweet potato, lemon, turmeric, ginger, chile and honey to taste (if using) in the Vitamix container. Secure the lid, remove the lid plug and insert the tamper. With the switch on Variable, select speed 1 and turn the machine on. Gradually increase the speed to 10, using the tamper to push the ingredients into the blades, then flip the switch to High and blend for about 1 minute or until there are no visible bits. Serve immediately.

Variation

For a creamy lassi, use almond or cashew milk, or even kefir, instead of water.

Tomato Kraut Cocktail

Fermented foods are a tasty way to get some probiotic lactobacteria while enjoying the complex flavors of cultured foods. Cabbage is already a healthful food, but when you ferment it, many of its anticancer compounds become more absorbable.

	MAKES 2 SERVINGS	
1 cup	water	250 mL
1/4 tsp	Worcestershire sauce	1 mL
1	medium tomato, cored	1
1/4 cup	sauerkraut, with juice (see tip)	60 mL

Tip

For maximum health benefit, always buy raw, refrigerated sauerkraut, not the pasteurized kraut in jars and cans on the shelf. The refrigerated kraut contains active cultures.

1. Place the water, Worcestershire sauce, tomato and sauerkraut in the Vitamix container. Secure the lid, remove the lid plug and insert the tamper. With the switch on Variable, select speed 1 and turn the machine on. Gradually increase the speed to 10, using the tamper to push the ingredients into the blades, then flip the switch to High and blend for about 1 minute or until there are no visible bits. Serve immediately.

Variation

Now that fermented foods are seeing a resurgence, you may see fermented carrots, red cabbage and other fun foods. Try them in this juice in place of the sauerkraut.

Tomato, Beet, Kimchi and Miso

This scarlet concoction is enlivened with spicy fermented kimchi and mild, salty fermented miso. Both contain probiotics and add a great deal of complex flavor to a sweet and tangy juice.

	MAKES 2 SERVINGS	
1 cup	water	250 mL
1	medium tomato, cored	1
1 tbsp	kimchi (or to taste)	15 mL
1 tsp	white miso	5 mL
1/2 cup	cubed beet	125 mL

Tips

Miso lasts for up to a year in the refrigerator and is a great addition to salad dressings and soups.

For a more prominent flavor, try red miso.

1. Place the water, tomato, kimchi, miso and beet in the Vitamix container. Secure the lid, remove the lid plug and insert the tamper. With the switch on Variable, select speed 1 and turn the machine on. Gradually increase the speed to 10, using the tamper to push the ingredients into the blades, then flip the switch to High and blend for about 1 minute or until there are no visible bits. Serve immediately.

Strawberry Kombucha Sipper

Kombucha is a wonderful source of probiotic bacteria and gives your juice a bit of a sweet-and-sour flavor, as well as some natural bubbles. Adding it to juice is a perfect way to keep your digestive tract happy and healthy.

MAKES 2 SERVINGS		
1 cup	plain kombucha	250 mL
1 cup	strawberries	250 mL
1	small red apple, quartered and cored	1

Tip

When local strawberries are in season, they will be at their peak of freshness and nutrient content.

1. Place the kombucha, strawberries and apple in the Vitamix container. Secure the lid, remove the lid plug and insert the tamper. With the switch on Variable, select speed 1 and turn the machine on. Gradually increase the speed to 10, using the tamper to push the ingredients into the blades, then flip the switch to High and blend for about 1 minute or until there are no visible bits. Serve immediately.

Variation

Kombucha comes in all sorts of flavors. Try this juice with pomegranate kombucha, for an even more brilliant red drink.

Green Apple Snap

Wake up your mouth with this snappy, slightly spicy juice. Arugula and mint combine for an herbal flavor that complements the tart green apple.

MAKES 2 SERVINGS		
1 cup	plain kombucha	250 mL
1	small green apple, quartered and cored	1
1 cup	arugula	250 mL
1/2 cup	lightly packed fresh mint stems and leaves	125 mL
1 cup	ice cubes	250 mL

Tip

Bags of small Granny Smith apples are usually a bargain, so opt for the little ones to save a little money.

1. Place the kombucha, apple, arugula, mint and ice cubes in the Vitamix container. Secure the lid, remove the lid plug and insert the tamper. With the switch on Variable, select speed 1 and turn the machine on. Gradually increase the speed to 10, using the tamper to push the ingredients into the blades, then flip the switch to High and blend for about 1 minute or until there are no visible bits. Serve immediately.

Variation

If you substitute spinach for arugula, the mint flavor will be more prominent.

Insightful Orange Juice

You probably learned that carrots are good for your eyes from watching cartoons, thanks to Bugs Bunny. Sweet corn is another eye health all-star, being rich in lutein, which is recommended to protect your eyes from macular degeneration.

MAKES 2 SERVINGS		
1 cup	plain kombucha	250 mL
1	large orange, peeled and seeded	1
1	large carrot, cut into chunks	1
1	ear sweet corn, kernels cut off the cob (or 1/2 cup/125 mL frozen corn kernels)	1

Tip

Look for yellow sweet corn, rather than white, for more of the healthful yellow pigments.

1. Place the kombucha, orange, carrot and corn in the Vitamix container. Secure the lid, remove the lid plug and insert the tamper. With the switch on Variable, select speed 1 and turn the machine on. Gradually increase the speed to 10, using the tamper to push the ingredients into the blades, then flip the switch to High and blend for about 1 minute or until there are no visible bits. Serve immediately.

Variation

Use sparkling water instead of kombucha for a fizzy sparkler.

Warrior's Blood

Beets and watermelon are both rich in nitrates that convert into nitric oxide, a compound that relaxes the lining of your circulatory system and measurably improves athletic performance. Non-athletes can benefit too, as nitric oxide also lowers blood pressure and boosts energy.

MAKES 2 SERVINGS		
1 cup	plain kombucha	250 mL
2 cups	cubed watermelon	500 mL
1	slice gingerroot	1
1/2	medium beet, cut into cubes	1/2

Tip

Peel and cube beets right before making this juice, as their antioxidant levels start to decrease as soon as they are cut.

1. Place the kombucha, watermelon, ginger and beet in the Vitamix container. Secure the lid, remove the lid plug and insert the tamper. With the switch on Variable, select speed 1 and turn the machine on. Gradually increase the speed to 10, using the tamper to push the ingredients into the blades, then flip the switch to High and blend for about 1 minute or until there are no visible bits. Serve immediately.

Variation

Add 1/4 lemon, peeled and seeded, for a little bit of sour with the sweet.

Heavy Metal Detox Juice

If you eat seafood, you may well have accumulated some mercury in your tissues. Cilantro juice is a natural remedy for heavy metal toxicity from exposure to metals like mercury, lead and cadmium. When you drink cilantro juice, it binds with heavy metals and removes them from your body. It's also pretty tasty.

MAKES 2 SERVINGS

1 cup	plain kombucha or water	250 mL
$1/2$	large cucumber, cut into chunks	$1/2$
$1/2$	large lemon, peeled and seeded	$1/2$
2	slices gingerroot	2
1	leaf kale	1
$1/2$ cup	lightly packed fresh cilantro (see tip)	125 mL
1 cup	ice cubes	250 mL

Tips

Cilantro stems are tender and juicy, so use them for this juice and save the leaves for salsa. Be sure to wash and dry cilantro well before use, as it tends to be gritty.

If you are particularly concerned about heavy metal toxicity, use double the cilantro and add a little extra liquid.

1. Place the kombucha, cucumber, lemon, ginger, kale, cilantro and ice cubes in the Vitamix container. Secure the lid, remove the lid plug and insert the tamper. With the switch on Variable, select speed 1 and turn the machine on. Gradually increase the speed to 10, using the tamper to push the ingredients into the blades, then flip the switch to High and blend for about 1 minute or until there are no visible bits. Serve immediately.

Broccoli Baby

Before everyone went crazy for kale, broccoli was the superfood hero, known for its anticancer benefits and for being rich in vitamins and minerals. It's still great, with large amounts of flavonoids and carotenoids that fight inflammation and oxidative stress.

MAKES 2 SERVINGS		
1 cup	plain kombucha	250 mL
2 cups	cubed honeydew melon	500 mL
1 cup	broccoli florets	250 mL
1	leaf kale	1

Tips

When you are cooking with broccoli, save the stems to use in this juice.

You'll need about half a 2-lb (1 kg) honeydew melon to get 2 cups (500 mL) cubes.

1. Place the kombucha, honeydew, broccoli and kale in the Vitamix container. Secure the lid, remove the lid plug and insert the tamper. With the switch on Variable, select speed 1 and turn the machine on. Gradually increase the speed to 10, using the tamper to push the ingredients into the blades, then flip the switch to High and blend for about 1 minute or until there are no visible bits. Serve immediately.

Variation

Broccolini is a slender, leafy cross between broccoli and turnips, and it would be a tasty substitute for broccoli in this juice.

Salad Greens in a Glass

Take a break from all that chewing and drink your salad — through a straw, if you like. A touch of lemon acts as a vinaigrette and makes the minerals in the romaine more absorbable.

MAKES 2 SERVINGS		
1 cup	plain kombucha	250 mL
1/2	large lemon, peeled and seeded	1/2
1	small heart of romaine, sliced (about 3 cups/750 mL)	1

Tip

Bagged hearts of romaine lettuce are widely available, or you can strip the outer leaves from a head of romaine and use them for salad, saving the pale inner heart for this drink.

1. Place the kombucha, lemon and romaine in the Vitamix container. Secure the lid, remove the lid plug and insert the tamper. With the switch on Variable, select speed 1 and turn the machine on. Gradually increase the speed to 10, using the tamper to push the ingredients into the blades, then flip the switch to High and blend for about 1 minute or until there are no visible bits. Serve immediately.

Variation

If you have a head of butter lettuce or leaf lettuce that you know you won't get to in the next couple of days, substitute it for romaine in this juice.

Probiotic Digestif

Drinking kombucha is a great way to keep your digestion in tip-top shape, and cider vinegar adds even more probiotics. Cucumber and ginger are both soothing to the digestive tract, and cabbage juice is recommended to cure acid reflux.

MAKES 2 SERVINGS

1 cup	plain kombucha	250 mL
1 tsp	apple cider vinegar	5 mL
1/2	large cucumber, cut into chunks	1/2
1	small apple, quartered and cored	1
1/2	medium carrot, cut into chunks	1/2
1	slice gingerroot	1
1/2 cup	sliced cabbage	125 mL

Tip

For optimal health benefits, always buy live, active apple cider vinegar, which is often cloudy and has gelatinous-looking blobs of "mother" starter floating in it, rather than pasteurized vinegar.

1. Place the kombucha, vinegar, cucumber, apple, carrot, ginger and cabbage in the Vitamix container. Secure the lid, remove the lid plug and insert the tamper. With the switch on Variable, select speed 1 and turn the machine on. Gradually increase the speed to 10, using the tamper to push the ingredients into the blades, then flip the switch to High and blend for about 1 minute or until there are no visible bits. Serve immediately.

Variation

Use red cabbage, for a burst of purple color.

BLENDER COCKTAILS

TIPS FOR SUCCESS

- Many of these recipes require you to freeze a mixture in an ice cube tray. You may well have discarded yours when you got an automatic ice maker, but fear not, ice cube trays are inexpensive and easy to find. A standard one holds about $1^1/_2$ cups (375 mL) of liquid.
- When foods and drinks are cold, their flavors are muted. That's why a frozen drink needs to have a concentrated burst of flavors in the base mixture.
- Keeping spirits like vodka and gin in the freezer will help you to make those drinks just a little bit colder.
- Chances are, you don't have a full set of every kind of barware. You can still enjoy your drinks in any glass you have. For reference, in the table below you'll find the capacities of some of the most popular glass sizes used for mixed drinks.

Type of Glass	Capacity
Margarita glass	12 oz (375 mL)
Old-fashioned glass	9 oz (270 mL)
Double old-fashioned glass	12 oz (375 mL)
Highball glass	17 oz (530 mL)
Large wine glass	16 oz (500 mL)
Flute	6 to 9 oz (175 mL to 270 mL)

Sea Breeze Freeze

The sea breeze is a refreshing blend of vodka and grapefruit and cranberry juices over ice. This frozen version employs whole cranberries and grapefruit, which give the drink a satisfyingly thick texture when blended with ice.

MAKES 4 SERVINGS

4 oz	vodka	125 mL
$1/_4$ cup	agave nectar	60 mL
1	large grapefruit, peeled and seeded	1
1 cup	frozen cranberries	250 mL
2 cups	ice cubes	500 mL

Tip

For a pale pink drink, use a pink grapefruit.

1. Place the vodka, agave nectar, grapefruit, cranberries and ice in the Vitamix container and secure the lid. With the switch on Variable, select speed 1 and turn the machine on. Gradually increase the speed to 10, then flip the switch to High and blend for about 30 seconds or until the ice no longer makes tinkling sounds on the blades.
2. Pour into four highball or other tall glasses and serve immediately.

Variation

Substitute gin for the vodka, for a little more complexity.

Lemon Thyme Vodka Slushy

If you like lemonade, you will love this cooling, zesty slush. You'll need to start a day or two before you want to drink it. Once you have the lemony syrup cubes in the freezer, you have delicious drinks in the bank, to dole out on hot afternoons, or for a party.

MAKES 4 SERVINGS

- **Fine-mesh sieve**
- **2 ice cube trays**
- **4 margarita glasses**

LEMON THYME ICE CUBES

3 cups	water	750 mL
1 cup	granulated sugar	250 mL
	Strips of zest from $1/2$ large lemon (see tip)	
35	sprigs fresh thyme	35
$1^1/4$ cups	freshly squeezed lemon juice	300 mL

SLUSHY

2 oz	vodka	60 mL
2 oz	limoncello	60 mL
12	Lemon Thyme Ice Cubes	12
1 cup	tonic water	250 mL
4	sprigs fresh thyme	4

Tips

For the strips of lemon zest, use a vegetable peeler or a sharp paring knife to pare off the yellow zest in wide strips, avoiding the white pith.

There's no need to remove the leaves from the thyme sprigs; both the stems and leaves will infuse flavor into the syrup.

1. *Ice Cubes:* Place the water and sugar in the Vitamix container and secure the lid. With the switch on Variable, select speed 1 and turn the machine on. Quickly increase the speed to 10, then flip the switch to High and blend for about 5 minutes, until the syrup is steaming.

2. Place the lemon zest and thyme in a 4-cup (1 L) glass measuring cup or heatproof container and pour in the hot syrup. Stir vigorously with a wooden spoon, pressing the zest and thyme up against the sides of the cup to release the flavors into the hot syrup. Cover and let steep at room temperature overnight.

3. Strain the syrup through the sieve into another measuring cup or bowl, pressing on the zest and thyme; discard solids. Stir lemon juice into syrup.

4. Pour into ice cube trays and freeze for about 8 hours, until solid. Once frozen, transfer to sealable freezer bags and store in the freezer for up to 3 weeks. (Makes enough ice cubes for 8 servings.)

5. *Slushy:* Place the vodka, limoncello and ice cubes in the Vitamix container and secure the lid. With the switch on Variable, select speed 1 and turn the machine on. Gradually increase the speed to 10, then flip the switch to High and blend for about 10 seconds or until slushy.

6. Turn the machine off and stir in tonic water. Pour into margarita glasses and garnish each with a sprig of thyme. Serve immediately.

Variation

Lemon-Thyme Mocktail Slushy: Omit the vodka and limoncello, and increase the tonic water to $1^1/2$ cups (375 mL), adding $1/2$ cup (125 mL) to the Vitamix with the ice cubes.

Bloody Mary Slushy

The bloody Mary is a cocktail that often seems to become a meal, with garnishes that tower over the glass. This slushy version is a refreshing summer drink with a more savory flavor profile than the usual frozen cocktail. Garnish as you will with speared chunks of pickle or cheese, celery stalks or bacon.

MAKES 2 SERVINGS

- **2 ice cube trays**

BLOODY MARY ICE CUBES

4 cups	tomato juice	1 L
2 tbsp	red miso	30 mL
2 tbsp	freshly squeezed lime juice	30 mL
1 tbsp	Worcestershire sauce	15 mL
1 tbsp	honey	15 mL
2 tsp	hot pepper sauce (or to taste)	10 mL
1/2 tsp	Dijon mustard	2 mL
8	drops Angostura bitters	8
2 tbsp	granulated sugar	30 mL

SLUSHY

2 oz	vodka	60 mL
6	Bloody Mary Ice Cubes	6

Tip

Miso and bitters add satisfying umami to this cocktail, giving it an almost meaty intensity.

1. *Ice Cubes:* Place the tomato juice, miso, lime juice, Worcestershire sauce, honey, hot pepper sauce, mustard, bitters and sugar in the Vitamix container and secure the lid. With the switch on Variable, select speed 1 and turn the machine on. Quickly increase the speed to 10, then flip the switch to High and blend for 10 seconds.

2. Pour into ice cube trays and freeze for about 3 hours, until solid. Once frozen, transfer to sealable freezer bags and store in the freezer for up to 3 weeks. (Makes enough ice cubes for 8 servings.)

3. *Slushy:* Place the vodka and ice cubes in the Vitamix container. Secure the lid, remove the lid plug and insert the tamper. With the switch on Variable, select speed 1 and turn the machine on. Gradually increase the speed to 10 and blend, using the tamper to push the cubes into the blades, until slushy (it should take under 10 seconds).

4. Transfer the slush to two 16-oz (500 mL) glasses. Serve immediately.

Variation

Bloody Mary Mocktail: Replace the vodka with water.

Chai Russians

This recipe takes a few steps, including making fresh almond milk and a chai spice mix, so plan accordingly. The bonus is that you will have enough spice left over to make another batch. This is also just a great recipe for Almond Chai, and you can keep the mixture in the refrigerator to drink with or without vodka.

๑๑ ๑๑ ๑๑ ๑๑ ๑๑ ๑๑ ๑๑ ๑๑ ๑๑ ๑๑ ๑๑ ๑๑ ๑๑ ๑๑ ๑๑ ๑๑ ๑๑

MAKES 8 SERVINGS

- **Nut milk straining bag or fine-mesh sieve lined with cheesecloth**

ALMOND MILK

3/4 cup	slivered almonds	175 mL
	Water	

CHAI SPICE MIX

4 tsp	cardamom seeds (removed from pods)	20 mL
4 tsp	ground ginger	20 mL
4 tsp	ground cinnamon	20 mL
1 tsp	whole cloves	5 mL
1 tsp	whole black peppercorns	5 mL
1/2 tsp	fennel seeds	2 mL

ALMOND CHAI TEA

4	black tea bags	4
2 cups	boiling water	500 mL
3/4 cup	liquid honey	175 mL

CHAI RUSSIANS

8 oz	vodka	250 mL
	Ice cubes (optional)	

1. *Almond Milk:* Place almonds in a bowl and add enough cool water to cover. Let soak at room temperature overnight. Drain.

2. Place 2 cups (500 mL) fresh water and the drained almonds in the Vitamix container and secure the lid. With the switch on Variable, select speed 1 and turn the machine on. Gradually increase the speed to 10, then flip the switch to High and blend for 2 to 3 minutes or until completely smooth.

3. Place the nut milk straining bag in a colander, or place a fine-mesh sieve lined with cheesecloth over a large bowl. Pour the almond milk through the bag or sieve. Squeeze the bag, or press with a rubber spatula through the sieve, to extract the milk. Set aside.

4. *Spice Mix:* Place the cardamom seeds, ginger, cinnamon, cloves, peppercorns and fennel seeds in the Vitamix container and secure the lid. With the switch on Variable, select speed 1 and turn the machine on. Gradually increase the speed to 10, then flip the switch to High and grind for about 40 seconds or until powdered.

5. Turn the machine off and let the spices settle before opening the container, then scrape them into a small bowl. Transfer 2 tbsp (30 mL) to a medium heatproof bowl. Store the remaining spice mix in an airtight container in a cool, dark place for up to 3 months.

6. *Chai Tea:* Add tea bags to the spice mixture, then pour in boiling water. Let steep for 4 minutes, then remove tea bags. Stir in honey until dissolved. Add the tea to the almond milk, whisking well.

Warm Chai Russians

7. For each portion, pour 1/2 cup (125 mL) warm tea into a teacup and stir in 2 tbsp (30 mL) vodka. Serve immediately.

Cold Chai Russians

7. Cover and refrigerate the tea for at least 3 hours, until chilled, or for up to 3 days. Pour the tea back into the Vitamix container, secure the lid and give it a quick spin. For each portion, pour 2 tbsp (30 mL) vodka into a tall glass and add ice cubes. Stir in 1/2 cup (125 mL) cold tea. Serve immediately.

Frosty Fresh Screwdrivers

The combination of orange juice and vodka is always delicious, and this frosty version is especially so on a summer day. Using whole oranges makes this cocktail extra-thick and tasty.

MAKES 2 SERVINGS		
4 oz	vodka	125 mL
1/4 cup	agave nectar	60 mL
2	large oranges, peeled and seeded	2
2 cups	ice cubes	500 mL

> **Tip**
> Use the biggest, best oranges you can find.

1. Place the vodka, agave nectar, oranges and ice cubes in the Vitamix container and secure the lid. With the switch on Variable, select speed 1 and turn the machine on. Gradually increase the speed to 10 and blend for about 40 seconds or until slushy.
2. Pour into two 16-oz (500 mL) glasses and serve immediately.

Variation

Use gin in place of the vodka, for a gin and juice.

Jazz and Blues

The distinctive sounds of jazz and blues echo through all of the music that has followed. Celebrate their unique sounds while sipping on a blue cocktail spiked with the jazzy flavor of gin.

MAKES 4 SERVINGS		
4 oz	gin	125 mL
2 tbsp	freshly squeezed lime juice	30 mL
2 tbsp	simple syrup (see tip)	30 mL
2 cups	frozen blueberries	500 mL
	Ice cubes	
1 cup	chilled ginger ale	250 mL
16	fresh blueberries	16

> **Tip**
> To make simple syrup, place 1 cup (250 mL) water and 1/2 cup (125 mL) granulated sugar in the Vitamix container and secure the lid. With the switch on Variable, select speed 1 and turn the machine on. Gradually increase the speed to 10, then flip the switch to High and blend for 4 minutes or until the syrup is steaming. You'll have more than enough for this recipe; store the remainder in a jar at room temperature for up to 1 month.

1. Place the gin, lime juice, simple syrup and frozen blueberries in the Vitamix container and secure the lid. With the switch on Variable, select speed 1 and turn the machine on. Gradually increase the speed to 10 and blend for 10 to 20 seconds or until smooth.
2. Place a few ice cubes in each of four highball glasses. Pour in blueberry mixture, dividing equally, then divide the ginger ale among the glasses. Garnish each glass with 4 blueberries. Serve immediately.

Variation

Replace the lime juice with lemon juice, for a classic pairing of blueberry and lemon.

Cashew Eggnog with Bourbon

This eggnog is so rich and creamy, you may not even need to mention that it is vegan. Creamy cashew milk, spiked with nutmeg and cinnamon, is such a treat, with or without the bourbon.

MAKES 4 SERVINGS		
1 cup	raw cashews	250 mL
	Water	
1/2 cup	pure maple syrup	125 mL
1/2 tsp	ground cinnamon	2 mL
1/2 tsp	ground nutmeg	2 mL
1/4 tsp	salt	1 mL
4 oz	bourbon	125 mL

Tips

Buy broken pieces of raw cashews; they are a bargain, and you are going to purée them anyway.

Instead of adding the bourbon to the blender, you can make the eggnog and add bourbon to each serving, allowing some of your guests to have a virgin version.

If desired, you can warm the eggnog in a small pot before serving.

1. Place cashews in a bowl and add enough cool water to cover. Let soak at room temperature overnight. Drain and rinse.

2. Place 2½ cups (625 mL) fresh water, the drained cashews, maple syrup, cinnamon, nutmeg and salt in the Vitamix container and secure the lid. With the switch on Variable, select speed 1 and turn the machine on. Gradually increase the speed to 10, then flip the switch to High and blend for 1 minute or until creamy and smooth.

3. Turn the machine off and add the bourbon. Replace the lid. With the switch on Variable, select speed 1 and turn the machine on. Gradually increase the speed to 5 and blend for 1 second.

4. Pour into four old-fashioned glasses and serve immediately.

Variation

Bourbon is sweet and mellow, but you may well enjoy a dark rum or even whisky in your eggnog.

Banana Daiquiris

Those frozen bananas you use in breakfast smoothies also make a creamy, delectable tropical cocktail.

∽∽∽∽∽∽∽∽∽∽∽∽∽∽∽∽∽∽∽∽∽∽∽∽∽∽∽∽∽∽∽

MAKES 2 SERVINGS

4 oz	white rum	125 mL
6 tbsp	liquid honey	90 mL
2 tsp	grated lime zest	10 mL
6 tbsp	freshly squeezed lime juice	90 mL
2	large frozen bananas, cut into chunks	2
1 cup	ice cubes	250 mL
	Fresh banana slices	

Tip

To garnish with a banana slice, cut the banana into 1/4-inch (0.5 cm) diagonal slices, then slice a lengthwise notch halfway across each and slide the notch over the rim of the glass.

1. Place the rum, honey, lime zest, lime juice, frozen bananas and ice cubes in the Vitamix container. Secure the lid, remove the lid plug and insert the tamper. With the switch on Variable, select speed 1 and turn the machine on. Gradually increase the speed to 10, using the tamper to push the ice cubes into the blades, then flip the switch to High and blend for about 20 seconds or until smooth.

2. Pour into two margarita glasses or large wine goblets and garnish with fresh banana slices. Serve immediately.

Variation

Use tequila in place of the rum.

Creamy Piña Coladas

Take a trip to the tropics with this classic concoction. While you sip, you can close your eyes and imagine that you are sitting in the sun on a white sand beach.

∽∽∽∽∽∽∽∽∽∽∽∽∽∽∽∽∽∽∽∽∽∽∽∽∽∽∽∽∽∽∽

MAKES 4 SERVINGS

1 cup	coconut milk	250 mL
8 oz	white rum	250 mL
1/2 cup	agave nectar or liquid honey	125 mL
1/4 cup	freshly squeezed lime juice	60 mL
3/4 cup	frozen pineapple chunks	175 mL
2 cups	ice cubes	500 mL

Tip

Always buy full-fat, not low-fat, coconut milk. Low-fat coconut milk is just regular coconut milk with more water added.

1. Place the coconut milk, rum, agave nectar, lime juice, pineapple and ice cubes in the Vitamix container. Secure the lid, remove the lid plug and insert the tamper. With the switch on Variable, select speed 1 and turn the machine on. Gradually increase the speed to 10, then flip the switch to high and, using the tamper to push the ice cubes into the blades, blend for 40 seconds or until thick and smooth. Turn the machine off. If you hear ice cubes hitting the blades as they fall to the bottom, blend for 5 more seconds.

2. Pour into four margarita glasses or other stemmed glasses. Serve immediately.

Frozen Ginger Mint Mojitos

Take the classic Cuban mojito flavors of mint and lime and add spicy fresh ginger, and you have a cocktail that works as well with Thai food as it does with Latin dishes. Tequila is delicious in this, but you can use the more traditional rum, if you prefer. Start this cocktail a day or two before serving, to give the syrup time to infuse.

MAKES 2 SERVINGS

- **Fine-mesh sieve**
- **3 ice cube trays**

GINGER MINT ICE CUBES

3 cups	water	750 mL
1¹/₂ cups	granulated sugar	375 mL
8	thin slices gingerroot	8
	Strips of zest from 1 large lime (see tip)	
1¹/₂ cups	freshly squeezed lime juice (8 to 12 medium limes)	375 mL
1¹/₂ cups	lightly packed fresh mint leaves	375 mL

MOJITOS

³/₄ cup	coconut water	175 mL
2 oz	tequila	60 mL
6	Ginger Mint Ice Cubes	6
	Fresh mint sprigs	

1. *Ice Cubes:* Place the water and sugar in the Vitamix container and secure the lid. With the switch on Variable, select speed 1 and turn the machine on. Quickly increase the speed to 10, then flip the switch to High and blend for about for 5 minutes or until the syrup is steaming.

2. Place the ginger and lime zest in a 4-cup (1 L) glass measuring cup or heatproof container and pour in the hot syrup. Stir vigorously with a wooden spoon, pressing the ginger and zest up against the sides of the cup to release the flavors into the hot syrup. Cover and let steep at room temperature overnight.

3. Strain the syrup through the sieve into another measuring cup or bowl, pressing on the ginger and zest; discard solids.

4. Place the syrup, lime juice and mint leaves in the Vitamix container and secure the lid. With the switch on Variable, select speed 1 and turn the machine on. Gradually increase the speed to 10 and blend for 5 seconds, just until the mint is chopped.

5. Pour into ice cube trays and freeze for about 3 hours, until solid. Once frozen, transfer to sealable freezer bags and store in the freezer for up to 3 weeks. (Makes enough for 6 servings.)

6. *Mojitos:* Place the coconut water, tequila and ice cubes in the Vitamix container. Secure the lid, remove the lid plug and insert the tamper. With the switch on Variable, select speed 1 and turn the machine on. Gradually increase the speed to 10, using the tamper to push the ice cubes into the blades, then flip the switch to High and blend for about 20 seconds or until slushy.

7. Pour into two highball glasses or large goblets and garnish with mint. Serve immediately.

Variation

Frozen Ginger Mint Mocktail Mojitos: Substitute coconut milk for the tequila.

Tips

For the strips of lime zest, use a vegetable peeler or a sharp paring knife to pare off the green zest in wide strips, avoiding white pith.

Keep the Ginger Mint Ice Cubes in the freezer, and you will be ready to make an exciting mojito for unexpected guests.

Spicy Cucumber Margaritas

If you like your drinks a little less sweet and a little more spicy, try this one. Cucumber gives it a subtle sweetness and a mild vegetal taste, to go with the mint.

∽ ∽

MAKES 2 SERVINGS

- **Margarita glasses**

2^1/$_2$ oz	white tequila	75 mL
1 oz	Grand Marnier or other orange liqueur	30 mL
^{1}/$_4$ cup	freshly squeezed lime juice	60 mL
^{1}/$_8$ tsp	hot pepper sauce	0.5 mL
^{1}/$_2$	large cucumber, peeled and seeded	^{1}/$_2$
3 tbsp	granulated sugar	45 mL
^{3}/$_4$ cup	chopped fresh mint	175 mL
12	ice cubes	12
	Coarse salt (optional)	
	Additional ice cubes	
2	cucumber slices	2

Tip

There are so many good hot sauces on the market, you probably already have a personal favorite. Classic Tabasco is good in this, but if you have another sauce you want to use, go for it.

---

1. Place the tequila, orange liqueur, lime juice, hot pepper sauce, cucumber, sugar, mint and ice cubes in the Vitamix container. Secure the lid, remove the lid plug and insert the tamper. With the switch on Variable, select speed 1 and turn the machine on. Gradually increase the speed to 10, using the tamper to push the ice cubes into the blades, and blend for about 40 seconds, just until the ice is slushy.

2. If desired, spread the salt on a small plate. Moisten the rims of the margarita glasses and dip them in salt.

3. Add a few ice cubes to each glass. Pour the margarita mixture into the glasses and garnish with cucumber slices. Serve immediately.

Variation

Spicy Cucumber Mocktail Margarita: Replace the tequila with tonic water, and replace the Grand Marnier with orange juice.

Tequila Lime Cocktails with Mango Ice Cubes

Add variety to a single drink by floating a sweet and tangy frozen burst of mango in it. As the cubes melt, the drink changes from a simple spritzer to a tropical blend.

∾ ∾

MAKES 2 SERVINGS

- **2 ice cube trays**

. . . .

MANGO ICE CUBES

1 cup	coconut water	250 mL
1 tbsp	freshly squeezed lime juice	15 mL
2	large mangos (each about 12 oz/375 g), peeled and pitted	2

TEQUILA LIME COCKTAILS

8	Mango Ice Cubes	8
4 oz	tequila	125 mL
1	large lime, cut in half	1
2 cups	ginger ale (approx.)	500 mL
	Fresh mint leaves	

Tips

Keeping the ice cubes in sealable freezer bags ensures that they won't absorb any off flavors from the freezer.

Put a swizzle stick or straw in each glass so you can stir it as the mango cubes melt and infuse the drink with fruity flavor.

---

1. *Ice Cubes:* Place the coconut water, lime juice and mangos in the Vitamix container and secure the lid. With the switch on Variable, select speed 1 and turn the machine on. Quickly increase the speed to 10 and blend for about 30 seconds or until smooth.

2. Pour into ice cube trays and freeze for about 3 hours, until solid. Once frozen, transfer to sealable freezer bags and store in the freezer for up to 3 weeks. (Makes enough for 6 servings.)

3. *Cocktails:* Place 4 mango ice cubes in each of two 16-oz (500 mL) glasses and add tequila, dividing equally. Squeeze $1/2$ lime into each glass, then add enough ginger ale to fill the glass. Garnish with mint. Serve immediately.

Variation

Use half papaya and half mango, for a more complex fruity flavor.

Frozen Berry Sangria

Sitting in a sidewalk café in Barcelona, it's easy to finish a pitcher of fruity, refreshing sangria. This version is a frosty, cooling purée of frozen berries, grapes and orange with red wine. Go for a Spanish red, such as Tempranillo, for a nod to the originators of a timeless drink.

MAKES 4 TO 6 SERVINGS

- **Minimum 8-cup (2 L) glass pitcher**
- **Large wine goblets**

1	bottle (750 mL) dry red wine, chilled, divided	1
2 oz	brandy	60 mL
2 tbsp	agave nectar or honey	30 mL
1	large orange, peeled and seeded	1
$^1/_2$	large lime, peeled	$^1/_2$
$1^3/_4$ cups	frozen strawberries	425 mL
2 cups	frozen red grapes	500 mL
2 cups	ice cubes	500 mL

Tip

Keep frozen grapes in a sealable bag in the freezer to use in this drink and in the Peanut Butter and Jelly Smoothie (page 229).

1. Pour half the wine into the pitcher and set aside.
2. Pour the remaining wine into the Vitamix container and add the brandy, agave nectar, orange, lime, strawberries, grapes and ice cubes. Secure the lid. With the switch on Variable, select speed 1 and turn the machine on. Gradually increase the speed to 10, then flip the switch to High and blend for about 40 seconds, just until smooth.
3. Pour into the pitcher and stir. Serve immediately in wine goblets.

Variation

Use frozen mixed berries in place of the strawberries.

Valentine's Raspberry Rosé Frappe

Every February we look for festive and romantic drinks that go with the Valentine's Day theme. This gorgeous rose-colored drink is garnished with rose petals, for a drink that charms and seduces. The low alcohol content will keep you from falling asleep after dinner.

MAKES 2 TO 4 SERVINGS

- **2 to 4 large wine goblets, chilled**

1	bottle (750 mL) dry rosé wine	1
2 oz	vodka	60 mL
1/2	large lemon, peeled and seeded	1/2
1/2 cup	powdered sugar (see page 13)	125 mL
2 cups	frozen raspberries	500 mL
	Rose petals (see tip)	

Tip

Use only organically grown, unsprayed rose petals for edible garnishes like this.

1. Pour the rosé into the Vitamix container and add the vodka, lemon, sugar and raspberries. Secure the lid. With the switch on Variable, select speed 1 and turn the machine on. Gradually increase the speed to 10 and blend for about 30 seconds or until smooth.

2. Pour into the chilled goblets and garnish with rose petals. Serve immediately. If there is any left over from the first pour, refrigerate it in the container and serve within 1 hour.

Variation

For a snazzy presentation, dip the rim of each goblet in water, then in raspberry sugar or another decorative large-crystal sugar.

Melon Mint Vinho Verde Coolers

Vinho Verde, or "green wine," is a simple, dry white wine that is often a little bit bubbly. It's perfect for summertime and makes a lovely counterpoint to the sweet melon in this drink. It's lower in alcohol than most wines, so you can serve these coolers to a group at a party and not worry about them overindulging.

MAKES 4 SERVINGS

- **Ice cube tray**

3 cups	cubed honeydew melon	750 mL
1/4 cup	granulated sugar	60 mL
1/2 cup	lightly packed fresh mint leaves	125 mL
1	bottle (750 mL) Vinho Verde	1
1 cup	ice cubes	250 mL

Tip

Buy the sweetest honeydew melon you can find. A ripe one will have a noticeable perfume. You'll need about 1 1/2 lbs (750 g) whole honeydew to get 3 cups (750 mL) of cubes.

1. Place the honeydew, sugar and mint in the Vitamix container and secure the lid. With the switch on Variable, select speed 1 and turn the machine on. Quickly increase the speed to 10 and blend for about 20 seconds or until smooth.

2. Pour into an ice cube tray and freeze for about 3 hours, until solid. Once frozen, transfer to sealable freezer bags and store in the freezer for up to 3 weeks.

3. To serve, pour the Vinho Verde into the Vitamix container and add the melon ice cubes and regular ice cubes. Secure the lid. With the switch on Variable, select speed 1 and turn the machine on. Gradually increase the speed to 10 and blend for about 30 seconds or until slushy.

4. Pour into four large wine glasses. Serve immediately.

Variation

The best melon is the ripest, sweetest one, so if the honeydew is not ready, go for another juicy, sweet-fleshed melon, such as Galia.

Peachy Pink Bellinis

In this pretty drink, frozen peach slices purée to a smooth, thick consistency, and bubbly prosecco gives the purée some lift. Strawberries add a hint of pink and a tart, sweet flavor.

MAKES 4 SERVINGS

- **4 large wine goblets, chilled**

2 oz	limoncello	60 mL
2 tbsp	honey	30 mL
2 cups	frozen sliced peaches	500 mL
1 cup	frozen strawberries	250 mL
1	bottle (750 mL) prosecco, chilled	1

1. Place the limoncello, honey, peaches and strawberries in the Vitamix container and secure the lid. With the switch on Variable, select speed 1 and turn the machine on. Gradually increase the speed to 10 and blend for about 30 seconds, just until smooth.
2. Turn the machine off, remove the lid and gradually pour in the prosecco down the side of the container, then gently and carefully stir until incorporated.
3. Pour into the chilled goblets and serve immediately.

Variation

Use raspberries instead of the strawberries.

Cantaloupe Bellinis with Vanilla

The original bellini was made with a purée of white-fleshed peaches stirred into a lively glass of prosecco. This frozen version is a blend of sweet orange cantaloupe with a hint of exotic vanilla, with the bubbles we all love.

MAKES 4 SERVINGS

- **4 large wine goblets, chilled**

1 oz	brandy	30 mL
2 tsp	vanilla extract	10 mL
4 cups	cubed cantaloupe	1 L
2 tbsp	powdered sugar (see page 13)	30 mL
2 cups	ice cubes	500 mL
1	bottle (750 mL) prosecco, chilled	1

1. Place the brandy, vanilla, cantaloupe, sugar and ice cubes in the Vitamix container and secure the lid. With the switch on Variable, select speed 1 and turn the machine on. Gradually increase the speed to 10, then flip the switch to High and blend for about 30 seconds or until the ice no longer makes tinkling sounds on the blades.
2. Turn the machine off, remove the lid and gradually pour in the prosecco down the side of the container, then gently and carefully stir until incorporated.
3. Pour into the chilled goblets. Serve immediately.

Tip

Prosecco is very bubbly, so pour it gradually down the side of the container and let it settle before stirring or serving.

Variation

These bellinis are delicious made with Galia or other kinds of melon in place of the cantaloupe.

Chocolate Stout Shake

Chocolate and stout have very similar flavor profiles if you look beyond the fact that one is a dessert and the other is beer. Dark chocolate and stout are both complex combinations of bitterness, fruitiness and sweet, malty flavors. In this shake, the beer goes in a sweet direction, with delectable results.

MAKES 2 SERVINGS

1	bottle (11.2 oz/330 mL) Guinness or other stout beer, divided	1
1/4 cup	half-and-half (10%) cream	60 mL
1/2 tsp	vanilla extract	2 mL
1/4 cup	powdered sugar (see page 13)	60 mL
2 tbsp	unsweetened cocoa powder	30 mL
2 cups	whole milk ice cubes (see tip, page 174)	500 mL

Tip

The craft beer movement has brought us all sorts of hefty stout beers, many on par with the famed Guinness. Your favorite 11- to 12-oz (312 to 340 mL) stout or porter will be delicious in this drink — just stick with sweet, not-too-hoppy beers.

1. Pour half the beer into the Vitamix container and add the cream, vanilla, sugar, cocoa and ice cubes. Secure the lid, remove the lid plug and insert the tamper. With the switch on Variable, select speed 1 and turn the machine on. Gradually increase the speed to 10, then flip the switch to High and, using the tamper to push the ice cubes into the blades, blend for 30 to 60 seconds or until thick and smooth. Turn the machine off. If you hear ice cubes hitting the blades as they fall to the bottom, pulse again.

2. Pour into two large glasses, then pour the remaining beer down the side of each glass, dividing equally. Serve immediately.

Variation

For a richer shake, replace the half-and-half cream with heavy or whipping (35%) cream.

SKIN TREATMENTS, SCRUBS, MASKS and LOTIONS

TIPS FOR SUCCESS

- Some of the scrubs may not feel as "scrubby" as you are accustomed to. Skin care doesn't have to feel like you are sanding your face. It's gentler and just as effective to use a scrub that is a little softer. Your skin will thank you.
- When using scrubs and masks based on whole foods, you will need to prevent the food from clogging the drain when you remove it from your face or body. Always use a washcloth or towel to remove the solids, shake it out over the garbage (or compost) and then rinse your skin. You may also wish to purchase a drain cover made of wire screen or perforated metal to place over the drain, to keep your body scrubs out of the pipes.
- Some of these mixtures will be very sticky to clean. Ingredients like shea butter, cocoa butter and lecithin will coat the inside of the blender container, and the usual automatic cleaning is not enough. You'll need to pour a good amount of dish soap on your sponge and carefully lather up the inside of the container, then run very hot water in the container and rinse. Repeat as needed.
- Vitamin E capsules are used in many of these skin treatments. To use them, pierce the gel caps with a paring knife and squeeze the oil out into your ingredients. Vitamin E is nourishing for your skin and also acts as a preservative for your lotion or other skin treatment.
- Aloe vera juice is a soothing jelly that calms irritated skin and can even help with eczema and psoriasis.
- Beeswax is in many skin care products as a thickener, and it also has beneficial effects on skin. Beeswax is antibacterial and is rich in vitamin A and anti-inflammatory chemicals. It draws moisture to the skin and seals it in without clogging pores.
- Sweet almond oil is used to fade dark spots and get a more even skin tone, as well as to moisturize.
- Grapeseed oil is lightly astringent and helps keep pores from clogging. It's also high in linoleic acid, which has anti-inflammatory qualities.
- The oils you use in your skin care can vary to suit your preferences and the seasons. The oils that absorb the fastest will feel lighter on your skin; these include grapeseed, jojoba, hemp seed and apricot kernel. You may want to use those as your liquid oils in the summer. For an oil that will seal in moisture a bit more, go with almond, avocado, flax, olive or sunflower. The heaviest oils are coconut, macadamia, evening primrose and palm. Don't substitute a light oil for a heavy one in these recipes, as it will change the end result.
- Essential oils are added to these skin care products for fragrance and aromatherapy. The table below provides a few recommendations for essential oils. Feel free to customize the recipes in this chapter to use the essential oils you prefer.

Energizing	Calming	Sensual
Eucalyptus	Thyme	Cinnamon
Lemon	Lavender	Geranium rose
Lemongrass	Myrrh	Jasmine
Rosemary	Neroli	Ylang-ylang

Rosehip Cleansing Gel

Rosehips, the dried bases of red roses, are packed with vitamin C. Making a strong infusion from them gives you a rosehip "hydrosol." The antioxidant and slightly astringent qualities of rosehips make this a good gentle cleanser. Adding a few pinches of guar gum to the hot infusion creates a stable, smooth gel that clings to your face while the other ingredients do their healing work.

MAKES ABOUT 3/4 CUP (175 ML)

3 tbsp	dried rosehips	45 mL
3/4 cup	boiling water	175 mL
1	vitamin E capsule	1
1/4 tsp	guar gum	1 mL
1 tsp	powdered vitamin C	5 mL
1 tbsp	glycerin	15 mL
5	drops rose essential oil	5

Tips

Guar gum is a powder used to gel foods and is often used in gluten-free baking. Here, it helps the mixture gel.

Food-grade glycerin is very good for helping your skin retain moisture, healing scars and holding the mixture in a creamy suspension.

1. Place rosehips in a heatproof bowl or cup. Pour in boiling water and let steep for at least 10 minutes or for up to 2 hours. Strain and measure 1/2 cup (125 mL) of the liquid and place in a small saucepan. Reserve any remaining infusion for another use, or add water and drink it as tea.

2. Place the saucepan over medium heat and warm the infusion to almost boiling.

3. Pour the infusion into the Vitamix container. Pierce the vitamin E capsule and squeeze the oil into the container, discarding the empty capsule. Secure the lid and remove the lid plug. With the switch on Variable, select speed 1 and turn the machine on. Gradually increase the speed to 5 and blend, using your fingers to drop tiny pinches of guar gum through the lid opening, then adding the vitamin C all at once, then drizzling in the glycerin and rose oil. Increase the speed to 10, then flip the switch to High and blend for 30 seconds or until smooth.

4. Transfer to a jar or other container and let cool, uncovered before use. Store in the refrigerator for up to 1 week.

To Use

Rub about 1 tbsp (15 mL) gel over your face and neck. Leave it on for about 5 minutes, then wipe off and discard solids. Rinse your skin with cool water.

Variation

If your skin is prone to breakouts, substitute tea tree oil for the rose oil.

Cucumber, Avocado and Turmeric Face Healer

Irritation and inflammation are the enemies of your skin and contribute to premature aging. This elixir is full of fresh, soothing ingredients. Avocado oil is high in sterols, which stimulate collagen and reduce age spots.

∽∽∽∽∽∽∽∽∽∽∽∽∽∽∽∽∽∽∽∽∽∽∽∽∽∽∽

MAKES ABOUT 1 CUP (250 ML)

1/4 cup	rose water	60 mL
1/2	medium cucumber, sliced	1/2
1/2	medium avocado	1/2
1/2	medium carrot, chopped	1/2
2	slices fresh turmeric, peeled	2

1. Place the rose water, cucumber, avocado, carrot and turmeric in the Vitamix container. Secure the lid, remove the lid plug and insert the tamper. With the switch on Variable, select speed 1 and turn the machine on. Gradually increase the speed to 7 as the mixture becomes creamy, using the tamper to push the ingredients into the blades, and blend for 10 seconds to fully emulsify.

2. Transfer to a jar and store in the refrigerator for up to 1 week.

To Use

Slather a thick layer on your face and neck every day and let dry for 10 to 15 minutes. Wipe off with a wet washcloth and enjoy your supple skin.

Okara Facial Mask

All that pulp left after making soy milk is a revered skin care ingredient in the East. Masks and scrubs made with okara are thought to increase collagen production, reduce wrinkles and brighten skin tone. Rosehips are packed with vitamin C, which also fights aging of the skin.

MAKES ABOUT ¹/₂ CUP (125 ML)

1 tbsp	dried rosehips	15 mL
¹/₂ cup	okara (see soy milk recipes, pages 216 and 217)	125 mL
2 tbsp	honey	30 mL
1 tsp	avocado oil or almond oil	5 mL
¹/₈ tsp	rose essential oil	0.5 mL

Tips

Dried rosehips are sold in the tea and supplements sections of supermarkets and natural foods stores. When brewed for tea, they make a brilliant red infusion that is very high in vitamin C.

Use the oil that meets your skin's needs. Avocado oil is very nourishing, while almond oil is light and easily absorbed (and easy to find).

1. Place rosehips in the Vitamix container and secure the lid. With the switch on High, turn the machine on and grind for about 40 seconds or until finely powdered.
2. Transfer powder to a bowl and stir in okara, honey, avocado oil and rose oil until well combined.
3. Store, tightly covered, in the refrigerator for up to 1 week.

To Use

Spread the mask thickly on your face and neck. Leave it on for 20 to 30 minutes as desired, then wipe off and discard solids. Rinse your face with cool water.

Carrot Turmeric Honey Mask

Carrots are good for your skin, both as a food and as a skin treatment. Rich in skin-supporting vitamin A, carrots speed the healing of acne and offer general support for younger-looking, brighter skin. Honey and yogurt are moisturizing.

〜〜〜〜〜〜〜〜〜〜〜〜〜〜〜〜〜〜〜〜〜〜〜〜〜〜〜〜〜〜

MAKES ABOUT 6 TBSP (90 ML), ENOUGH FOR 1 OR 2 MASKS		
2 tbsp	quick-cooking rolled oats	30 mL
1/2	large carrot, cut into chunks	1/2
2	slices fresh turmeric	2
1/4 cup	plain full-fat yogurt	60 mL
1 tbsp	raw honey	15 mL

1. Place the oats in the Vitamix container and secure the lid. With the switch on Variable, select speed 1 and turn the machine on. Quickly increase the speed to 10, then flip the switch to High and grind for 30 seconds to a fine powder. Transfer oats to a medium bowl.

2. Replace the lid on the container and remove the lid plug. With the switch on Variable, select speed 3 and turn the machine on. Drop in the carrot pieces, one at a time, through the lid opening and blend until finely chopped, then drop in the turmeric and blend until finely minced.

3. Turn the machine off and scrape the mixture out of the corners of the container. Add the yogurt and honey. Replace the lid, select speed 1 and turn the machine on. Blend for about 30 seconds, then gradually increase the speed to 3, increasing only as long as the mixture is engaging the blades.

4. Turn the machine off and scrape the mixture to the center of the container. Replace the lid, select speed 1 and turn the machine on, slowly increasing the speed until the mixture is puréed.

5. Scrape the carrot mixture into the bowl with the oats and stir together. Let stand for 10 minutes to allow the oats to absorb the liquids.

6. Use immediately and store any leftover mask, tightly covered, in the refrigerator for up to 3 days. The mask will thicken; just stir in a little water or yogurt to thin.

To Use

Apply a thick layer of the mask to your face and neck while lying on your back, patting the mixture on. Be careful, as turmeric will stain light-colored surfaces. Let the mask dry on your face for about 30 minutes, then wipe off and discard solids. Rinse your skin with cool water.

Tips

Fresh turmeric is full of antioxidants and helps to protect your skin. It may stain your countertops, but it won't stain your skin.

If you can't find fresh turmeric, substitute 1/2 tsp (2 mL) ground turmeric.

Cucumber Tea Tree Mask for Breakouts

When your skin is prone to breakouts, try this gentle, natural mask. Kefir and cucumber are soothing, and tea tree oil is a potent antibacterial. Baking soda balances pH and brightens your skin.

∾ ∾

MAKES ABOUT 1/2 CUP (125 ML)

1 tbsp	plain kefir or yogurt	15 mL
1/2 tsp	tea tree oil	2 mL
1/2	large cucumber, peeled and cut into chunks	1/2
1 tbsp	baking soda	15 mL
2 tsp	chia seeds	10 mL

Tip

Be patient and stay on lower speeds until the ingredients are finely minced, then gradually increase the speed.

1. Place the kefir, tea tree oil, cucumber, baking soda and chia seeds in the Vitamix container. Secure the lid, remove the lid plug and insert the tamper. With the switch on Variable, select speed 1 and turn the machine on. Using the tamper to push the ingredients into the blades, gradually increase the speed to 3 and blend until minced. Gradually increase the speed to 5 and blend for about 30 seconds or until the mixture is flowing around the blades. Flip the switch to High and blend for 30 seconds or until smooth.

2. Transfer to a small jar and store in the refrigerator for up to 3 days.

To Use

Apply the mask to areas prone to breakouts three times a day. Leave it on for 20 minutes, then wipe off and discard solids. Rinse your skin with cool water.

Variation

For a serious breakout, you can increase the tea tree oil to 1 tsp (5 mL).

Almond, Honey and Aloe Scrub and Mask

After you make almond milk, save some of the strained pulp to make this skin-loving blend. The synergy of consuming almond milk and applying almond pulp to your skin is a beautiful thing: the protein, zinc and fat in the milk feed your skin from the inside, and the fibrous pulp is a gentle exfoliant.

∽∾ ∽∾

MAKES 3 TBSP (45 ML)		
1 tbsp	almond pulp (see Almond Milk recipe, page 212)	15 mL
1 tbsp	aloe vera juice	15 mL
1 tbsp	liquid honey	15 mL

Tips

After making almond milk, measure out the strained pulp by tablespoonfuls (15 mL) onto a pan lined with parchment paper and freeze until solid, then transfer to a sealable freezer bag and store in the freezer. Thaw a portion whenever you want to make this scrub.

If you haven't made almond milk and saved the pulp, secure the lid on the Vitamix container and remove the lid plug. With the switch on Variable, select speed 5 and turn the machine on. Drop in 4 whole almonds, one at a time, through the lid opening and grind for 20 seconds. Gradually increase the speed to 10, then flip the switch to High and grind for 4 to 5 seconds to a fine powder. Proceed with the recipe, stirring in more aloe vera juice as needed to make it creamy.

1. In a small bowl, stir together almond pulp, aloe vera juice and honey. Let stand for 5 minutes.
2. Store, tightly covered, in the refrigerator for up to 4 days.

To Use

Rub about 1 tbsp (15 mL) of the scrub on your face 15 minutes before you take a bath or shower. Massage the scrub onto your face, let it set for 15 minutes, then wipe off and discard solids. Rinse your face with warm water.

Carrot Walnut Scrub

Fresh carrots release their beta-carotene to nourish your skin, and walnuts replenish with their skin-healing oil. Adding vitamin C helps reverse skin aging, fade dark spots and fight wrinkles.

∾ ∾

MAKES ABOUT 2¹/₂ TBSP (37 ML)

4	raw walnut halves	4
2 tbsp	sliced carrots	30 mL
2 tbsp	full-fat plain yogurt	30 mL
¹/₂ tsp	vitamin C powder	2 mL

1. Secure the lid on the Vitamix container and remove the lid plug. With the switch on Variable, select speed 5 and turn the machine on. Drop in the walnuts, one piece at a time, through the lid opening, holding a folded towel over the opening so they don't fly out, and grind for about 40 seconds or until the walnuts stop flying around in the container.

2. Turn the machine off and scrape the walnuts to the center of the container. Replace the lid and grind again, gradually increasing the speed to 10. Repeat the scraping and grinding one more time. Scrape the powder into a small bowl.

3. Replace the lid on the container. Select speed 5 and turn the machine on. Drop in the carrots, a few pieces at a time, through the lid opening and blend until finely minced. Turn the machine off and scrape the container. Replace the lid and blend for a few seconds.

4. Turn the machine off and add the yogurt. Replace the lid, select speed 1 and blend for 30 seconds or until incorporated.

5. Scrape the carrot mixture into the bowl with the walnut powder and stir in the vitamin C powder.

6. Use immediately or store, tightly covered, in the refrigerator for up to 1 week.

To Use

Place a washcloth or towel on the sink to catch any bits of carrot that may fall as you apply the scrub, so they will not clog the drain. Apply the scrub to your face, using a circular motion to scrub the skin gently. Leave it on for 5 minutes, then wipe off and discard solids. Rinse your face with cool water.

Variation

For very dry skin, add a few drops of walnut oil with the yogurt.

Tip

Vitamin C powder is sold in the supplements section of supermarkets, pharmacies and natural foods stores, often in bulk, where you can scoop and bag just a few spoonfuls. It acts as a natural preservative and will keep this scrub fresh if you store it for a week.

Sweet Potato Spice Body Scrub

Sweet potatoes are a great source of vitamin A, which is often added to skin creams to speed healing, reduce wrinkles and fade dark spots. With some crunchy sugar added, this mix is a gentle scrub, because you really don't need to use harsh abrasives.

MAKES ABOUT 1 CUP (250 ML)

1 cup	cubed sweet potato (4 oz/125 g)	250 mL
1 tsp	ground cinnamon	5 mL
1/2 tsp	ground allspice	2 mL
1/2 tsp	ground cloves	2 mL
1 cup	turbinado sugar	250 mL

1. Place the sweet potato in the Vitamix container and secure the lid. With the switch on Variable, select speed 1 and turn the machine on. Gradually increase the speed to 5 and blend for about 10 seconds or until finely minced.

2. Turn the machine off and scrape down the sides of the container. Replace the lid, select speed 1 and blend until the sweet potato is evenly minced.

3. Turn the machine off and add the cinnamon, allspice and cloves. Replace the lid and pulse three times to blend the spices. Remove the lid and add the sugar. Replace the lid, gradually increase the speed to 5 and blend for 5 to 10 seconds or until the sugar is incorporated.

4. Scrape out into a bowl or jar and store, tightly covered, in the refrigerator for up to 1 week.

To Use

Place a bathtub drain screen in the drain. Sitting in the tub, spread the scrub on your skin and scrub in small circular motions. Wipe off and discard solids, then rinse your skin.

Parsley and Oats Body Scrub

If you have ever used a body scrub with plastic scrubbing beads, please stop immediately. Those beads never biodegrade, and they end up in the waterways, where fish eat them and often die. Far better to use real food ingredients you already have in your kitchen. You will be able to buff your skin to a fresh and lovely look with skin-loving oats and parsley.

MAKES ABOUT ¹/₂ CUP (125 ML)

¹/₂ cup	quick-cooking rolled oats	125 mL
2 tbsp	coarse salt	30 mL
2 tbsp	dried parsley	30 mL
15	drops essential oil (see tip)	15

Tips

In the summertime, you'll want to use this scrub to polish away dry skin and make your skin glow. In the winter, your parched skin will thank you for the moisture.

To energize and uplift, use lemon or orange oil; for a calming feeling, use lavender.

1. Place the oats in the Vitamix container and secure the lid. With the switch on Variable, select speed 1 and turn the machine on. Quickly increase the speed to 10, then flip the switch to High and grind for 30 seconds to a fine powder.

2. Turn the machine off and add the salt and parsley. Replace the lid and pulse three times to blend.

3. Scrape into a medium bowl. Toss the mixture with a spoon as you sprinkle in the essential oil, coating evenly.

4. Transfer to a jar and store, tightly covered, in the refrigerator for up to 1 week.

To Use

Measure 2 to 3 tbsp (30 to 45 mL) scrub for just your legs, or more for the rest of your body. Stir in 2 tsp (10 mL) water for each 1 tbsp (15 mL) scrub. Place a bathtub drain screen in the drain. Sitting in the tub, apply the scrub to your skin and massage in a circular motion. Leave it on for about 5 minutes, then wipe off and discard solids and rinse your skin.

Coffee and Kelp Cellulite Body Wrap

High-end spas offer treatments like this one, where they cover you with herbs, seaweed and other things, then wrap you in a hot cloth to steep. In this mix, coffee acts as a diuretic, tightening your skin and making your thighs look smaller. Seaweed is a skin care star, drawing toxins and excess fluid from the skin while supplying lots of minerals and B vitamins.

MAKES ABOUT 3/4 CUP (175 ML), ENOUGH FOR 1 THIGH TREATMENT

1/2 cup	coffee beans	125 mL
1/2 oz	wakame seaweed	15 g
3/4 cup	aloe vera juice	175 mL

Tip

Look for fine, thin wakame, which will mince easily in the Vitamix.

1. Place the coffee beans and seaweed in the Vitamix container and secure the lid. With the switch on Variable, select speed 1 and turn the machine on. Gradually increase the speed to 5, blending just until the seaweed and coffee are ground.

2. Turn the machine off and add the aloe vera juice. Replace the lid and turn the machine on. Gradually increase the speed to 10 and blend to a smooth paste. Scrape out into a medium bowl and use immediately.

To Use

Place a towel in the bathtub, to lie on as you do your treatment. Bring a box of plastic wrap and a timer — and a book if you want to read once the treatment is in progress.

Place a length of plastic wrap under each thigh, long enough to wrap around it with several inches of overlap. Apply the mixture to each thigh, on top and underneath, massaging it as you go. Some of the paste on the underside of your thigh will fall onto the plastic wrap; lift up the wrap and press it back on. Cover the thighs with paste, then wrap in plastic wrap as tightly as you can. Lie there for at least 30 minutes or for up to 1 hour.

Wipe off the coffee mixture and bundle it up in the plastic wrap (so you won't clog the drain). Place the bundle in the sink while you rinse off your legs. Apply lotion and proceed as usual. Discard the used coffee mixture.

Variation

Use half cacao nibs and half coffee beans, for a chocolate-scented wrap.

Creamy Lemon Lotion

Lotion is one of those products you buy in a bottle and never think about, isn't it? Well, too many lotions are full of ingredients you would rather not have on your skin, if you could figure out what they are. With your Vitamix, making your own creamy lotion is as easy as making a sauce.

MAKES ABOUT ¹/₂ CUP (125 ML)

- **Fine–mesh sieve**
- **Double boiler**

3 tbsp	quick-cooking rolled oats	45 mL
³/₄ cup	boiling water	175 mL
3 tbsp	shea butter	45 mL
2 tbsp	melted coconut oil	30 mL
2 tsp	liquid lecithin	10 mL
2	capsules vitamin E oil	2
10	drops lemon essential oil or other essential oil	10

Tip

The temperature at which the two solutions are combined is very important to the success of the lotion. It pays to invest in a good instant-read thermometer.

1. Place oats in a medium heatproof bowl and pour in boiling water. Stir a few times, then let steep for 5 minutes. Strain through the sieve into a measuring cup to make ¹/₂ cup (125 mL). Sip or discard extra liquid; discard solids.

2. Transfer liquid to a small saucepan and heat over low heat to 170°F (77°C).

3. Meanwhile, in the top of the double boiler, over simmering water, combine shea butter, coconut oil and lecithin. Pierce the vitamin E capsules and squeeze the oil into the double boiler, discarding the empty capsules. Heat, stirring constantly, to 170°F (77°C).

4. When the oil mixture and oat water are both at 170°F (77°C), pour the oat water into the Vitamix container. Secure the lid and remove the lid plug. With the switch on Variable, select speed 1 and turn the machine on. Very slowly pour the oil mixture in a thin stream through the lid opening, blending until incorporated. Pour in the lemon oil, gradually increase the speed to 10 and blend for 30 seconds or until smooth and emulsified.

5. Transfer to a jar and store in the refrigerator for up to 3 weeks. If the lotion separates, shake it well.

To Use

Remove enough lotion from the refrigerator for 2 or 3 days at a time, so it doesn't spoil. Apply the lotion to your skin as desired after bathing. This lotion can also be used as a shaving cream for your legs.

Variation

Grapefruit, tangerine and orange essential oils also make lovely scented lotions.

Vanilla Rosemary Almond Lotion

Almond oil is popular in skin care because it absorbs quickly into the skin and is rich in vitamins E and A. It's also rich in oleic acid, linoleic acids and antioxidants, all of which benefit the skin. Smelling like vanilla is a wonderful thing, too.

MAKES ABOUT ⅔ CUP (150 ML)

- **Fine-mesh sieve**
- **Double boiler**

2 tsp	chia seeds	10 mL
¾ cup	boiling water	175 mL
3 tbsp	shea butter	45 mL
2 tbsp	almond oil	30 mL
2 tsp	liquid lecithin	10 mL
½ tsp	vanilla extract	2 mL
2	capsules vitamin E oil	2
10	drops rosemary essential oil	10

Tips

Chia seeds are nutrition powerhouses, with protein, fiber and essential fats. You extract some of those fats and vitamin E for this lotion, plus the lotion benefits from the thickening properties of chia.

The temperature at which the two solutions are combined is very important to the success of the lotion. It pays to invest in a good instant-read thermometer.

1. Place chia seeds in a medium heatproof bowl and pour in boiling water. Stir a few times, then let steep for 5 minutes. Strain through the sieve into a measuring cup to make ½ cup (125 mL). Sip or discard extra liquid; discard solids.

2. Transfer liquid to a small saucepan and heat over low heat to 170°F (77°C).

3. Meanwhile, in the top of the double boiler, over simmering water, combine shea butter, almond oil, lecithin and vanilla. Pierce the vitamin E capsules and squeeze the oil into the double boiler, discarding the empty capsules. Heat, stirring constantly, to 170°F (77°C).

4. When the oil mixture and chia water are both at 170°F (77°C), pour the chia water into the Vitamix container. Secure the lid and remove the lid plug. With the switch on Variable, select speed 1 and turn the machine on. Very slowly pour the oil mixture in a thin stream through the lid opening, blending until incorporated. Pour in the rosemary oil, gradually increase the speed to 10 and blend for 30 seconds or until creamy and emulsified.

5. Transfer to a jar and store in the refrigerator for up to 3 weeks. If the lotion separates, shake it well.

To Use

Remove enough lotion from the refrigerator for 2 or 3 days at a time, so it doesn't spoil. Apply the lotion to your skin as desired after bathing. This lotion can also be used as a shaving cream for your legs.

Variation

Add ½ tsp (2 mL) almond extract with the vanilla for an even more luscious scent.

Black Tea and Colloidal Oat Lotion

Black tea is full of potent antioxidants, and high-end skin care lines are often based on the antiaging properties of tea. And you'll often see "colloidal oatmeal" on lotion ingredient lists. It's finely ground oats suspended in water, and it soothes and protects your skin. This lotion is unscented, but you can always add a few drops of essential oil to give it a scent.

∾ ᘒ ∾ ᘒ ∾ ᘒ ∾ ᘒ ∾ ᘒ ∾ ᘒ ∾ ᘒ ∾ ᘒ ∾ ᘒ ∾ ᘒ ∾ ᘒ ∾ ᘒ ∾ ᘒ ∾ ᘒ ∾ ᘒ ∾ ᘒ ∾ ᘒ

MAKES ABOUT 2¼ CUPS (550 ML)

- Fine-mesh sieve

. . . .

2¹/₂ cups	boiling water	625 mL
4	black tea bags	4
¹/₄ cup	quick-cooking rolled oats	60 mL
¹/₂ cup	aloe vera juice	125 mL
1 tsp	liquid lecithin	5 mL
2 tbsp	melted coconut oil	30 mL
¹/₂ cup	grapeseed oil	125 mL

1. In a heatproof measuring cup or teapot, combine boiling water and tea bags. Let steep for 5 minutes. Remove the tea bags and measure 2 cups (500 mL) of brewed tea. Transfer to a small saucepan and set aside.

2. Place the oats in the Vitamix container and secure the lid. With the switch on Variable, select speed 1 and turn the machine on. Gradually increase the speed to 10, then flip the switch to High and grind for about 30 seconds to a fine powder.

3. Sprinkle the oat powder into the tea in the saucepan while whisking it in. Bring to a boil over medium-high heat, whisking constantly. Reduce heat to low, cover and simmer, stirring occasionally, for 20 minutes. Remove from heat, uncover and let cool slightly.

4. Set the sieve over a bowl and pour in oat paste. Using a spatula, scrape to force the paste through the sieve.

5. Pour the oat paste into the Vitamix container and add the aloe vera juice. Secure the lid. With the switch on Variable, select speed 1 and turn the machine on. Gradually increase the speed to 10 and blend for 30 seconds.

6. Turn the machine off and add the lecithin. Replace the lid, select speed 1 and turn the machine on. Gradually increase the speed to 10 and blend for 20 seconds. Turn the machine off.

7. In a small saucepan, combine coconut oil and grapeseed oil. Heat over medium heat, stirring, until the mixture reaches 170°F (77°C).

8. Remove the lid plug, select speed 5 and turn the machine on. Gradually drizzle in the oil mixture through the lid opening, then increase the speed to 10 and blend for 20 seconds or until smooth and emulsified.

9. Transfer to a jar or airtight container and store in the refrigerator for up to 2 weeks.

To Use

Remove enough lotion from the refrigerator for 2 or 3 days at a time, so it doesn't spoil. Apply the lotion to your skin as desired after bathing. This lotion can also be used as a shaving cream for your legs.

Variation

Green tea is also good for your skin, and you can substitute it for black.

Tip

Use organic tea to avoid chemicals.

Lavender Lotion Disks

Lotion disks are the most durable of your homemade lotion options because they will stay solid in a cool room and, as long as you keep them tightly covered, will hold their scent and texture for a month or so. They make lovely gifts, too.

∽∾ ∽∾

MAKES 12 DISKS

- **12-cup mini muffin pan, lined with paper liners**

$1/4$ cup	melted coconut oil	60 mL
3 oz	cocoa butter	90 g
$2^1/2$ oz	beeswax pastilles or minced beeswax	75 g
2	capsules vitamin E oil	2
1 tsp	lavender essential oil	5 mL

Tips

Coconut oil is most accurately measured in liquid form. If yours is solid, either place the jar in a bowl of warm water or remove the lid and microwave the jar for 45 seconds.

For gift-giving, use pretty decorative paper liners for the muffin pan. Put several of the disks in a candy box or a decorative jar and give them to friends and family.

1. Place the coconut oil, cocoa butter and beeswax in the Vitamix container and secure the lid. With the switch on Variable, select speed 1 and turn the machine on. Gradually increase the speed to 10, then flip the switch to High and blend for about 2 minutes or until the beeswax is melted and the mixture is combined.

2. Turn the machine off and scrape down the sides of the container. Replace the lid and blend on High for 1 minute.

3. Turn the machine off and remove the lid plug. With the switch on Variable, select speed 7 and turn the machine on. Pierce the vitamin E capsules and squeeze the oil through the lid opening, discarding the empty capsules. Pour in the lavender oil and blend until incorporated.

4. While the mixture is still hot, pour it into the prepared muffin cups, dividing equally. Let cool completely.

5. Store in a tightly sealed jar or other airtight container in a cool place for up to 1 month.

To Use

Rub a disk between your palms to soften the surface, then rub the disk over your skin.

Variation

Lavender is a soothing scent, but you may want to try an invigorating one, like rosemary or citrus, in its place.

Moisturizing Chocolate "Truffles"

These luscious little lotion bombs make your skin smell like a brownie and even give you a little temporary tint if you are very pale-skinned. If you are a generous person, these make great gifts, especially in wintertime, when everyone has dry skin and needs some comfort.

MAKES 24 TRUFFLES

- Double boiler
- #70 scoop (see tip, page 189)
- Two 12-cup mini muffin pans, lined with paper liners

3 oz	cocoa butter, finely chopped	90 g
2¹/₂ oz	beeswax pastilles or minced beeswax	75 g
2	capsules vitamin E oil	2
¹/₄ cup	melted coconut oil	60 mL
3 tbsp	unsweetened cocoa powder	45 mL
1 tsp	powdered vitamin C	5 mL
1 tsp	chocolate extract	5 mL
¹/₂ tsp	vanilla extract	2 mL
	Additional unsweetened cocoa powder (optional)	

1. Place cocoa butter and beeswax in the top of the double boiler and heat over simmering water just until melted. Remove from heat and let stand for a few seconds.

2. Pierce the vitamin E capsules and squeeze the oil into the Vitamix container, discarding the empty capsules. Add the coconut oil, cocoa and vitamin C. Secure the lid and remove the lid plug. With the switch on Variable, select speed 1 and turn the machine on. Gradually increase the speed to 5, then pour the melted cocoa butter mixture through the lid opening and blend for about 1 minute or until well mixed.

3. Turn the machine off and scrape down the sides of the container. Replace the lid, turn the machine on and pour in the chocolate and vanilla extracts through the lid opening, blending until incorporated.

4. Scrape into a bowl and let stand at room temperature until firm (about 30 to 60 minutes, depending on the temperature of the room).

5. Using the scoop, scoop out balls of the mixture and drop each one in a prepared muffin cup. Refrigerate for about 1 hour or until set. If desired, roll each ball between your palms to make it smooth. Dust with additional cocoa powder, if desired.

To Use

Rub a truffle between your palms to soften the surface, then rub the truffle over your skin.

Variations

For a "flavored" truffle, add ¹/₂ tsp (2 mL) hazelnut extract with the other extracts.

To make disks instead of truffles, pour the warm mixture into the prepared muffin cups, dividing equally. (If it starts to harden and become difficult to pour, blend again for 1 minute to warm it.) Let cool completely.

Tip

Craft stores sell colorful mini muffin paper liners in all sorts of colors and designs to match the season. Just make sure that the receiver of your gift knows that these truffles are not edible!

Avocado Jojoba Hair Mask

The oils in avocado and jojoba are rare in that they can actually penetrate into the hair shaft. Avocado also nourishes the scalp, to fight thinning hair, and egg gives your hair a protein boost. Use a hair mask once a week for the best results.

MAKES 1 TREATMENT		
1	large egg	1
1/2	large avocado	1/2
1 tsp	jojoba oil	5 mL
10	drops rosemary or lavender essential oil (see tip)	10

Tips

Use up those avocados that are getting a little mushy for this hair treatment. As long as they are not turning brown inside, they are still good for this.

If jojoba oil is not available, you can use olive oil in its place.

For thinning hair, use rosemary essential oil; for normal hair, use lavender essential oil.

1. Place the egg, avocado, jojoba oil and essential oil in the Vitamix container and secure the lid. With the switch on Variable, select speed 1 and turn the machine on. Very gradually increase the speed to 4 or 5, increasing only as long as the avocado is engaged with the blades.

2. Turn the machine off and scrape down the sides of the container. Replace the lid, select speed 1 and turn the machine on. Gradually increase to speed 5 and blend until smooth. Transfer to a bowl and use immediately.

To Use

Wrap a towel around your shoulders and stand over the sink as you work the mask into your scalp and hair. Leave on for 20 minutes. Shampoo in cold water with a mild shampoo and condition as usual.

ACKNOWLEDGMENTS

I am eternally grateful for the support and encouragement of my sweetheart, Stan. I'd also like to thank my mom, Marilyn Calhoun, for a lifetime of love and celebration, and for letting me work on the book at her house.

Working with the talented people at Robert Rose and PageWave Graphics has been a pleasure. My thanks to editors Sue Sumeraj and Jennifer MacKenzie, designer Daniella Zanchetta, Colin Erricson's photography team, proofreader Kelly Jones and indexer Gillian Watts. Special thanks to publisher Bob Dees for the inspiration and guidance.

I couldn't have done this without the recipe testing help of Kristine Vick, Diane Jackson, Lisa Genis and Kate Selner. My cocktail consultant, Bret Bannon, also played a pivotal role.

Big thanks to the people at Vitamix for sending blenders and answering my technical questions. Bob's Red Mill also contributed a selection of top-quality whole grains for recipe development and testing, and I thank them.

INDEX

Library and Archives Canada Cataloguing in Publication

Asbell, Robin, author
    300 best blender recipes : using your Vitamix / Robin Asbell.

Includes index.
ISBN 978-0-7788-0558-8 (paperback)

    1. Blenders (Cooking). 2. Vitamix Corporation. 3. Cookbooks. I. Title. II. Title: Three hundred best blender recipes.

TX840.B5A83 2017   641.5'893   C2016-906075-6